America Firsthand

SIXTH EDITION

America Firsthand

SIXTH EDITION

Volume Two
Readings from Reconstruction to the Present

Robert D. Marcus
*Late of the State University
of New York College at Brockport*

David Burner
State University of New York at Stony Brook

Anthony Marcus
University of Melbourne

BEDFORD/ST. MARTIN'S
Boston ◆ New York

FOR BEDFORD/ST. MARTIN'S

Publisher for History: Patricia A. Rossi
Director of Development for History: Jane Knetzger
Developmental Editor: Sarah Barrash Wilson
Production Editor: Arthur Johnson
Production Supervisor: Jennifer Wetzel
Marketing Manager: Jenna Bookin Barry
Editorial Assistant: Rachel L. Safer
Production Assistant: Tina Lai
Copyeditor: Mary Lou Wilshaw-Watts
Cover Design: Donna Lee Dennison
Cover Art: "Renovation work on the Statue of Liberty," September 1938. © Hulton-Deutsch Collection/CORBIS.
Composition: Pine Tree Composition, Inc.
Printing and Binding: R.R. Donnelley & Sons Company

President: Joan E. Feinberg
Editorial Director: Denise B. Wydra
Director of Marketing: Karen Melton
Director of Editing, Design, and Production: Marcia Cohen
Managing Editor: Elizabeth M. Schaaf

Library of Congress Control Number: 2003101706

For information, write: Bedford/St. Martin's, 75 Arlington Street, Boston, MA 02116 (617-399-4000)

ISBN: 0–312–40362–3

Acknowledgments

Bracketed numbers indicate selection numbers.

[1] "African Americans during Reconstruction" from B. A. Botkin, ed., *Lay My Burden Down: A Folk History of Slavery.* Copyright © 1945 by B. A. Botkin. Reprinted by permission of Curtis Brown, Ltd.
[11] "Antilynching Campaign in Tennessee" from Alfreda M. Duster, ed., *Crusade for Justice: The Autobiography of Ida B. Wells.* Copyright © 1970 by The University of Chicago Press. Reprinted by permission of The University of Chicago Press.
[15] "A Bintel Brief" from Isaac Metzker, *A Bintel Brief: Sixty Years of Letters from the Lower East Side to the JEWISH DAILY FORWARD.* Copyright © 1971 by Isaac Metzker. Reprinted with the permission of Isaac Metzker and the *Jewish Daily Forward.*

Acknowledgments and copyrights are continued at the back of the book on pages 342–44, which constitute an extension of the copyright page. It is a violation of the law to reproduce these selections by any means whatsoever without the written permission of the copyright holder.

This book is dedicated to Robert Marcus, who died in October 2000; he was one of the two creators and coeditors of America Firsthand. *At the time of Bob's death, his doctoral sponsor Robert Wiebe—soon to pass away himself—eulogized that Bob had "a first-rate mind, was ingenious, versatile, and brimming over with fresh ideas." We remember Bob as an original thinker, a thoughtful scholar, and a true friend.*

Preface

This sixth edition of *America Firsthand* continues to pursue the goal of previous editions: to give center stage to ordinary Americans who speak directly of their own lives. As much as possible, individuals speak in their own words and in selections long enough to be memorable, personal, and immediate. The accounts of indentured servants, Southern aristocrats, runaway slaves, Western explorers, civil rights activists, immigrants, and many others expose students to a wide range of American life and human experience.

In addition, this revision retains two features unique to *America Firsthand*, the Points of View selections and the visual portfolios. The part-opening Points of View sections pair counterpoint readings on a specific event or topic, exposing different viewpoints and offering opportunities for analysis. For instance, students encounter both British and colonial accounts of the Boston Massacre, as well as the contrasting testimony of an independent craftsman and a manufacturer on industrialism in the late nineteenth century. Critical-thinking questions help students sift through the evidence, make connections, and analyze the readings in relation to each other. The four visual portfolios in each volume provide students with the opportunity to extend historical analysis from text to images. Focusing on a theme such as "Slavery and Freedom" or "The Western Landscape," each portfolio is accompanied by a short introduction, a brief narrative describing the images, and questions to help students make comparisons and draw inferences from the visual depictions.

The team of authors for this new edition was changed by the untimely death of Robert Marcus in October of 2000. Robert Marcus and his longtime collaborator David Burner brought the series into the world and developed it over five editions. Marcus was a scholar and educator whose lifelong commitment was, as he wrote in the preface to the fifth edition, to "include people from many groups whose experience has been, until recently, largely lost in mainstream history." In attempting to uphold this commitment to inclusiveness and pedagogical excellence, Robert Marcus's son Anthony Marcus joins David Burner in producing this sixth edition. Presently a lecturer in cultural anthropology, he has taught college students for over ten years and has published on race and ethnicity in Latin America and the United States. Anthony collaborated with his father once before on the two-volume documentary history of U.S. trials and court proceedings, *On Trial.*

This edition of *America Firsthand* features an entirely new final part in the second volume. With five new readings and a visual portfolio about September 11 and its aftermath, this section reflects the passing of post–World War II America and the arrival of a new set of challenges and historical problems in the post–cold war era. The opening Points of View selections offer the views of an Arab American woman who argues in favor of racial profiling at airports alongside those of an African American man who insists that racial profiling is an injustice. Part Seven also includes selections on illegal Mexican immigrants, the Rodney King beating and riots, Matthew Shepard's death, and September 11.

The new Points of View readings at the end of the second volume join two new Points of View sections in the first volume. These include Bartolomé de Las Casas and Bernal Díaz del Castillo's conflicting views on European contact with natives of the Americas as well as views of the Mexican-American War from opposite sides of the battlefield. Like those Points of View pairings that were retained from the previous edition, these new selections present differing perspectives and offer opportunities for critical thinking.

This edition also includes three new visual portfolios, each connected to a number of the preceding selections and carefully annotated with background information and questions that link the images presented with the readings. The first volume incorporates a new visual essay on colonial architecture, and the second volume includes new portfolios on advertising in the 1920s and on September 11.

Throughout, we have retained readings that users wanted to continue teaching and dropped less successful ones. New selections in the first volume include a description of the Revolutionary War and its aftermath by an African American loyalist soldier; dispatches from an officer in New Mexico during the Mexican-American War; a presentation of everyday life on a nineteenth-century Connecticut whaling vessel in the southern Indian Ocean; the remarkable tale of Henry "Box" Brown, a slave who mailed himself to freedom; an account of a sixteen-year-old who helped John Brown free slaves in Kansas; and the correspondence of a black Civil War journalist who experienced the fall of Richmond in 1865. Fresh selections in the second volume include Jane Addams on industrialism and the Pullman Strike; Kate Richards O'Hare's statements in her own defense during a World War I sedition trial; the comments of a journalist at *The Nation* about the Scopes trial; remembrances by a member of the Puerto Rican radical group the Young Lords; and a memoir of being held hostage in the American embassy in Tehran in 1980.

As in previous editions, carefully written headnotes before the selections prepare students for each reading and help place personalities in their times and places. Questions immediately following the headnotes enable students and instructors to give attention to specific passages and issues that can provide points for discussion as well as material for testing or essays. Glosses within the accounts identify unfamiliar names or terms.

America Firsthand, Sixth Edition, presents the American experience through the perspectives of diverse people who have in common a vivid record of the world they inhabited and of the events they experienced. We hope that the readings will serve as fertile ground in which students can begin to root their own interest in history and deepen their understanding of the times in which they live.

ACKNOWLEDGMENTS

We would like to thank all the instructors who graciously provided helpful comments for improving *America Firsthand:* Jamie Bronstein, New Mexico State University; Elizabeth Clement, University of Utah; Benton Gates, Indiana University–Purdue University, Fort Wayne; James W. Hilty, Temple University; D. Carol Hunter, Earlham College; Anne Keary, University of Utah; Cynthia A. Kierner, University of North Carolina–Charlotte; Molly Ladd-Taylor, York University, Toronto; Jennifer A. Lee, University of Florida; Kathy S. Mason, Southwest Missouri State University; David McCreery, Georgia State University; Beth Ruffin McIntyre, Southwest Missouri State University; Kelly A. Minor, University of Florida; David W. Moore, Loyola University, New Orleans; Penne Restad, University of Texas, Austin; Rebecca S. Shoemaker, Indiana State University; Julie L. Smith, University of North Carolina–Pembroke; Cherry L. Spruill, Indiana University–Purdue University, Indianapolis; and David Stowe, Michigan State University.

We also wish to extend great thanks to Jo Sanson, whose assistance enabled us to produce the best sixth edition possible. Cary Wintz and Timothy More also provided valuable research to the project. The many people associated with Bedford/St. Martin's who worked on the sixth edition need to be acknowledged as well: Joan Feinberg, Denise Wydra, Patricia Rossi, Jane Knetzger, Sarah Barrash Wilson, Rachel Safer, Amy Langlais, Elizabeth Schaaf, Arthur Johnson, and Donna Dennison.

Contents

Preface   vii

PART ONE
After the War: New South and New West   1

Points of View: Dilemmas of Reconstruction (1865–1877)

1. AFRICAN AMERICANS DURING RECONSTRUCTION   2
   Felix Haywood et al.
   In interviews conducted in the 1930s, Felix Haywood and other
   former slaves tell about their lives immediately following the
   Civil War.

2. WHITE SOUTHERNERS' REACTIONS
   TO RECONSTRUCTION   8
   Caleb G. Forshey and the Reverend James Sinclair
   Testimony by Caleb Forshey and the Reverend James Sinclair before
   a joint congressional committee shows reactions of Southern
   whites to Reconstruction policies.

FOR CRITICAL THINKING   16

3. THE MURDER OF JIM WILLIAMS   17
   Rosy Williams et al.
   Testimony of Rosy Williams, John Caldwell, and Dr. James R. Bratton
   describes the 1871 hanging of Jim Williams by the Ku Klux Klan in
   Yorkville, South Carolina.

4. VENGEANCE AGAINST "LONG HAIR"   27
   She Walks with Her Shawl and One Bull
   Lakota and Cheyenne Indians remember the Little Big Horn encounter
   of 1876 in which more than four thousand warriors defeated Custer and his
   regiment in southern Montana.

5. WORK UNDER SHARECROPPER AND LABOR CONTRACTS   33
   Grimes Family and Swindell Brothers
   Grimes family and Swindell Brothers contracts provide examples
   of new economic arrangements from Reconstruction through the 1880s.

6. SCHOOL DAYS OF AN INDIAN GIRL   37
   Zitkala-Ša (Gertrude Simmons Bonnin)
   A South Dakota Sioux recalls her experiences at a boarding school for
   Native American children in the 1880s and later at college.

VISUAL PORTFOLIO: *The Western Landscape*   **45**

PART TWO
The Gilded Age: A New Industrial Commonwealth   **55**

Points of View: Industrialism and Progress (1882)

7. THE DECLINE OF THE INDEPENDENT CRAFTSMAN   56
   Joseph T. Finnerty
   Joseph T. Finnerty, a brass worker, criticizes the growing scale
   of industry before a Senate Committee.

8. WORKERS PROSPER AS INDUSTRY GROWS   64
   William Steinway
   The piano manufacturer William Steinway defends industrial
   growth before a Senate committee.

FOR CRITICAL THINKING   **73**

9. GEORGE RICE LOSES OUT TO STANDARD OIL   74
   George Rice
   In 1898, George Rice exposes the business practices of Standard Oil, a trust
   that destroyed his refining business.

10. HONEST AND DISHONEST GRAFT   81
    George Washington Plunkitt
    The Tammany Hall politician George Washington Plunkitt reflects on the
    meaning of political corruption during the Gilded Age in a selection from 1905.

11. ANTILYNCHING CAMPAIGN IN TENNESSEE 89
Ida B. Wells-Barnett

Ida B. Wells-Barnett, an African American journalist, remembers the 1892 lynching of three Memphis friends who owned a grocery store in her community.

12. A MODERN LEAR 95
Jane Addams

The pioneering social worker and reformer Jane Addams criticizes the paternalism of industrialist and philanthropist George M. Pullman during the 1894 strike at his factory.

PART THREE
An Age of Reform: Responses to Industrial America 103

Points of View: The Triangle Shirtwaist Fire (1911)

13. CONDITIONS AT THE TRIANGLE SHIRTWAIST COMPANY 104
Pauline Newman et al.

Pauline Newman and four other women describe the fire that broke out in the Triangle Shirtwaist Company and the hazardous safety conditions that led to it.

14. A FIRE TRAP 109
William Gunn Shepherd

A special morning edition of the New York World, *March 26, 1911, recounts the tragedy in which over 140 people died.*

FOR CRITICAL THINKING 115

15. A BINTEL BRIEF 116
Abraham Cahan

Letters to the Jewish Daily Forward *and Abraham Cahan's answers reflect the concerns of new immigrants adjusting to American life in the early 1900s.*

16. CONDITIONS AT THE SLAUGHTERHOUSE 123
Upton Sinclair

An excerpt from Upton Sinclair's book The Jungle, *published in 1906, graphically describes unsanitary practices in the meat-packing industry.*

17. LETTERS FROM THE GREAT MIGRATION 131
Emmett J. Scott et al.

Letters from 1916 and 1917 document the "great migration" of African Americans looking for new opportunities in Northern cities.

18. THE TRIAL OF KATE RICHARDS O'HARE   135
    Kate Richards O'Hare et al.

    *The socialist Kate Richards O'Hare is found guilty in a North Dakota court
    in 1917 of disrupting recruitment for World War I.*

VISUAL PORTFOLIO: *Urban Industrial America*   143

PART FOUR
A New Society: Between the Wars   153

Points of View: The Scopes Trial (1925)

19. IN DEFENSE OF THE BIBLE   154
    William Jennings Bryan and Clarence Darrow

    *William Jennings Bryan testifies against the theory of evolution
    during the famous Tennessee "monkey trial."*

20. TENNESSEE'S DILEMMA   161
    Joseph Wood Krutch

    *The critic Joseph Wood Krutch reflects on the issues of political
    leadership, citizenship, and education raised by the Scopes trial.*

FOR CRITICAL THINKING   164

21. THE HARLEM RENAISSANCE   165
    Langston Hughes

    Langston Hughes evokes Harlem in the 1920s.

22. MY FIGHT FOR BIRTH CONTROL   175
    Margaret Sanger

    *Margaret Sanger recounts a tragic incident that inspired her renowned
    crusade to offer contraceptive information to women in the 1920s.*

23. DOWN AND OUT IN THE GREAT DEPRESSION   182
    Anonymous

    *Ordinary citizens describe their plight in anonymous letters to Franklin D.
    and Eleanor Roosevelt and to various government officials in the 1930s.*

24. THE SIT-DOWN STRIKES   190
    Henry Kraus

    *The 1936 "Battle of Bull's Run" became a legendary moment in the
    American labor movement.*

VISUAL PORTFOLIO: *Advertising in the 1920s*   197

PART FIVE
"The American Century": War, Affluence, and Uncertainty   209

Points of View: Building an Atomic Bomb (1942–1945)

25. LETTERS FROM LOS ALAMOS   210
    Phyllis Fisher
    *Phyllis Fisher, the wife of a nuclear physicist working with
    J. Robert Oppenheimer, writes to her parents between 1944
    and 1945.*

26. TO BUILD A BOMB   216
    J. Robert Oppenheimer
    *J. Robert Oppenheimer recounts the drive to recruit almost four
    thousand scientists for the Manhattan Project and speaks about the
    reaction to the success of the project.*

FOR CRITICAL THINKING   224

27. ROSIE THE RIVETER   225
    Fanny Christina Hill
    *Fanny Christina Hill, an African American, remembers her
    employment in defense work during World War II.*

28. MEMORIES OF THE INTERNMENT CAMP   232
    Ben Yorita and Philip Hayasaka
    *Ben Yorita and Philip Hayasaka, Japanese Americans, recall their
    lives at a "relocation center" during World War II.*

29. THE BATAAN DEATH MARCH   239
    Blair Robinett et al.
    *Private First Class Blair Robinett and fellow soldiers relate gruesome
    details of survival and death during this infamous World War II
    event.*

30. POST–WORLD WAR II "RED SCARE"   247
    Mark Goodson
    *CBS executive Mark Goodson describes entertainment industry blacklisting
    during the McCarthy era.*

PART SIX

Contested Boundaries: Moral Dilemmas
at Home and Abroad

253

Points of View: The My Lai Incident (1968–1970)

31. DISBELIEF AND CORROBORATION   254
    Ronald L. Ridenhour et al.

    A letter from a former infantryman asks for an investigation
    of the My Lai Massacre, and testimony and army reports
    examine the slaughter.

32. COVER-UP AND OUTCOME   261
    General Westmoreland, President Nixon, et al.

    More testimony and reports coupled with reflections by General
    William Westmoreland and President Richard Nixon shed light
    on how the incident happened and why public reaction was so
    explosive.

    FOR CRITICAL THINKING   **269**

---

33. BETTY FRIEDAN STARTS A REVOLUTION   270
    Betty Friedan et al.

    Betty Friedan writes about and readers respond to her 1963 book,
    The Feminine Mystique.

34. MISSISSIPPI FREEDOM SUMMER   276
    Student Workers

    Participants in the 1964 Mississippi Freedom Summer project document
    their experiences and emotions in letters home.

35. THE YOUNG LORDS   284
    Pablo Guzmán

    Pablo Guzmán recounts his own involvement in the early 1970s
    as a young Puerto Rican radical in the left-wing political group the
    Young Lords.

36. AN AMERICAN HOSTAGE IN TEHRAN   292
    Barry Rosen

    The press attaché for the American embassy in Iran tells of the 1979
    storming of the embassy by Islamic students and the beginning of his
    long ordeal.

PART SEVEN
New World Order? Angry Realignments
after the Cold War   299

Points of View: Racial Profiling (1998–2002)

37. DRIVING WHILE BLACK   301
    James Campbell
    *James Campbell, an African American reporter, tells his nephew of the
    dangers of "driving while black."*

38. LET THEM PROFILE ME   304
    Fedwa Malti-Douglas
    *An Arab American scholar explains why she accepts being profiled at
    airports after the attacks of September 11.*

    FOR CRITICAL THINKING   306

39. CROSSING THE RIO GRANDE   307
    Al Santoli
    *The lives and dreams of two illegal immigrants living in El Paso,
    Texas, in the 1980s are revealed in first-person narratives.*

40. RODNEY KING AND THE LOS ANGELES RIOTS   315
    Stan Chambers
    *The veteran reporter Stan Chambers recounts first reactions to the
    videotaped beating of Rodney King in 1991, and his view from a
    helicopter of the Los Angeles riots of a year later.*

41. HOMOPHOBIA IN THE HEARTLAND   320
    Dennis W. Shepard
    *Matthew Shepard's father addresses the men who killed his son in 1998 and
    the court that found them guilty.*

42. SEPTEMBER 11 AND THE AFTERMATH   326
    Kimberly Morales, Daniel Harris, Diana Hoffman,
    Amber Amundson
    *A student watches the towers burn, a man reflects on the public's reactions to
    the attacks, and two women urge different responses from the government.*

VISUAL PORTFOLIO: *9/11*   335

America Firsthand

SIXTH EDITION

PART ONE

After the War

New South and New West

"I have vowed that if I should have children—the first ingredient of the first principle of their education shall be uncompromising hatred & contempt of the Yankee," declared a white Southerner toward the end of the Civil War. "I'm free as a frog!" exulted one former slave. You will read similar responses from both white Southerners like Caleb Forshey and black Southerners like Felix Haywood facing the future after the war. High hopes or extreme bitterness promised a painful future for the South.

While slavery had effectively met its end, victory for the Union did not resolve questions about the roles that African American men and women would play in American life. The first attempts to secure rights for the former slaves, known as Reconstruction, produced three new amendments to the Constitution, which initiated a movement toward equality that today, more than a century later, is far from over. Despite federal laws mandating economic freedom for African Americans, determined opposition from white Southerners largely defeated Reconstruction. In part, this resistance took legal forms such as marshaling public opinion, applying economic power, and organizing politically. But the resort to terror came early and continued in various forms for generations. The Ku Klux Klan, arising soon after the war, quickly became an armed conspiracy intimidating, whipping, and killing African Americans like Rosy Williams's husband Jim and their white allies.

In the end, three institutions replaced slavery in the postwar South—Jim Crow or segregation in social affairs, a whites-only Democratic Party in politics, and sharecropping in economics. Southern farmers developed arrangements such as the Grimes family's sharecrop contract, which offered neither slavery nor full freedom to work where one chose, while in the North parallel restrictions on free labor like the Swindell Brothers' contract appeared.

At the same time that the former slaves' hopes for freedom were being dashed in the South, the West—with its vast opportunities and awesome landscape—

drew capital and population and stirred the American imagination (as illustrated in the visual portfolio "The Western Landscape," which begins on page 45). However, the completion of the first transcontinental railroad link in 1869, the renewed movement westward that it generated, and the collapse of the buffalo herds that fed and sheltered the Plains Indians helped to decimate the remaining independent Native American cultures. The Battle of Little Big Horn (1876), remembered here in accounts by She Walks with Her Shawl and other Indians, was the last Native American victory in centuries of sporadic warfare between Indians and newer Americans. As Native Americans were shunted to reservations often far distant from their ancestral homes, their young people were placed in boarding schools to educate them in the ways of the dominant society. The struggles of Zitkala-Ša, a Sioux from the Yankton reservation in South Dakota, to find her place in both the Sioux and the white worlds indicate the complexities lurking behind the stereotypes.

POINTS OF VIEW
Dilemmas of Reconstruction (1865–1877)

1
African Americans during Reconstruction
Felix Haywood et al.

Wherever travelers went in the months following Appomattox, they saw abandoned fields, twisted rails, burned buildings, white men hobbling about on one leg or dangling an empty sleeve, and former slaves exploring their new freedom or searching for food, shelter, and work. The war had settled some things: secession and slavery were dead. The South was desperately impoverished, its prewar economy gone with the wind.

All else was confusion. Freedmen struggled to define their freedom. Some left the plantations to which they had been bound and found family separated by slavery and war. Many—perhaps most—saw freedom in the ownership of land, a dream encouraged by a field order issued by General William Tecumseh Sherman in January 1865 that assigned some vacant lands to former slaves. As a black soldier told his white officer: "Every colored man will be a slave and feel himself a slave until he could raise his own bale of cotton and put his own mark upon it and say, 'Dis is mine!'"

"African Americans React to Reconstruction," from B. A. Botkin, ed., *Lay My Burden Down: A Folk History of Slavery* (Chicago: University of Chicago Press, 1945), pp. 65–70, 223–24, 241–42, 246–47.

Yet soon after the first jubilee of freedom, the Andrew Johnson administration, falling under the influence of former Confederates, revoked Sherman's order assigning land to former slaves and stood by as white Southerners began to force the freedmen back into old patterns—assigning them work under coercive labor contracts and governing their daily activities by "black codes" that denied them their civil rights. When these policies provoked a political reaction in the North, Republicans in Congress took control of Southern policy through a series of Reconstruction Acts. While restoring civil rights and providing military protection, these acts failed to provide land to the freedmen. The Thirteenth (1865), Fourteenth (1868), and Fifteenth Amendments (1870) to the U.S. Constitution decreed an equality between the races that did not become a reality in African Americans' daily lives in either the North or the South. For about a decade the federal government made vigorous efforts to help freedmen gain education, legal and medical services, reasonable employment contracts, and a measure of political power. But those efforts were abandoned once the Northern public, tired of disorder in the South and wary of government intervention, abandoned the former slaves to their old masters. African Americans were soon left to respond however they could to the social revolution brought about by emancipation, the war's impoverishment of the South, and the violence of groups like the Ku Klux Klan.

Historians have pieced together the story of the freedmen's actions from a multiplicity of sources. Interviews with former slaves collected in the 1930s, a sample of which you will read here, are an important source for comprehending the lives of those freed, and then abandoned, after the Civil War.

BEFORE YOU READ

1. Judging from these accounts, what were the major problems that former slaves faced after the war?
2. What did these former slaves expect of freedom?
3. Why did some freedmen continue to work for their former masters?

FELIX HAYWOOD

San Antonio, Texas. Born in Raleigh,
North Carolina. Age at interview: 88.

The end of the war, it come just like that—like you snap your fingers. . . . How did we know it! Hallelujah broke out—

> Abe Lincoln freed the nigger
>   With the gun and the trigger;
> And I ain't going to get whipped any more.
>   I got my ticket,
>   Leaving the thicket,
>   And I'm a-heading for the Golden Shore!

Soldiers, all of a sudden, was everywhere—coming in bunches, crossing and walking and riding. Everyone was a-singing. We was all walking on golden clouds. Hallelujah!

Union forever,
  Hurrah, boys, hurrah!
Although I may be poor,
  I'll never be a slave—
Shouting the battle cry of freedom.

Everybody went wild. We felt like heroes, and nobody had made us that way but ourselves. We was free. Just like that, we was free. It didn't seem to make the whites mad, either. They went right on giving us food just the same. Nobody took our homes away, but right off colored folks started on the move. They seemed to want to get closer to freedom, so they'd know what it was— like it was a place or a city. Me and my father stuck, stuck close as a lean tick to a sick kitten. The Gudlows started us out on a ranch. My father, he'd round up cattle—unbranded cattle—for the whites. They was cattle that they belonged to, all right; they had gone to find water 'long the San Antonio River and the Guadalupe. Then the whites gave me and my father some cattle for our own. My father had his own brand—7 B)—and we had a herd to start out with of seventy.

We knowed freedom was on us, but we didn't know what was to come with it. We thought we was going to get rich like the white folks. We thought we was going to be richer than the white folks, 'cause we was stronger and knowed how to work, and the whites didn't, and they didn't have us to work for them any more. But it didn't turn out that way. We soon found out that freedom could make folks proud, but it didn't make 'em rich.

Did you ever stop to think that thinking don't do any good when you do it too late? Well, that's how it was with us. If every mother's son of a black had thrown 'way his hoe and took up a gun to fight for his own freedom along with the Yankees, the war'd been over before it began. But we didn't do it. We couldn't help stick to our masters. We couldn't no more shoot 'em than we could fly. My father and me used to talk 'bout it. We decided we was too soft and freedom wasn't going to be much to our good even if we had a education.

WARREN McKINNEY

Hazen, Arkansas. Born in South Carolina.
Age at interview: 85.

I was born in Edgefield County, South Carolina. I am eighty-five years old. I was born a slave of George Strauter. I remembers hearing them say, "Thank God, I's free as a jay bird." My ma was a slave in the field. I was eleven years old when freedom was declared. When I was little, Mr. Strauter whipped my ma. It hurt me bad as it did her. I hated him. She was crying. I chunked him with rocks. He run after me, but he didn't catch me. There was twenty-five or thirty hands that worked in the field. They raised wheat, corn, oats, barley, and cotton. All the children that couldn't work stayed at one house. Aunt Mat kept the babies and small children that couldn't go to the field. He had a gin and a shop. The shop was at the fork of the roads. When the war come on, my papa went to built forts. He quit Ma and took another woman. When the war close, Ma took her four children, bundled 'em up and went to Augusta. The government give out rations there. My ma washed and ironed. People died in piles. I don't know till yet what was the matter. They said it was the change of living. I seen five or six wooden, painted coffins piled up on wagons pass by our house. Loads passed every day like you see cotton pass here. Some said it was cholera and some took consumption. Lots of the colored people nearly starved. Not much to get to do and not much houseroom. Several families had to live in one house. Lots of the colored folks went up North and froze to death. They couldn't stand the cold. They wrote back about them dying. No, they never sent them back. I heard some sent for money to come back. I heard plenty 'bout the Ku Klux. They scared the folks to death. People left Augusta in droves. About a thousand would all meet and walk going to hunt work and new homes. Some of them died. I had a sister and brother lost that way. I had another sister come to Louisiana that way. She wrote back.

I don't think the colored folks looked for a share of land. They never got nothing 'cause the white folks didn't have nothing but barren hills left. About all the mules was wore out hauling provisions in the army. Some folks say they ought to done more for the colored folks when they left, but they say they was broke. Freeing all the slaves left 'em broke.

That reconstruction was a mighty hard pull. Me and Ma couldn't live. A man paid our ways to Carlisle, Arkansas, and we come. We started working for Mr. Emenson. He had a big store, teams, and land. We liked it fine, and I been here fifty-six years now. There was so much wild game, living was not so hard. If a fellow could get a little bread and a place to stay, he was all right. After I come to this state, I voted some. I have farmed and worked at odd jobs. I farmed mostly. Ma went back to her old master. He persuaded her to come back home. Me and her went back and run a farm four or five years before she died. Then I come back here.

LEE GUIDON

South Carolina. Born in South Carolina.
Age at interview: 89.

Yes, ma'am, I sure was in the Civil War. I plowed all day, and me and my sister helped take care of the baby at night. It would cry, and me bumping it [in a straight chair, rocking]. Time I git it to the bed where its mama was, it wake up and start crying all over again. I be so sleepy. It was a puny sort of baby. Its papa was off at war. His name was Jim Cowan, and his wife Miss Margaret Brown 'fore she married him. Miss Lucy Smith give me and my sister to them. Then she married Mr. Abe Moore. Jim Smith was Miss Lucy's boy. He lay out in the woods all time. He say no need in him gitting shot up and killed. He say let the slaves be free. We lived, seemed like, on 'bout the line of York and Union counties. He lay out in the woods over in York County. Mr. Jim say all the fighting 'bout was jealousy. They caught him several times, but every time he got away from 'em. After they come home Mr. Jim say they never win no war. They stole and starved out the South. . . .

After freedom a heap of people say they was going to name theirselves over. They named theirselves big names, then went roaming round like wild, hunting cities. They changed up so it was hard to tell who or where anybody was. Heap of 'em died, and you didn't know when you hear about it if he was your folks hardly. Some of the names was Abraham, and some called theirselves Lincum. Any big name 'cepting their master's name. It was the fashion. I heard 'em talking 'bout it one evening, and my pa say, "Fine folks raise us and we gonna hold to our own names." That settled it with all of us. . . .

I reckon I do know 'bout the Ku Kluck. I knowed a man named Alfred Owens. He seemed all right, but he was a Republican. He said he was not afraid. He run a tanyard and kept a heap of guns in a big room. They all loaded. He married a Southern woman. Her husband either died or was killed. She had a son living with them. The Ku Kluck was called Upper League. They get this boy to unload all the guns. Then the white men went there. The white man give up and said, "I ain't got no gun to defend myself with. The guns all unloaded, and I ain't got no powder and shot." But the Ku Kluck shot in the houses and shot him up like lacework. He sold fine harness, saddles, bridles— all sorts of leather things. The Ku Kluck sure run them outen their country. They say they not going to have them round, and they sure run them out, back where they came from. . . .

For them what stayed on like they were, Reconstruction times 'bout like times before that 'cepting the Yankee stole out and tore up a scandalous heap. They tell the black folks to do something, and then come white folks you live with and say Ku Kluck whup you. They say leave, and white folks say better not listen to them old yankees. They'll git you too far off to come back, and you freeze. They done give you all the use they got for you. How they do? All sorts of ways. Some stayed at their cabins glad to have one to live in and farmed on. Some running round begging, some hunting work for money, and nobody had no money 'cepting the Yankees, and they had no homes or land and mighty little work for you to do. No work to live on. Some going every day to the city. That winter I heard 'bout them starving and freezing by the wagon loads. I never heard nothing 'bout voting till freedom. I don't think I ever voted till I come to Mississippi. I votes Republican. That's the party of my color, and I stick to them as long as they do right. I don't dabble in white folks' business, and that white folks' voting is their business. If I vote, I go do it and go on home.

I been plowing all my life, and in the hot days I cuts and saws wood. Then when I gets outa cotton-picking, I put each boy on a load of wood and we sell wood. The last years we got $3 a cord. Then we clear land till next spring. I don't find no time to be loafing. I never missed a year farming till I got the Bright's disease [one of several kinds of kidney ailments] and it hurt me to do hard work. Farming is the best life there is when you are able. . . .

When I owned most, I had six head mules and five head horses. I rented 140 acres of land. I bought this house and some other land about. The anthrax killed nearly all my horses and mules. I got one big fine mule yet. Its mate died. I lost my house. My son give me one room, and he paying the debt off now. It's hard for colored folks to keep anything. Somebody gets it from 'em if they don't mind.

The present times is hard. Timber is scarce. Game is about all gone. Prices higher. Old folks cannot work. Times is hard for younger folks too. They go to town too much and go to shows. They going to a tent show now. Circus coming, they say. They spending too much money for foolishness. It's a fast time. Folks too restless. Some of the colored folks work hard as folks ever did. They spends too much. Some folks is lazy. Always been that way.

I signed up to the government, but they ain't give me nothing 'cepting powdered milk and rice what wasn't fit to eat. It cracked up and had black something in it. A lady said she would give me some shirts that was her husband's. I went to get them, but she wasn't home. These heavy shirts give me heat. They won't give me the pension, and I don't know why. It would help me buy my salts and pills and the other medicines like Swamp Root. They won't give it to me.

TOBY JONES

Madisonville, Texas. Born in South Carolina.
Age at interview: 87.

I worked for Massa 'bout four years after freedom, 'cause he forced me to, said he couldn't 'ford to let me go. His place was near ruint, the fences burnt, and the house would have been, but it was rock. There was a battle fought near his place, and I taken Missy to a hideout in the mountains to where her father was, 'cause there was bullets flying everywhere. When the war was over, Massa come home and says, "You son of a gun, you's supposed to be free, but you ain't, 'cause I ain't gwine give you freedom." So I goes on working for him till I gits the chance to steal a hoss from him. The woman I wanted to marry, Govie, she 'cides to come to Texas with me. Me and Govie, we rides the hoss 'most a hundred miles, then we turned him a-loose and give him a scare back to his house, and come on foot the rest the way to Texas.

All we had to eat was what we could beg, and sometimes we went three days without a bite to eat. Sometimes we'd pick a few berries. When we got cold we'd crawl in a brushpile and hug up close together to keep warm. Once in a while we'd come to a farmhouse, and the man let us sleep on cottonseed in his barn, but they was far and few between, 'cause they wasn't many houses in the country them days like now.

When we gits to Texas, we gits married, but all they was to our wedding am we just 'grees to live together as man and wife. I settled on some land, and we cut some trees and split them open and stood them on end with the tops together for our house. Then we deadened some trees, and the land was ready to farm. There was some wild cattle and hogs, and that's the way we got our start, caught some of them and tamed them.

I don't know as I 'spected nothing from freedom, but they turned us out like a bunch of stray dogs, no homes, no clothing, no nothing, not 'nough food to last us one meal. After we settles on that place, I never seed man or woman, 'cept Govie, for six years, 'cause it was a long ways to anywhere. All we had to farm with was sharp sticks. We'd stick holes and plant corn, and when it come up we'd punch up the dirt round it. We didn't plant cotton, 'cause we couldn't eat that. I made bows and arrows to kill wild game with, and we never went to a store for nothing. We made our clothes out of animal skins.

WHY ADAM KIRK WAS A DEMOCRAT

House Report No. 262, 43 Cong., 2 Sess., p. 106.
Statement of an Alabama Negro (1874)

A white man raised me. I was raised in the house of old man Billy Kirk. He raised me as a body servant. The class that he belongs to seems nearer to me than the Northern white man, and actually, since the war, everything I have got is by their aid and their assistance. They have helped me raise up my family and have stood by me, and whenever I want a doctor, no matter what hour of the day or night, he is called in whether I have got a cent or not. And when I want any assistance I can get it from them. I think they have got better principles and better character than the Republicans.

2

White Southerners' Reactions to Reconstruction

Caleb G. Forshey and the Reverend James Sinclair

Like their former slaves, white Southerners at the end of the Civil War exhibited a wide variety of attitudes. Granted generous surrender terms that protected them from charges of treason and allowed them to keep horses and mules "to put in a crop," returning Confederate soldiers at first were more resigned to the outcome of the war than those who stayed at home. "I seen our 'Federates go off laughin' an' gay; full of life an' health," recalled a former slave. "Dey was big an' strong, asingin' Dixie an' dey jus knowed dey was agoin' to win. I seen 'em come back skin an' bone, dere eyes all sad an' hollow, an' dere clothes all ragged. Dey was all lookin' sick. De sperrit dey lef' wid jus' been done whupped ooutten dem." That would change as Northern indecision and con-

The Report of the Committees of the House of Representatives Made during the First Session, Thirty-Ninth Congress, 1865–1866, vol. 2 (Washington, D.C.: Government Printing Office, 1866); Forshey: pp. 129–32; Sinclair: pp. 168–71.

flict between Congress and President Andrew Johnson encouraged more organized aggression by white Southerners. In a few years, Confederate veterans would form the core of the Ku Klux Klan.

Those who stayed home had had less opportunity to discharge their anger during the war. After it ended, Southern women were proud to insult Union officers. An innkeeper complained that the Yankees, who had killed his sons, burned down his house, and stolen his slaves, had left him with but "one inestimable privilege — to hate 'em. I git up at half-past four in the morning, and sit up till twelve at night, to hate 'em." A substantial minority, however, had opposed secession and looked forward to expressing those sentiments they had suppressed through the war years. Many Southerners were ready to accept peace on the conqueror's terms. But Northern uncertainty as to what these terms should be made those Southerners waver and encouraged those already angry. The president called for one policy and Congress for another. Northerners elected a Republican Congress that demanded freedom, civil rights, even the franchise for former slaves living in the South, and yet the same Northerners tolerated the denial of civil rights to African Americans living in the North. In the fall of 1865, three Republican states — Connecticut, Wisconsin, and Minnesota — voted down amendments to their constitutions that would have enfranchised blacks. This fueled resistance to Republican demands among white Southerners.

Assembled to examine Southern representation in Congress, the Congressional Joint Committee of Fifteen was part of the Republican Congress's opposition to President Andrew Johnson's plan of Reconstruction. In 1866, the committee held hearings as part of its effort to develop the Fourteenth Amendment. Despite the president's veto, Congress had already enlarged the scope of the Freedmen's Bureau to care for displaced former slaves and to try by military commission those accused of depriving freedmen of civil rights.

Of the two white Southerners whose interviews with the committee are included here, Caleb Forshey had supported secession while James Sinclair, although a slaveholder, had opposed it. A Scottish-born minister who had moved to North Carolina in 1857, Sinclair's Unionist sentiments led to the loss of his church and then to his arrest during the war. In 1865, he was working with the Freedmen's Bureau.

BEFORE YOU READ

1. What did Caleb Forshey think of Union efforts to protect former slaves through military occupation and the Freedmen's Bureau?

2. What were Forshey's beliefs about African Americans?

3. What was the plight of former slaves and white Unionists according to James Sinclair?

CALEB G. FORSHEY

Washington, D.C., March 28, 1866

Question: Where do you reside?
Answer: I reside in the State of Texas.

Question: How long have you been a resident of Texas?

Answer: I have resided in Texas and been a citizen of that State for nearly thirteen years.

Question: What opportunities have you had for ascertaining the temper and disposition of the people of Texas towards the government and authority of the United States?

Answer: For ten years I have been superintendent of the Texas Military Institute, as its founder and conductor. I have been in the confederate service in various parts of the confederacy; but chiefly in the trans-Mississippi department, in Louisiana and Texas, as an officer of engineers. I have had occasion to see and know very extensively the condition of affairs in Texas, and also to a considerable extent in Louisiana. I think I am pretty well-informed, as well as anybody, perhaps, of the present state of affairs in Texas.

Question: What are the feelings and views of the people of Texas as to the late rebellion, and the future condition and circumstances of the State, and its relations to the federal government?

Answer: After our army had given up its arms and gone home, the surrender of all matters in controversy was complete, and as nearly universal, perhaps, as anything could be. Assuming the matters in controversy to have been the right to secede, and the right to hold slaves, I think they were given up tee-totally, to use a strong Americanism. When you speak of feeling, I should discriminate a little. The feeling was that of any party who had been cast in a suit he had staked all upon. They did not return from feeling, but from a sense of necessity, and from a judgment that it was the only and necessary thing to be done, to give up the contest. But when they gave it up, it was without reservation; with a view to look forward, and not back. That is my impression of the manner in which the thing was done. There was a public expectation that in some very limited time there would be a restoration to former relations. . . . It was the expectation of the people that, as soon as the State was organized as proposed by the President, they would be restored to their former relations, and things would go on as before.

Question: What is your opinion of a military force under the authority of the federal government to preserve order in Texas and to protect those who have been loyal, both white and black, from the aggressions of those who have been in the rebellion?

Answer: My judgment is well founded on that subject: that wherever such military force is and has been, it has excited the very feeling it was intended to prevent; that so far from being necessary it is very pernicious everywhere, and without exception. The local authorities and public sentiment are ample for protection. I think no occasion would occur, unless some individual case that our laws would not reach. We had an opportunity to test this after the surrender and before any authority was there. The military authorities, or the military officers, declared that we were without laws, and it was a long time before the governor appointed arrived there, and then it was sometime before we could effect anything in the way of organization. We were a people without law, order, or anything; and it was a time for violence if it would occur. I think it is a great credit to our civilization that, in that state of affairs, there was nowhere any instance of violence. I am proud of it, for I expected the contrary; I expected that our soldiers on coming home, many of them, would be dissolute, and that many of them would oppress the class of men you speak of; but it did not occur. But afterwards, wherever soldiers have been sent, there have been little troubles, none of them large; but personal collisions between soldiers and citizens.

Question: What is your opinion as to the necessity and advantages of the Freedmen's Bureau, or an agency of that kind, in Texas?

Answer: My opinion is that it is not needed; my opinion is stronger than that—that the effect of it is to irritate, if nothing else. While in New York city recently I had a conversation with some friends from Texas, from five distant points in the State. We met together and compared opinions; and the opinion of each was the same, that the negroes had generally gone to work since January; that except where the Freedmen's Bureau had interfered, or rather encouraged troubles, such as little complaints, especially between negro and negro, the negro's disposition was very good, and they had generally gone to work, a vast majority of them with their former masters. . . . The impression in Texas at present is that the negroes under the influence of the Freedmen's Bureau do worse than without it.

I want to state that I believe all our former owners of negroes are the friends of the negroes; and that the antagonism paraded in the papers of the north does not exist at all. I know the fact is the very converse of that; and good feeling always prevails between the masters and the slaves. But the negroes went off and left them in the lurch; my own family was an instance of it. But they came back after a time, saying they had been free enough and wanted a home.

Question: Do you think those who employ the negroes there are willing to make contracts with them, so that they shall have fair wages for their labor?

Answer: I think so; I think they are paid liberally, more than the white men in this country get; the average compensation to negroes there is greater than the average compensation of free laboring white men in this country. It seems to have regulated itself in a great measure by what each neighborhood was doing; the negroes saying, "I can get thus and so at such a place." Men have hired from eight to fifteen dollars per month during the year, and women at about two dollars less a month; house-servants at a great deal more.

Question: Do the men who employ the negroes claim to exercise the right to enforce their contract by physical force?

Answer: Not at all; that is totally abandoned; not a single instance of it has occurred. I think they still chastise children, though. The negro parents often neglect that, and the children are still switched as we switch our own children. I know it is done in my own house; we have little house-servants that we switch just as I do our own little fellows.

Question: What is your opinion as to the respective advantages to the white and black races, of the present free system of labor and the institution of slavery?

Answer: I think freedom is very unfortunate for the negro; I think it is sad; his present helpless condition touches my heart more than anything else I ever contemplated, and I think that is the common sentiment of our slaveholders. I have seen it on the largest plantations, where the negro men had all left, and where only women and children remained, and the owners had to keep them and feed them. The beginning certainly presents a touching and sad spectacle. The poor negro is dying at a rate fearful to relate.

I have some ethnological theories that may perhaps warp my judgment; but my judgment is that the highest condition the black race has ever reached or can reach, is one where he is provided for by a master race. That is the result of a great deal of scientific investigation and observation of the negro character by me ever since I was a man. The labor question had become a most momentous one, and I was studying it. I undertook to investigate the condition of the negro from statistics under various circumstances, to treat it purely as a matter of statistics from the census tables of this country of ours. I found that the free blacks of the north decreased 8 per cent.; the free blacks of the south increased 7 or 8 per cent., while the slaves by their sides increased 34 per cent. I inferred from the doctrines of political economy that the race is in the best condition when it procreates the fastest; that, other things being equal, slavery is of vast advantage to the negro. I will mention one or two things in connexion with this as explanatory of that result. The negro will not take care of his offspring unless required to do it, as compared with the whites. The little children will die; they do die, and hence the necessity of very rigorous regulations on our plantations which we have adopted in our nursery system.

Another cause is that there is no continence among the negroes. All the continence I have ever seen among the negroes has been enforced upon plantations, where it is generally assumed there is none. For the sake of procreation, if nothing else, we compel men to live with their wives. The discipline of the plantation was more rigorous, perhaps, in regard to men staying with their wives, than in regard to anything else; and I think the procreative results, as shown by the census tables, is due in a great measure to that discipline. . . .

Question: What is the prevailing inclination among the people of Texas in regard to giving the negroes civil or political rights and privileges?

Answer: I think they are all opposed to it. There are some men—I am not among them—who think that the basis of intelligence might be a good basis for the elective franchise. But a much larger class, perhaps nine-tenths of our people, believe that the distinctions between the races should not be broken down by any such community of interests in the management of the affairs of the State. I think there is a very common sentiment that the negro, even with education, has not a mind capable of appreciating the political institutions of the country to such an extent as would make him a good associate for the white man in the administration of the government. I think if the vote was taken on the question of admitting him to the right of suffrage there would be a very small vote in favor of it—scarcely respectable: that is my judgment.

THE REVEREND JAMES SINCLAIR

Washington, D.C., January 29, 1866

Question: What is generally the state of feeling among the white people of North Carolina towards the government of the United States?

Answer: That is a difficult question to answer, but I will answer it as far as my own knowledge goes. In my opinion, there is generally among the white people not much love for the government. Though they are willing, and I believe determined, to acquiesce in what is inevitable, yet so far as love and affection for the government is concerned, I do not believe that they have any of it at all, outside of their personal respect and regard for President Johnson.

Question: How do they feel towards the mass of the northern people — that is, the people of what were known formerly as the free States?

Answer: They feel in this way: that they have been ruined by them. You can imagine the feelings of a person towards one whom he regards as having ruined him. They regard the northern people as having destroyed their property or taken it from them, and brought all the calamities of this war upon them.

Question: How do they feel in regard to what is called the right of secession?

Answer: They think that it was right . . . that there was no wrong in it. They are willing now to accept the decision of the question that has been made by the sword, but they are not by any means converted from their old opinion that they had a right to secede. It is true that there have always been Union men in our State, but not Union men without slavery, except perhaps among Quakers. Slavery was the central idea even of the Unionist. The only difference between them and the others upon that question was, that they desired to have that institution under the aegis of the Constitution, and protected by it. The secessionists wanted to get away from the north altogether. When the secessionists precipitated our State into rebellion, the Unionists and secessionists went together, because the great object with both was the preservation of slavery by the preservation of State sovereignty. There was another class of Unionists who did not care anything at all about slavery, but they were driven by the other whites into the rebellion for the purpose of preserving slavery. The poor whites are to-day very much opposed to conferring upon the negro the right of suffrage; as much so as the other classes of the whites. They believe it is the intention of government to give the negro rights at their expense. They cannot see it in any other light than that as the negro is elevated they must proportionately go down. While they are glad that slavery is done away with, they are bitterly opposed to conferring the right of suffrage on the negro as the most prominent secessionists; but it is for the reason I have stated, that they think rights conferred on the negro must necessarily be taken from them, particularly the ballot, which was the only bulwark guarding their superiority to the negro race.

Question: In your judgment, what proportion of the white people of North Carolina are really, and truly, and cordially attached to the government of the United States?

Answer: Very few, sir; very few. . . .

Question: Is the Freedmen's Bureau acceptable to the great mass of the white people in North Carolina?

Answer: No, sir; I do not think it is; I think the most of the whites wish the bureau to be taken away.

Question: Why do they wish that?

Answer: They think that they can manage the negro for themselves: that they understand him better than northern men do. They say, "Let us understand what you want us to do with [the] negro—what you desire of us; lay down your conditions for our readmission into the Union, and then we will know what we have to do, and if you will do that we will enact laws for the government of these negroes. They have lived among us, and they are all with us, and we can manage them better than you can." They think it is interfering with the rights of the State for a bureau, the agent and representative of the federal government, to overslaugh the State entirely, and interfere with the regulations and administration of justice before their courts.

Question: Is there generally a willingness on the part of the whites to allow the freedmen to enjoy the right of acquiring land and personal property?

Answer: I think they are very willing to let them do that, for this reason; to get rid of some portion of the taxes imposed upon their property by the government. For instance, a white man will agree to sell a negro some of his land on condition of his paying so much a year on it, promising to give him a deed of it when the whole payment is made, taking his note in the mean time. This relieves that much of the land from taxes to be paid by the white man. All I am afraid of is, that the negro is too eager to go into this thing; that he will ruin himself, get himself into debt to the white man, and be forever bound to him for the debt and never get the land. I have often warned them to be careful what they did about these things.

Question: There is no repugnance on the part of the whites to the negro owning land and personal property?

Answer: I think not.

Question: Have they any objection to the legal establishment of the domestic relations among the blacks, such as the relation of husband and wife, of parent and child, and the securing by law to the negro the rights of those relations?

Answer: That is a matter of ridicule with the whites. They do not believe the negroes will ever respect those relations more than the brutes. I suppose I have married more than two hundred couples of negroes since the war, but the whites laugh at the very idea of the thing. Under the old laws a slave could not marry a free woman of color; it was made a penal offence in North Carolina for any one to perform such a marriage. But there was in my own family a slave who desired to marry a free woman of color, and I did what I conceived to be my duty, and married them, and I was presented to the grand jury for doing so, but the prosecuting attorney threw out the case and would not try it. In former times the officiating clergyman marrying slaves, could not use the usual formula: "Whom God has joined together let no man put asunder"; you could not say, "According to the ordinance of God I pronounce you man and wife; you are no longer two but one." It was not legal for you to do so.

Question: What, in general, has been the treatment of the blacks by the whites since the close of hostilities?

Answer: It has not generally been of the kindest character, I must say that; I am compelled to say that.

Question: Are you aware of any instance of personal ill treatment towards the blacks by the whites?

Answer: Yes, sir.

Question: Give some instances that have occurred since the war.

Answer: [Sinclair describes the beating of a young woman across her buttocks in graphic detail.]

Question: What was the provocation, if any?

Answer: Something in regard to some work, which is generally the provocation.

Question: Was there no law in North Carolina at that time to punish such an outrage?

Answer: No, sir; only the regulations of the Freedmen's Bureau; we took cognizance of the case. In old times that was quite allowable; it is what was called "paddling."

Question: Did you deal with the master?

Answer: I immediately sent a letter to him to come to my office, but he did not come, and I have never seen him in regard to the matter since. I had no soldiers to enforce compliance, and I was obliged to let the matter drop.

Question: Have you any reason to suppose that such instances of cruelty are frequent in North Carolina at this time—instances of whipping and striking?

Answer: I think they are; it was only a few days before I left that a woman came there with her head all bandaged up, having been cut and bruised by her employer. They think nothing of striking them.

Question: And the negro has practically no redress?

Answer: Only what he can get from the Freedmen's Bureau.

Question: Can you say anything further in regard to the political condition of North Carolina—the feeling of the people towards the government of the United States?

Answer: I for one would not wish to be left there in the hands of those men; I could not live there just now. But perhaps my case is an isolated one from the position I was compelled to take in that State. I was persecuted, arrested, and they tried to get me into their service; they tried everything to accomplish their purpose, and of course I have rendered myself still more obnoxious by accepting an appointment under the Freedmen's Bureau. As for myself I would not be allowed to remain there. I do not want to be handed over to these people. I know it is utterly impossible for any man who was not true to the Confederate States up to the last moment of the existence of the confederacy, to expect any favor of these people as the State is constituted at present.

Question: Suppose the military pressure of the government of the United States should be withdrawn from North Carolina, would northern men and true Unionists be safe in that State?

Answer: A northern man going there would perhaps present nothing obnoxious to the people of the State. But men who were born there, who have been true to the Union, and who have fought against the rebellion, are worse off than northern men. . . .

Question: In your judgment, what effect has been produced by the liberality of the President in granting pardons and amnesties to rebels in that State — what effect upon the public mind?

Answer: On my oath I am bound to reply exactly as I believe; that is, that if President Johnson is ever a candidate for re-election he will be supported by the southern States, particularly by North Carolina; but that his liberality to them has drawn them one whit closer to the government than before, I do not believe. It has drawn them to President Johnson personally, and to the Democratic party, I suppose.

FOR CRITICAL THINKING

1. Reading the accounts of these former slaves, what do you think they most needed during the Reconstruction era to establish themselves in Southern society?

2. How did the views of Forshey and Sinclair differ on Reconstruction policy? On what principles do you think those differences were based?

3. Was there a basis for agreement between Southern African Americans and whites on how to rebuild the South after the Civil War? Did the activities of the Union — such as military occupation, the Freedmen's Bureau, and passage of the Thirteenth, Fourteenth, and Fifteenth Amendments — help or hinder the redevelopment of the South?

3

The Murder of Jim Williams
Rosy Williams et al.

There have been three distinct Ku Klux Klans: they flourished in the 1860s and 1870s, from the 1920s to the early 1940s, and from the 1950s through to the present. The first, which concerns us here, began as a fraternity in Tennessee in 1866 but soon turned into a violent organization dedicated to defeating Republican Reconstruction governments in the South and intimidating and controlling African Americans. In rural counties in many parts of the region, the Klan, its members sworn to secrecy on penalty of "death, death, death," controlled regions for months or even years, destroying the property of blacks or their white allies, driving people away, assaulting, and killing. Local governments and law enforcement agencies, dominated by or simply intimidated by the Klan, failed to stop these activities. Nationally, Republicans demanded action against the Klan while Democrats discounted its activities. In 1871, the Republicans, who then controlled both houses of Congress, established a joint House-Senate committee chaired by Senator John Scott of Pennsylvania to investigate the Klan. Its twelve-volume report is our main source of knowledge of the first Klan.

The climax of Klan activity came in 1871 with a reign of terror in a number of South Carolina counties. President Ulysses S. Grant, who since taking office had been reluctant to intervene in the South, requested from Congress a bill to put down the mounting atrocities in South Carolina and elsewhere. The result was the Ku Klux Act of 1871. It allowed the president to suspend the writ of habeas corpus, *which in turn enabled federal military authorities to arrest Klansmen when local authorities refused to do so. This was not, as some alleged, martial law, since all such prisoners were eventually tried in federal courts.*

The hanging on March 6, 1871, of Jim Williams, an outspoken enemy of the Klan and the captain of a black militia unit, became the single most famous event in the history of the South Carolina Klan. One of Yorkville's most prominent citizens, Dr. J. Rufus Bratton, was called to testify before the Committee and was later accused of leading the raid. As soon as the suspension of habeas corpus *threatened his arrest, he fled to Canada, where he lived in exile until 1877, when President Rutherford B. Hayes, as part of the many deals that finally ended Reconstruction, dropped all charges against him. Bratton returned to Yorkville as something of a local hero. The Klan's day had ended, but few Klansmen were ever punished for their actions.*

United States, Cong., *Testimony Taken by the Joint Select Committee to Inquire into the Condition of Affairs in the Late Insurrectionary States, South Carolina* [usually referred to as the *KKK Report*] (Washington, D.C.: Government Printing Office, 1872), vol. 3, pp. 1720–21; *KKK Report, South Carolina*, vol. 3, pp. 1724–27; *KKK Report, South Carolina*, vol. 3, pp. 1342–59 passim.

BEFORE YOU READ

1. What happened on the night of March 6, 1871, when Jim Williams was hanged? Piece together an account of events from the testimony.

2. What does this incident tell you about relations between blacks and whites in this part of South Carolina?

3. How widespread was membership in the Klan among whites in this area?

TESTIMONY OF MRS. ROSY WILLIAMS

Mrs. Rosy Williams, (colored,) widow of Jim Williams, was the eighth witness called for the prosecution. She was sworn, and testified as follows:

Direct examination by Mr. Corbin:

Question: Are you the wife of Jim Williams?

Answer: Yes, sir.

Question: Where do you live; where did you live when Jim Williams was living?

Answer: On Bratton's place.

Question: In what county, York County?

Answer: Yes, sir.

Question: When was Jim Williams killed—your husband?

Answer: The 7th of March.

Question: Tell the court and jury all about it—all you know about it.

Answer: They came to my house about two o'clock in the night; came in the house and called him.

Question: Who came?

Answer: Disguised men. I can't tell who it was. I don't know any of them.

Question: What do you call them?

Answer: I call them Ku-Klux.

Question: How many came?

Answer: I don't know how many there was.

Question: How many do you think?

Answer: I reckon about nine or ten came into the house, as nigh as I can guess it.

Question: What did they do?

Answer: He went under the house before they came, and after they came in he came up in the house and gave them the guns; there were but two in the house, and then they asked him for the others, and cussed, and told him to come out. He told them he had never had any of the guns. He went with them, and after they had took him out-doors they came in the house after me, and said there were some guns hid. I told them there was not; and after I told them that they went out, and after they had went out there I heard him make a fuss like he was strangling.

Question: Who?

Answer: Williams. Then I went to the door and pulled the door open, and allowed to go down and beg them not to hurt him. They told me not to go out there. Well, I didn't go out. Then they told me to shut the door and take my children and go to bed. I shut the door but didn't go to bed. I looked out of the crack after them until they got under the shadows of the trees. I couldn't see them then.

Question: Did they take Jim Williams?

Answer: Yes, sir; but I couldn't tell him from the rest.

Question: Was that the last you ever saw him alive?

Answer: Yes, sir.

Question: Or did you see him again?

Answer: No, sir; the next morning I went and looked for him, but I didn't find him. I was scared, too. Then I went for my people, to get some one to go help me look for him; and I met an old man who told me they had found him, and said he was dead. They had hung him; but I didn't go out there until 12 o'clock.

Question: Did you go out there then—did you see him?

Answer: Yes, sir.

Question: What was his condition?

Answer: He was hung on a pine tree.

Question: With a rope around his neck?

Answer: Yes, sir.

Question: Dead?

Answer: Yes, sir; he was dead.

TESTIMONY OF JOHN CALDWELL

John Caldwell was the next witness called, who, being duly sworn, testified as follows:

Direct examination by Mr. Corbin:

Question: What is your name?

Answer: John Caldwell. . . .

Question: How long have you resided in York county?

Answer: Twenty-seven years. I was born and raised there.

Question: How old are you?

Answer: About twenty-seven years.

Question: In what portion of York county do you reside?

Answer: In the western portion.

Question: Have you ever been a member of the Ku-Klux organization in York County?

Answer: Yes, sir; I have.

Question: When did you join the order?

Answer: In 1868.

Question: Where was that?

Answer: At Yorkville.

Question: Who initiated you?

Answer: Major J. W. Avery.

Question: What was his relation to the order at that time?

Answer: He just came to me and asked me to walk up to his store. He took me into a room and said he wanted me to join an order. I asked him what he was getting it up for. He said it was in self-defense.

Question: Were you initiated by him then? Did he administer the oath? Can you tell us about what that oath was?

Answer: I cannot remember.

Question: Can you tell us the substance of it?

Answer: Only the last portion of it.

Question: What was that?

Answer: I understood that any person who divulged the secrets of the organization should "suffer death, death, death."

Question: Do you think you would recognize the oath were you to hear it again?

Answer: No, sir; only that portion of it. . . .

Question: Commence at the beginning and describe the raid on Jim Williams; when you got the order to go; where you went to muster; who took command of the men, and what road you traveled; what you did when you got to Jim Williams's house, and all about the matter.

Answer: The first I heard of it was at Yorkville; I was told there by Dr. Bratton that they were going down to McConnellsville; I asked him what he was going after; he said he was going for some guns; he asked me if I would go, and I said I would have nothing to do with it; I had never been on a raid; he asked me the name of the chief man in our county; I told him I understood it was William Johnson or Alonzo Brown was the leading man in our county.

Question: Do you mean in your portion of the county?

Answer: Yes, sir.

Question: Go on and tell all you know.

Answer: Johnson came to me and told me to meet him at the muster-patch; that was William Johnson.

Question: What is his relation to the order?

Answer: He was chief.

Question: Of what Klan?

Answer: Of the Rattlesnake Klan. I went out to the muster-ground that night; it is called the brier-patch; I met several men there. . . . Dr. Bratton came there, and Lindsay Brown and Rufus McLain.

Question: Did you put on your disguise at the brier-patch?

Answer: Yes, sir.

Question: What sort of disguises are they?

Answer: Most of them were black gowns, with heads and false-faces.

Question: What sort of heads were they?

Answer: They were made out of black cloth, or dark cloth.

Question: How were they ornamented?

Answer: Some had horns, and some had not.

Question: Had you horses there?

Answer: Yes, sir.

Question: Were the men armed?

Answer: No, sir. I don't believe I saw a gun in the party.

Question: Had they pistols?

Answer: I didn't see any pistols.

Question: Now tell us where they went.

Answer: We went down to the Pinckney road, and there we met another party of men. . . .

Question: What did they do there?

Answer: We stopped then, and there were four men initiated there. . . .

Question: Who was in command of the party?

Answer: Bratton was at the head of the party. He was riding in front.

Question: What Bratton was that?

Answer: Dr. J. Rufus Bratton, of Yorkville.

Question: Go on with what you had to say.

Answer: We went on then to McConnellsville; and about 200 or 300 yards from there we halted; and they said there were some guns down at that place, and they sent a party to search and get them. A man then came from the party that went forward and said, bring up the horses; and they took them down. They said there was a gun at Mr. Moore's; and they went up there for a black man; but I don't know who he was.

Question: At whose place was this?

Answer: They said it was Mr. Moore's place.

Question: What did they do with the black man?

Answer: They asked him about Jim Williams; how far away he lived. They asked him if he knew if Williams had any guns. He said he thought there were twelve or fifteen guns there. Then they took this black-masked man and mounted him on a horse or mule, and carried him a piece; then they halted and turned the black man loose, and he went back home. Then they went on from there about three miles, and stopped in a thicket, and a party of ten went off—I don't know whether there were more than ten—and were gone probably an hour.

Question: Can you describe the place?

Answer: It was in an old piney thicket on the side of a hill.

Question: What did you do?

Answer: I remained there with the horses. I was not well, and I just remained there with the horses.

Question: Did the party go forward?

Answer: Yes, sir. Before I got off my horse I heard some one call for ten men, and that party then went off. I saw them go off; and they were gone probably one hour when they returned.

Question: Did you hear anything of them while they were gone?

Answer: Not a word.

Question: Did the same crowd return?

Answer: Yes, sir.

Question: What was said by any of them as to what they had done?

Answer: I asked if they had found the black man Jim Williams, and if they saw him. I got no answer, and they just got on their horses to leave.

Question: Who ordered them?

Answer: I heard some man say, "Mount your horses," and then they mounted and took across over the fence, and I got up forward to the foremost man — Dr. Bratton. I asked him if he had found the negro. He said yes. Said I, "Where, where is he?" Said he, "He is in hell, I expect."

Question: What further was said?

Answer: I asked him, "You didn't kill him?" He said, "We hung him." I said, "Dr. Bratton, you ought not to have done that." He then pulled out his watch, and said, "We have no time to spare; we have to call on one or two more."

TESTIMONY OF DR. JAMES R. BRATTON

James R. Bratton sworn and examined.

By the Chairman:

Question: Do you reside in this place?

Answer: Yes, sir, and have been residing here for twenty-five years.

Question: Are you a native of this State?

Answer: Yes, sir; of this county.

Question: What is your occupation?

Answer: I have been practicing medicine here for twenty-five years.

Question: Have you had an opportunity of becoming acquainted with the people of this county generally?

Answer: Yes, sir, I think I have.

Question: Does your practice extend through the county?

Answer: Through the different sections of the county.

Question: Our purpose is to inquire into the security of life, person, and property through this county, and the manner in which the laws are executed. Have you any knowledge of any offenses against the law, or against the security of person and property, that have not been redressed in the ordinary courts of justice?

Answer: I have no personal knowledge of anything of the kind. I merely hear rumors and reports. Personally, I know nothing about it.

Question: Have you been called upon, as a physician, to either testify before, or certify upon, any inquests on the bodies of dead men?

Answer: I have not. I have only heard these reports from the coroner's inquests; that is the way I get my information about these cases.

Question: How many persons have you heard of who have been killed in this county within the last six or eight months?

Answer: There was a man up here named Tom Black, or Roundtree, that they say was killed — I cannot tell when. One report says he was killed by negroes for his money; another, that it was by white men in disguise. He had been to Charlotte a few days before that, to sell his cotton, and, when killed, his money could not be found; but who killed him I cannot tell. . . .

Question: Any others?

Answer: Yes, sir; a negro was hung about twelve miles below by some persons, who I cannot tell.

Question: What was his name?

Answer: Williams.

Question: Was he a militia captain?

Answer: He was.

Question: When was that?

Answer: That was some time in this year, in February or March; in the latter part of February or the first of March; I do not remember the date exactly.

Question: Do you recollect the day of the week?

Answer: No, sir, I do not remember it.

Question: Do you recollect the day you heard it?

Answer: No, sir; nor the day it was done; it was some time in the latter part of February or the first of March.

Question: Was that done by men in disguise?

Answer: Yes, sir, it was so reported; that was the testimony at the coroner's inquest.

Question: Were you at that inquest?

Answer: I was not; but it was so reported to me by the coroner.

Question: Was that in February or March?

Answer: Yes, sir.

Question: Are those the only cases you have known of?

Answer: I do not know any other cases that I can think of now. I have not fixed any other cases upon my mind. Let me see, there may have been other cases.

Question: Those are cases of actual death about which I am inquiring now?

Answer: What do you mean by that?

Question: Persons killed.

Answer: Those three are negroes killed. I do not know any other cases to my knowledge. . . .

Question: Do you discredit the statements of negroes who say they were whipped?

Answer: In many cases I do.

Question: Do you think the men who disguise themselves could be easily told?

Answer: I do not say that, but a great many of these people dislike to work, and if they can get the protection of the State or the United States to relieve them from work they will do it, and I have no faith in their testimony.

Question: In negro testimony?

Answer: I have not.

Question: Is there any concerted arrangement here for the purpose of intimidating the negroes either with regard to their political rights or their making complaints against those who have whipped them or otherwise committed violence upon them?

Answer: I know nothing of the kind. The truth is this, I think it is just the reverse. If ever our people were earnest in anything it is to teach the negro his duty to be quiet and passive and attend to his duty; to let public meetings alone; to go and vote as he pleases, allowing no man to interfere with him. I do not know any cases where a darkey has been interfered with at the polls.

Question: Is attendance at a political meeting considered imprudent or wrong in them?

Answer: When they attend in large numbers they create great confusion and annoyance; but I do not know a procession that has been interfered with.

Question: Is that the light in which the white people view that subject, that the negroes had better stay away altogether from political meetings?

Answer: Yes, sir. Our advice is "have as little to do with politics as possible; if you want to vote, vote, but vote for no dishonest, vicious, ignorant, and wicked man; vote for whom you please, so he is honest, whether a radical or a democrat." That has been my advice to them all.

Question: Do you know of no organization in this county intended to prevent negroes from voting as they saw proper?

Answer: I don't; and that has not been the case.

Question: Do you know anything of this organization commonly called Ku-Klux?

Answer: I am no member of the Ku-Klux, and know nothing of their proceedings. . . .

[Bratton is presented with an article on the Klan from the local newspaper.]

Question: Now, Doctor, having stated your belief that there is a Ku-Klux organization, since you saw this notice in the paper, state who in your belief compose it.

Answer: I cannot tell you that, sir.

Question: What class of people, sir?

Answer: I cannot tell you who compose that organization. I know nothing about them. I do not belong, and have no means of knowing.

Question: Have you no idea who compose it?

Answer: No, sir; I have no means of knowing. . . .

Question: Have you any knowledge of the men who participated in the hanging of Captain Williams?

Answer: I have no knowledge of that fact.

Question: Has no man said anything to you about it?

Answer: No, sir; no man has said, "I did it," or "he did." I know nothing about it as to who hung him.

Question: Either from those who participated in it or from any other person?

Answer: No, sir.

Question: Did you learn that he was hanged?

Answer: Yes, sir.

Question: That that was the mode of his killing—that he was hung?

Answer: Yes, sir.

Question: Were you upon the inquest of any one of these men who were murdered by violence in this county?

Answer: No, sir. I was engaged all the time in other business. Generally in these cases in the country they take the nearest physician. . . .

Question: What, in your opinion, have been the causes of whatever disturbances have occurred in this county within a year; what are the principal leading causes of any troubles that may have existed, whether breaking out by Ku-Klux acts or any other mode of proceeding?

Answer: Why, sir, my opinion is this: that these burnings of people's houses and barns and gin-houses produced this disturbance.

Question: Was that last summer?

Answer: That was last fall and winter, and this spring. I do not know that there were any burnings last summer that I remember. I think it was all this winter.

Question: You have given an estimate of the number of the whippings of negroes, whether by Ku-Klux or other negroes, or somebody else for private reasons, at twelve or fifteen. What is the probable number of burnings of gin-houses in this county in the last year?

Answer: I will have to count them up. Thomason, stables and barn; Warren, gin-houses; Miller, gin-house; Crosby, gin-house; Preacher Castle, barn; my brother's thrashing-house was burnt the other night. A boy confessed it afterward. He simply did it because my brother had told him not to go into his select orchard. He had a large orchard and told him that he and the rest of the colored people might go in there, but not in the garden. He did go into the garden. He caught him there and cursed him a little, and, in a few days, this fire took place. . . .

Question: Out of these six cases [of arson], is there any evidence to connect the negroes, as a class, with the burning?

Answer: No, sir.

Question: Yet you give these burnings as the outrages against the negroes?

Answer: That is the general impression among the people.

Question: What justice is there in charging the negroes, as a class, with burning, any more than the murderers who are operating through the country?

Answer: Let me tell you. These people are easily excited to action, and when we had the candidates last fall, strange to say, one candidate actually made this speech: "You have to succeed in this county if you have to burn every blade of grass," or something to that effect.

Question: Did you hear it?

Answer: No, sir.

Question: Who reported it to you?

Answer: I do not know.

Question: Who made the speech?

Answer: Doctor Neagle.

Question: Who heard it?

Answer: Almost any citizen you can take up.

Question: You cannot swear that he said it?

Answer: No, sir.

Question: You are willing to believe it?

Answer: Yes, sir.

Question: And that the negroes did these burnings, incited by that?

Answer: I am more disposed to think that the negroes did it than that white persons did it.

Question: And yet you have no opinion as to the murderers in this county?

Answer: No, sir.

4

Vengeance against "Long Hair"
She Walks with Her Shawl
and One Bull

Americans vividly remember the Plains Indians, whose last great victory came at the Little Big Horn in 1876, the "feather-streaming, buffalo-chasing, wild-riding, recklessly fighting Indian of the plains," as the historian William Brandon describes their young male warriors. In most American imaginations they are the archetype of the American Indian.

The reality is far more complex, however. The religion, elaborate warrior code, fierce grief for the dead, and stunning rituals and visions of other worlds were largely borrowed from the many Indian cultures these nomads briefly conquered as they swept across the plains in the eighteenth and nineteenth centuries on horses first brought to the Americas by the Spanish conquistadors. Not the tomahawk but the rifle, acquired from French, English, and, later, American traders, was their main weapon. And their beads were all from Europe. Anthropologists use the term syncretic *to describe the culture of nomadic Plains Indians like the Lakota Sioux: a magnificent amalgam of all the peoples they had encountered. Native American, surely, but in this they were also quintessentially American.*

The horse and rifle brought wealth and military might. The plains became a terrain of ritual hunting and warfare, and prosperity permitted extensive trade and the elaboration of Indian cultures. For about a century, competing powers hindered white conquest. But over time the French, Spanish, English, and Mexicans ceased to be counterweights to the rising power of the Anglo-Americans. Emigrants to the West Coast and then settlers disrupted Indian life, and the Civil War divided and weakened the Western Indians even as it strengthened the federal government. Then came the wasteful white buffalo hunters, the miners, the railroads, rushes of settlers, and a determined U.S. Army. A series of Indian wars, beginning during the Civil War, rapidly resulted in all but a few Plains Indians being pushed onto reservations.

By 1876 the great Western saga—"America's Iliad," as Brandon calls it—appeared about over. But thousands of Sioux and Northern Cheyenne, still off of or escaping from the reservations, gathered briefly at the Little Big Horn to enjoy religious rituals, hunting, and their defiance of the U.S. Army. General George Armstrong Custer and his premier Indian fighters, the Seventh Cavalry, found them there and promptly attacked.

Jerome A. Greene, ed., *Lakota and Cheyenne, Indian Views of the Great Sioux War, 1876–1877* (Norman: University of Oklahoma Press, 1994), pp. 42–46, 54–59.

We see the ensuing battle through the eyes of a Hunkpapa Lakota woman, She Walks with Her Shawl, and a Minneconjou Lakota man, One Bull, the adopted son of Sitting Bull. Keep in mind that both accounts are filtered through white interviewers.

BEFORE YOU READ

1. Observe in each account how these informants reacted to the battle. What role did each assume? What can you learn about Lakota culture from their actions?

2. What can you infer about Sitting Bull's role from One Bull's account?

3. On the basis of these accounts, does the usual characterization of the battle as a "massacre" seem accurate? Why or why not?

SHE WALKS WITH HER SHAWL (HUNKPAPA LAKOTA)

Account given to Walter S. Campbell in 1931

I was born seventy-seven winters ago, near Grand River, [in present] South Dakota. My father, Slohan, was the bravest man among our people. Fifty-five years ago we packed our tents and went with other Indians to Peji-slawakpa (Greasy Grass). We were then living on the Standing Rock Indian reservation [Great Sioux Reservation, Standing Rock Agency]. I belonged to Sitting Bull's band. They were great fighters. We called ourselves Hunkpapa. This means confederated bands. When I was still a young girl (about seventeen) I accompanied a Sioux war party which made war against the Crow Indians in Montana. My father went to war 70 times. He was wounded nearly a dozen times.

But I am going to tell you of the greatest battle. This was a fight against Pehin-hanska (General Custer). I was several miles from the Hunkpapa camp when I saw a cloud of dust rise beyond a ridge of bluffs in the east. The morning was hot and sultry. Several of us Indian girls were digging wild turnips. I was then 23 years old. We girls looked towards the camp and saw a warrior ride swiftly, shouting that the soldiers were only a few miles away and that the women and children including old men should run for the hills in an opposite direction.

I dropped the pointed ash stick which I had used in digging turnips and rans towards my tipi. I saw my father running towards the horses. When I got to my tent, mother told me that news was brought to her that my brother had been killed by the soldiers. My brother had gone early that morning in search for a horse that strayed from our herd. In a few moments we saw soldiers on horseback on a bluff just across the Greasy Grass (Little Big Horn) river. I knew that there would be a battle because I saw warriors getting their horses and tomahawks.

I heard Hawkman shout, Ho-ka-he! Ho-ka-he! (Charge.) The soldiers began firing into our camp. Then they ceased firing. I saw my father preparing to go to battle. I sang a death song for my brother who had been killed.

My heart was bad. Revenge! Revenge! For my brother's death. I thought of the death of my young brother, One Hawk. Brown Eagle, my brother's companion on that morning had escaped and gave the alarm to the camp that the soldiers were coming. I ran to a nearby thicket and got my black horse. I painted my face with crimson and unbraided my black hair. I was mourning. I was a woman, but I was not afraid.

By this time the soldiers (Reno's men) were forming a battle line in the bottom about a half mile away. In another moment I heard a terrific volley of carbines. The bullets shattered the tipi poles. Women and children were running away from the gunfire. In the tumult I heard old men and women singing death songs for their warriors who were now ready to attack the soldiers. The chanting of death songs made me brave, although I was a woman. I saw a warrior adjusting his quiver and grasping his tomahawk. He started running towards his horse when he suddenly recoiled and dropped dead. He was killed near his tipi.

Warriors were given orders by Hawkman to mount their horses and follow the fringe of a forest and wait until commands were given to charge. The soldiers kept on firing. Some women were also killed. Horses and dogs too! The camp was in great commotion.

Father led my black horse up to me and I mounted. We galloped towards the soldiers. Other warriors joined in with us. When we were nearing the fringe of the woods an order was given by Hawkman to charge. Ho-ka-he! Ho-ka-he! Charge! Charge! The warriors were now near the soldiers. The troopers were all on foot. They shot straight, because I saw our leader killed as he rode with his warriors.

The charge was so stubborn that the soldiers ran to their horses and, mounting them, rode swiftly towards the river. The Greasy Grass river was very deep. Their horses had to swim to get across. Some of the warriors rode into the water and tomahawked the soldiers. In the charge the Indians rode among the troopers and with tomahawks unhorsed several of them. The soldiers were very excited. Some of them shot into the air. The Indians chased the soldiers across the river and up over a bluff.

Then the warriors returned to the bottom where the first battle took place. We heard a commotion far down the valley. The warriors rode in a column of fives. They sang a victory song. Someone said that another body of soldiers were attacking the lower end of the village. I heard afterwards that the soldiers were under the command of Long Hair (Custer). With my father and other youthful warriors I rode in that direction.

We crossed the Greasy Grass below a beaver dam (the water is not so deep there) and came upon many horses. One soldier was holding the reins of eight or ten horses. An Indian waved his blanket and scared all the horses. They got away from the men (troopers). On the ridge just north of us I saw blue-clad men running up a ravine, firing as they ran.

The dust created from the stampeding horses and powder smoke made everything dark and black. Flashes from carbines could be seen. The valley was dense with powder smoke. I never heard such whooping and shouting. "There was never a better day to die," shouted Red Horse. In the battle I heard cries from troopers, but could not understand what they were saying. I do not speak English.

Long Hair's troopers were trapped in an enclosure. There were Indians everywhere. The Cheyennes attacked the soldiers from the north and Crow King from the South. The Sioux Indians encircled the troopers. Not one got away! The Sioux used tomahawks. It was not a massacre, but [a] hotly contested battle between two armed forces. Very few soldiers were mutilated, as oft has been said by the whites. Not a single soldier was burned at the stake. Sioux Indians do not torture their victims.

After the battle the Indians took all the equipment and horses belonging to the soldiers. The brave men who came to punish us that morning were defeated; but in the end, the Indians lost. We saw the body of Long Hair. Of course, we did not know who the soldiers were until an interpreter told us that the men came from Fort Lincoln, then [in] Dakota Territory. On the saddle blankets were the cross saber insignia and the letter seven.

The victorious warriors returned to the camp, as did the women and children who could see the battle from where they took refuge. Over sixty Indians were killed and they were also brought back to the camp for scaffold-burial. The Indians did not stage a victory dance that night. They were mourning for their own dead. . . .

ONE BULL (MINNECONJOU LAKOTA)

Account given to John P. Everett in the 1920s

I was in Sitting Bull's camp on [Little] Big Horn River, One Horn Band Hinkowoji [Minneconjou] Tepee. They were called that because they planted their gardens near the river. Itazipco (Without Bow [Sans Arc]) was another band. Ogalala [Oglala] was the Red Cloud band. Another band, Schiyeio means Cheyenne. They were a different tribe, not Lakota. They were friends of Lakota.

Pizi (Gall) had another band. All the different bands camped together. There were many other chiefs with their bands. Four Horn and Two Moon and many others. Whenever the chiefs held a council they went to Sitting Bull's camp because he was a good medicine man.

Lakota and Cheyennes had gone to this camp to look after their buffalo and so young men and women could get acquainted. White men had driven our buffalo away from Lakota land. So we went where buffalo were to take care of them and keep white men away.

I was a strong young man 22 years old. On the day of the fight I was sitting in my tepee combing my hair. I don't know what time it was. About this time maybe. (Two P.M.) Lakota had no watches in those days. I had just been out and picketed my horses and was back in my tepee. I saw a man named Fat Bear come running into camp and he said soldiers were coming on the other side of the river and had killed a boy named Deeds who went out to picket a horse. Then I came out of my tepee and saw soldiers running their horses toward our camp on same side of the river. We could hear lots of shooting. I went to tepee of my uncle, Sitting Bull, and said I was going to go take part in the battle. He said, "Go ahead, they have already fired."

I had a rifle and plenty of shells, but I took that off and gave it to Sitting Bull and he gave me a shield. Then I took the shield and my tomahawk and got on my horse and rode up to where the soldiers were attacking us. They were firing pretty heavy. They were all down near the river in the timber. Lakota were riding around fast and shooting at them. I rode up to some Lakota and said, "Let's all charge at once." I raised my tomahawk and said, "Wakontanka help me so I do not sin but fight my battle." I started to charge. There were five Lakota riding behind me. We charged for some soldiers that were still fighting and they ran to where their horses were in the timber. Then the soldiers all started for the river. I turned my horse and started that way too and there was a man named Mato Washte (Pretty Bear) right behind me and he and his horse were shot down. I followed the soldiers. They were running for the river. I killed two with my tomahawk. Then the soldiers got across the river. I came back to where Pretty Bear was and got him up on my horse. He was wounded and covered with blood. I started my horse toward the river where the soldiers were, trying to get across.

Then I let Pretty Bear get off my horse and I went across the river after the soldiers. I killed one more of them with my tomahawk.

Then I saw four soldiers ahead of me running up the hill. I was just about to charge them when someone rode along beside me and said, "You better not go any farther. You are wounded." That was Sitting Bull. I was not wounded but I was all covered with blood that got on me when I had Pretty Bear on my horse. So I did what Sitting Bull told me. Then Sitting Bull rode back but I went on. Another Lakota went after these four soldiers. He had a rifle and shot one of them off his horse. One of the soldiers kept shooting back but without hitting us. The man that was with me was a Lakota but I did not know who he was. Now the soldiers were getting together up on the hill and we could see the other soldiers coming with the pack mules a long way off.

Then I went back across the river and rode down it a way, then I rode with the man who was shooting at the four soldiers and we crossed the river again just east of Sitting Bull's camp. We saw a bunch of horsemen up on a hill to the north and they were Lakotas. We rode up to them and I told them I had killed a lot of soldiers and showed them my tomahawk. Then I said I was going up and help kill Custer's soldiers, but Sitting Bull told me not to go so I didn't go but we rode up where we could see the Lakotas and Cheyennes killing Custer's men. They had been shooting heavy but the Indians charged them straight from the west and then some rode around them shooting and the Indians were knocking them off their horses and killing them with tomahawks and clubs. THEY WERE ALL KILLED. There were a lot of Sioux killed. The others were picking them up on their horses and taking them back to camp.

Then we had a war dance all night and in the morning we heard that the soldiers with the pack mules were up on the hill and the Sioux started up after them. I went with Sitting Bull and volunteered to go help kill these soldiers but

Sitting Bull said no. So we watched the fight from a hill. I didn't have my rifle with me then, just my tomahawk. The Sioux surrounded them and they fought that way all day. The soldiers had ditches dug all around the hill. Then along towards sundown the Sioux broke camp and went [south] to the mountains.

The Sioux did not take any prisoners that I know of. I didn't see any. I don't know how many Indians there were, but it was a very big band. Many bands together. The Indians had rifles with little short cartridges. I didn't use mine.

After the fight we all stayed in the Big Horn Mountains about ten days. After that they broke camp and went north following along the Tongue River. Then we went to the Little Missouri, and we found a place where there must have been some soldiers for we found a lot of sacks of yellow corn piled up. Then some of the bands went one way and some went another. One little band went to Slim Buttes and they were all killed by soldiers.

I was with Sitting Bull all the time we were in camp on the [Little] Big Horn and saw him during the battle. He was telling his men what to do. The first I knew of any soldiers was when they killed the boy who went to picket his horse across the river from Sitting Bull's camp. Before we broke camp that night we saw the walking soldiers coming from down the river but my uncle said, "We won't fight them. We have killed enough. We will go. . . ."

5

Work under Sharecropper and Labor Contracts

Grimes Family and Swindell Brothers

The end of slavery and the impoverishment of the South in the aftermath of the Civil War seriously disrupted Southern agriculture. Five years after the war's end, Southern cotton production was still only about half of what it had been in the 1850s. The large plantations, no longer tended by gangs of slaves or hired freedmen, were broken up into smaller holdings, but the capital required for profitable agriculture meant that control of farming remained centralized in a limited elite of merchants and large landholders.

Various mechanisms arose to finance Southern agriculture. Tenants worked on leased land, and small landowners gave liens on their crops to get financing. But the most common method of financing agriculture was sharecropping. Agreements like the Grimes family's sharecrop contract determined the economic life of thousands of poor rural families in the southern United States after the Civil War. Families, both African American and white, lacking capital for agriculture were furnished seed, implements, and a line of credit for food and other necessities to keep them through the growing season. Accounts were settled in the winter after crops were in. Under these conditions a small number of farmers managed to make money and eventually became landowners, but the larger part found themselves in ever deeper debt at the end of the year, with no choice but to contract again for the next year.

Another form of labor contract was the agreement, like that of the Swindell Brothers' firm, to pay the passage to America for immigrants with needed skills in return for their agreeing to work for a fixed period of time. Under pressure from labor organizations, this form of recruitment, legalized during the Civil War, was banned in 1885.

BEFORE YOU READ

1. What restrictions on the freedom of sharecroppers were built into the contract?
2. Which restrictions might have been the most significant in preventing sharecroppers from achieving independence?
3. Why would labor organizations object to agreements like the Swindell contract?
4. What would motivate workers to enter into such contracts?

From the Grimes Family Papers (#3357), 1882, held in the Southern Historical Collection, University of North Carolina, Chapel Hill; Wayne Moquin, ed., *Makers of America*, vol. 4, *Seekers after Wealth* (Chicago: Encyclopaedia Britannica Educational Corp., 1971).

GRIMES FAMILY PAPERS

To every one applying to rent land upon shares, the following conditions must be read, and *agreed to.*

To every 30 or 35 acres, I agree to furnish the team, plow, and farming implements, except cotton planters, and I *do not* agree to furnish a cart to every cropper. The croppers are to have half of the cotton, corn and fodder (and peas and pumpkins and potatoes if any are planted) if the following conditions are complied with, but—if not—they are to have only two fifths (2/5). Croppers are to have no part or interest in the cotton seed raised from the crop planted and worked by them. No vine crops of any description, that is, no watermelons, muskmelons, . . . squashes or anything of that kind, except peas and pumpkins, and potatoes, are to be planted in the cotton or corn. All must work under my direction. All plantation work to be done by the croppers. My part of the crop to be *housed* by them, and the fodder and oats to be hauled and put in the house. All the cotton must be topped about 1st August. If any cropper fails from any cause to save all the fodder from his crop, I am to have enough fodder to make it equal to one half of the whole if the whole amount of fodder had been saved.

For every mule or horse furnished by me there must be 1000 good sized rails . . . hauled, and the fence repaired as far as they will go, the fence to be torn down and put up from the bottom if I so direct. All croppers to haul rails and work on fence whenever I may order. Rails to be split when I may say. Each cropper to clean out every ditch in his crop, and where a ditch runs between two croppers, the cleaning out of that ditch is to be divided equally between them. Every ditch bank in the crop must be shrubbed down and cleaned off before the crop is planted and must be cut down every time the land is worked with his hoe and when the crop is "laid by," the ditch banks must be left clean of bushes, weeds, and seeds. The cleaning out of all ditches must be done by the first of October. The rails must be split and the fence repaired before corn is planted.

Each cropper must keep in good repair all bridges in his crop or over ditches that he has to clean out and when a bridge needs repairing that is outside of all their crops, then any one that I call on must repair it.

Fence jams to be done as ditch banks. If any cotton is planted on the land outside of the plantation fence, I am to have *three fourths* of all the cotton made in those patches, that is to say, no cotton must be planted by croppers in their home patches.

All croppers must clean out stables and fill them with straw, and haul straw in front of stables whenever I direct. All the cotton must be manured, and enough fertilizer must be brought to manure each crop highly, the croppers to pay for one half of all manure bought, the quantity to be purchased for each crop must be left to me.

No cropper to work off the plantation when there is any work to be done on the land he has rented, or when his work is needed by me or other croppers. Trees to be cut down on Orchard, House field & Evanson fences, leaving such as I may designate.

Road field to be planted from the *very edge of the ditch to the fence*, and all the land to be planted close up to the ditches and fences. *No stock of any kind* belonging to croppers to run in the plantation after crops are gathered.

If the fence should be blown down, or if trees should fall on the fence outside of the land planted by any of the croppers, any one or all that I may call upon must put it up and repair it. Every cropper must feed, or have fed, the team he works, Saturday nights, Sundays, and every morning before going to work, beginning to feed his team (morning, noon, and night *every day* in the week) on the day he rents and feeding it to and including the 31st day of December. If any cropper shall from any cause fail to repair his fence as far as 1000 rails will go, or shall fail to clean out any part of his ditches, or shall fail to leave his ditch banks, any part of them, well shrubbed and clean when his crop is laid by, or shall fail to clean out stables, fill them up and haul straw in front of them whenever he is told, he shall have only two-fifths (2/5) of the cotton, corn, fodder, peas and pumpkins made on the land he cultivates.

If any cropper shall fail to feed his team Saturday nights, all day Sunday and all the rest of the week, morning/noon, and night, for every time he so fails he must pay me five cents.

No corn nor cotton stalks must be burned, but must be cut down, cut up and plowed in. Nothing must be burned off the land except when it is *impossible* to plow it in.

Every cropper must be responsible for all gear and farming implements placed in his hands, and if not returned must be paid for unless it is worn out by use.

Croppers must sow & plow in oats and haul them to the crib, but *must have no part of them.* Nothing to be sold from their crops, nor fodder nor corn to be carried out of the fields until my rent is all paid, and all amounts they owe me and for which I am responsible are paid in full.

I am to gin & pack all the cotton and charge every cropper an eighteenth of his part, the cropper to furnish his part of the bagging, ties, & twine.

The sale of every cropper's part of the cotton to be made by me when and where I choose to sell, and after deducting all they owe me and all sums that I may be responsible for on their accounts, to pay them their half of the net proceeds. Work of every description, particularly the work on fences and ditches, to be done to my satisfaction, and must be done over until I am satisfied that it is done as it should be.

No wood to burn, nor light wood, nor poles, nor timber for boards, nor wood for any purpose whatever must be gotten above the house occupied by Henry Beasley—nor must any trees be cut down nor any wood used for any purpose, except for firewood, without my permission.

SWINDELL BROTHERS CONTRACT

Antwerp, Dec. 15, 1882

Agreement between the firm of Swindell Bros. of the first part, and John Schmidt, gatherer, and Carl Wagner, blower, of the second part.

The undersigned, of the second part, covenants and agrees with the party of the first part that they will for two consecutive years, beginning January 1, 1882, work and duly perform such duties as instructed by the party of the first part or his superintendents. The party of the first part covenants and agrees to pay the undersigned, who may duly perform their duties, the price generally paid by Baltimore manufacturers for the size of 16 by 24 inches, and all sheets shall be estimated at eight sheet of 36 by 54 inches for 100 square feet. The party of the first part covenants and agrees that the wages of each glassblower shall be an average of $80 per calendar month, on condition that he makes 180 boxes of 100 square feet per calendar month.

The gatherer shall receive 65 percent of the sum paid the blower for wages per calendar month for actual work performed during the fire. It is agreed that the party of the first part shall retain 10 percent of the wages of each and every workman until the expiration of this contract as a guarantee of the faithful performance of the provisions of this contract. The aforesaid 10 percent shall be forfeited by each and every workman who shall fail to comply with the provisions of this contract.

It is further agreed that the party of the first part shall advance the passage money for the parties of the second part.

It is further agreed that the party of the first part have the right to discharge any of the workmen for drunkenness or neglect of duty, or for disturbing the peace, or creating dissatisfaction among them, or for joining any association of American workmen.

The said Swindell Bros., their heirs, and assigns, shall be considered the parties of the first part, and they agree to pay each blower $12 per week and the gatherer $9.00 per week, on condition that each perform his work faithfully at every blowing. The parties of the first part agrees to make monthly settlements for the parties of the second part, after the advances for the passage, etc., shall have been repaid. Provided you faithfully perform your work for the term of contract (two years), we will pay back the passage money from Europe to America.

Swindell Bros.
Yohonn Schmidt, *Gatherer*
Carl Wagener, *Blower*

6

School Days of an Indian Girl
Zitkala-Ša (Gertrude Simmons Bonnin)

From the mid-1880s to the 1930s, the thrust of American Indian policy was to assimilate Native Americans into the larger society. Boarding schools for Native American children became a common strategy for inducting promising young Native Americans into white culture. Officials were particularly eager to educate girls, hoping to alter the domestic culture of the Indians.

Zitkala-Ša, or Red Bird (1876–1938), a Sioux from the Yankton reservation in South Dakota, described in a series of articles in the Atlantic Monthly *in 1900 her experiences at a Quaker missionary school for Native Americans in Wabash, Indiana, which she attended from age eight to eleven. She remarked that she came back to the reservation "neither a wild Indian nor a tame one."*

Red Bird returned to the school four years later to complete the course of study and then attended Earlham College in Richmond, Indiana, somehow acquiring the capacity to succeed in the white world without losing her Native American heritage. After returning to the Sioux country, she married a Sioux and began a lifetime of work to improve the status and condition of Indian peoples. In a long career that ended with her death in 1938, she played an influential role in the organization of Native American communities, which led to major though not thoroughly satisfying federal reforms in the late 1920s and 1930s.

BEFORE YOU READ

1. What do you think Zitkala-Ša meant when she said she returned to the reservation "neither a wild Indian nor a tame one"? What did she reject about her education, and what did she accept?

2. Given the pain of her school experience, what reasons can you suggest for Zitkala-Ša's return to school?

3. What did Zitkala-Ša mean by her final comment about the Indian schools: "[F]ew there are who have paused to question whether real life or long-lasting death lies beneath this semblance of civilization"?

The first turning away from the easy, natural flow of my life occurred in an early spring. It was in my eighth year; in the month of March, I afterward learned. At this age I knew but one language, and that was my mother's native tongue. . . .

Zitkala-Ša (Gertrude Simmons Bonnin), "The School Days of an Indian Girl," *Atlantic Monthly* 89 (January–March 1900), pp. 45–47, 190, 192–94.

"Mother, my friend Judéwin is going home with the missionaries. She is going to a more beautiful country than ours; the palefaces told her so!" I said wistfully, wishing in my heart that I too might go.

Mother sat in a chair, and I was hanging on her knee. Within the last two seasons my big brother Dawée had returned from a three years' education in the East, and his coming back influenced my mother to take a farther step from her native way of living. First it was a change from the buffalo skin to the white man's canvas that covered our wigwam. Now she had given up her wigwam of slender poles, to live, a foreigner, in a home of clumsy logs.

"Yes, my child, several others besides Judéwin are going away with the palefaces. Your brother said the missionaries had inquired about his little sister," she said, watching my face very closely.

My heart thumped so hard against my breast, I wondered if she could hear it.

"Did he tell them to take me, mother?" I asked, fearing lest Dawée had forbidden the palefaces to see me, and that my hope of going to the Wonderland would be entirely blighted.

With a sad, slow smile, she answered: "There! I knew you were wishing to go, because Judéwin has filled your ears with the white men's lies. Don't believe a word they say! Their words are sweet, but, my child, their deeds are bitter. You will cry for me, but they will not even soothe you. Stay with me, my little one! Your brother Dawée says that going East, away from your mother, is too hard an experience for his baby sister."

Thus my mother discouraged my curiosity about the lands beyond our eastern horizon; for it was not yet an ambition for Letters that was stirring me. But on the following day the missionaries did come to our very house. I spied them coming up the footpath leading to our cottage. A third man was with them, but he was not my brother Dawée. It was another, a young interpreter, a paleface who had a smattering of the Indian language. I was ready to run out to meet them, but I did not dare to displease my mother. With great glee, I jumped up and down on our ground floor. I begged my mother to open the door, that they would be sure to come to us. Alas! They came, they saw, and they conquered!

Judéwin had told me of the great tree where grew red, red apples; and how we could reach out our hands and pick all the red apples we could eat. I had never seen apple trees. I had never tasted more than a dozen red apples in my life; and when I heard of the orchards of the East, I was eager to roam among them. The missionaries smiled into my eyes, and patted my head. I wondered how mother could say such hard words against them.

"Mother, ask them if little girls may have all the red apples they want, when they go East," I whispered aloud in my excitement.

The interpreter heard me, and answered: "Yes, little girl, the nice red apples are for those who pick them; and you will have a ride on the iron horse if you go with these good people."

I had never seen a train, and he knew it.

"Mother, I'm going East! I like big red apples, and I want to ride on the iron horse! Mother, say yes!" I pleaded.

My mother said nothing. The missionaries waited in silence; and my eyes began to blur with tears, though I struggled to choke them back. The corners of my mouth twitched, and my mother saw me.

"I am not ready to give you any word," she said to them. "Tomorrow I shall send you my answer by my son."

With this they left us. Alone with my mother, I yielded to my tears, and cried aloud, shaking my head so as not to hear what she was saying to me. This was the first time I had ever been so unwilling to give up my own desire that I refused to hearken to my mother's voice.

There was a solemn silence in our home that night. Before I went to bed I begged the Great Spirit to make my mother willing I should go with the missionaries.

The next morning came, and my mother called me to her side. "My daughter, do you still persist in wishing to leave your mother?" she asked.

"Oh, mother, it is not that I wish to leave you, but I want to see the wonderful Eastern land," I answered.

My dear old aunt came to our house that morning, and I heard her say, "Let her try it."

I hoped that, as usual, my aunt was pleading on my side. My brother Dawée came for mother's decision. I dropped my play, and crept close to my aunt.

"Yes, Dawée, my daughter, though she does not understand what it all means, is anxious to go. She will need an education when she is grown, for then there will be fewer real Dakotas, and many more palefaces: This tearing her away, so young, from her mother is necessary, if I would have her an educated woman. The palefaces, who owe us a large debt for stolen lands, have begun to pay a tardy justice in offering some education to our children. But I know my daughter must suffer keenly in this experiment. For her sake, I dread to tell you my reply to the missionaries. Go, tell them that they may take my little daughter, and that the Great Spirit shall not fail to reward them according to their hearts." . . .

THE CUTTING OF MY LONG HAIR

The first day in the land of apples was a bitter-cold one; for the snow still covered the ground, and the trees were bare. A large bell rang for breakfast, its loud metallic voice crashing through the belfry overhead and into our sensitive ears. The annoying clatter of shoes on bare floors gave us no peace. The constant clash of harsh noises, with an undercurrent of many voices murmuring an unknown tongue, made a bedlam within which I was securely tied. And though my spirit tore itself in struggling for its lost freedom, all was useless.

A paleface woman, with white hair, came up after us. We were placed in a line of girls who were marching into the dining room. These were Indian girls, in stiff shoes and closely clinging dresses. The small girls wore sleeved aprons and shingled hair. As I walked noiselessly in my soft moccasins, I felt like sinking to the floor, for my blanket had been stripped from my shoulders. I looked hard at the Indian girls, who seemed not to care that they were even more immodestly dressed than I, in their tightly fitting clothes. While we marched in, the boys entered at an opposite door. I watched for the three young braves who came in our party. I spied them in the rear ranks, looking as uncomfortable as I felt.

A small bell was tapped, and each of the pupils drew a chair from under the table. Supposing this act meant they were to be seated, I pulled out mine and at once slipped into it from one side. But when I turned my head, I saw that I was the only one seated, and all the rest at our table remained standing. Just as I began to rise, looking shyly around to see how chairs were to be used, a second bell was sounded. All were seated at last, and I had to crawl back into my chair again. I heard a man's voice at one end of the hall, and I looked around to see him. But all the others hung their heads over their plates. As I glanced at the long chain of tables, I caught the eyes of a paleface woman upon me. Immediately I dropped my eyes, wondering why I was so keenly watched by the strange woman. The man ceased his mutterings, and then a third bell was tapped. Every one picked up his knife and fork and began eating. I began crying instead, for by this time I was afraid to venture anything more.

But this eating by formula was not the hardest trial in that first day. Late in the morning, my friend Judéwin gave me a terrible warning. Judéwin knew a few words of English; and she had overhead the paleface woman talk about cutting our long, heavy hair. Our mothers had taught us that only unskilled warriors who were captured had their hair shingled by the enemy. Among our people, short hair was worn by mourners, and shingled hair by cowards!

We discussed our fate some moments, and when Judéwin said, "We have to submit, because they are strong," I rebelled.

"No, I will not submit! I will struggle first!" I answered.

I watched my chance, and when no one noticed I disappeared. I crept up the stairs as quietly as I could in my squeaking shoes, — my moccasins had been exchanged for shoes. Along the hall I passed, without knowing whither I was going. Turning aside to an open door, I found a large room with three white beds in it. The windows were covered with dark green curtains, which made the room very dim. Thankful that no one was there, I directed my steps toward the corner farthest from the door. On my hands and knees I crawled under the bed, and cuddled myself in the dark corner.

From my hiding place I peered out, shuddering with fear whenever I heard footsteps near by. Though in the hall loud voices were calling my name, and I knew that even Judéwin was searching for me, I did not open my mouth to answer. Then the steps were quickened and the voices became excited. The sounds came nearer and nearer. Women and girls entered the room. I held my breath and watched them open closet doors and peep behind large trunks. Some one threw up the curtains, and the room was filled with sudden light. What caused them to stoop and look under the bed I do not know. I remember being dragged out, though I resisted by kicking and scratching wildly. In spite of myself, I was carried downstairs and tied fast in a chair.

I cried aloud, shaking my head all the while until I felt the cold blades of the scissors against my neck, and heard them gnaw off one of my thick braids.

Then I lost my spirit. Since the day I was taken from my mother I had suffered extreme indignities. People had stared at me. I had been tossed about in the air like a wooden puppet. And now my long hair was shingled like a coward's! In my anguish I moaned for my mother, but no one came to comfort me. Not a soul reasoned quietly with me, as my own mother used to do; for now I was only one of many little animals driven by a herder.

IRON ROUTINE

A loud-clamoring bell awakened us at half past six in the cold winter mornings. From happy dreams of Western rolling lands and unlassoed freedom we tumbled out upon chilly bare floors back again into a paleface day. We had short time to jump into our shoes and clothes, and wet our eyes with icy water, before a small hand bell was vigorously rung for roll call. . . .

A paleface woman, with a yellow-covered roll book open on her arm and a gnawed pencil in her hand, appeared at the door. Her small, tired face was coldly lighted with a pair of large gray eyes. . . .

Relentlessly her pencil black-marked our daily records if we were not present to respond to our names, and no chum of ours had done it successfully for us. No matter if a dull headache or the painful cough of slow consumption had delayed the absentee, there was only time enough to mark the tardiness. It was next to impossible to leave the iron routine after the civilizing machine had once begun its day's buzzing; and as it was inbred in me to suffer in silence rather than to appeal to the ears of one whose open eyes could not see my pain, I have many times trudged in the day's harness heavy-footed, like a dumb sick brute. . . .

I grew bitter, and censured the woman for cruel neglect of our physical ills. I despised the pencils that moved automatically, and the one teaspoon which dealt out, from a large bottle, healing to a row of variously ailing Indian children. I blamed the hard-working, well-meaning, ignorant woman who was inculcating in our hearts her superstitious ideas. Though I was sullen in all my little troubles, as soon as I felt better I was ready again to smile upon the cruel woman. Within a week I was again actively testing the chains which tightly bound my individuality like a mummy for burial. . . .

INCURRING MY MOTHER'S DISPLEASURE

In the second journey to the East I had not come without some precautions. I had a secret interview with one of our best medicine men, and when I left his wigwam I carried securely in my sleeve a tiny bunch of magic roots. This possession assured me of friends wherever I should go. So absolutely did I believe in its charms that I wore it through all the school routine for more than a year. Then, before I lost my faith in the dead roots, I lost the little buckskin bag containing all my good luck.

At the close of this second term of three years I was the proud owner of my first diploma. The following autumn I ventured upon a college career against my mother's will.

I had written for her approval, but in her reply I found no encouragement. She called my notice to her neighbors' children, who had completed their education in three years. They had returned to their homes, and were then talking English with the frontier settlers. Her few words hinted that I had better give up my slow attempt to learn the white man's ways, and be content to roam over the prairies and find my living upon wild roots. I silenced her by deliberate disobedience.

Thus, homeless and heavy-hearted, I began anew my life among strangers.

As I hid myself in my little room in the college dormitory, away from the scornful and yet curious eyes of the students, I pined for sympathy. Often I wept in secret, wishing I had gone West, to be nourished by my mother's love, instead of remaining among a cold race whose hearts were frozen hard with prejudice.

During the fall and winter seasons I scarcely had a real friend, though by that time several of my classmates were courteous to me at a safe distance. . . .

. . . I appeared as the college representative in [an oratorical] contest. This time the competition was among orators from different colleges in our state. It was held at the state capital, in one of the largest opera houses.

Here again was a strong prejudice against my people. In the evening, as the great audience filled the house, the student bodies began warring among themselves. Fortunately, I was spared witnessing any of the noisy wrangling before the contest began. The slurs against the Indian that stained the lips of our opponents were already burning like a dry fever within my breast.

But after the orations were delivered a deeper burn awaited me. There, before that vast ocean of eyes, some college rowdies threw out a large white flag, with a drawing of a most forlorn Indian girl on it. Under this they had printed in bold black letters words that ridiculed the college which was represented by a "squaw." Such worse than barbarian rudeness embittered me. While we waited for the verdict of the judges, I gleamed fiercely upon the throngs of palefaces. My teeth were hard set, as I saw the white flag still floating insolently in the air.

Then anxiously we watched the man carry toward the stage the envelope containing the final decision.

There were two prizes given, that night, and one of them was mine!

The evil spirit laughed within me when the white flag dropped out of sight, and the hands which furled it hung limp in defeat.

Leaving the crowd as quickly as possible, I was soon in my room. The rest of the night I sat in an armchair and gazed into the crackling fire. I laughed no more in triumph when thus alone. The little taste of victory did not satisfy a hunger in my heart. In my mind I saw my mother far away on the Western plains, and she was holding a charge against me.

RETROSPECTION

Leaving my mother, I returned to the school in the East. As months passed over me, I slowly comprehended that the large army of white teachers in Indian schools had a larger missionary creed than I had suspected.

It was one which included self-preservation quite as much as Indian education. When I saw an opium-eater holding a position as teacher of Indians, I did not understand what good was expected, until a Christian in power replied that this pumpkin-colored creature had a feeble mother to support. An inebriate paleface sat stupid in a doctor's chair, while Indian patients carried their ailments to untimely graves, because his fair wife was dependent upon him for her daily food. . . .

My illness, which prevented the conclusion of my college course, together with my mother's stories of the encroaching frontier settlers, left me in no mood to strain my eyes in searching for latent good in my white co-workers.

At this stage of my own evolution, I was ready to curse men of small capacity for being the dwarfs their God had made them. In the process of my education I had lost all consciousness of the nature world about me. Thus, when a hidden rage took me to the small white-walled prison which I then called my room, I unknowingly turned away from my one salvation.

Alone in my room, I sat like the petrified Indian woman of whom my mother used to tell me. I wished my heart's burdens would turn me to unfeeling stone. But alive, in my tomb, I was destitute!

For the white man's papers I had given up my faith in the Great Spirit. For these same papers I had forgotten the healing in trees and brooks. On account of my mother's simple view of life, and my lack of any, I gave her up, also. I made no friends among the race of people I loathed. Like a slender tree, I had been uprooted from my mother, nature, and God. I was shorn of my branches, which had waved in sympathy and love for home and friends. The natural coat of bark which had protected my oversensitive nature was scraped off to the very quick.

Now a cold bare pole I seemed to be planted in a strange earth. Still, I seemed to hope a day would come when my mute aching head, reared upward to the sky, would flash a zigzag lightning across the heavens. With this dream of vent for a long-pent consciousness, I walked again amid the crowds.

At last, one weary day in the schoolroom, a new idea presented itself to me. It was a new way of solving the problem of my inner self. I liked it. Thus I resigned my position as teacher; and now I am in an Eastern city, following the long course of study I have set for myself. Now, as I look back upon the recent past, I see it from a distance, as a whole. I remember how, from morning till evening, many specimens of civilized peoples visited the Indian school. The city folks with canes and eyeglasses, the countrymen with sunburnt cheeks and clumsy feet, forgot their relative social ranks in an ignorant curiosity. Both sorts of these Christian palefaces were alike astounded at seeing the children of savage warriors so docile and industrious.

As answers to their shallow inquiries they received the students' sample work to look upon. Examining the neatly figured pages, and gazing upon the Indian girls and boys bending over their books, the white visitors walked out of the schoolhouse well satisfied: they were educating the children of the red man! They were paying a liberal fee to the government employees in whose able hands lay the small forest of Indian timber.

In this fashion many have passed idly through the Indian schools during the last decade, afterward to boast of their charity to the North American Indian. But few there are who have paused to question whether real life or long-lasting death lies beneath this semblance of civilization.

The Western Landscape

The American West has spawned countless myths surrounding its dramatic scenery and frontier hardships. As if to compensate for the discomforts of resettling in so strange and remote an environment, fantastic images and the large-scale projection of human desires accompanied the move West. Many Americans envisioned a West conquered strictly by white males, ignoring the important roles played by women and by Native Americans, Mexicans, African Americans, and Chinese. The West also generated images of the solitary, independent American—the Western Hero, the Marlboro Man—though the Western region has received more support from the U.S. government than any other section of the country. Most Western artists portrayed a world of soldiers and settlers defending themselves against Indian attacks while the U.S. Army emptied the last pockets of Native American resistance. These myths have endured in American politics and popular culture.

The values of Western settlers and representations of the West by publicists and artists betrayed a dual vision. On the one hand, the Far West was nature at its most sublime: mysterious, glorious, to be celebrated in paintings and photographs and to be preserved in parks and forests. At the same time, a guidebook written to attract settlers envisioned the rapid transformation of these lands into "one grand scene of continuous improvements, universal enterprise, and unparalleled commerce." The West, then, was like no place else, yet the goal of its settlers was to transform it into a region much like the urban and industrialized East they had left behind.

The settlement of the West was contemporaneous with the growth of outdoor photography. Artists like Alfred Bierstadt used photography to capture scenes to be painted later, and by the 1870s scientific expeditions to the West routinely employed photographers to document their progress, as did the railroads. The American public began to see images of the West in stereographs, in albums and slides used in lectures, and in magazine and book illustrations. The images that follow include portraits of unsullied nature as well as scenes of the construction and subsequent destruction that transformed the Western landscape.

Plate 1. William H. Bartlett, "A Settlement on the Frontier," *The Literary Emporium: A Compendium of Religious, Literary and Philosophical Knowledge,* 1845

Plate 2. Unknown artist, "The Devil's Gate: California Overland Route," *Ballou's Dollar Monthly Magazine,* April 1862

Plate 3. Unknown artist, "Caravan of Emigrants to California Crossing the Great
American Desert in Nebraska," from Henry Howe, *Historical Collections of the Great
West: Containing Narratives of the Most Important and Interesting Events in Western
History*, 1857

The economic depression of 1837 to 1843 greatly increased interest in cheap
Western land. In 1842 the first large group of migrants moved across the
Oregon Trail, the long route to California. Contemporaries called it "Oregon
fever." "There is nothing like a new country for poor folks," declared one farmer
setting off on the westward journey with his family. In the next twenty-five
years, as many as half a million people made the dangerous two-thousand-mile
trek through the Great Plains and Rocky Mountains. Not all reached their destination: tens of thousands died en route (only a few hundred in conflicts with
Indians). This migration swelled further in 1846 when the Mormons crossed
the plains to their new Zion in the Great Salt Lake basin. Then in 1849 the
massive gold rush to California created a substantial population on the West
Coast. This led to the need for rapid statehood for California, which upset the
balance of power between slave and free states and increased the threat of civil
war for the nation. What messages do the illustrations in Plates 1, 2, and 3 —
taken from popular books and magazines of the 1840s, 1850s, and 1860s —
deliver about the westward movement?

Plate 4. Unknown artist, "The Course of Empire," *Harper's New Monthly Magazine*, June 1, 1867

By the 1860s, Americans moving west were no longer depicted simply as small figures on a great landscape. Why is Plate 4, from a popular magazine, entitled "The Course of Empire"? What is suggested here about the relationship of those moving west and the Native American inhabitants of the region? Plate 5 presents an impressive piece of the Western landscape—Citadel Rock, Wyoming, in the Green River Valley. The rock itself is quite a marvel, but so too is the sight of such industry. This is near where Union Pacific Railroad workers set a short-lived record by laying almost eight miles of track in one day. (A few months later, Central Pacific workers laid over ten miles of track in a single day.) Plate 6 depicts the ceremony that was held when Union Pacific workers reached the Continental Divide on August 8, 1868. In her speech at this occasion, Mrs. Clayton, a woman accompanying the party, announced: "We consecrate this flag to the glory of God, the benefit of civilization and the happiness of mankind." By Plate 6, then, the once antlike figures on an empty landscape have grown to dominate the picture of the West.

Above: Plate 5. Andrew Russell, "Citadel Rock, Green River Valley," from F. V. Hayden, *Sun Pictures of Rocky Mountain Scenery*, New York, 1870

Below: Plate 6. Unknown artist, "Mrs. Clayton Planting the National Flag on the Summit of the Rocky Mountains 1868," from *The World of Wonders: A Record of Things Wonderful in Nature, Science, and Art*, 1869

The fame of Yosemite Valley as an example of nature at its most sublime owes much to the work of nineteenth-century photographers such as Carleton E. Watkins and Eadweard Muybridge. Their images, of which Plate 7 is an example, popularized the natural beauty of the West and began a tradition of Western photography that continues into the present. Compare this image of the unspoiled West with the building of the Central Pacific Railroad in Plate 8 and the destruction wrought by gold mining in Colorado in Plate 9. All document the West. Do you think the differences among them reflect the intentions of the artists, or do the differences lie in the eye of the beholder?

Left: Plate 7. Carleton E. Watkins, "No. A12. Mirror Lake View from Cathedral Rocks, Yosemite," c. 1865–1866

Right: Plate 8. Alfred A. Hart, "No. 152. Bear River Valley near Gold Run. Little York Mines in the Distance," c. 1867–1869

Below right: Plate 9. Unknown artist, "Hydraulic Mines, Gold Run, Colorado Territory," c. 1870s

Plate 10. William H. Jackson, "No. 65. North from Barthold Pass," *U.S. Geological Survey of the Territories. Department of the Interior, Professor F. V. Hayden in Charge,* 1874

utiful View!

Plate 11. Erdlen's Photograph Gallery, Salida, Colorado, "Beautiful View," c. 1885

The romantic image shown in Plate 10—William H. Jackson's 1874 photograph of the guide for one of pioneer geologist Ferdinand V. Hayden's exploratory parties into the Rocky Mountains—seems to embody the essence of the American scientific discovery of the West. Jackson's photographs of this still largely unexplored country were so startling and exciting to the public that it is claimed Hayden successfully used Jackson's photographs of the Yellowstone area to lobby the U.S. Congress to establish the first national park. Yet within a generation the Western landscape is no longer depicted as unknown and unexplored territory but instead (in Plate 11) appears as a "Beautiful View!" that is easily accessed and enjoyed even by little girls in pinafores. How do the two artists use the human figure in the landscape, and what do their methods suggest about perceptions of the West?

PART TWO

The Gilded Age

A New Industrial Commonwealth

Remarkable economic growth affected virtually all of America outside of the South during and after the Civil War. In 1882, when the Senate Committee on Education and Labor held hearings on the relations between labor and capital, it heard much on both the hardships and opportunities of this new economy. Brass worker Joseph T. Finnerty detailed the uncomfortable changes for industrial workers as enterprises grew, while the piano manufacturer William Steinway extolled the opportunities and higher standards of living created by vast manufactures. George Rice learned that it was not just workers who were threatened by the new economy when he was driven out of business by Standard Oil. His fight against monopolies as a plaintiff in a famous case against John D. Rockefeller would eventually spur the passage of antitrust laws.

The upward and outward expansion of cities matched the growth of industry. Both immigrants and Americans leaving farms and small towns swelled the raw, booming cities. Corrupt political organizations, usually called "machines," often managed the political needs of these new urbanites. Full-time politicians, like George Washington Plunkitt, who rewarded their constituents in return for their votes, ran these organizations. In the process, such amenities as public buildings, sewers, and water were provided but, reformers complained, often at too high a price or too low a quality.

Cities generally were violent places, but Southern cities like Memphis, Tennessee, shared with the Southern countryside a particularly horrendous form of violence: lynching, which swept through the South in the 1880s. The journalist Ida B. Wells-Barnett's account of the first lynchings in Memphis details how she became a leader in the battle against this method of terrorizing African Americans. For most of its long history, this battle was dominated by women who recognized that using false accusations of rape, specifically the rape of white women by black men, was a means of subjugating women as well as African Americans.

But the Gilded Age was far more than bankers and industrialists enriching themselves while small businessmen and African Americans struggled. It was also the period when progressive middle-class reformers like the social worker Jane Addams started to take up the cause of immigrants, poor people, blacks, and the rapidly expanding industrial working class. Her support of the Pullman strike of 1894, described in "A Modern Lear," was one of dozens of issues of social justice and public life that she took up in her long career.

POINTS OF VIEW
Industrialism and Progress (1882)

7

The Decline of the Independent Craftsman
Joseph T. Finnerty

By 1860, the United States was already among the richest of nations, its prosperity based on producing food and raw materials for its own people and for consumers elsewhere in the Atlantic world. In the half century that followed, it became the world's largest industrial power. While agriculture continued to grow, vast expansion of industry gave the era its particular character. In 1859, 140,000 establishments might have been called factories, most of them tiny undertakings with one owner and four or five workers. In 1914, the United States had 268,000 factories, many of them large firms with hundreds of workers.

Americans who lived through the half century of growth did not need to see figures and graphs to understand what had taken place. Lying over the Lehigh Valley of eastern Pennsylvania, the Mahoning Valley of eastern Ohio, and the Ohio Valley at Pittsburgh, layers of smog covered steel and glass mills. Other than in the most rural and isolated areas, time was marked off by the rude blast of factory whistles summoning employees to work early in the morning and signaling an end to the day. Everywhere new cities and towns sprung up to shelter people at the newly opened mines and factories.

Industrial workers experienced these changes in a poignant way. As late as 1870, few Americans worked for wages. Those who did usually labored side by side with their employers. Joseph T. Finnerty recalls here how labor and management worked

Testimony of Joseph T. Finnerty, *Report of the Committee of the Senate upon the Relations between Labor and Capital*, 5 vols. (Washington, D.C.: Government Printing Office, 1885), vol. 1, pp. 740–46.

closely together in the years after the Civil War. Many city artisans still worked in jobs like that of silversmith or cabinetmaker, cobblers made shoes by hand, and chandlers dipped tapers in hot wax one at a time. Individuals often took enormous pride in their work. By 1900, however, about two-thirds of the labor force consisted of wage earners rather than self-employed people, and conditions between management and labor had deteriorated as firms grew larger. "The employer," one laborer observed, "has pretty much the same feeling toward the men that he has toward his machinery."

The rising number of industrial workers, increasingly frequent strikes occasioned by swings in the economy, and growing friction between labor and management became issues for national political debate. With economic statistics still primitive, arguments raged over whether workers were prospering or suffering in the new economy and whether their living and working conditions had deteriorated. In 1882, the United States Senate unanimously adopted a resolution directing its Committee on Education and Labor to conduct a broad investigation into "the relations between labor and capital, the wages and hours of labor, the condition of the laboring classes in the United States, and their relative condition and wages as compared with similar classes abroad, and to inquire into the division of labor and capital of their joint productions in the United States; also, the subject of labor strikes." In hearings held in various parts of the country the following year, the committee collected testimony from an unusually wide array of witnesses: industrialists, reformers, union leaders, workers, clergymen, and an assortment of unclassifiable crackpots. The senators on the panel did themselves great honor by their unfailing courtesy to witnesses, avoidance of partisan bickering, and welcoming stance to ordinary workers like Joseph T. Finnerty, giving the testimony permanent value in considering the impact of industrialism on working people.

BEFORE YOU READ

1. To what extent do you think Joseph T. Finnerty's testimony should be read as that of a worker and to what extent as that of a representative of the Central Labor Union of New York?

2. What, according to Finnerty, were the main changes in the life of bronze workers over the previous fifteen years?

3. What were the effects of doing bronze work on the workers? Why did they tend to drink heavily?

TESTIMONY INTRODUCED BY THE
CENTRAL LABOR UNION OF NEW YORK

New York, August 28, 1883

Joseph T. Finnerty sworn and examined.

By Mr. George:

Question. Please state your age and occupation? —*Answer.* I am thirty-two years old; I am a brass worker.

Q. How long have you been a brass worker? —*A.* Fourteen years.

Q. What were the wages that you received, say, fourteen years ago—I mean brass workers generally?

Decreased Wages

A. The wages paid in the trade fourteen years ago were from $18 to $21 a week.

Q. What are the wages now of the same class of workmen, with the same skill, and working the same number of hours—if they do work the same number of hours now?—*A.* From $12 to $18 a week; on an average $15 a week.

Q. Do you think $15 a week is a fair statement of the average now?—*A.* Yes, sir; it is rather above than below the average.

Division of Labor in the Trades

Q. Has there been any change in the last fourteen or fifteen years in the mode of working brass, as to the part that the brass worker performs in the business of production in that industry? If so, state what that change is?—*A.* There has been a change. Fourteen years ago the workman was supposed to finish all his own work right through, with a very small exception. To-day the trade is so broken up that it takes eight men to finish the same job.

Q. What do you call a "job"? Explain that?—*A.* Well, to make a water-cock or a chandelier, or a steam valve, all such things as those are "jobs." The making of a water-cock is broken up now into twelve different parts.

Q. You say that fifteen years ago each man did one of these jobs complete?—*A.* Yes, sir; a man who was making a chandelier made it right through, a valve-maker made his work right through, and a cock-maker made his work right through.

Q. But now I understand you to say that in making a chandelier a man does but one-tenth of the work?—*A.* Yes; one-tenth or one-twelfth, and in making a brass cock or steam-valve he does only about one-fourth of it.

Q. How has that change been brought about?—*A.* Principally by the introduction of machinery for turning out the work faster and cheaper. A man now being employed on the machine gets no chance of learning the trade beyond the particular branch that he works at, and, being kept constantly at that one branch, he becomes very expert and turns that part of the work out quicker and cheaper than it could be done on the old plan.

Q. You say it takes twelve men now to make a brass cock; are there four different machines that are used in making a thing of that kind?—*A.* There are four different operations and machines; three lathes and a polishing machine. Fourteen years ago there was only one lathe used to do that job but now there are four besides the polishing machine.

Q. How is it in making a chandelier?—*A.* There are polishers, dippers, buffers, chasers, filers, and all of these have their own special branches and do nothing else.

Q. And each one of them, I suppose, does his part by the aid of a machine?—*A.* Yes, sir; with the exception of the dipper or bronzer, the man that gives the color. He puts it on by hand. All the others do their parts by machinery.

Q. The man's principal business, then, is to adjust the machine to the piece of brass, or the brass to the machine, and to keep it there till the work is done?—A. Yes, sir; but he has got to exercise a little skill, of course.

Q. Yes; of course, he must have sense enough to adjust it properly, but his principal duty is to keep the brass in the proper position with reference to the machine, and then the machine will do the work; is that correct?—A. That is correct as to one man, the dipper. The others have the machine running and it does the work. Formerly it was all done by hand.

Q. Then the result is that a man who works in brass now with this machinery never becomes a perfect workman—that is, he never learns to turn out a job complete?—A. No, sir.

Q. In other words he learns to do only one-tenth or one-fourth of a job, as the case may be. He does not learn the other parts of the trade?—A. No, sir; he does not.

Q. Of course, this subdivision of labor and this introduction of machinery has added very much to the production of brass work?—A. Yes, sir.

Production Increased—Quality Deteriorated

Q. Explain to the committee, in your own way, the difference in amount between the production of one man, say fifteen years ago, and what one man can now produce with the aid of machinery? Or, take a group of men, four, or five, or six, and explain to us how much value each man can impart to this work by the aid of machinery?—A. I think the best way I can explain that to the committee is to take some one article for an illustration? I will take a chandelier for instance. Fourteen years ago a man working one week at $21 a week would finish a chandelier and it could be sold for $300. To-day, with all the machinery and all the branches of the business combined, eight or ten men can turn out thirty-six chandeliers, which can be sold at $150 apiece; making in the neighborhood of $4,000, for the week's work of the eight men.

Q. You say that formerly one man in a week would make a chandelier worth about $300?—A. Yes.

Q. And that now eight men working the one week and using machinery can make thirty-six chandeliers worth each $150?—A. Well, worth from $100 to $150.

Q. Would $125 be the average selling price of those chandeliers?—A. Yes, sir.

Q. So that one man fifteen years ago produced in a week a manufactured article worth $300?—A. Yes, sir.

Q. And now eight men working the same time produce articles worth about $4,350, which makes an average of about $540 for each man's work. Is that about correct?—A. Well, say $450. The other figure might be a little too high. I want to keep right down to the bottom facts.

Q. What was the value of the raw material put into a chandelier fifteen yeas ago?—A. The chandelier that was made fourteen or fifteen years ago was all solid bronze work—genuine work. The chandeliers that are made to-day are nothing but a mere hollow shell. There is considerable less bronze used in all bronze work now than there was fourteen years ago. Things were made solid and reliable at that time and intended to last, but now it is not so.

Q. About how much less material is used now in the manufacture of such an article?—A. I would say about one-quarter less; but that is only a guess.

Q. Do you mean one-quarter less or do you mean that there was four times as much bronze put into chandeliers fourteen years ago as there is now?—A. That is what I mean.

The Social Condition of the Men Getting Worse

Q. Tell us now, if you can, about the social condition of the bronze workers as compared with their condition fourteen or fifteen years ago, and whether it has grown better or worse.—A. Well, I remember that fourteen years ago the workmen and the foremen and the boss were all as one family; it was just as easy and as free to speak to the boss as any one else, but now the boss is superior, and the men all go to the superintendent or to the foreman; but we would not think of looking the foreman in the face now any more than we would the boss.

Q. Is that so when you are off duty as well as when you are on?—A. Off duty as well as on duty, we would not dream of speaking to him on the street, unless he was a personal acquaintance or some old reliable hand in the shop that might have grown up there. The average hand growing up in the shop now would not think of speaking to the boss, would not presume to recognize him, nor the boss would not recognize him either.

Q. By the "boss" I suppose you mean the owner of the factory?—A. Yes, sir.

Q. You have told us that the wages have been reduced. How is it as to the style of living of the workmen now compared with how they lived fourteen or fifteen years ago?—A. That appears to be about the same as far as house rent is concerned. There was a reduction of house rents some years ago, but they have reached up again.

Q. Are other things about equal?—A. About equal.

Q. Let me see if I understand you fully. You get less wages than you did fifteen years ago?—A. Yes.

Q. Now, do you mean to say that the wages which you receive at present will buy as much of the comforts of life as the wages which you received then would?—A. By no means. I say that the rents are the same as they were fourteen years ago, but the man who had apartments of four or five rooms at that time is confining himself to perhaps three rooms now.

Q. How are the social surroundings of the workingmen now, as to the character of the neighborhoods in which they live; for I have noticed that there are some very fine neighborhoods in this city and some others that are very poor.—A. The bronze workers as a rule live in tenement houses. They are surrounded by the poorest class, the cheapest class; the cheapest element of the laboring people, and they are no better than anybody else.

Q. Was that so fifteen years ago, or is there a difference since that time? — *A.* It was different then. A mechanic was considered somebody, and he felt that he was somebody; he was a skilled mechanic, and he was considered above the poor laborer on the street.

Q. How is it as to the neighborhoods where they live and the character of their dwellings at present as compared with fifteen years ago; are they better or worse than they were then? —*A.* If there is any change, it is for the worse; the tendency is to get worse.

Q. Are you a married man? —*A.* Yes.

Q. How long have you been married? —*A.* Six years.

Q. State now what opportunities you have of supporting your family comfortably and giving your children such social privileges and enjoyments as are necessary for their comfort and happiness. —*A.* I have not any other facilities beyond the average workingmen's opportunity to train up their children; that is, to send them to the public schools. We cannot go any further than that on our wages.

Q. Is that about the average condition of the bronze workers in this city? — *A.* The average is a little worse than my case; the average of the brass workers could not live as well as I do, because their average wages is only $15 a week, while my wages is $20 a week.

Impossibility of Saving from Present Wages

Q. Do the bronze workers who are married men lay up anything, as a general rule? —*A.* No, sir; they do not. If they happen to be able to make both ends meet at the end of the year they are doing wonders. Of course in every class of people there may be one or two in a hundred that would get rich, no matter what wages they received, but the bronze worker generally saves no money, and if he can keep his family in food and clothes and pay his rent he feels that he is doing wonders.

Q. Before the introduction of this machinery, by which the man has been reduced to being one-tenth or one-fourth of a complete tradesman, how much capital did it take to become a brass worker on one's own account?

Increased Difficulty of Starting in Business

A. At that time a man that had $300 or $400 could start a brass shop himself and make a living out of it, but to-day no man who understands the condition of the trade would start with less than $5,000. He would need that much to supply machinery and start his shop, and then he would have a hard road to travel.

Q. At that time, if a man had a room large enough to work in, and had his tools and a little money to buy the raw material, he could become an independent workman, you say, making his brass work himself and selling it to the public? —*A.* Yes, sir.

Q. But now the conditions have changed so much that it would take $5,000 even to start a shop and fit it up with the necessary machinery? —*A.* Yes, sir. There is one thing about brass shops that you had better understand, and that is that almost every brass shop has special patents and its own special line of business, and one does not compete with the others in their lines. In chandeliers, for instance, some make high-priced chandeliers, while others make a specialty of the cheap chandelier, and the regular brass shops each make a specialty of one department. John Mathews, for example, makes soda-water fountains; another shop makes a specialty of injectors, and another of pumps. So that, to a certain extent, each of these shops has got a monopoly of its own line of business. At the same time they may have the facilities for making anything that comes in their line, but their prices are so high for anything outside of their regular work, their specialty, that a man who wants any article will go to some shop that make a specialty of the kind of work he wants; a man who wants a pump will go to a pump factory, or a man who wants a soda-water fountain will go to a soda-fountain factory.

Q. Fourteen years ago, as I understand you, a brass worker might hope, by prudence and economy, to become an independent worker for himself? — *A.* Yes, sir; but now the trade is controlled by the larger companies. They have their drummers or agents in different parts of the country, and it takes capital to carry on the business in that way; and in order to establish an independent brass shop you have to have your connections made all through the country, something which a poor man cannot do.

Q. So you consider that it is about hopeless for a brass worker now to aspire to the condition of brass manufacturer? — *A.* Yes, sir; it is hopeless, and I think they will not try it any more.

Q. Has that change any effect on the habits of saving of the working men? — *A.* No, sir; I cannot say that it has any effect. They are living up to the way they are accustomed to live, and the minute you undertake to drive them down any lower than that there is a row.

Q. What I mean is this: Has the stimulus, the inducement to save by close living, and all that sort of thing been lessened in any degree by the fact that there is now no hope of a workman ever becoming a boss or having an independent establishment of his own? — *A.* All the brass worker cares about now is to hold his job, and he will put up with any kind of abuse as long as he is not discharged.

Q. But fourteen years ago you say it was different. — *A.* Yes, sir. He would not stand any abuse at all then, and no abuse would be offered to him then; he was treated as a skilled workman.

Q. Did many of the workers in brass fourteen years ago actually get into the position of independent brass manufacturers? — *A.* Oh, yes, sir. There are some of our leading firms to-day that started under the different condition that existed fourteen or fifteen years ago.

Q. Were these men more provident or economical or stingy at that time, as a rule, than the workmen are now, when they have no hope of becoming independent workers? — *A.* The men who are bosses now, and who were workmen at that time, were not saving or stingy, and while they were merely getting journeymen's wages they did not save anything; but when they got to be foremen, then they commenced to save, and when they became superintendents they made enough money to start for themselves.

The Brass Workers' Organization

Q. Is there a labor organization of the brass workers? —*A.* There is.

Q. Do you belong to it? —*A.* I do.

Q. Have they ever made a strike? —*A.* Only once — for eight hours — and they failed to get it. They have never struck for higher wages.

Q. Have you any rule in your organization limiting the number of apprentices that shall be taken into the shops? —*A.* No, sir. The organization does not attempt at all to interfere with the rights of the shop; we could not do it. In the first place the boss has entire power to hire whoever he pleases — boys or men; he can put in forty or fifty boys, and there is nobody going to object.

Brass Working Unhealthy

There is one thing that I want to say a word about, and that is the health of the men in the trade. Brass working is very injurious to the health. The polishers and the molders are all the time breathing the vapors or the particles that are floating around in the air, and the average life is only about thirty-five years among the molders, and out of every forty molders thirty are compelled to drink strong drink to drown this breathing of the vapors.

By the Chairman:

Q. Do you mean that they have to take it medicinally? —*A.* Yes, sir; either beer or whisky; in order to cure the effects of the fumes. Before they pour the metal they go out and take a drink; the fumes flow up and around slowly, and the men have to keep in the fumes until they have all their metals poured. Then they are perspiring, and they go out and have another drink; so that they are generally hard drinkers, and the trade makes them so.

Q. Your idea is that the alcohol in the drinks operates as a medicine to counteract the poisonous effects of the fumes that you speak of? —*A.* Yes, sir; they take it to drown the effects of the fumes. Polishers are always breathing the particles that float in the atmosphere. Polishing and molding are two branches of the trade that are very hard and laborious.

Q. How long have you worked at the business? —*A.* Fourteen years.

Q. What is your age? —*A.* Thirty-two years.

Q. How old is the oldest man in your employment that you are acquainted with who has pursued the business continually? —*A.* The oldest man I know is sixty years of age. There are only very few old men in the trade, which numbers about 4,000 men. I do not suppose you could raise a dozen old men in the trade. As soon as they get up to be a certain age they drop the trade or there is fault found with their work.

Q. Do you expect to follow the business for the remainder of your life? —*A.* No, sir; I expect to get out of it as soon as I can.

Q. Do you think you would live to be forty-five years old if you continued at your business? —*A.* I might.

Q. You are a pretty strong, healthy man naturally? —*A.* Yes, sir.

By Mr. George:

Q. Do your employers generally want apprentices, or are they required in the business? —A. There is no system of apprenticeship such as you mean known in a brass shop. If there are any boys wanted they advertise for them and take them and break them in on a lathe, and that is all there is about the boy business in a brass shop. In every shop, on an average, there is about one boy to four men.

8

Workers Prosper as Industry Grows
William Steinway

The national wealth of the United States increased in the last half of the nineteenth century from about $4.5 billion to nearly $64 billion. This enormous growth materially benefited most of the American people, including wage workers, whose real wages rose substantially. Nonetheless, workers gave much evidence of what the commissioner of the Connecticut Bureau of Labor Statistics described as "the feeling of bitterness which so frequently manifests itself in their utterances." And workers showed their discontent not only in utterances: labor disturbances formed a regular part of the landscape of the Gilded Age. Some—like the great railroad strike of 1877, the Homestead walkout of 1892, and the Pullman strike of 1894—made dramatic national headlines. Less remembered are the smaller strikes occurring each year by the hundreds and then thousands in the last quarter of the nineteenth century.

Those who were socially conscious worried especially about the many working people in the great cities who lived in flimsy overcrowded housing with inadequate sanitation that quickly degenerated into disease-ridden slums. In these substandard environments, crime and immorality flourished. People in such circumstances had no protection against dips in the economy. They could not grow their own food or retreat to ancestral farms to weather hard times. Nor could they afford to educate their children, whose labor was too soon needed for family survival. "If a man has not got a boy to act as 'back boy' [earning wages]," a Massachusetts textile worker asserted, "it is very hard for him to get along."

Contemporaries struggled to explain—or explain away—such problems. The Senate Committee on the Relations between Labor and Capital of 1883 (see Selection 7) heard many theories about the sources of labor discontent. The explanations offered by the piano manufacturer William Steinway, excerpted here, were characteristic of the beliefs of successful businessmen. Social mobility, he argued, was not only still possible but was increasingly available with industrial growth; Steinway pointed to his own experience of rising from apprentice to industrialist as proof. Educational improvements and other practical reforms would render workers prosperous and content within the current economic system. He especially urged apprenticeships and industrial schooling as

Testimony of William Steinway, *Report of the Committee of the Senate upon the Relations between Labor and Capital*, 5 vols. (Washington, D.C.: Government Printing Office, 1885), vol. 2, pp. 1085–95.

well as the dispersal of industry from downtown locations into suburbs where workers could secure good housing at reasonable prices.

Steinway's experiences with his workers and his activities on their behalf foreshadow what came in the next century to be called "welfare capitalism." In the interest of suburbanizing industry, he bought land in what is now part of Astoria, Queens, and moved his piano manufacturing from Manhattan to this less crowded location. He chaired the commission that began the New York City subway system and started the project that led to a subway line under the East River—long called the Steinway tunnel—to connect his new community to the city.

Yet much of Steinway's experience was atypical of American industrial development. The Steinway piano was an exotic bloom in nineteenth-century America. The nation had risen to industrial preeminence by supplying materials like steel and oil for industry and by creating inexpensive goods like Kodak cameras or cheap brass chandeliers for mass markets. It is hard to think of another nineteenth-century American product like the Steinway, a luxury good that competed against the finest European products. In fact, it can be argued that the Steinway was a German product made in the United States. The Steinway family had learned to manufacture great pianos in Germany, almost all Steinway's skilled employees in America had learned their trade in Germany, and Steinway paid for German instruction in the public schools his workers attended in Queens. Nonetheless, nothing could have been more American than his testimony to the senators about his unaided rise to the apex of piano manufacturing, his faith in education, or his optimism that all social conflict could be resolved and that every worthy citizen could prosper.

BEFORE YOU READ

1. What is William Steinway's view of labor unions?
2. What is Steinway's view of the condition of labor in the United States?
3. How does Steinway think the conditions of workers in the United States compare with conditions in Europe? In what areas is the United States ahead? In what areas is Europe ahead?
4. What does he think is needed to improve the conditions of workers in the United States?

New York, September 27, 1883

William Steinway examined.

By Mr. Call:

Question. Have you seen the resolution under which the committee is conducting this examination?—*Answer.* Yes, sir.

Mr. Call. The committee will be glad to hear from you any facts or opinions you may have to present on the several subjects mentioned in the resolution, first stating your residence and occupation and your connection with labor in this country and abroad.

The Witness. I was born in Brunswick, Germany, in 1836, and came to the city of New York in the spring of 1850, when fourteen years of age, with my father, mother, and the rest of our family. We worked for three years in the factories here, learning the language and the customs of the people, and in March, 1853, started the business of Steinway & Sons—my father, my two brothers, and myself—which has now become the most extensive establishment of its kind in existence. We have three distinct establishments, manufactories rather, our New York factory, at Fourth avenue and Fifty-second and Fifty-third streets; a large establishment at Astoria, N.Y., opposite One hundred and twentieth street, where we employ over 400 men, and where we have carried out our ideas of improving the condition of the workingmen by giving them light and air and good houses to live in, building them public baths, and laying out a public park, keeping up at our own expense in the public school a teacher who teaches German and music free of charge, and various other advantages. We employ about 1,000 workmen, a great majority of whom are skilled workmen. I will remark that in the first three years when I worked as an apprentice and journeyman, and in the first few years when our business was small, I had ample opportunities of studying the lot of the workingman by actual experience, also the way that workingmen worked, and I can say that skilled artisans to-day are far better off than they were a third of a century ago. At that time but very few people, even skilled laborers, were able to save money and put it in bank. To-day the skilled laborers, more especially in the piano-forte trade, and the wood-working establishments, have wages double what they were in those times; and from my experience also as director in savings banks, &c., I find that a great many skilled artisans, those blessed with health, have constituted a great portion of the depositors in banks. The wages in the piano-forte trade, that is to say, the skilled laborers, have averaged $20 per week (ranging from $15 to $30).

We ourselves have a branch establishment in Hamburg, and from my travels in Europe and my study of the condition of the workingmen in both hemispheres, especially in the piano-forte trade, I will say here that of my own personal knowledge the wages of skilled artisans in the piano-forte trade in the cities of New York, Boston, Baltimore, and Philadelphia, where they are most densely congregated, average precisely three times the amount that the skilled artisans of Europe do in the same trade.

The introduction of machinery in our business, and in the wood-working establishments, has been of great benefit by doing the hard work which formerly imperiled the health and lives of the skilled artisans. I will further state that of the about one hundred piano-forte manufacturers of the United States, which are chiefly concentrated in the four cities I have named, nearly all have been workingmen themselves.

Labor Ought to Organize

The relations between ourselves and our men have always been very good until lately disturbed by the entrance of the socialistic and the communistic element in the labor unions. I myself think that labor ought to organize, as it has organized. I am not opposed to labor unions, and any labor union that is carried on in a sensible way can do a great deal, not only toward bettering their own condition in the way of wages, but also in equalizing wages in the various cities, and in resisting in times of depression the great deterioration and fall of wages. We have gone through very hard strikes. We have been singled out. Our house being the strongest and largest, has been made the target of strikes. It is just about a year ago now that one of the most senseless strikes was inaugurated during my absence in Europe by the socialistic and communistic element inducing our men to strike against an honest, faithful bookkeeper, against whom they were unable to allege the slightest grievance, except that they did not want him, and that their union had so ordered. They were unsuccessful, however. The strike lasted over nine weeks, and inflicted a loss upon us of $75,000. Furthermore, of late years the labor union, especially the piano-forte maker's union, which claims three thousand members, in order to induce everybody to join strikes ordered by them, exercise over them a terror of the idea that unless they go with them they will be treated as "scabs" and be driven out of every shop in the city of New York, or in the United States. Many of our older men, who have been with us twenty and twenty five years, and quite a number of whom own houses, both in Astoria and New York, have come to me personally or written me letters about this terrorism exercised by members of the trades unions; but, as I said, with the exception of that, I am not opposed to labor unions; but on the contrary will here give it as my opinion that strikes are a necessity and should not be legislated against, and cannot be legislated against. The fierce competition of manufacturers, and especially in our trade, makes it impossible that any manufacturer could arbitrarily raise his price unless he is forced to do so by a strike for higher wages. It would be simply impossible for him, and he would be laughed at by his customers if he attempted to do so.

Manufacturers Miscalled Capitalists

A great mistake is also made by the workingmen and the professional agitators, who foment strikes, by calling manufacturers capitalists.

Of about 100 piano-forte manufacturers in the United States known throughout the world to make the best pianos in existence, and conceded so by musical talent and authority in Europe, there are but four wealthy houses—about 20 to 25 people of moderate means—and the rest, that is, 60 or 70 manufacturers in the piano-forte trade, just manage to eke out a hand-to-mouth existence. These are hard words, but they are literally true.

The Horrors of the Tenement House System

. . . I consider one of the greatest evils under which workingmen live, especially in the city of New York, is the horrors of the tenement houses—the terrible rents that they have to pay. The average workingman's family has one room in which they cook, wash, iron, and live, and one or two, or possibly three, bed rooms, of which generally one or two are dark rooms, without any windows, or without admitting God's pure air. This is a terrible evil, which is, however, chiefly caused by the insular position of the city of New York, where, in winter, in times of ice and fog, it is impossible that workingmen should come long distances and be in time for their work.

The horrors of the tenement houses are having a very baneful effect upon the morals and character of the coming generation; in fact, I may say a terrible effect. But I do not see what legislation can do. Capitalists consider tenement houses a poor investment, paying poor returns. The only thing that I can imagine is to do as *we* have done, remove the very large factories requiring much room and many men from out of the city of New York into the suburbs.

Want of an Apprentice Law

A second great evil under which we are suffering, and it seems to me it is an evil that has been increasing from year to year, is, that in no country of the wide world, as I have found during my experience and my extensive travels, are there so many young men growing up without learning a trade or any particular calling, as in the United States. We have no apprentice law. In our own business, as well as the wood-working business, everybody is unwilling to take an apprentice, for the simple reason that it is a well known fact that the first year or two when a boy is learning a trade he will produce nothing, and will spoil a great deal, and will take up the time of a skilled man to teach him, and yet the moment he has learned one little branch of the trade he leaves, shifts for himself. He has not learned the business properly, and the consequence is that he is dependent, and, in times of great depression, cannot find employment. Hence we have no supply of skilled artisans growing up, and have to draw for our extra skilled labor on Europe. When I came to this country, in 1850, the majority, indeed I might say seven-eighths, of the journeyman piano makers were Americans, skilled workmen. Through our apprentice law, or rather through the total want of one, the entire native element has been thrown out of the piano business, and to-day seven-eighths of the workingmen in the piano shops, and over one-half in the New England States, are Germans.

By the Chairman:

Q. Is that for lack of an apprentice law as much as it is from the fact that skilled labor already trained has found its way here from abroad and has entered into competition, and made the employment of apprentices by employers a thing undesirable on their part? —*A.* No, sir; I attribute it entirely, or chiefly, to the lack of a proper apprentice law.

Industrial Schools

The total want of industrial schools in this city is a very great evil. There ought to be industrial schools all over each city where boys can go and find for what business they have aptitude and talent. Then, under regular apprentice laws, under which a boy could be bound for, say, five years at rising wages, commencing at $3 a week for the first year, getting $3.50 the second year, $4 a week the third year, and so on, they would learn a trade well. During the last two or three years the employer could have the advantage, since during the first one or two years he lost. . . .

Q. When you first came here you found that seven-eighths of the piano-makers were Americans? —*A.* Yes.

Q. Was there an apprentice law then? —*A.* Yes; and I myself offered to bind myself for seven years in a factory, commencing at seventeen and rising yearly.

Q. That law has been abrogated?—*A.* Yes. After a few years I suddenly found nobody would take apprentices, and could not hold them if they did. That is a great evil. That is a subject on which I think legislation would do a great deal of good.

Compulsory Education

I would also advocate a law compelling every child between the ages of six and fourteen to go to school. I have found in my experience as an employer and executor, and as worker in benevolent enterprises in which I have been engaged, that there is a great deal more ignorance in reading and writing among young men and women growing up in this city—mostly children of foreigners—than anybody has any idea of. During the war we raised a fund to assist the wives of men that went to the war, and I found that one-half of those who had grown up in this country, or had come here when they were little children, were unable to sign their names. I never would have believed it possible if I had not myself experienced it. Hence I think that a compulsory law compelling every child between the ages of six and fourteen years to be sent to school should be enacted, and that parents should be punished if they did not enforce it. . . .

Independence of Skilled Artisans

Having gone through the panics of 1861, 1867, and 1873, I know that skilled artisans are absolutely independent of bad times, for a skilled workman will always find employment. It is so in the piano-forte trade and in the kindred trade in wood. . . . I found that all the skilled piano-forte manufacturers and those in the wood-working trades readily retained and found employment at remunerative wages; whereas the half skilled men who knew only one little branch of a trade were thrown out of employment. Hence the necessity of educating our young men who wish to learn trades to make them thorough skilled workingmen. In other words, do away with the curse of the American mechanics—young men learning only one portion of a skilled trade, and being then absolutely dependent upon that because they do not know anything else. . . .

Relative Condition of Workingmen
in Europe and America

The Chairman. The resolution calls attention to the relative conditions of all working people abroad, and working people in America, specific and general classes. What is your observation in that respect?

A. I have paid a great deal of attention to the condition of the workingmen, and, as I before stated, in our own business and kindred trades I find that first-class skilled artisans in this country earn from double to three times as much as skilled artisans of the same rank do in Europe. In unskilled labor I find the proportion is not so favorable to the American laborer. It is true that they earn more money here, but the cost of living, especially rents, is so much enhanced that they are not much better off in a pecuniary way than the workingman in Europe. But their social position here is much higher than that in Europe, and they have a much better chance here to get along than they have in

Europe where every thing is more limited. But the skilled artisans are far better off in this country; they wear better clothing, have better food, and have a chance to live better, move in better society, and in fact their condition is in every way far superior. Still there remains a great deal to be done, and a great deal could be done to improve their condition in this country in the way I have indicated. . . .

Merchants, Manufacturers, etc. —
Their Relative Conditions in Europe and America

Q. How in regard to the relative condition of merchants, of manufacturers, of the ordinary class of business men on this side of the ocean and the corresponding class on the other side of the ocean—those who manage the business affairs of communities?—*A.* The manufacturers of Europe do not work nearly as hard as our Americans do, who are on their feet from morning to night, and on whom the rack and tear of business wears very fast. The manufacturers in Europe have this advantage: they have much cheaper money than manufacturers in America, who have to depend upon outside help, and who have to borrow money for that purpose. And I think that, as a general thing, the European manufacturers are just as well off as our own. . . .

I found that in Europe there are a great many more manufacturing establishments where the business has been handed down from father to son—they are long established trades—whereas, in this country, manufacturers have generally worked their own way up from nothing, through their own energy, and have, after awhile, accumulated a competence. . . .

Operative Classes—Their Wages and Conditions
in Europe and America Contrasted

Q. Have you any general information as to the condition of the laboring classes employed in manufacturing—as to their food, and their dwelling places, as compared with the same classes in this country?—*A.* I made a special study of that. At Mulhausen, in Alsace, in the city of Crefeld, in Rhenish Prussia, a great silk center, and several other places, I found that they have wretched habitations, and are very poorly clad and ill-fed, not nearly so well as the operatives in this country.

Q. How is it as to the wages that those classes receive there and here?— *A.* From what I observed I found that the wages are considerably less in Europe than those paid here, even setting aside our own business.

Q. The skilled laborers are paid less there—how about the labor that is not so much skilled?—*A.* Unskilled labor is also paid less. In other words, it is very rare to see a workingman in Europe whose family can lay by anything, whereas here thrifty, skilled mechanics, blessed with health, and not meeting with sickness or other misfortune, have a chance to save money and do save money.

Q. Then you say that in this country the laborer is much better off in his social and pecuniary conditions, and in the means of enjoying the comforts of life?—*A.* Undoubtedly.

Mr. Pugh. That is one great reason why there is so much immigration to this country, I suppose.

The Witness. Certainly. I have been called upon while in Europe, my name being so well known, and my arrival being mentioned in the newspapers, by dozens of mechanics who wanted to come to America, and who would have done so if they had had the money. Of course there is great dissatisfaction with their condition there, especially in the industrial districts of Westphalia, Saxony, and Silicia.

Education of the Working Classes in Europe and America

By the Chairman:

Q. How do they compare with our own working people in the matter of education? —A. In Germany, where, since 1818, school attendance has been compulsory, there is hardly a person to be found who cannot read and write. Every child between the age of five and fourteen must attend school, and if not attending school the parents would be punished. The result is, that a person unable to read and write, unless they are very old people, is unknown.

By Mr. Call:

Q. That is true throughout Germany generally, is it? —A. Yes. In France and England it is not so favorable, nor in Belgium, because up to a few years ago there was no law compelling children to go to school.

By the Chairman:

Q. Do you think that education is improving the condition of the laboring people in those countries? —A. It undoubtedly has done so. It has given them greater intelligence and better knowledge of their trades.

Industrial Schools in Germany

By Mr. Call:

Q. How about industrial schools there? —Are they extensive? —A. Yes; they are. I have seen several myself.

Q. People are taught their trades in the public schools, are they? —A. Yes; boys of fourteen to fifteen years of age are taken, and it is ascertained what trades they have aptitudes for, thus preparing them for learning their trades. One of the greatest boons that education could bestow upon boys here would be to give them a similar opportunity.

Q. For that reason you find skilled labor far more abundant there than here? —A. Yes. Here, in good times, there is a great want of skilled labor, and there there is always a greater supply than demand. Hence the great immigration of skilled artisans to this country. . . .

Q. I understood you to say that you worked as a journeyman yourself in this country? —A. Yes.

Q. Had you greater opportunities outside your own knowledge and capacity for building up the vast business that you have built up—greater opportunities than many others who were your contemporaries? —*A.* To be just, I think that, being father and sons, we were possessed of some greater advantages when we came here—we had great advantages over one single individual. I am modest enough to say that I personally could not have done so but for the harmony and good management that prevailed in our firm by reason of our relationship.

Q. Any other family with the same advantages would have had the same results? —*A.* Yes.

Q. The point I wanted to get at was that it was not due to any adventitious aid of capital, but to yourselves as workingmen and economists? —*A.* Yes.

Q. You do not consider that you owe this success to anything outside of yourselves, do you? —*A.* No; I think not. But it was simply because we were all skilled artisans and had learned the trade thoroughly, and had special talents. We had no outside help at all. We worked our way up, and I know dozens of others who have done the same thing.

Q. Do you know anything in the relations of capital, as it is called (as a general name for an economical cause), anything in the relations of capital and labor unfriendly to the success of the workingman in becoming a director of labor, and of a great combination of labor in this country? —*A.* Not at all. I think, under the institutions of our country, if an individual has the talent, the energy, and the industry he has as good a chance to-day as ever to work himself up.

Legislative Measures; Child Labor; Industrial Schools, etc.

Q. Is there anything in the shape of public legislation or voluntary action that you would suggest that will improve that opportunity? —*A.* I think that is one of the greatest problems, and I do not see that legislation can do much more than it has done now, with the exception of what I have indicated. There should be an apprentice law and a stringent law against child-labor, so as to give the children of the poor people a chance to perfect their education, and the industrial schools could be established and every effort made toward giving artisans and laboring people healthy, happy homes.

Q. With those things supplied, either by public law or voluntary action, would you consider the relations now existing under our institutions as favorable as they could be made? —*A.* As favorable as it is possible to make them, in my opinion. Anything further would simply help one class in opposition to another. In this country it must be left to individual talent and industry. I think in this country a young man has a better chance to work up in the world than anywhere else that I have seen. . . .

Removal of City Factories

By Mr. Pugh:

Q. I understood you to condemn the presence of those large manufacturing establishments in our cities, and to charge the discomfort of the operatives in them to the fact largely of the presence of such establishments in cities? —*A.* Yes; I think every effort ought to be directed to having the large establishments go out to the suburbs of the city, in order to give the workingmen a change to live as human beings ought to live. . . .

Q. Your factory, I understand you to say, is removed from New York? — A. We still have a large factory, which we call our "finishing" factory, in New York. It is the case-making factory. The iron and steel works for making the hardware, &c., has been removed over to Astoria, and one department after another has been added thereto, and within a few years the entire establishment will be removed from New York to Astoria.

Q. Do your artisans there live in rented houses? —A. Some of our artisans have already acquired homes of their own, but others of them live in rented houses, and not more than two families in one house, where they have gas, water, free baths, free schools, and every advantage. We have upwards of four hundred men there.

Q. At Astoria? —A. At Astoria.

Q. And you have found them able to improve their condition there? — A. Oh, yes; very much so. There is no sickness or anything of that kind there, and they are all feeling comfortable and happy, and I think the large wealthy manufacturers should also remove their factories from the cities and establish them somewhere in the suburbs, and do something for their workingmen in that way.

Q. You think that that would be a solution of a great part of the trouble arising between labor and capital? —A. Certainly a solution of the tenement-house trouble.

Q. And that, you think, is a large part of the cause of distress and dissatisfaction among the people? —A. Yes; I think it is a great cause of dissatisfaction among the workingmen — the bad places that they have to live in, and the high rents they have to pay. Yet tenement houses are considered a very poor investment by capitalists.

FOR CRITICAL THINKING

1. How is it possible for Joseph T. Finnerty to see a decline in the situation of working people and at the same time for William Steinway to see their lot improving? Is one person right and the other wrong, or are they talking about different things?

2. How do you think Finnerty would respond to the proposals for improvement put forward by William Steinway? Are Steinway's suggestions responsive to the problems in bronze workers' lives that Finnerty outlines?

3. If you were one of the senators on the Committee on the Relations between Labor and Capital, what, if any, legislation would you suggest to improve the situation of workers based on the testimonies of Finnerty and Steinway?

George Rice Loses Out to Standard Oil

George Rice

*Even the optimistic Andrew Carnegie noted in his lecture to young men that "as busi-
ness gravitates more and more to immense concerns," opportunity might be threatened.
George Rice (1835–1905) did all that Carnegie would have suggested. Entering the oil
business early, he kept, as Carnegie advised, all his eggs in one basket and watched the
basket closely. What he saw was the Standard Oil Company under John D. Rockefeller
undercut his operation and eventually drive him out of business.*

*Rice's legal and intellectual counterattack on Standard Oil led the charge against
"the trusts." He supplied information to two of the major writers on that corporation,
Henry Demerest Lloyd and Ida Tarbell, whose books and articles encouraged antitrust
legislation. And he spent considerable time in legal pursuit of Standard Oil, a quest
that never met with success during his lifetime but that eventually inspired efforts that
led to the breakup of the giant corporation in 1911.*

*After a dramatic personal encounter in 1898 with John D. Rockefeller during de-
positions for one of Rice's many suits against Standard Oil, a reporter for the* New
York World *interviewed Rice. Here is his explanation of how Standard Oil operated.*

BEFORE YOU READ

1. How, according to Rice, did Standard Oil undercut its competitors?
2. Do you agree with Rice that this constituted unfair competition?
3. What was Rice's attitude toward large corporations, and how did it reflect popular feelings?

"I have been twenty years fighting John D. Rockefeller and the Standard Oil
Trust, and I am not through yet."

The man who said this was George Rice, of Marietta, O. He is the man
who told John D. Rockefeller to his face last Wednesday in the New Netherland Hotel, where Mr. Rockefeller had been testifying before the State Commission sent from Ohio to get evidence in proceedings intended to prove him
guilty of contempt of the Ohio Supreme Court, that his great wealth was built
on wrecks of other men's business.

It was a dramatic scene. Mr. Rockefeller and Mr. Rice have known each other
well for a generation. In a twenty-year fight men are apt to get well acquainted.

New York World, October 16, 1898, p. 25.

But when the great multi-millionaire walked across the parlor, and, extending his hand—which was not taken—said to George Rice in a suave tenor voice: "HOW ARE YOU, GEORGE! WE ARE GETTING TO BE GRAY-HAIRED MEN NOW, AIN'T WE? DON'T YOU WISH YOU HAD TAKEN MY ADVICE YEARS AGO?" the group of onlookers were not prepared for what followed.

George Rice drew himself up to his full height, which is about 6 feet 2 inches, his bright gray eyes flashed fire, and his massive frame visibly vibrated with suppressed anger, as he looked the great oil magnate straight in the face and said: "Perhaps it would have been better for me if I had. YOU HAVE CERTAINLY RUINED MY BUSINESS, AS YOU SAID YOU WOULD."

Mr. Rockefeller recoiled and his face showed a shade of pallor. The words of Rice had evidently stung him. Quickly recovering himself he turned from his accuser, saying, "Oh, pshaw, that isn't so, George!"

"But I say it is so," was the instant rejoinder of George Rice, and, raising his voice so that everybody in the room could hear him, he pointed his index finger at the Oil King, and added: "You know well that by the power of your great wealth you have ruined my business, and you cannot deny it."

MR. RICE TELLS HIS EXPERIENCE TO THE WORLD

This ended the episode in the hotel parlor. A few hours later, sitting in his private room, Mr. Rice gave to a *World* representative the full story of how he was ruined as an oil refiner by the machinations of the great Standard Oil Laocoon in whose coils an uncounted multitude of competitors have been crushed to death.

"I am but one of many victims of Rockefeller's colossal combination," said Mr. Rice, "and my story is not essentially different from the rest. You ask me to tell you what I meant by telling Mr. Rockefeller, as I did publicly to-day, that he had ruined my business. The whole story, with all its inside details of intrigue and conspiracy, would require a volume to tell. I will tell you as much of it as you choose to ask me for. What particular phase of my experience do you care to have me relate?"

"Give me your personal story, Mr. Rice—just what happened to you in your own business."

"Well, I went into the oil-producing business in West Virginia in 1872, and in 1876 I went into the oil-refining business. Immediately I did that my fight with the Standard Oil people began. I established what was known as the Ohio Oil Works, which had a capacity of about 100,000 barrels of crude oil per annum. I found to my surprise at first, though I afterward understood it perfectly, that the Standard Oil Company was offering the same quality of oil at much lower prices than I could do—from one to three cents a gallon less than I could possibly sell it for.

"I sought for the reason and found that the railroads were in league with the Standard Oil concern at every point, giving it discriminating rates and privileges of all kinds as against myself and all outside competitors.

"For instance, I found that the railroads would not furnish tank-cars to any competitors, while the Standard combination was able by its immense wealth to buy its own cars. It owns from 8,000 to 10,000 tank-cars, and the railroads pay them sufficient mileage on the use of those Standard Oil cars to pay for the first cost of the cars inside of three years. A tank-car, when it comes back empty, cannot bring any goods. The transcontinental lines charge $105 to return an empty cylinder tank-car from the Pacific coast to the Missouri River, while they charge the trust nothing at all for the return of their own exclusive box tank-cars. This gives the trust an advantage of over $100 a car.

"Again, the independent competitor, like myself, was obliged to ship his oil in box-cars and pay 25 per cent more freight on the weight of the wooden barrels, while no charge at all was made to the Standard Oil Trust on the weight of the iron cylinders.

"Again, the railroads deduct 63 gallons (or over 400 pounds) from the filled capacity of each Standard Oil tank-car, which is the same as carrying 1 1/4 per cent of their rail products entirely free of cost. This went on up to March 15, 1890, and was one of the things that helped to wreck my business. Yet another thing helped to ruin me. The railroads allowed the trust to deliver its oils in less than carload quantities at the same rates as for full carloads. They allowed the trust to stop its cars, whether carrying oil in bulk or barrels, at different stations and take it off in small quantities without paying the higher rates which independent competitors were always charged for small quantities thus delivered. Of course, against such discriminations as these the independent competitor of moderate capital could not contend. He was driven to the wall every time, as I was."

MIGHT HAVE BEEN WORTH
A MILLION

"My refinery," continued Mr. Rice, "has been shut down for two years. If I had had a fair and equal show with the railroads my refinery plant to-day would have been easily worth a million dollars and would have been growing all the time. As it is, I am out of the business, my plant is worthless and the men whom it would have employed are either idle or finding other work. These discriminations of which I have spoken are as bad to-day as they have ever been. The public needs to understand that the railroads and Standard Oil monopoly are really one and the same thing. The officers and directors of the Oil Trust are also the presidents and directors of one-fifth of the total railroad mileage of the United States. This is no mere statement of mine. It is proved by *Poor's Manual*.

"The trust was formed in January, 1882, and from that time the lines were drawn tighter and tighter to oppress and strangle every competitor. It was the highwayman's policy of 'stand and deliver.' I had my choice offered me to either give up my business at a price far less than I knew it to be worth, or to be robbed of it under forms of law. I chose not to accept the price and my business was destroyed. The threat of the trust was made good, and I suppose that is what John D. Rockefeller must have meant when he asked me if I didn't wish I had been wiser and listened to him years ago."

"Well, do you now wish, Mr. Rice, that you had knuckled to the trust and saved your money?"

"Not a bit of it," replied the "ruined" but plucky oil refiner of Marietta. "I have made a fight for principle, and I am neither sorry for it nor ashamed of it. I have been before the courts many times; I have been before Congressional committees; and I have appeared time and time again before the Interstate Commerce Commission, all the time trying to get relief from these gross discriminations. I confess I have made very little headway as yet. I shall go on with the fight as long as I live, and it may be that I shall never win. But, sooner or later, in my lifetime or afterward, the people of this country will surely take up this fight as their own and settle the question of whether they will rule the railroads and the trusts or be ruled by them."

LAWS NOT ENFORCED

"I have made a mistake, apparently, in supposing that the laws of our country could and would be enforced. I supposed the courts and the other authorities of the land would support me in my right to a free and equal chance in business with all my fellow-citizens, John D. Rockefeller included. But I have learned by long years of conflict and trial and tribulation, which have cost me untold worry and a lot of money, that this is not so; that I have no business rights which the railroads and this great trust can be made to respect.

"The Interstate Commerce Commission is all right in theory, but it does not have the courage of its powers; it suffers from the paralysis of political influences. The laws are neither feared nor respected by the men of many millions."

"Tell me just how the shoe was made to pinch you personally. How did the trust manage to close your refinery at Marietta?"

"Why, that's easy to tell. Every car of oil that I sent into any part of the United States the trust would jump on it and cut the life out of it. I mean to say that as soon as my oil arrived at the point to which it was shipped the trust would cut the price, so that the man who bought my oil lost money on the sale of it. They would not cut the prices to the whole town, but only to my one customer, and the whole town knew of this man's having lost money by trading with me. From that time forward, of course, I could get no orders in that town. . . .

"In 1872, the trunk lines of railroads made a contract with a corporation called 'The South Improvement Company,' which was only another name for the Standard Oil Company, under which the Standard Oil Company was allowed the most outrageous discriminating freight rates. It seems incredible that these contracts should have been made. They not only gave the Standard Oil Company heavy rebates on their own shipments of oil, but gave them rebates on the shipments of their competitors. At that time the Standard Oil Company only had 10 per cent of the petroleum industry of the country, while their competitors had 90 per cent. The rebates allowed to the Standard people were from 40 cents to $1.06 per barrel on crude petroleum, and from 50 cents to $1.32 per barrel on refined petroleum. Thus the Standard Oil Company received nine times as much for rebates on the shipments of its competitors than it did on its own.

"In 1874," continued Mr. Rice, "the railroads forced the independent pipe lines of the country to sell out their plants to the Standard Oil Company at the price of old junk, and gave to the latter, besides, still further discriminating rebates on freight. A circular was issued on Sept. 9, 1874, known as "The Rutter Circular," from the freight office of the New York Central and Hudson River Railroad Company, establishing new rates on refined and crude oil. Under this circular the Standard Oil Company was given an advantage of 20 cents a barrel in the freight charges on crude oil connected with its pipe-line system, which the independent refineries did not have. In that same year the Standard company secured the railroad terminal oil facilities of all the trunk lines centering in New York City. Many fortunes invested in the independent pipe lines were wrecked by that move, through no fault of their managers and no lack of business skill, but simply because the Standard Oil officials, acting in collusion with the railroad officials, had established these unfair discriminations in freight rates between the oil that came through the Standard pipes and that which came through other pipes.

"To show you how the rebate system worked in my own case, let me say that in 1885, I was charged 25 cents a barrel for carrying oil from Macksburg to Marietta, a distance of twenty-five miles, while the Standard Oil Company only paid 10 cents a barrel for the same distance. More than this, out of the 35 cents a barrel that I paid the trust actually received 25 cents. In other words, the trust received about two-thirds of all the money I paid for freight."

TRUST "GREATER" THAN THE COURTS OR THE COUNTRY

"You spoke of your having fought the trust for twenty years. Give me a general outline of your encounter with it."

"Well, about 1879 or 1880 I, with others, brought about a public investigation by the Legislature of Ohio as to the discriminations by the railroads of which I have spoken. Nothing came of that investigation except that we proved any number of facts on which further agitation and action was based. I have gone before the Interstate Commerce Commission in many cases trying to get these discriminations stopped. I brought an action through the Attorney-General of Ohio in 1887 to forfeit the charters of two railroads for gross discrimination, and I proved my case. The courts decided, clear up to the highest court, that these two railroads could not make those discriminating charges.

"I obtained at great cost a decree of the Court to that effect. Apparently it was a conclusive victory. In reality it was of no account. The discriminating rates went on as before, and they are still going on to-day. There is no use in trying to stop it. In March, 1892, the Ohio Supreme Court rendered a judgment against the Standard Oil Company, of Ohio, ordering it to discontinue all business relations with the trust.

"The company has pretended to comply with the decree. In fact the trust still exists and the Standard Oil Company, of Ohio, is still a part of it. The way they have got around it is this: On March 21, 1892, the trust resolved on paper to wind up its affairs, and trustees were appointed for that purpose. Then they issued another kind of trust certificate, called an 'Assignment of Legal Title,' which they made marketable and allowed to be transferred from one holder to another on their trust transfer books, which makes this certificate just as negotiable and salable as the old original trust certificate."

$140,060,000 PROFITS IN SIX YEARS

"In this way the trust is still kept intact. In proof of this fact the trust is known to have declared and paid since March, 1892, up to September of this year, 26 regular quarterly dividends of 3 per cent., and 59 per cent. besides in special dividends, or a total of 137 per cent.—dividends, which, based on their reported capitalization of $102,230,700, amounts to $140,060,000 paid in dividends since its pretended dissolution. No more proof is required that the trust has not been dissolved and that the decree of the Supreme Court of Ohio has been treated with contempt."

"But while you have been ruined, Mr. Rice, it is said, you know, that the mass of consumers have gained—that the price of oil is cheaper, because of the trust. What do you say to this suggestion that you, and others like you, have been crushed for the general good?"

"It is a trust lie," replied Mr. Rice warmly. "There is not the least truth in it. Refined oil for general consumption is as much higher in price as these gross rebates and discriminations amount to, because it is fair to assume, on general principles, that the railroads are making money on the transportation of Standard oil. It only costs three-eighths of a cent a gallon to refine oil. The Standard Oil Trust may possibly save one-eighth of a cent on that, but not more. How much does that amount to in the problem of the cost of oil to the retail consumer?

"Refined oil would certainly have been cheaper right along for the last twenty years but for the Standard combination. If the railroad rates had been honest, and the allowances for rebate had been fair and square to all oil producers and refiners, the mass of the people must and would have got the benefit of it. There is no question that the people have paid millions more for oil than they would have done if the laws against conspiracies and combinations in restriction of fair trade could have been enforced. The price of refined oil is notoriously high to-day compared with the low price of crude oil. There is a difference of from 100 to 300 per cent between crude and refined oil prices, when we all know that crude oil can be turned into refined oil and sold all within thirty days."

"Do you see no remedy ahead for the condition of things which ruined your business as a refiner?"

THE REMEDY—ENFORCE THE LAW

"No, I see no remedy, so long as the railroads are under their present management. I have myself tried every known avenue of relief, and my experience has satisfied me that Blackstone did not foresee the conditions of law and justice now prevailing in this country when he wrote his famous maxim, "There is no wrong without a legal remedy." There is no relief for present conditions in this country except by the Government's acquiring ownership of the railroads. There is plenty of law existing now, but it cannot be enforced. It is a dead letter. The Interstate Commerce act has been law for ten years, and the penalty for the violation of it is a fine of $500 and two years in the State prison. It is violated every day, and it has been violated every day for ten years past, but I observe that no one has yet been sent to prison, and I do not believe that any violator of this law ever expects to be."

Speaking of Mr. Rockefeller, the man who said to him at the public hearing at the New Netherland Hotel, Thursday: "We are getting to be gray-haired men now, aren't we, George? Don't you wish you had taken my advice years ago?" Mr. Rice said: "There is no doubt whatever that Mr. Rockefeller, through the operations of the Standard Oil Trust, is the richest man in the world to-day. I know their business, because it is also mine, and I believe that the Rockefellers are now worth $200,000,000.

"John D. Rockefeller's personal income from the trust and other sources has for several years exceeded $12,000,000 per annum."

10

Honest and Dishonest Graft
George Washington Plunkitt

Reformers such as Lincoln Steffens blamed most of the ills of large cities on the political organizations or "machines" that often ran them. In New York City, the most powerful machine was the Democratic Party's Tammany Hall. The following selection, by Tammany politician George Washington Plunkitt (1843–1924), offers a view of the political machine that differs from that presented by Steffens.

Plunkitt's reflections of his political experience were published, edited, and perhaps embroidered on by newspaperman William L. Riordon in 1905. Plunkitt's view of American politics directly contravened the opinions typical of the Progressive Era. While the thrust of reformers, through civil service laws and other programs, was to limit the power of political parties and their machines, Plunkitt argued that parties and political machines performed vital functions. "Honest graft" was, he said, the oil that kept the machines, and government, in motion.

BEFORE YOU READ

1. What, according to George Washington Plunkitt, is the distinction between honest graft and dishonest graft? Why does he consider this distinction important? Is it considered important today?

2. What is Plunkitt's argument against civil service reform? Why does it not benefit his particular constituents?

3. What, according to Plunkitt, is the basis for his political success?

HONEST GRAFT AND DISHONEST GRAFT

"Everybody is talkin' these days about Tammany men growin' rich on graft, but nobody thinks of drawin' the distinction between honest graft and dishonest graft. There's all the difference in the world between the two. Yes, many of our men have grown rich in politics. I have myself. I've made a big fortune out of the game, and I'm gettin' richer every day, but I've not gone in for dishonest graft—blackmailin' gamblers, saloon-keepers, disorderly people, etc.—and neither has any of the men who have made big fortunes in politics.

"There's an honest graft, and I'm an example of how it works. I might sum up the whole thing by sayin': 'I seen my opportunities and I took 'em.'

William L. Riordon, *Plunkitt of Tammany Hall* (New York: McClure, Phillips, 1905), pp. 3–10, 19–28, 46–55.

"Just let me explain by examples. My party's in power in the city, and it's goin' to undertake a lot of public improvements. Well, I'm tipped off, say, that they're going to lay out a new park at a certain place.

"I see my opportunity and I take it. I go to that place and I buy up all the land I can in the neighborhood. Then the board of this or that makes its plan public, and there is a rush to get my land, which nobody cared particular for before.

"Ain't it perfectly honest to charge a good price and make a profit on my investment and foresight? Of course, it is. Well, that's honest graft.

"Or, supposin' it's a new bridge they're goin' to build. I get tipped off and I buy as much property as I can that has to be taken for approaches. I sell at my own price later on and drop some more money in the bank.

"Wouldn't you? It's just like lookin' ahead in Wall Street or in the coffee or cotton market. It's honest graft, and I'm lookin' for it every day in the year. I will tell you frankly that I've got a good lot of it, too.

"I'll tell you of one case. They were goin' to fix up a big park, no matter where. I got on to it, and went lookin' about for land in that neighborhood.

"I could get nothin' at a bargain but a big piece of swamp, but I took it fast enough and held on to it. What turned out was just what I counted on. They couldn't make the park complete without Plunkitt's swamp, and they had to pay a good price for it. Anything dishonest in that?

"Up in the watershed I made some money, too. I bought up several bits of land there some years ago and made a pretty good guess that they would be bought up for water purposes later by the city.

"Somehow, I always guessed about right, and shouldn't I enjoy the profit of my foresight? It was rather amusin' when the condemnation commissioners came along and found piece after piece of the land in the name of George Plunkitt of the Fifteenth Assembly District, New York City. They wondered how I knew just what to buy. The answer is—I seen my opportunity and I took it. I haven't confined myself to land; anything that pays is in my line.

"For instance, the city is repavin' a street and has several hundred thousand old granite blocks to sell. I am on hand to buy, and I know just what they are worth.

"How? Never mind that. I had a sort of monopoly of this business for a while, but once a newspaper tried to do me. It got some outside men to come over from Brooklyn and New Jersey to bid against me.

"Was I done? Not much. I went to each of the men and said: 'How many of these 250,000 stones do you want?' One said 20,000, and another wanted 15,000, and another wanted 10,000. I said: 'All right, let me bid for the lot, and I'll give each of you all you want for nothin'.

"They agreed, of course. Then the auctioneer yelled: 'How much am I bid for these 250,000 fine pavin' stones?'

"'Two dollars and fifty cents,' says I.

"'Two dollars and fifty cents!' screamed the auctioneer. 'Oh, that's a joke! Give me a real bid.'

"He found the bid was real enough. My rivals stood silent. I got the lot for $2.50 and gave them their share. That's how the attempt to do Plunkitt ended, and that's how all such attempts end.

"I've told you how I got rich by honest graft. Now, let me tell you that most politicians who are accused of robbin' the city get rich the same way.

"They didn't steal a dollar from the city treasury. They just seen their opportunities and took them. That is why, when a reform administration comes in and spends a half million dollars in tryin' to find the public robberies they talked about in the campaign, they don't find them.

"The books are always all right. The money in the city treasury is all right. Everything is all right. All they can show is that the Tammany heads of departments looked after their friends, within the law, and gave them what opportunities they could to make honest graft. Now, let me tell you that's never goin' to hurt Tammany with the people. Every good man looks after his friends, and any man who doesn't isn't likely to be popular. If I have a good thing to hand out in private life, I give it to a friend. Why shouldn't I do the same in public life?

"Another kind of honest graft. Tammany has raised a good many salaries. There was an awful howl by the reformers, but don't you know that Tammany gains ten votes for every one it lost by salary raisin'?

"The Wall Street banker thinks it shameful to raise a department clerk's salary from $1500 to $1800 a year, but every man who draws a salary himself says: 'That's all right. I wish it was me.' And he feels very much like votin' the Tammany ticket on election day, just out of sympathy.

"Tammany was beat in 1901 because the people were deceived into believin' that it worked dishonest graft. They didn't draw a distinction between dishonest and honest graft, but they saw that some Tammany men grew rich, and supposed they had been robbin' the city treasury or levyin' blackmail on disorderly houses, or workin' in with the gamblers and lawbreakers.

"As a matter of policy, if nothing else, why should the Tammany leaders go into such dirty business, when there is so much honest graft lyin' around when they are in power? Did you ever consider that?

"Now, in conclusion, I want to say that I don't own a dishonest dollar. If my worst enemy was given the job of writin' my epitaph when I'm gone, he couldn't do more than write:

"'George W. Plunkitt. He Seen His Opportunities, and He Took 'Em.'"

THE CURSE OF CIVIL SERVICE REFORM

"This civil service law is the biggest fraud of the age. It is the curse of the nation. There can't be no real patriotism while it lasts. How are you goin' to interest our young men in their country if you have no offices to give them when they work for their party? Just look at things in this city to-day. There are ten thousand good offices, but we can't get at more than a few hundred of them. How are we goin' to provide for the thousands of men who worked for the Tammany ticket? It can't be done. These men were full of patriotism a short time ago. They expected to be servin' their city, but when we tell them that we can't place them, do you think their patriotism is goin' to last? Not much. They say: 'What's the use of workin' for your country anyhow? There's nothin' in the game.' And what can they do? I don't know, but I'll tell you what I do know. I know more than one young man in past years who worked for the ticket and was just overflowin' with patriotism, but when he was knocked out by the civil service humbug he got to hate his country and became an Anarchist.

"This ain't no exaggeration. I have good reason for sayin' that most of the Anarchists in this city to-day are men who ran up against civil service examinations. Isn't it enough to make a man sour on his country when he wants to serve it and won't be allowed unless he answers a lot of fool questions about the number of cubic inches of water in the Atlantic and the quality of sand in the Sahara desert? There was once a bright young man in my district who tackled one of these examinations. The next I heard of him he had settled down in Herr Most's saloon smokin' and drinkin' beer and talkin' socialism all day. Before that time he had never drank anything but whisky. I knew what was comin' when a young Irishman drops whisky and takes to beer and long pipes in a German saloon. That young man is to-day one of the wildest Anarchists in town. And just to think! He might be a patriot but for that cussed civil service.

"Say, did you hear about the Civil Service Reform Association kickin' because the tax commissioners want to put their fifty-five deputies on the exempt list, and fire the outfit left to them by Low? That's civil service for you. Just think! Fifty-five Republicans and mugwumps[1] holdin' $3000 and $4000 and $5000 jobs in the tax department when 1555 good Tammany men are ready and willin' to take their places! It's an outrage! What did the people mean when they voted for Tammany? What is representative government, anyhow? Is it all a fake that this is a government of the people, by the people and for the people? If it isn't a fake, then why isn't the people's voice obeyed and Tammany men put in all the offices?

"When the people elected Tammany, they knew just what they were doin'. We didn't put up any false pretences. We didn't go in for humbug civil service and all that rot. We stood as we have always stood, for rewardin' the men that won the victory. They call that the spoils system. All right; Tammany is for the spoils system, and when we go in we fire every anti-Tammany man from office that can be fired under the law. It's an elastic sort of law and you can bet it will be stretched to the limit. Of course the Republican State Civil Service Board will stand in the way of our local Civil Service Commission all it can; but say!— suppose we carry the State some time won't we fire the up-State Board all right? Or we'll make it work in harmony with the local board, and that means that Tammany will get everything in sight. I know that the civil service humbug is stuck into the constitution, too, but, as Tim Campbell said: 'What's the constitution among friends?'

"Say, the people's voice is smothered by the cursed civil service law; it is the root of all evil in our government. You hear of this thing or that thing goin' wrong in the nation, the State or the city. Look down beneath the surface and you can trace everything wrong to civil service. I have studied the subject and I know. The

1. **mugwumps:** "good government" bolters from the Republican Party in 1884.

civil service humbug is underminin' our institutions and if a halt ain't called soon this great republic will tumble down like a Park-avenue house when they were buildin' the subway, and on its ruins will rise another Russian government.

"This is an awful serious proposition. Free silver and the tariff and imperialism and the Panama Canal are triflin' issues when compared to it. We could worry along without any of these things, but civil service is sappin' the foundation of the whole shootin' match. Let me argue it out for you. I ain't up on sillygisms, but I can give you some arguments that nobody can answer.

"First, this great and glorious country was built up by political parties; second, parties can't hold together if their workers don't get the offices when they win; third, if the parties go to pieces, the government they built up must go to pieces, too; fourth, then there'll be h _ _ _ to pay.

"Could anything be clearer than that? Say, honest now; can you answer that argument? Of course you won't deny that the government was built up by the great parties. That's history, and you can't go back of the returns. As to my second proposition, you can't deny that either. When parties can't get offices, they'll bust. They ain't far from the bustin' point now, with all this civil service business keepin' most of the good things from them. How are you goin' to keep up patriotism if this thing goes on? You can't do it. Let me tell you that patriotism has been dying out fast for the last twenty years. Before then when a party won, its workers got everything in sight. That was somethin' to make a man patriotic. Now, when a party wins and its men come forward and ask for their reward, the reply is, 'Nothin' doin', unless you can answer a list of questions about Egyptian mummies and how many years it will take for a bird to wear out a mass of iron as big as the earth by steppin' on it once in a century?'

"I have studied politics and men for forty-five years, and I see how things are driftin'. Sad indeed is the change that has come over the young men, even in my district, where I try to keep up the fire of patriotism by gettin' a lot of jobs for my constituents, whether Tammany is in or out. The boys and men don't get excited any more when they see a United States flag or hear the 'Star Spangled Banner.' They don't care no more for fire-crackers on the Fourth of July. And why should they? What is there in it for them? They know that no matter how hard they work for their country in a campaign, the jobs will go to fellows who can tell about the mummies and the bird steppin' on the iron. Are you surprised then that the young men of the country are beginnin' to look coldly on the flag and don't care to put up a nickel for fire-crackers?

"Say, let me tell of one case. After the battle of San Juan Hill, the Americans found a dead man with a light complexion, red hair and blue eyes. They could see he wasn't a Spaniard, although he had on a Spanish uniform. Several officers looked him over, and then a private of the Seventy-first Regiment saw him and yelled, 'Good Lord, that's Flaherty.' That man grew up in my district, and he was once the most patriotic American boy on the West Side. He couldn't see a flag without yellin' himself hoarse.

"Now, how did he come to be lying dead with a Spanish uniform on? I found out all about it, and I'll vouch for the story. Well, in the municipal campaign of 1897, that young man, chockful of patriotism, worked day and night for the Tammany ticket. Tammany won, and the young man determined to devote his life to the service of the city. He picked out a place that would suit him, and sent in his application to the head of department. He got a reply that he must take a civil service examination to get the place. He didn't know what these examinations were, so he went, all lighthearted, to the Civil Service Board. He read the questions about the mummies, the bird on the iron, and all the other fool questions—and he left that office an enemy of the country that he had loved so well. The mummies and the bird blasted his patriotism. He went to Cuba, enlisted in the Spanish army at the breakin' out of the war, and died fightin' his country.

"That is but one victim of the infamous civil service. If that young man had not run up against the civil examination, but had been allowed to serve his country as he wished, he would be in a good office today, drawin' a good salary. Ah, how many young men have had their patriotism blasted in the same way!

"Now, what is goin' to happen when civil service crushes out patriotism? Only one thing can happen: the republic will go to pieces. Then a czar or a sultan will turn up, which brings me to the fourthly of my argument—that is, there will be h _ _ _ to pay. And that ain't no lie."

TO HOLD YOUR DISTRICT—STUDY HUMAN NATURE AND ACT ACCORDIN'

"There's only one way to hold a district; you must study human nature and act accordin'. You can't study human nature in books. Books is a hindrance more than anything else. If you have been to college, so much the worse for you. You'll have to unlearn all you learned before you can get right down to human nature, and unlearnin' takes a lot of time. Some men can never forget what they learned at college. Such men may get to be district leaders by a fluke, but they never last.

"To learn real human nature you have to go among the people, see them and be seen. I know every man, woman, and child in the Fifteenth District, except them that's been born this summer—and I know some of them, too. I know what they like and what they don't like, what they are strong at and what they are weak in, and I reach them by approachin' at the right side.

"For instance, here's how I gather in the young men. I hear of a young feller that's proud of his voice, thinks that he can sing fine. I ask him to come around to Washington Hall and join our Glee Club. He comes and sings, and he's a follower of Plunkitt for life. Another young feller gains a reputation as a baseball player in a vacant lot. I bring him into our baseball club. That fixes him. You'll find him workin' for my ticket at the polls next election day. Then there's the feller that likes rowin' on the river, the young feller that makes a name as a waltzer on his block, the young feller that's handy with his dukes—I rope them all in by givin' them opportunities to show themselves off. I don't trouble them with political arguments. I just study human nature and act accordin'.

"But you may say this game won't work with the high-toned fellers, the fellers that go through college and then join the Citizens' Union. Of course it wouldn't work. I have a special treatment for them. I ain't like the patent medicine man that gives the same medicine for all diseases. The Citizens' Union kind of a young man! I love him! He's the daintiest morsel of the lot, and he don't often escape me.

"Before telling you how I catch him, let me mention that before the election last year, the Citizens' Union said they had four hundred or five hundred enrolled voters in my district. They had a lovely headquarters, too, beautiful roll-top desks and the cutest rugs in the world. If I was accused of havin' contributed to fix up the nest for them, I wouldn't deny it under oath. What do I mean by that? Never mind. You can guess from the sequel, if you're sharp.

"Well, election day came. The Citizens' Union's candidate for Senator, who ran against me, just polled five votes in the district, while I polled something more than 14,000 votes. What became of the 400 or 500 Citizens' Union enrolled voters in my district? Some people guessed that many of them were good Plunkitt men all along and worked with the Cits just to bring them into the Plunkitt camp by election day. You can guess that way, too, if you want to. I never contradict stories about me, especially in hot weather. I just call your attention to the fact that on last election day 395 Citizens' Union enrolled voters in my district were missin' and unaccounted for.

"I tell you frankly, though, how I have captured some of the Citizens' Union's young men. I have a plan that never fails. I watch the City Record to see when there's civil service examinations for good things. Then I take my young Cit in hand, tell him all about the good thing and get him worked up till he goes and takes an examination. I don't bother about him any more. It's a cinch that he comes back to me in a few days and asks to join Tammany Hall. Come over to Washington Hall some night and I'll show you a list of names on our rolls marked 'C.S.' which means, 'bucked up against civil service.'

"As to the older voters, I reach them, too. No, I don't send them campaign literature. That's rot. People can get all the political stuff they want to read—and a good deal more, too—in the papers. Who reads speeches, nowadays, anyhow? It's bad enough to listen to them. You ain't goin' to gain any votes by stuffin' their letter-boxes with campaign documents. Like as not you'll lose votes, for there's nothin' a man hates more than to hear the letter-carrier ring his bell and go to the letter-box expectin' to find a letter he was lookin' for, and find only a lot of printed politics. I met a man this very mornin' who told me he voted the Democratic State ticket last year just because the Republicans kept crammin' his letter-box with campaign documents.

"What tells in holdin' your grip on your district is to go right down among the poor families and help them in the different ways they need help. I've got a regular system for this. If there's a fire in Ninth, Tenth, or Eleventh Avenue, for example, any hour of the day or night, I'm usually there with some of my election district captains as soon as the fire-engines. If a family is burned out I don't ask whether they are Republicans or Democrats, and I don't refer them to the Charity Organization Society, which would investigate their case in a month or two and decide they were worthy of help about the time they are dead from starvation. I just get quarters for them, buy clothes for them if their clothes were burned up, and fix them up till they get things runnin' again. It's philanthropy, but it's politics, too—mighty good politics. Who can tell how many votes one of the fires bring me? The poor are the most grateful people in the world, and, let me tell you, they have more friends in their neighborhoods than the rich have in theirs.

"If there's a family in my district in want I know it before the charitable societies do, and me and my men are first on the ground. I have a special corps to look up such cases. The consequence is that the poor look up to George W. Plunkitt as a father, come to him in trouble—and don't forget him on election day.

"Another thing, I can always get a job for a deservin' man. I make it a point to keep on the track of jobs, and it seldom happens that I don't have a few up my sleeve ready for use. I know every big employer in the district and in the whole city, for that matter, and they ain't in the habit of sayin' no to me when I ask them for a job.

"And the children—the little roses of the district! Do I forget them? Oh, no! They know me, every one of them, and they know that a sight of Uncle George and candy means the same thing. Some of them are the best kind of vote-getters. I'll tell you a case. Last year a little Eleventh Avenue rosebud whose father is a Republican, caught hold of his whiskers on election day and said she wouldn't let go till he'd promise to vote for me. And she didn't."

ON *THE SHAME OF THE CITIES*

"I've been readin' a book by Lincoln Steffens on *The Shame of the Cities.* Steffens means well but, like all reformers, he don't know how to make distinctions. He can't see no difference between honest graft and dishonest graft and, consequent, he gets things all mixed up. There's the biggest kind of a difference between political looters and politicians who make a fortune out of politics by keepin' their eyes wide open. The looter goes in for himself alone without considerin' his organization or his city. The politician looks after his own interests, the organization's interests, and the city's interests all at the same time. See the distinction? For instance, I ain't no looter. The looter hogs it. I never hogged. I made my pile in politics, but, at the same time, I served the organization and got more big improvements for New York City than any other livin' man. And I never monkeyed with the penal code."

11

Antilynching Campaign in Tennessee
Ida B. Wells-Barnett

Lynching — the murder, especially by hanging, of a person accused of some offense, real or imagined, by a mob — is an old crime in the United States. The word can be traced back to the way Colonel Charles Lynch and his fellow patriots in revolutionary Virginia dealt with suspected Tories. Lynchings, especially of blacks, began to increase in the 1880s and peaked in 1892, the worst year in American history for this brutal crime.

Thomas Moss, Calvin McDowell, and Henry Stewart, friends of Ida B. Wells-Barnett (1864–1931) and respectable and successful members of the Memphis African American community, were among the approximately two hundred fifty Americans whose lynchings were recorded in 1892. (There were doubtless more of which no record was made.) The murder of her friends changed Wells-Barnett's entire life. Already well known as a leading African American journalist and reformer — she had sued a railroad company in 1883 for forcing her to leave a "whites-only" car — she left Memphis after her angry editorial on the lynchings put her life in danger, and she became a lifelong activist against the crime. Her campaign helped make opposition to lynching a leading cause among African American activists until World War II, when lynchings largely — but not completely — ceased.

In answering the accusation that lynching was the response to "the new Negro crime" — the propensity of black men to rape white women — Wells-Barnett researched in detail the circumstances of the 728 lynchings of the previous ten years that she was able to authenticate. Her evidence refuted the excuse that the victims had committed rape. Only a third of black lynching victims were even accused of rape. Many died for crimes like "race prejudice," "making threats," or "quarreling with whites." Some of the victims were women and even children.

BEFORE YOU READ

1. How does Wells-Barnett explain the lynchings of her friends and others? Do you agree with her?

2. What is Wells-Barnett's strategy for Memphis's African Americans to respond to the lynchings? What do you think of it?

3. Do you agree with Wells-Barnett that "every white man in Memphis who consented" to the lynchings and rioting "is as guilty as those who fired the guns"?

Alfreda M. Duster, ed., *Crusade for Justice: The Autobiography of Ida B. Wells* (Chicago: University of Chicago Press, 1970), pp. 47–52.

While I was thus carrying on the work of my newspaper, happy in the thought that our influence was helpful and that I was doing the work I loved and had proved that I could make a living out of it, there came the lynching in Memphis which changed the whole course of my life. . . .

Thomas Moss, Calvin McDowell, and Henry Stewart owned and operated a grocery store in a thickly populated suburb [of Memphis]. Moss was a letter carrier and could only be at the store at night. Everybody in town knew and loved Tommie. An exemplary young man, he was married and the father of one little girl, Maurine, whose godmother I was. He and his wife Betty were the best friends I had in town. And he believed, with me, that we should defend the cause of right and fight wrong wherever we saw it.

He delivered mail at the office of the *Free Speech*, and whatever Tommie knew in the way of news we got first. He owned his little home, and having saved his money he went into the grocery business with the same ambition that a young white man would have had. He was the president of the company. His partners ran the business in the daytime.

They had located their grocery in the district known as the "Curve" because the streetcar line curved sharply at that point. There was already a grocery owned and operated by a white man who hitherto had had a monopoly on the trade of this thickly populated colored suburb. Thomas's grocery changed all that, and he and his associates were made to feel that they were not welcome by the white grocer. The district being mostly colored and many of the residents belonging either to Thomas's church or to his lodge, he was not worried by the white grocer's hostility.

One day some colored and white boys quarreled over a game of marbles and the colored boys got the better of the fight which followed. The father of the white boys whipped the victorious colored boy, whose father and friends pitched in to avenge the grown white man's flogging of a colored boy. The colored men won the fight, whereupon the white father and grocery keeper swore out a warrant for the arrest of the colored victors. Of course the colored grocery keepers had been drawn into the dispute. But the case was dismissed with nominal fines. Then the challenge was issued that the vanquished whites were coming on Saturday night to clean out the People's Grocery Company.

Knowing this, the owners of the company consulted a lawyer and were told that as they were outside the city limits and beyond police protection, they would be justified in protecting themselves if attacked. Accordingly the grocery company armed several men and stationed them in the rear of the store on that fatal Saturday night, not to attack but to repel a threatened attack. And Saturday night was the time when men of both races congregated in their respective groceries.

About ten o'clock that night, when Thomas was posting his books for the week and Calvin McDowell and his clerk were waiting on customers preparatory to closing, shots rang out in the back room of the store. The men stationed there had seen several white men stealing through the rear door and fired on them without a moment's pause. Three of these men were wounded, and others fled and gave the alarm.

Sunday morning's paper came out with lurid headlines telling how officers of the law had been wounded while in the discharge of their duties, hunting up criminals whom they had been told were harbored in the People's Grocery Company, this being "a low dive in which drinking and gambling were carried on: a resort of thieves and thugs." So ran the description in the leading white journals of Memphis of this successful effort of decent black men to carry on a legitimate business. The same newspaper told of the arrest and jailing of the proprietor of the store and many of the colored people. They predicted that it would go hard with the ringleaders if these "officers" should die. The tale of how the peaceful homes of that suburb were raided on that quiet Sunday morning by police pretending to be looking for others who were implicated in what the papers had called a conspiracy, has been often told. Over a hundred colored men were dragged from their homes and put in jail on suspicion.

All day long on that fateful Sunday white men were permitted in the jail to look over the imprisoned black men. Frenzied descriptions and hearsays were detailed in the papers, which fed the fires of sensationalism. Groups of white men gathered on the street corners and meeting places to discuss the awful crime of Negroes shooting white men.

There had been no lynchings in Memphis since the Civil War, but the colored people felt that anything might happen during the excitement. Many of them were in business there. Several times they had elected a member of their race to represent them in the legislature in Nashville. And a Negro, Lymus Wallace, had been elected several times as a member of the city council and we had had representation on the school board several times. Mr. Fred Savage was then our representative on the board of education.

The manhood which these Negroes represented went to the county jail and kept watch Sunday night. This they did also on Monday night, guarding the jail to see that nothing happened to the colored men during this time of race prejudice, while it was thought that the wounded white men would die. On Tuesday following, the newspapers which had fanned the flame of race prejudice announced that the wounded men were out of danger and would recover. The colored men who had guarded the jail for two nights felt that the crisis was past and that they need not guard the jail the third night.

While they slept a body of picked men was admitted to the jail, which was a modern Bastile. This mob took out of their cells Thomas Moss, Calvin McDowell, and Henry Stewart, the three officials of the People's Grocery Company. They were loaded on a switch engine of the railroad which ran back of the jail, carried a mile north of the city limits, and horribly shot to death. One of the morning papers held back its edition in order to supply its readers with the details of that lynching.

From its columns was gleaned the above information, together with details which told that "It is said that Tom Moss begged for his life for the sake of his wife and child and his unborn baby"; that when asked if he had anything to say, told them to "tell my people to go West—there is no justice for them here"; that Calvin McDowell got hold of one of the guns of the lynchers and because they could not loosen his grip a shot was fired into his closed fist. When the three bodies were found, the fingers of McDowell's right hand had been shot to pieces and his eyes were gouged out. This proved that the one who wrote that news report was either an eyewitness or got the facts from someone who was.

The shock to the colored people who knew and loved both Moss and McDowell was beyond description. Groups of them went to the grocery and elsewhere and vented their feelings in talking among themselves, but they offered no violence. Word was brought to the city hall that Negroes were massing at the "Curve" where the grocery had been located. Immediately an order was issued by the judge of the criminal court sitting on the bench, who told the sheriff to "take a hundred men, go out to the Curve at once, and shoot down on sight any Negro who appears to be making trouble."

The loafers around the courts quickly spread the news, and gangs of them rushed into the hardware stores, armed themselves, boarded the cars and rushed out to the Curve. They obeyed the judge's orders literally and shot into any group of Negroes they saw with as little compunction as if they had been on a hunting trip. The only reason hundreds of Negroes were not killed on that day by the mobs was because of the forebearance of the colored men. They realized their helplessness and submitted to outrages and insults for the sake of those depending upon them.

This mob took possession of the People's Grocery Company, helping themselves to food and drink, and destroyed what they could not eat or steal. The creditors had the place closed and a few days later what remained of the stock was sold at auction. Thus, with the aid of the city and county authorities and the daily papers, that white grocer had indeed put an end to his rival Negro grocer as well as to his business.

As said before, I was in Natchez, Mississippi, when the worst of this horrible event was taking place. Thomas Moss had already been buried before I reached home. Although stunned by the events of that hectic week, the *Free Speech* felt that it must carry on. Its leader for that week said:

> The city of Memphis has demonstrated that neither character nor standing avails the Negro if he dares to protect himself against the white man or become his rival. There is nothing we can do about the lynching now, as we are outnumbered and without arms. The white mob could help itself to ammunition without pay, but the order was rigidly enforced against the selling of guns to Negroes. There is therefore only one thing left that we can do; save our money and leave a town which will neither protect our lives and property, nor give us a fair trial in the courts, but takes us out and murders us in cold blood when accused by white persons.

This advice of the *Free Speech*, coupled with the last words of Thomas Moss, was taken up and reechoed among our people throughout Memphis. Hundreds disposed of their property and left. Rev. R. N. Countee and Rev. W. A. Brinkley, both leading pastors, took their whole congregations with them as they, too, went West. Memphis had never seen such an upheaval among colored people. Business was practically at a standstill, for the Negro was famous then, as now, for spending his money for fine clothes, furniture, jewelry, and pianos and other musical instruments, to say nothing of good things to eat. Music houses had more musical instruments, sold on the installment plan, thrown back on their hands than they could find storage for.

Six weeks after the lynching the superintendent and treasurer of the City Railway Company came into the office of the *Free Speech* and asked us to use our influence with the colored people to get them to ride on the streetcars again. When I asked why they came to us the reply was that colored people had been their best patrons, but that there had been a marked falling off of their patronage. There were no jim crow[1] streetcars in Memphis then. I asked what they thought was the cause. They said they didn't know. They had heard Negroes were afraid of electricity, for Memphis already had streetcars run by electricity in 1892. They wanted us to assure our people that there was no danger and to tell them that any discourtesy toward them would be punished severely.

But I said that I couldn't believe it, because "electricity has been the motive power here for over six months and you are just now noticing the slump. How long since you have observed the change?" "About six weeks," said one of them. "You see it's a matter of dollars and cents with us. If we don't look after the loss and remedy the cause the company will get somebody else who will."

"So your own job then depends on Negro patronage?" I asked. And although their faces flushed over the question they made no direct reply. "You see it is like this," said the superintendent. "When the company installed electricity at a cost of thousands of dollars last fall, Negro labor got a large share of it in wages in relaying tracks, grading the streets, etc. And so we think it is only fair that they should give us their patronage in return."

Said I, "They were doing so until six weeks ago, yet you say you don't know the cause of the falling off. Why, it was just six weeks ago that the lynching took place." "But the streetcar company had nothing to do with the lynching," said one of the men. "It is owned by northern capitalists." "And run by southern lynchers," I retorted. "We have learned that every white man of any standing in town knew of the plan and consented to the lynching of our boys. Did you know Tom Moss, the letter carrier?" "Yes," he replied.

"A finer, cleaner man than he never walked the streets of Memphis," I said. "He was well liked, a favorite with everybody; yet he was murdered with no more consideration than if he had been a dog, because he as a man defended his property from attack. The colored people feel that every white man in Memphis who consented to his death is as guilty as those who fired the guns which took his life, and they want to get away from this town.

"We told them the week after the lynching to save their nickels and dimes so that they could do so. We had no way of knowing that they were doing so before this, as I have walked more than I ever did in my life before. No one has been arrested or punished about that terrible affair nor will they be because all are equally guilty."

"Why don't the colored people find the guilty ones?" asked one of them.

---

1. **jim crow:** discrimination against African Americans in public places, such as streetcars.

"As if they could. There is strong belief among us that the criminal court judge himself was one of the lynchers. Suppose we had the evidence; could we get it before that judge? Or a grand jury of white men who had permitted it to be? Or force the reporter of the *Appeal* to tell what he saw and knows about that night? You know very well that we are powerless to do any of these things."

"Well we hope you will do what you can for us and if you know of any discourtesy on the part of our employees let us know and we will be glad to remedy it."

When they left the office I wrote this interview for the next issue of the *Free Speech* and in the article told the people to keep up the good work. Not only that, I went to the two largest churches in the city the next Sunday, before the paper came out, and told them all about it. I urged them to keep on staying off the cars.

Every time word came of people leaving Memphis, we who were left behind rejoiced. Oklahoma was about to be opened up, and scores sold or gave away property, shook Memphis dust off their feet, and went out West as Tom Moss had said for us to do.

12

A Modern Lear

Jane Addams

The Pullman strike of 1894 became the first national strike in U.S. history, spreading across twenty-seven states and territories and involving 150,000 workers who succeeded in paralyzing the nation's rail systems. George M. Pullman was an industrialist whose factories built luxury and sleeper rail cars. In Illinois he had built what he claimed to be a model town for his workers, just south of Chicago, that he called Pullman. He provided schooling, health care, parks, and a library for his workers and prided himself on being a great philanthropist. But when the severe depression of the early 1890s struck, he cut wages by twenty-five percent. His workers formed a committee to ask that the rent on company houses, which all Pullman's workers had to live in, also be lowered. Pullman refused and fired three of the committee members.

On May 10, 1894, workers in his factory went on strike. In June, members of the American Railway Union, under the leadership of future Socialist Party presidential candidate Eugene Debs, decided to "hot-cargo," or refuse to handle, trains with Pullman cars. Though the strike was peaceful, President Grover Cleveland believed that it represented a threat to mail delivery. His attorney general issued a federal injunction against the strike, making it illegal. Despite pleas by Illinois governor John Peter Altgeld to allow local law enforcement and National Guardsmen to deal with the situation, Cleveland sent in federal troops in an attempt to decisively put down the strike.

Federal troops arrived in Chicago on July 3, 1894, and the next day, Independence Day, Chicago exploded in rioting and street battles between strikers, federal troops, and National Guardsmen. Seven hundred rail cars were destroyed, at least four rioters were shot dead by guardsmen, and Debs was arrested for ignoring the federal injunction. In the end, the strikers were unable to defeat the federal government, and the labor action gradually petered out until the Pullman plant reopened in August, with no reduction in rent for the workers' houses and with none of the strike leaders rehired.

In this well-known article, the pioneering social worker and reformer Jane Addams, while not being uncritical of the workers, laid blame for the turmoil at the feet of Pullman. She recognized in him a genuine moral code but one rendered obsolete by new industrial conditions. Addams compared Pullman's paternalism toward his workers to the relationship between Shakespeare's King Lear and Lear's daughter Cordelia. In the play, Lear's belief in his own generosity to Cordelia creates a sense of self-righteousness and stubbornness that blinds him to her true aspirations. Pullman, similarly, could see only the material benefits that he had offered his workers, without recognizing their desire to have some control over their working and living conditions.

Jane Addams, "A Modern Lear," *Survey* 29 (November 2, 1912), pp. 131–37.

BEFORE YOU READ

1. On what grounds did Addams support the side of the striking workers?

2. What does Addams's writing suggest about industrial relations in the late nineteenth century?

3. Do you think the comparison between a parent and an employer is a valid and useful one in helping to determine ethical forms of behavior in industrial relations?

Those of us who lived in Chicago during the summer of 1894 were confronted by a drama which epitomized and, at the same time, challenged the code of social ethics under which we live, for a quick series of unusual events had dispelled the good nature which in happier times envelops the ugliness of the industrial situation. It sometimes seems as if the shocking experiences of that summer, the barbaric instinct to kill, roused on both sides, the sharp division into class lines, with the resultant distrust and bitterness, can only be endured if we learn from it all a great ethical lesson. To endure is all we can hope for. It is impossible to justify such a course of rage and riot in a civilized community to whom the methods of conciliation and control were open. Every public-spirited citizen in Chicago during that summer felt the stress and perplexity of the situation and asked himself, "How far am I responsible for this social disorder? What can be done to prevent such outrageous manifestations of ill-will?" . . .

During the discussions which followed the Pullman strike, the defenders of the situation were broadly divided between the people pleading for individual benevolence and those insisting upon social righteousness; between those who held that the philanthropy of the president of the Pullman company had been most ungratefully received and those who maintained that the situation was the inevitable outcome of the social consciousness developing among working people.

In the midst of these discussions the writer found her mind dwelling upon a comparison which modified and softened all her judgments. Her attention was caught by the similarity of ingratitude suffered by an indulgent employer and an indulgent parent. King Lear came often to her mind. We have all shared the family relationship and our code of ethics concerning it is somewhat settled. We also bear a part in the industrial relationship, but our ethics concerning that are still uncertain. A comparative study of these two relationships presents an advantage, in that it enables us to consider the situation from the known experience toward the unknown. The minds of all of us reach back to our early struggles, as we emerged from the state of self-willed childhood to a recognition of the family claim.

We have all had glimpses of what it might be to blaspheme against family ties; to ignore the elemental claim that they make upon us, but on the whole we have recognized them, and it does not occur to us to throw them over. The industrial claim is so difficult; the ties are so intangible that we are constantly ignoring them and shirking the duties which they impose. It will probably be easier to treat of the tragedy of the Pullman strike as if it were already long past when we compare it to the family tragedy of Lear which has already become historic to our minds and which we discuss without personal feeling.

Historically considered, the relation of Lear to his children was archaic and barbaric, holding in it merely the beginnings of a family life, since developed. We may in later years learn to look back upon the industrial relationships in which we are now placed as quite as incomprehensible and selfish, quite as barbaric and undeveloped, as was the family relationship between Lear and his daughters. We may then take the relationship of this unusually generous employer at Pullman to his own townful of employes as at least a fair one, because so exceptionally liberal in many of its aspects. King Lear doubtless held the same notion of a father's duty that was held by the other fathers of his time; but he alone was a king and had kingdoms to bestow upon his children. He was unique, therefore, in the magnitude of his indulgence, and in the magnitude of the disaster which followed it. The sense of duty held by the president of the Pullman company doubtless represents the ideal in the minds of the best of the present employers as to their obligations toward their employes, but he projected this ideal more magnificently than the others. He alone gave his men so model a town, such perfect surroundings. The magnitude of his indulgence and failure corresponded and we are forced to challenge the ideal itself: the same deal which, more or less clearly defined, is floating in the minds of all philanthropic employers.

This older tragedy implied mal-adjustment between individuals; the forces of the tragedy were personal and passionate. This modern tragedy in its inception is a mal-adjustment between two large bodies of men, an employing company and a mass of employes. It deals not with personal relationships, but with industrial relationships.

Owing, however, to the unusual part played in it by the will of one man, we find that it closely approaches Lear in motif. The relation of the British King to his family is very like the relation of the president of the Pullman company to his town; the denouement of a daughter's break with her father suggests the break of the employes with their benefactor. If we call one an example of the domestic tragedy, the other of the industrial tragedy, it is possible to make them illuminate each other.

It is easy to discover striking points of similarity in the tragedies of the royal father and the philanthropic president of the Pullman company. The like quality of ingratitude they both suffered is at once apparent. It may be said that the ingratitude which Lear received was poignant and bitter to him in proportion as he recalled the extraordinary benefits he had heaped upon his daughters, and that he found his fate harder to bear because he had so far exceeded the measure of a father's duty, as he himself says. What, then, would be the bitterness of a man who had heaped extraordinary benefits upon those toward whom he had no duty recognized by common consent; who had not only exceeded the righteousness of the employer, but who had worked out original and striking methods for lavishing goodness and generosity? More than that, the president had been almost persecuted for this goodness by the more utilitarian members of his company and had at one time imperilled his business reputation for the sake of the benefactions to his town, and he had thus reached the height of sacrifice for it. This model town embodied not only his hopes and ambitions, but stood for the peculiar effort which a man makes for that which is misunderstood.

It is easy to see that although the heart of Lear was cut by ingratitude and by misfortune, it was cut deepest of all by the public pity of his people, in that they should remember him no longer as a king and benefactor, but as a defeated man who had blundered through oversoftness. So the heart of the Chicago man was cut by the unparalleled publicity which brought him to the minds of thousands as a type of oppression and injustice, and to many others as an example of the evil of an irregulated sympathy for the "lower classes." He who had been dined and feted throughout Europe as the creator of a model town, as the friend and benefactor of workingmen, was now execrated by workingmen throughout the entire country. He had not only been good to those who were now basely ungrateful to him, but he felt himself deserted by the admiration of his people.

In shops such as those at Pullman, indeed, in all manufacturing affairs since the industrial revolution, industry is organized into a vast social operation. The shops are managed, however, not for the development of the workman thus socialized, but for the interests of the company owning the capital. The divergence between the social form and the individual aim becomes greater as the employes are more highly socialized and dependent, just as the clash in a family is more vital in proportion to the development and closeness of the family tie. The president of the Pullman company went further than the usual employer does. He socialized not only the factory but the form in which his workmen were living. He built and, in a great measure, regulated an entire town. This again might have worked out into a successful associated effort, if he had had in view the sole good of the inhabitants thus socialized, if he had called upon them for self-expression and had made the town a growth and manifestation of their wants and needs. But, unfortunately, the end to be obtained became ultimately commercial and not social, having in view the payment to the company of at least 4 per cent on the money invested, so that with this rigid requirement there could be no adaptation of rent to wages, much less to needs. The rents became statical and the wages competitive, shifting inevitably with the demands of trade. The president assumed that he himself knew the needs of his men, and so far from wishing them to express their needs he denied to them the simple rights of trade organization, which would have been, of course, the merest preliminary to an attempt at associated expression. If we may take the dictatorial relation of Lear to Cordelia as a typical and most dramatic example of the distinctively family tragedy, one will asserting its authority through all the entanglement of wounded affection, and insisting upon its selfish ends at all cost, may we not consider the absolute authority of this employer over his town as a typical and dramatic example of the industrial tragedy? One will directing the energies of many others, without regard to their desires, and having in view in the last analysis only commercial results?

It shocks our ideal of family life that a man should fail to know his daughter's heart because she awkwardly expressed her love, that he should refuse to comfort and advise her through all difference of opinion and clashing of will. That a man should be so absorbed in his own indignation as to fail to apprehend his child's thought; that he should lose his affection in his anger, is really no more unnatural than that the man who spent a million of dollars on a swamp to make it sanitary for his employes, should refuse to speak to them for ten minutes, whether they were in the right or wrong; or that a man who had given them his time and thought for twenty years should withdraw from them his guidance when he believed them misled by ill-advisers and wandering in a mental fog; or that he should grow hard and angry when they needed tenderness and help.

Lear ignored the common ancestry of Cordelia and himself. He forgot her royal inheritance of magnanimity, and also the power of obstinacy which he shared with her. So long had he thought of himself as the noble and indulgent father that he had lost the faculty by which he might perceive himself in the wrong. Even when his spirit was broken by the storm he declared himself more sinned against than sinning. He could believe any amount of kindness and goodness of himself, but could imagine no fidelity on the part of Cordelia unless she gave him the sign he demanded.

The president of the Pullman company doubtless began to build his town from an honest desire to give his employes the best surroundings. As it developed it became a source of pride and an exponent of power, that he cared most for when it gave him a glow of benevolence. . . . He cultivated the great and noble impulses of the benefactor, until the power of attaining a simple human relationship with his employes, that of frank equality with them, was gone from him. He, too, lost the faculty of affectionate interpretation, and demanded a sign. He and his employes had no mutual interest in a common cause. . . .

. . . Without pressing the analogy too hard may we not compare the indulgent relation of this employer to his town to the relation which existed between Lear and Cordelia? He fostered his employes for many years, gave them sanitary houses and beautiful parks, but in their extreme need, when they were struggling with the most difficult question which the times could present to them, when, if ever, they required the assistance of a trained mind and a comprehensive outlook, he lost his touch and had nothing wherewith to help them. He did not see the situation. He had been ignorant of their gropings toward justice. His conception of goodness for them had been cleanliness, decency of living, and above all, thrift and temperance. He had provided them means for all this; had gone further, and given them opportunities for enjoyment and comradeship. But he suddenly found his town in the sweep of a world-wide moral impulse. A movement had been going on about him and through the souls of his workingmen of which he had been unconscious. He had only heard of this movement by rumor. The men who consorted with him at his club and in his business had spoken but little of it, and when they had discussed it had contemptuously called it the "Labor Movement," headed by deadbeats and agitators. Of the force and power of this movement, of all the vitality within it, of that conception of duty which induces men to go without food and to see their wives and children suffer for the sake of securing better wages for fellow-workmen whom they have never seen, this president had dreamed absolutely nothing. But his town had at last become swept into this larger movement, so that the giving up of comfortable homes, of beautiful surroundings, seemed as naught to the men within its grasp.

Outside the ken of this philanthropist, the proletariat had learned to say in many languages that "the injury of one is the concern of all." Their watchwords were brotherhood, sacrifice, the subordination of individual and trade interests to the good of the working class; and their persistent striving were toward the ultimate freedom of that class from the conditions under which they now labor.

Compared to these watchwords the old ones which the philanthropic employer had given this town were negative and inadequate.

When this movement finally swept in his own town, or, to speak more fairly, when in their distress and perplexity his own employes appealed to the organized manifestation of this movement, they were quite sure that simply because they were workmen in distress they would not be deserted by it. This loyalty on the part of a widely ramified and well organized union toward the workmen in a "scab shop," who had contributed nothing to its cause, was certainly a manifestation of moral power.

That the movement was ill-directed, that it was ill-timed and disastrous in results, that it stirred up and became confused in the minds of the public with the elements of riot and bloodshed, can never touch the fact that it started from an unselfish impulse.

In none of his utterances or correspondence did the president of the company for an instant recognize this touch of nobility, although one would imagine that he would gladly point out this bit of virtue, in what he must have considered the moral ruin about him. He stood throughout pleading for the individual virtues, those which had distinguished the model workman of his youth, those which had enabled him and so many of his contemporaries to rise in life, when "rising in life" was urged upon every promising boy as the goal of his efforts. Of the new code of ethics he had caught absolutely nothing. The morals he had taught his men did not fail them in their hour of confusion. They were self-controlled and destroyed no property. They were sober and exhibited no drunkenness, even though obliged to hold their meetings in the saloon hall of a neighboring town. They repaid their employer in kind, but he had given them no rule for the higher fellowship and life of association into which they were plunged.

The virtues of one generation are not sufficient for the next, any more than the accumulations of knowledge possessed by one age are adequate to the needs of another.

Of the virtues received from our fathers we can afford to lose none. We accept as a precious trust those principles and precepts which the race has worked out for its highest safeguard and protection. But merely to preserve those is not enough. A task is laid upon each generation to enlarge their application, to ennoble their conception, and, above all, to apply and adapt them to the peculiar problems presented to it for solution.

The president of this company desired that his employes should possess the individual and family virtues, but did nothing to cherish in them those social virtues which his own age demanded. He rather substituted for that sense of responsibility to the community, a feeling of gratitude to himself, who had provided them with public buildings, and had laid out for them a simulacrum of public life.

Is it strange that when the genuine feeling of the age struck his town this belated and almost feudal virtue of personal gratitude fell before it?

Day after day during that horrible suspense, when the wires constantly reported the same message, "The president of the company holds that there is nothing to arbitrate," one longed to find out what was in the mind of this man, to unfold his ultimate motive. One concludes that he must have been sustained by the consciousness of being in the right. Only that could have held him against the great desire for fair play which swept over the country. Only the training which an arbitrary will receives by years of consulting first its own personal and commercial ends could have made it strong enough to withstand the demands for social adjustment. He felt himself right from the *commercial* standpoint, and could not see the situation from the *social* standpoint. For years he had gradually accustomed himself to the thought that his motive was beyond reproach; that his attitude to this town was always righteous and philanthropic. Habit held him persistent in this view of the case through all the changing conditions. . . .

PART THREE

An Age of Reform

Responses to Industrial America

.

While the middle class flourished at the turn of the twentieth century, the labor movement grew on the recognition that "once a worker" most likely meant "always a worker," particularly for women, children, immigrants, and members of other groups for whom opportunities for a better life would not often materialize. Working conditions at the Triangle Shirtwaist Company offered a warning of the uneven effects of industrial growth. By the time the Triangle fire occurred, American society was only beginning to recognize the new workers in their midst and the peculiar dangers they faced. As they sewed garments that defined middle-class style in new but uninspected high-rise factory buildings, young immigrant women were risking their lives in unsafe conditions for low wages.

While intending to alleviate the economic misery of working people, Upton Sinclair instead improved the sanitary conditions in meat-packing houses—which illustrates both the capacity of American society to respond to social problems and the limits of that capacity. And nowhere were the perils and promises of the time more inextricably mixed than in the lives of new immigrants like those who wrote to the "Bintel Brief" advice column of the *Jewish Daily Forward* with questions about their attempts to adjust to and succeed in a new and often bewildering society. The images in the visual portfolio "Urban Industrial America" (page 143) illuminate this rich and frightening land of contrasts and show how photographers struggled to understand this new world.

World War I multiplied both the perils and promises of American life. This war, like the Korean and Vietnam Wars later on, stirred social discontent. The war exacerbated tensions between older Americans and immigrants, raising questions of who was an American (or an Irish American, a German American, and so on), who was loyal, and who was not; hundreds of socialists and antiwar activists like Kate Richards O'Hare were imprisoned for opposing the war. Another major change wrought by the war was the movement of African Americans to Northern cities. As the letters assembled by Emmett J. Scott reveal, fresh opportunities in war industries combined with the depredations of the boll weevil on cotton crops stimulated a great folk migration. Further fueled by the next great war and the ensuing era of cold war prosperity, this population shift would transform race relations and the nature of American cities for generations to come.

POINTS OF VIEW

The Triangle Shirtwaist Fire (1911)

13

Conditions at the
Triangle Shirtwaist Company

Pauline Newman et al.

"I think if you want to go into the . . . twelve-, fourteen- or fifteen-story buildings they call workshops," New York City's fire chief testified in 1910, *"you will find it very interesting to see the number of people in one of these buildings with absolutely not one fire protection, without any means of escape in case of fire."* At the time, over half a million New Yorkers worked eight or more floors above ground level, beyond the eighty-five-foot reach of the fire fighters' ladders. When the shirtwaist makers struck in 1909, they demanded improved safety and sanitary conditions as well as better wages. The strikers did not win most of their demands, and fire safety in particular did not improve.

On Saturday, March 25, 1911, the issues of the strike received renewed meaning when fire broke out in the shop of the Triangle Shirtwaist Company on the eighth, ninth, and tenth floors of a modern, fireproof loft building in lower Manhattan. The number of exits was inadequate, doors were locked to prevent pilfering, other doors opened inward, and the stairwell had no exit to the roof. Hundreds of workers were trapped; within half an hour, 146 of them, mostly young immigrant women, had died. The owners of the Triangle Shirtwaist Company were later tried for manslaughter, found not guilty, and collected insurance to replace their factory.

The fire evoked a public cry for labor reform. More than 120,000 people attended a funeral for the unclaimed dead. The International Ladies Garment Workers Union and the Women's Trade Union League, both supporters of previous strikes and safety protests, were now joined by New York City's leading civic organizations in protest meetings and demands—eventually heeded by the state legislature—for factory safety legislation.

Barbara Mayer Wertheimer, *We Were There: The Story of Working Women in America* (New York: Pantheon, 1977), pp. 294–95; Leon Stein, *The Triangle Fire* (Philadelphia: Lippincott, 1962), pp. 55–56, 59–60, 144–45, 191–92.

In a speech many years later to a group of trade union women, Pauline Newman, who became the first woman organizer for the International Ladies Garment Workers Union, recounts what it was like to work at the Triangle Company. Kate Alterman, Anna Gullo, and Ida Nelson testified at the company owners' trial about their experience during that terrible half hour. Rose Schneiderman's speech at the fashionable memorial meeting held at the Metropolitan Opera House on April 2, 1911, to commemorate the victims created a sensation and began the twenty-nine-year-old Schneiderman's career in labor reform.

BEFORE YOU READ

1. What were the main abuses that Newman reported?
2. How did Kate Alterman, Anna Gullo, and Ida Nelson manage to survive the fire?
3. Would a speech like Rose Schneiderman's help the cause of factory safety, or would it alienate potential supporters?

PAULINE NEWMAN

I'd like to tell you about the kind of world we lived in 75 years ago because all of you probably weren't even born then. Seventy-five years is a long time, but I'd like to give you at least a glimpse of that world because it has no resemblance to the world we live in today, in any respect.

That world 75 years ago was a world of incredible exploitation of men, women, and children. I went to work for the Triangle Shirtwaist Company in 1901. The corner of a shop would resemble a kindergarten because we were young, eight, nine, ten years old. It was a world of greed; the human being didn't mean anything. The hours were from 7:30 in the morning to 6:30 at night when it wasn't busy. When the season was on we worked until 9 o'clock. No overtime pay, not even supper money. There was a bakery in the garment center that produced little apple pies the size of this ashtray [*holding up ashtray for group to see*] and that was what we got for our overtime instead of money.

My wages as a youngster were $1.50 for a seven-day week. I know it sounds exaggerated, but it isn't; it's true. If you worked there long enough and you were satisfactory you got 50 cents a week increase every year. So by the time I left the Triangle Waist Company in 1909, my wages went up to $5.50, and that was quite a wage in those days.

All shops were as bad as the Triangle Waist Company. When you were told Saturday afternoon, through a sign on the elevator, "If you don't come in on Sunday, you needn't come in on Monday," what choice did you have? You had no choice.

I worked on the 9th floor with a lot of youngsters like myself. Our work was not difficult. When the operators were through with sewing shirtwaists, there was a little thread left, and we youngsters would get a little scissors and trim the threads off.

And when the inspectors came around, do you know what happened? The supervisors made all the children climb into one of those crates that they ship

material in, and they covered us over with finished shirtwaists until the inspector had left, because of course we were too young to be working in the factory
legally.

The Triangle Waist Company was a family affair, all relatives of the owner
running the place, watching to see that you did your work, watching when you
went into the toilet. And if you were two or three minutes longer than foreman
or foreladies thought you should be, it was deducted from your pay. If you came
five minutes late in the morning because the freight elevator didn't come down
to take you up in time, you were sent home for half a day without pay.

Rubber heels came into use around that time and our employers were the
first to use them; you never knew when they would sneak up on you, spying, to
be sure you did not talk to each other during working hours.

Most of the women rarely took more than $6.00 a week home, most less.
The early sweatshops were usually so dark that gas jets (for light) burned day
and night. There was no insulation in the winter, only a pot-bellied stove in the
middle of the factory. If you were a finisher and could take your work with you
(finishing is a hand operation) you could sit next to the stove in winter. But if
you were an operator or a trimmer it was very cold indeed. Of course in the
summer you suffocated with practically no ventilation.

There was no drinking water, maybe a tap in the hall, warm, dirty. What were
you going to do? Drink this water or none at all. Well, in those days there were
vendors who came in with bottles of pop for 2 cents, and much as you disliked to
spend the two pennies you got the pop instead of the filthy water in the hall.

The condition was no better and no worse than the tenements where we
lived. You got out of the workshop, dark and cold in winter, hot in summer,
dirty unswept floors, no ventilation, and you would go home. What kind of
home did you go to? You won't find the tenements *we* lived in. Some of the
rooms didn't have any windows. I lived in a two-room tenement with my
mother and two sisters and the bedroom had no windows, the facilities were
down in the yard, but that's the way it was in the factories too. In the summer
the sidewalk, fire escapes, and the roof of the tenements became bedrooms just
to get a breath of air.

We wore cheap clothes, lived in cheap tenements, ate cheap food. There
was nothing to look forward to, nothing to expect the next day to be better.

Someone once asked me; "How did you survive?" And I told him, what al-
ternative did we have? You stayed and you survived, that's all.

KATE ALTERMAN

At the Fire

Then I went to the toilet room. Margaret [Schwartz] disappeared from me and
I wanted to go up Greene Street side, but the whole door was in flames, so I
went and hid myself in the toilet rooms and bent my face over the sink, and
then I ran to the Washington side elevator, but there was a big crowd and I
couldn't pass through there. Then I noticed someone, a whole crowd around

the door and I saw Bernstein, the manager's brother, trying to open the door, and there was Margaret near him. Bernstein tried the door, he couldn't open it.

And then Margaret began to open the door. I take her on one side — I pushed her on the side and I said, "Wait, I will open that door." I tried, pulled the handle in and out, all ways and I couldn't open it. She pushed me on the other side, got hold of the handle and then she tried. And then I saw her bending down on her knees, and her hair was loose, and the trail of her dress was a little far from her, and then a big smoke came and I couldn't see.

I just know it was Margaret, and I said, "Margaret," and she didn't reply. I left Margaret, I turned my head on the side and I noticed the trail of her dress and the ends of her hair begin to burn. Then I ran in, in a small dressing room that was on the Washington side, there was a big crowd and I went out from there, stood in the center of the room, between the machines and between the examining tables.

I noticed afterwards on the other side, near the Washington side windows, Bernstein, the manager's brother throwing around like a wildcat at the window, and he was chasing his head out of the window, and pull himself back in — he wanted to jump, I suppose, but he was afraid. And then I saw the flames cover him. I noticed on the Greene Street side someone else fell down on the floor and the flames cover him.

And then I stood in the center of the room, and I just turned my coat on the left side with the fur to my face, the lining on the outside, got hold of a bunch of dresses that was lying on the examining table not burned yet, covered my head and tried to run through the flames on the Greene Street side. The whole door was a red curtain of fire, but a young lady came and she wouldn't let me in. I kicked her with my foot and I don't know what became of her.

I ran out through the Greene Street side door, right through the flames on to the roof.

ANNA GULLO

At the Fire

[T]he flames came up higher. I looked back into the shop and saw the flames were bubbling on the machines. I turned back to the window and made the sign of the cross. I went to jump out of the window. But I had no courage to do it. . . .

. . . I had on my fur coat and my hat with two feathers. I pulled my woolen skirt over my head. Somebody had hit me with water from a pail. I was soaked.

At the vestibule door there was a big barrel of oil. I went through the staircase door. As I was going down I heard a loud noise. Maybe the barrel of oil exploded. I remember when I passed the eighth floor all I could see was a mass of flames. The wind was blowing up the staircase.

When I got to the bottom I was cold and wet. I was crying for my sister. I remember a man came over to me. I was sitting on the curb. He lifted my head and looked into my face. It must have been all black from the smoke of the fire.

He wiped my face with a handkerchief. He said, "I thought you were my sister." He gave me his coat.

I don't know who he was. I never again found my sister alive. I hope he found his.

IDA NELSON

At the Fire

I don't know what made me do it but I bent over and pushed my pay into the top of my stocking. Then I ran to the Greene Street side and tried to get into the staircase. . . .

[But where Anna Gullo had just exited, there was now a wall of fire.] I couldn't get through. The heat was too intense.

I ran back into the shop and found part of a roll of piece goods. I think it was lawn;[1] it was on the bookkeeper's desk. I wrapped it around and around me until only my face showed.

Then I ran right into the fire on the stairway and up toward the roof. I couldn't breathe. The lawn caught fire. As I ran, I tried to keep peeling off the burning lawn, twisting and turning as I ran. By the time I passed the tenth floor and got to the roof, I had left most of the lawn in ashes behind me. But I still had one end of it under my arm. That was the arm that got burned.

ROSE SCHNEIDERMAN

At the Memorial Meeting
at the Metropolitan Opera House

I would be a traitor to those poor burned bodies if I were to come here to talk good fellowship. We have tried you good people of the public—and we have found you wanting.

The old Inquisition had its rack and its thumbscrews and its instruments of torture with iron teeth. We know what these things are today: the iron teeth are our necessities, the thumbscrews are the high-powered and swift machinery close to which we must work, and the rack is here in the firetrap structures that will destroy us the minute they catch fire.

This is not the first time girls have been burned alive in this city. Every week I must learn of the untimely death of one of my sister workers. Every year thousands of us are maimed. The life of men and women is so cheap and property is so sacred! There are so many of us for one job, it matters little if 140-odd are burned to death.

We have tried you, citizens! We are trying you now and you have a couple of dollars for the sorrowing mothers and brothers and sisters by way of a charity gift. But every time the workers come out in the only way they know to protest

1. **lawn:** a thin cotton or linen fabric.

against conditions which are unbearable, the strong hand of the law is allowed
to press down heavily upon us.

Public officials have only words of warning for us—warning that we must
be intensely orderly and must be intensely peaceable, and they have the work-
house just back of all their warnings. The strong hand of the law beats us back
when we rise—back into the conditions that make life unbearable.

I can't talk fellowship to you who are gathered here. Too much blood has
been spilled. I know from experience it is up to the working people to save
themselves. And the only way is through a strong working-class movement.

14

A Fire Trap

William Gunn Shepherd

*On the afternoon of March 25, 1911, when fire broke out in the loft building at Wash-
ington Place and Greene Street in lower Manhattan that housed the Triangle Shirtwaist Company, the* New York World *reporter William Gunn Shepherd (1878–1933)
happened to be in the vicinity. Finding a telephone in a store across the street, he reported the scene before him to a relay of four men at the newspaper. Then the exhausted
Shepherd returned to the* World *building further downtown at Park Row to rewrite
his dispatches. Accompanying his story were pictures, diagrams of the scene, reports
from other journalists, and a list of the dead. The first six pages of the newspaper's next
edition were wholly given over to the fire.*

*This article is a remarkably complete eyewitness account of a great public disaster.
Given that it appeared in a conservative and respected newspaper, it suggests—both by
what it says and what it does not—a great deal about how respectable people of the period thought about the victims and heroes of such an event.*

BEFORE YOU READ

1. Did Shepherd connect the fire to concerns that had led to the earlier strike?
2. How did he deal with the issue of criminal liability?
3. What picture do you get of the men and women involved?

At 4.35 o'clock yesterday afternoon fire springing from a source that may
never be positively identified was discovered in the rear of the eighth floor of
the ten-story building at the northwest corner of Washington place and
Greene street, the first of three floors occupied as a factory of the Triangle
Waist Company.

New York World, March 26, 1911.

At 11.30 o'clock Chief Croker made this statement:

Every body has been removed. The number taken out, which includes those who jumped from the windows, is 141. The number of those that have died so far in the hospitals is seven, which makes the total number of deaths at this time 148.

At 2 o'clock this morning Chief Croker estimated the total dead as one hundred and fifty-four. He said further: "I expected something of this kind to happen in these so-called fire-proof buildings, which are without adequate protection as far as fire-escapes are concerned."

More than a third of those who lost their lives did so in jumping from windows. The firemen who answered the first of the four alarms turned in found 30 bodies on the pavements of Washington place and Greene street. Almost all of these were girls, as were the great majority of them all.

A single fire escape, a single stairway, one working passenger elevator and one working freight elevator offered the only means of escape from the building. A loft building under the specifications of the law, no other ways of egress were required, and to this fact, which also permitted the use of the building as a factory, the dreadful toll may be traced. Two other elevators were there, but were not in operation.

The property damage resulting from the fire did not exceed $100,000.

To accommodate the unprecedented number of bodies, the Charities pier at the foot of East Twenty-sixth street was opened, for the first time since the Slocum disaster,[1] with which this will rank, for no fire in a building in New York ever claimed so many lives before.

Inspection by Acting Superintendent of Buildings Ludwig will be made the basis for charges of criminal negligence on the ground that the fire-proof doors leading to one of the inclosed tower stairways were locked.

The list of dead and injured will be found on page 4.

STREETS LITTERED WITH BODIES
OF MEN AND WOMEN

It was the most appalling horror since the Slocum disaster and the Iroquois Theatre fire in Chicago. Every available ambulance in Manhattan was called upon to cart the dead to the Morgue—bodies charred to unrecognizable blackness or reddened to a sickly hue—as was to be seen by shoulders or limbs protruding through flame eaten clothing. Men and women, boys and girls were of the dead that littered the street; that is actually the condition—the streets were littered.

The fire began in the eighth story. The flames licked and shot their way up through the other two stories. All three floors were occupied by the Triangle Waist Company. The estimate of the number of the employees at work is made by Chief Croker at about 1,000. The proprietors of the company say 700 men and girls were in their place.

1. **Slocum disaster:** the *General Slocum*, an excursion steamship, caught fire in the East River in 1904, killing more than a thousand of its passengers and crew.

Whatever the number, they had no chance of escape. Before smoke or flame gave signs from the windows the loss of life was fully under way. The first signs that persons in the street knew that these three top stories had turned into red furnaces in which human creatures were being caught and incinerated was when screaming men and women and boys and girls crowded out on the many window ledges and threw themselves into the streets far below.

They jumped with their clothing ablaze. The hair of some of the girls streamed up of flame as they leaped. Thud after thud sounded on the pavements. It is the ghastly fact that on both the Greene street and the Washington place sides of the building there grew mounds of the dead and dying.

And the worst horror of all was that in this heap of the dead now and then there stirred a limb or sounded a moan.

Within the three flaming floors it was as frightful. There flames enveloped many so that they died instantly. When Fire Chief Croker could make his way into the three floors he found sights that utterly staggered him—that sent him, a man used to viewing horrors, back and down into the street with quivering lips.

The floors were black with smoke. And then he saw as the smoke drifted away bodies burned to bare bones. There were skeletons bending over sewing machines.

The elevator boys saved hundreds. They each made twenty trips from the time of the alarm until twenty minutes later when they could do no more. Fire was streaming into the shaft, flames biting at the cables. They fled for their own lives.

Some—about seventy—chose a successful avenue of escape. They clambered up a ladder to the roof. A few remembered the fire escape. Many may have thought of it, but only as they uttered cries of dismay.

Wretchedly inadequate was this fire escape—a lone ladder running down a rear narrow court, which was smoke filled as the fire raged, one narrow door giving access to the ladder. By the scores they fought and struggled and breathed fire and died trying to make that needle-eye road to self-preservation.

Those who got the roof—got life. Young men of the University of New York Commercial and Law School, studious young fellows who had chosen to spend their Saturday afternoon in study, answered the yells for aid that came from the smoking roof by thrusting ladders from the upper windows of their class rooms to the frantic men and women on the roofs.

None of the fire-besieged hesitated an instant. In going down on all fours and struggling across these slender bridges—eighty feet above the paved court—to the out-thrust arms of the students. It is a fact that none of the men on the roof, wild with excitement as they were, made a movement toward the ladder till the girls had crossed to safety.

Those who did make the fire escape—and these were but the few who had, in spite of panic, first thought of it—huddled themselves into what appeared as bad a trap as the one from which they had escaped. They found themselves let down into an absolutely closed court; and when through the cellar of the Asch

Building they sought to make their way to the street, they encountered on the ground floor iron shutters securely clamped into place.

For a time they stood around or knelt in prayer, not knowing when the burning building might crash in upon them. Some of these dashed back and screamed, in the hope of attracting the attention of the law students in the university building. But there were so many agonized cries ringing in the air that the youths never heard the shouts from below.

Those who had got down the fire escape and found themselves cut off from the street by the iron shutters rushed frantically back to the court and ran around distraught, until firemen putting their implements to the iron shutters rushed through the Greene street entrance. They herded the wild-eyed group to the street.

Shivering at the chasm below them, scorched by the fire behind, there were some that still held positions on the window sills when the first squad of the firemen arrived.

The nets were spread below with all promptness. Citizens were commandeered into the service—as the firemen necessarily gave their attention to the one engine and hose of the force that first arrived.

The catapult force that the bodies gathered in the long plunges made the nets utterly without avail. Screaming girls and men, as they fell, tore the nets from the grasp of the holders and the bodies struck the sidewalks and lay just as they fell. Some of the bodies ripped big holes through the life-nets.

The curious, uncanny feature about this deadly fire is that it was not spectacular from flame and smoke. The city had no sign of the disaster that was happening. The smoke of the fire scarcely blackened the sky. No big, definite clouds arose to blot out the sunshine and the springtime brightness of the blue above.

Concentrated, the fire burned within. The flames caught all the flimsy lace stuff and linens that go into the making of spring and summer shirt-waists and fed eagerly upon the rolls of silk.

The cutting room was laden with the stuff on long tables. The employees were toiling over such material at the rows and rows of machines. Sinisterly the spring day gave aid to the fire. Many of the window panes facing south and east were drawn down. Draughts had full play.

It was the first fire with heavy loss of life in a skyscraper factory building in this city, but it bore out Fire Chief Croker's predictions of several years' standing. These were that such a fire would absolutely mean disaster! The walls of such buildings are fireproof, but the contents of the buildings—as in this case—are highly inflammable. The fire, having no manner of eating into the walls, concentrates on all the food it can find in the interior. The result is a furnace, with the flames fighting upward till they strike the roof. Then the fire mushrooms and starts back down the walls.

This is what happened in the Asch Building yesterday. Before a curl of smoke sifted outward through the windows the flames had swept and swirled around the rooms and mercilessly killed.

FOUR THOUSAND OUT BEFORE THE FIRE

Four thousand workers most fortunately had left the building about an hour and a half before—had tripped along toward the east side laughingly, buoyantly. For this was their fine day—pay day. These were the girls and boys and men and women from the factories and waterooms on the seven lower floors and the shipping departments in the basement.

All the places except the Triangle Waist Company's factory closed down at 3 o'clock yesterday. The Triangle Waist Company does not recognize the union. Around their big shop a strike centered not long ago. The delay in the filling of orders caused by the strike had made it necessary for the toilers to work overtime. That was why they sat bent over their machines and otherwise were busy at their tasks yesterday afternoon.

Those of the Triangle factory had, many of them, drawn their pay. Detectives were placed on guard over the bodies till they were taken to the Morgue, lest vandals should seek to rob. But no such creature appeared on the scene of the disaster. When darkness came upon the rows of bodies huddled under brown tarpaulins the vigilance was renewed. But no ghoul attempted to prowl among the dead.

So swift and unwarningly did the fire come that the first man on the street aware of it saw no smoke at all. He saw only a girl standing on a window ledge on the ninth floor of the building, waving her arms and shrieking that she was going to jump. He yelled back at her to stand where she was. And then as he stared, wonderingly, he saw a mere puff of smoke, such as a man might blow from a cigarette.

This man, John Maron of No. 116 Waverly Place, suddenly took panic as he saw the girl lean far over the sill and come tumbling down, with a flutter of her skirts. He saw her fall past floor after floor and strike the pavement on her head.

A man who later gave his name as R. Garner, but would not tell his address, had seen Maron and heard him shout, without realizing what it meant until the girl's body on the pavement came across his vision. Then he too looked upward.

What he saw made him rush for the nearest fire box at an opposite corner, about one hundred feet away. He had seen countless windows crowded with white faces and he had heard a frantic, swelling call for help.

He tore at the key of the fire box. And he said last night that somehow before he turned he became conscious that there was a frightful rain of bodies from the windows.

The first fireman to arrive took but a single glance at the tall building, saw with a gasp the heap of bodies and rushed to summon all the help available. Police whistles began to shrill their calls, and from opposite buildings hundreds were leaning out of windows, shouting insanely in their agony at the sight.

It seemed a long time to the helpless watchers before wailing sirens of many fire engines, the rattling bells of patrol wagons and ambulances sounded near by. Reserve after reserve squad of police from everywhere in the city were shunted to the neighborhood. Fifteen ambulances took stations along Washington Place. Calls for more ambulances went out.

In less than half an hour ten thousand persons were pressing the swiftly constructed police lines. Thousands ran down the side streets from Broadway. A huge crowd lined along the lawns of Washington Square, peering down Washington Place. For the most part the crowd could barely see the evidence of the horror that had happened—could make out but vaguely the black objects on the water blackened sidewalks.

WOMEN GOT FIRST CHANCE AT THE WINDOWS

From all that could be learned it appears that the men among these shirt waist workers were really men—pallid faced weaklings as they might have appeared as they threaded their way to the shop early yesterday morning. It appears that even the boys acted in fine, manly fashion.

Eye witnesses of those who saw the wild leaps from the windows declared that the girls were given first chance at even this miserable prospect of saving their lives. Men could be seen in the reddening rooms helping the girls to the window sills for a final breath of life sustaining air.

On the ledge of a ninth story window two girls stood silently watching the arrival of the first fire apparatus. Twice one of the girls made a move to jump. The other restrained her, tottering in her foothold as she did so. They watched firemen rig the ladders up against the wall. They saw the last ladder lifted and pushed into place. They saw that it reached only the seventh floor.

For the third time the more frightened girl tried to leap. The bells of arriving fire wagons must have risen to them. The other girl gesticulated in the direction of the sounds. But she talked to ears that could no longer hear. Scarcely turning, her companion dived head first into the street.

The other girl drew herself erect. The crowd in the street were stretching their arms up at her shouting and imploring her not to leap. She made a steady gesture, looking down as if to assure them she would remain brave.

But a thin flame shot out of the window at her back and touched her hair. In an instant her head was aflame. She tore at her burning hair, lost her balance and came shooting down upon the mound of bodies below.

ELEVATOR BOYS MADE TWENTY TRIPS

If it had not been for the courage of the elevator boys the disaster might have been doubly if not trebly appalling. These young men, John Vito and Joseph Gasper, ran their cars up and down until the shafts were ablaze. Each made no less than twenty trips up and down after the first alarm was given.

And Vito attributes fine heroism to Maurice Blanck and Isaac Harris, the owners of the Triangle Waist Company. He says the partners stood by the shafts, holding back men who would have pressed forward and calling to him to take only the women down. Vito showed bloody hands to indicate how he had fought back the few cowardly men who had tried to overrun the women.

Blanck's two little children and their governess were with him when the alarm came. He had just ordered a taxicab and was awaiting its arrival before starting for his home. Blanck and his children and his partner, Harris, managed afterward to make their way to the roof and the men handed the governess and the children over the ladder to the students of the University Law School and then themselves crawled to safety.

FOR CRITICAL THINKING

1. How would an event similar to the Triangle Shirtwaist fire be covered today on television news? How would the tone and attitude of the coverage be different from that of the *New York World* story? Would present-day journalists delve into aspects of the story that their 1911 counterparts would not?

2. The role of government in regulating working conditions was controversial in 1911 when the Triangle Shirtwaist fire occurred, and it remains controversial in the present as indicated by extensive criticism of the Occupational Safety and Health Administration (OSHA) for restricting economic growth. Should local, state, and federal government have the responsibility to inspect and regulate working conditions at privately owned enterprises, or should this be an issue between workers and management?

3. How does Shepherd's report compare to the survivors' accounts?

15

A Bintel Brief

Abraham Cahan

Years before Ann Landers and Dear Abby, there was "A Bintel Brief." In 1906 the Jewish Daily Forward, *a Yiddish-language newspaper addressing the more than half a million Jewish immigrants in New York City, began running an advice column under a title that translates as "a bundle of letters." The column spoke to Jews from Russia, Hungary, Poland, Romania, and the Middle East, with different traditions and dialects as well as skills and opportunities, struggling with each other as well as their new circumstances in some of the most crowded urban neighborhoods in the world. These immigrants and their neighborhoods were among the subjects of reform journalist Jacob Riis, whose images of poverty so influenced Americans' vision of the cities. (See the visual portfolio "Urban Industrial America" on page 143.)*

The editor of the Jewish Daily Forward *was Abraham Cahan (1860–1951), who also wrote several novels about immigrant life. Cahan contributed some of the letters as well as the responses. "A Bintel Brief" gave advice on all kinds of personal problems. These excerpts from the early years of the column offer fascinating glimpses into Jewish immigrant life at the turn of the century and speak of issues central to the experiences of most immigrants.*

BEFORE YOU READ

1. What are the major tensions of immigrant life as revealed in the letters?
2. What values did Cahan represent in his answers?
3. How does Cahan's advice compare to that given today in similar newspaper columns and on daytime talk shows?

Worthy Editor,

We are a small family who recently came to the "Golden Land." My husband, my boy and I are together, and our daughter lives in another city.

I had opened a grocery store here, but soon lost all my money. In Europe we were in business; we had people working for us and paid them well. In short, there we made a good living but here we are badly off.

My husband became a peddler. The "pleasure" of knocking on doors and ringing bells cannot be known by anyone but a peddler. If anybody does buy

Isaac Metzker, *A Bintel Brief: Sixty Years of Letters from the Lower East Side to the* JEWISH DAILY FOR-WARD (New York: Doubleday, 1971), pp. 42–44, 49–51, 54–55, 58–59, 63–64, 68–70, 109–10, 117–18.

anything "on time," a lot of the money is lost, because there are some people who never intend to pay. In addition, my husband has trouble because he has a beard, and because of the beard he gets beaten up by the hoodlums.

Also we have problems with our boy, who throws money around. He works every day till late at night in a grocery for three dollars a week. I watch over him and give him the best because I'm sorry that he has to work so hard. But he costs me plenty and he borrows money from everybody. He has many friends and owes them all money. I get more and more worried as he takes here and borrows there. All my talking doesn't help. I am afraid to chase him away from home because he might get worse among strangers. I want to point out that he is well versed in Russian and Hebrew and he is not a child any more, but his behavior is not that of an intelligent adult.

I don't know what to do. My husband argues that he doesn't want to continue peddling. He doesn't want to shave off his beard, and it's not fitting for such a man to do so. The boy wants to go to his sister, but that's a twenty-five-dollar fare. What can I do? I beg you for a suggestion.

Your Constant reader,
F. L.

Answer:

Since her husband doesn't earn a living anyway, it would be advisable for all three of them to move to the city where the daughter is living. As for the beard, we feel that if the man is religious and the beard is dear to him because the Jewish law does not allow him to shave it off, it's up to him to decide. But if he is not religious, and the beard interferes with his earnings, it should be sacrificed.

Dear Editor,

For a long time I worked in a shop with a Gentile girl, and we began to go out together and fell in love. We agreed that I would remain a Jew and she a Christian. But after we had been married for a year, I realized that it would not work.

I began to notice that whenever one of my Jewish friends comes to the house, she is displeased. Worse yet, when she sees me reading a Jewish newspaper her face changes color. She says nothing, but I can see that she has changed. I feel that she is very unhappy with me, though I know she loves me. She will soon become a mother, and she is more dependent on me than ever.

She used to be quite liberal, but lately she is being drawn back to the Christian religion. She gets up early Sunday mornings, runs to church and comes home with eyes swollen from crying. When we pass a church now and then, she trembles.

Dear Editor, advise me what to do now. I could never convert, and there's no hope for me to keep her from going to church. What can we do now?

Thankfully,
A Reader

Answer:

Unfortunately, we often hear of such tragedies, which stem from marriages between people of different worlds. It's possible that if this couple were to move to a Jewish neighborhood, the young man might have more influence on his wife.

Dear Editor,

I am a girl from Galicia and in the shop where I work I sit near a Russian Jew with whom I was always on good terms. Why should one worker resent another?

But once, in a short debate, he stated that all Galicians were no good. When I asked him to repeat it, he answered that he wouldn't retract a word, and that he wished all Galician Jews dead.

I was naturally not silent in the face of such a nasty expression. He maintained that only Russian Jews are fine and intelligent. According to him, the *Galitzianer* are inhuman savages, and he had the right to speak of them so badly.

Dear Editor, does he really have a right to say this? Have the Galician Jews not sent enough money for the unfortunate sufferers of the pogroms in Russia? When a Gentile speaks badly of Jews, it's immediately printed in the newspapers and discussed hotly everywhere. But that a Jew should express himself so about his own brothers is nothing? Does he have a right? Are Galicians really so bad? And does he, the Russian, remain fine and intelligent in spite of such expressions?

As a reader of your worthy newspaper, I hope you will print my letter and give your opinion.

With thanks in advance,
B. M.

Answer:

The Galician Jews are just as good and bad as people from other lands. If the Galicians must be ashamed of the foolish and evil ones among them, then the Russians, too, must hide their heads in shame because among them there is such an idiot as the acquaintance of our letter writer.

Worthy Editor,

I am eighteen years old and a machinist by trade. During the past year I suffered a great deal, just because I am a Jew.

It is common knowledge that my trade is run mainly by the Gentiles and, working among the Gentiles, I have seen things that cast a dark shadow on the American labor scene. Just listen:

I worked in a shop in a small town in New Jersey, with twenty Gentiles. There was one other Jew besides me, and both of us endured the greatest hardships. That we were insulted goes without saying. At times we were even beaten up. We work in an area where there are many factories, and once, when we were leaving the shop, a group of workers fell on us like hoodlums and beat us. To top it off, we and one of our attackers were arrested. The hoodlum was let out on bail, but we, beaten and bleeding, had to stay in jail. At the trial, they fined the hoodlum eight dollars and let him go free.

After that I went to work on a job in Brooklyn. As soon as they found out that I was a Jew they began to torment me so that I had to leave the place. I have already worked at many places, and I either have to leave, voluntarily, or they fire me because I am a Jew.

Till now, I was alone and didn't care. At this trade you can make good wages, and I had enough. But now I've brought my parents over, and of course I have to support them.

Lately I've been working on one job for three months and I would be satisfied, but the worm of anti-Semitism is beginning to eat at my bones again. I go to work in the morning as to Gehenna,[1] and I run away at night as from a fire. It's impossible to talk to them because they are common boors, so-called "American sports." I have already tried in various ways, but the only way to deal with them is with a strong fist. But I am too weak and there are too many.

Perhaps you can help me in this matter. I know it is not an easy problem.

Your reader,
E. H.

Answer:

In the answer, the Jewish machinist is advised to appeal to the United Hebrew Trades and ask them to intercede for him and bring up charges before the Machinists Union about this persecution. His attention is also drawn to the fact that there are Gentile factories where Jews and Gentiles work together and get along well with each other.

Finally it is noted that people will have to work long and hard before this senseless racial hatred can be completely uprooted.

Worthy Editor,

I was born in America and my parents gave me a good education. I studied Yiddish and Hebrew, finished high school, completed a course in bookkeeping and got a good job. I have many friends, and several boys have already proposed to me.

Recently I went to visit my parents' home in Russian Poland. My mother's family in Europe had invited my parents to a wedding, but instead of going themselves, they sent me. I stayed at my grandmother's with an aunt and uncle and had a good time. Our European family, like my parents, are quite well off and they treated me well. They indulged me in everything and I stayed with them six months.

It was lively in the town. There were many organizations and clubs and they all accepted me warmly, looked up to me—after all, I was a citizen of the free land, America. Among the social leaders of the community was an intelligent young man, a friend of my uncle's, who took me to various gatherings and affairs.

He was very attentive, and after a short while he declared his love for me in a long letter. I had noticed that he was not indifferent to me, and I liked him as well. I looked up to him and respected him, as did all the townsfolk. My family

---

1. **Gehenna:** hell.

became aware of it, and when they spoke to me about him, I could see they thought it was a good match.

He was handsome, clever, educated, a good talker and charmed me, but I didn't give him a definite answer. As my love for him grew, however, I wrote to my parents about him, and then we became officially engaged.

A few months later we both went to my parents in the States and they received him like their own son. My bridegroom immediately began to learn English and tried to adjust to the new life. Yet when I introduced him to my friends they looked at him with disappointment. "This 'greenhorn'[2] is your fiancé?" they asked. I told them what a big role he played in his town, how everyone respected him, but they looked at me as if I were crazy and scoffed at my words.

At first I thought, Let them laugh, when they get better acquainted with him they'll talk differently. In time, though, I was affected by their talk and began to think, like them, that he really was a "greenhorn" and acted like one.

In short, my love for him is cooling off gradually. I'm suffering terribly because my feelings for him are changing. In Europe, where everyone admired him and all the girls envied me, he looked different. But, here, I see before me another person.

I haven't the courage to tell him, and I can't even talk about it to my parents. He still loves me with all his heart, and I don't know what to do. I choke it all up inside myself, and I beg you to help me with advice in my desperate situation.

Respectfully,
A Worried Reader

Answer:

The writer would make a grave mistake if she were to separate from her bridegroom now. She must not lose her common sense and be influenced by the foolish opinions of her friends who divided the world into "greenhorns" and real Americans.

We can assure the writer that her bridegroom will learn English quickly. He will know American history and literature as well as her friends do, and be a better American than they. She should be proud of his love and laugh at those who call him "greenhorn."

Dear Editor,

Since I do not want my conscience to bother me, I ask you to decide whether a married woman has the right to go to school two evenings a week. My husband thinks I have no right to do this.

I admit that I cannot be satisfied to be just a wife and mother. I am still young and I want to learn and enjoy life. My children and my house are not neglected, but I go to evening high school twice a week. My husband is not

2. **greenhorn:** newly arrived immigrant.

pleased and when I come home at night and ring the bell, he lets me stand outside a long time intentionally, and doesn't hurry to open the door.

Now he has announced a new decision. Because I send out the laundry to be done, it seems to him that I have too much time for myself, even enough to go to school. So from now on he will count out every penny for anything I have to buy for the house, so I will not be able to send out the laundry any more. And when I have to do the work myself there won't be any time left for such "foolishness" as going to school. I told him that I'm willing to do my own washing but that I would still be able to find time for study.

When I am alone with my thoughts, I feel I may not be right. Perhaps I should not go to school. I want to say that my husband is an intelligent man and he wanted to marry a woman who was educated. The fact that he is intelligent makes me more annoyed with him. He is in favor of the emancipation of women, yet in real life he acts contrary to his beliefs.

Awaiting your opinion on this, I remain,

Your reader,
The Discontented Wife

Answer:

Since this man is intelligent and an adherent of the women's emancipation movement, he is scolded severely in the answer for wanting to keep his wife so enslaved. Also the opinion is expressed that the wife absolutely has the right to go to school two evenings a week.

Dear Editor,

I plead with you to open your illustrious newspaper and take in my "Bintel Brief" in which I write about my great suffering.

A long gloomy year, three hundred and sixty-five days, have gone by since I left my home and am alone on the lonely road of life. Oh, my poor dear parents, how saddened they were at my leaving. The leave-taking, their seeing me on my way, was like a silent funeral.

There was no shaking of the alms box, there was no grave digging and no sawing of boards, but I, myself, put on the white shirt that was wet with my mother's tears, took my pillow, and climbed into the wagon. Accompanying me was a quiet choked wail from my parents and friends.

The wheels of the wagon rolled farther and farther away. My mother and father wept for their son, then turned with heavy hearts to the empty house. They did not sit shive[3] even though they had lost a child.

I came to America and became a painter. My great love for Hebrew, for Russian, all of my other knowledge was smeared with paint. During the year that I have been here I have had some good periods, but I am not happy, because I have no interest in anything. My homesickness and loneliness darken my life.

---

3. **shive:** period of mourning.

Ah, home, my beloved home. My heart is heavy for my parents whom I left behind. I want to run back, but I am powerless. I am a coward, because I know that I have to serve under *"Fonie"*[4] for three years. I am lonely in my homesickness and I beg you to be my counsel as to how to act.

Respectfully,
V. A.

Answer:

The answer states that almost all immigrants yearn deeply for dear ones and home at first. They are compared with plants that are transplanted to new ground. At first it seems that they are withering, but in time most of them revive and take root in the new earth.

The advice to this young man is that he must not consider going home, but try to take root here. He should try to overcome all these emotions and strive to make something of himself so that in time he will be able to bring his parents here.

---

4. *"Fonie"*: the czar.

16

Conditions at the Slaughterhouse

Upton Sinclair

Exposing the meat-packing industry was not Upton Sinclair's main purpose in writing
The Jungle. *A recent convert to socialism, Sinclair (1878–1968) had received a five-
hundred-dollar advance from* The Appeal to Reason, *the nation's leading socialist
newspaper. Choosing to write about packing-house workers who had recently lost a labor
strike in the summer of 1904, he went to Chicago, infiltrated the stockyards, and wrote
a novel exposing the miseries of the workers there.*

The publication of The Jungle *in 1906 was one of the major events of the Progressive Era. Intended as a plea for socialism, the book, which is excerpted here, was
read by a shocked public as an exposé not of the economic system but of the sanitary conditions in Chicago meat-packing houses. Sinclair himself said that he had taken aim at
America's heart and hit instead its stomach. Evidently the empty stomachs of the book's
immigrant workers Jurgis and Ona mattered less to the public than its own, which it
feared might be filled with packing-house wastes mixed with food. Sinclair's book and
President Theodore Roosevelt's leadership persuaded Congress to enact the first national
meat inspection and pure food and drug laws.*

BEFORE YOU READ

1. What comparison did Sinclair make between the animals and the workers in the
slaughterhouse?
2. What are the psychological effects of the work on Jurgis and Ona?
3. Why do you think the account of sanitary conditions impressed the public so
much more sharply than the account of workers' lives?

Entering one of the Durham buildings, they found a number of other visitors
waiting; and before long there came a guide, to escort them through the place.
They make a great feature of showing strangers through the packing plants, for
it is a good advertisement. But *ponas*[1] Jokubas whispered maliciously that the
visitors did not see any more than the packers wanted them to.

They climbed a long series of stairways outside of the building, to the top of
its five or six stories. Here was the chute, with its river of hogs, all patiently toiling

1. *ponas:* Mister (Lith.).

Upton Sinclair, *The Jungle*, 5th ed. (New York: Viking Penguin, 1946), pp. 33–40, 94–99, 135–37.

upward; there was a place for them to rest to cool off, and then through another passageway they went into a room from which there is no returning for hogs.

It was a long, narrow room, with a gallery along it for visitors. At the head there was a great iron wheel, about twenty feet in circumference, with rings here and there along its edge. Upon both sides of this wheel there was a narrow space, into which came the hogs at the end of their journey; in the midst of them stood a great burly Negro, bare-armed and bare-chested. He was resting for the moment, for the wheel had stopped while men were cleaning up. In a minute or two, however, it began slowly to revolve, and then the men upon each side of it sprang to work. They had chains which they fastened about the leg of the nearest hog, and the other end of the chain they hooked into one of the rings upon the wheel. So, as the wheel turned, a hog was suddenly jerked off his feet and borne aloft.

At the same instant the ear was assailed by a most terrifying shriek; the visitors started in alarm, the women turned pale and shrank back. The shriek was followed by another, louder and yet more agonizing—for once started upon that journey, the hog never came back; at the top of the wheel he was shunted off upon a trolley, and went sailing down the room. And meantime another was swung up, and then another, and another, until there was a double line of them, each dangling by a foot and kicking in frenzy—and squealing. The uproar was appalling, perilous to the eardrums; one feared there was too much sound for the room to hold—that the walls must give way or the ceiling crack. There were high squeals and low squeals, grunts, and wails of agony; there would come a momentary lull, and then a fresh outburst, louder than ever, surging up to a deafening climax. It was too much for some of the visitors—the men would look at each other, laughing nervously, and the women would stand with hands clenched, and the blood rushing to their faces, and the tears starting in their eyes.

Meantime, heedless of all these things, the men upon the floor were going about their work. Neither squeals of hogs nor tears of visitors made any difference to them; one by one they hooked up the hogs, and one by one with a swift stroke they slit their throats. There was a long line of hogs, with squeals and lifeblood ebbing away together; until at last each started again, and vanished with a splash into a huge vat of boiling water.

It was all so very businesslike that one watched it fascinated. It was porkmaking by machinery, porkmaking by applied mathematics. And yet somehow the most matter-of-fact person could not help thinking of the hogs. . . .

One could not stand and watch very long without becoming philosophical, without beginning to deal in symbols and similes, and to hear the hog squeal of the universe. Was it permitted to believe that there was nowhere upon the earth, or above the earth, a heaven for hogs, where they were requited for all this suffering? Each one of these hogs was a separate creature. Some were white hogs, some were black; some were brown, some were spotted; some were old, some young; some were long and lean, some were monstrous. And each of them had an individuality of his own, a will of his own, a hope and a heart's desire; each was full of self-confidence, of self-importance, and a sense of dignity.

And trusting and strong in faith he had gone about his business, the while a black shadow hung over him and a horrid Fate waited in his pathway. Now suddenly it had swooped upon him, and had seized him by the leg. Relentless, remorseless, it was; all his protests, his screams, were nothing to it—it did its cruel will with him, as if his wishes, his feelings, had simply no existence at all; it cut his throat and watched him gasp out his life. And now was one to believe that there was nowhere a god of hogs, to whom this hog personality was precious, to whom these hog squeals and agonies had a meaning? Who would take this hog into his arms and comfort him, reward him for his work well done, and show him the meaning of his sacrifice? Perhaps some glimpse of all this was in the thoughts of our humble-minded Jurgis, as he turned to go on with the rest of the party, and muttered: "*Dieve*—but I'm glad I'm not a hog!"

The carcass hog was scooped out of the vat by machinery, and then it fell to the second floor, passing on the way through a wonderful machine with numerous scrapers, which adjusted themselves to the size and shape of the animal, and sent it out at the other end with nearly all of its bristles removed. It was then again strung up by machinery, and sent upon another trolley ride; this time passing between two lines of men, who sat upon a raised platform, each doing a certain single thing to the carcass as it came to him. One scraped the outside of a leg; another scraped the inside of the same leg. One with a swift stroke cut the throat; another with two swift strokes severed the head, which fell to the floor and vanished through a hole. Another made a slit down the body; a second opened the body wider; a third with a saw cut the breastbone; a fourth loosened the entrails; a fifth pulled them out—and they also slid through a hole in the floor. There were men to scrape each side and men to scrape the back; there were men to clean the carcass inside, to trim it and wash it. Looking down this room, one saw, creeping slowly, a line of dangling hogs a hundred yards in length; and for every yard there was a man, working as if a demon were after him. At the end of this hog's progress every inch of the carcass had been gone over several times; and then it was rolled into the chilling room, where it stayed for twenty-four hours, and where a stranger might lose himself in a forest of freezing hogs.

Before the carcass was admitted here, however, it had to pass a government inspector, who sat in the doorway and felt of the glands in the neck for tuberculosis. This government inspector did not have the manner of a man who was worked to death; he was apparently not haunted by a fear that the hog might get by him before he had finished his testing. If you were a sociable person, he was quite willing to enter into conversation with you, and to explain to you the deadly nature of the ptomaines[2] which are found in tubercular pork; and while he was talking with you you could hardly be so ungrateful as to notice that a dozen carcasses were passing him untouched. This inspector wore a blue uniform, with brass buttons, and he gave an atmosphere of authority to the scene, and, as it were, put the stamp of official approval upon the things which were done in Durham's.

2. **ptomaines:** bacteria causing food poisoning.

Jurgis went down the line with the rest of the visitors, staring open-mouthed, lost in wonder. He had dressed hogs himself in the forest of Lithuania; but he had never expected to live to see one hog dressed by several hundred men. It was like a wonderful poem to him, and he took it all in guilelessly—even to the conspicuous signs demanding immaculate cleanliness of the employees. Jurgis was vexed when the cynical Jokubas translated these signs with sarcastic comments, offering to take them to the secret rooms where the spoiled meats went to be doctored.

The party descended to the next floor, where the various waste materials were treated. Here came the entrails, to be scraped and washed clean for sausage casings; men and women worked here in the midst of a sickening stench, which caused the visitors to hasten by, gasping. To another room came all the scraps to be "tanked," which meant boiling and pumping off the grease to make soap and lard; below they took out the refuse, and this, too, was a region in which the visitors did not linger. In still other places men were engaged in cutting up the carcasses that had been through the chilling rooms. First there were the "splitters," the most expert workmen in the plant, who earned as high as fifty cents an hour, and did not a thing all day except chop hogs down the middle. Then there were "cleaver men," great giants with muscles of iron; each had two men to attend him—to slide the half carcass in front of him on the table, and hold it while he chopped it, and then turn each piece so that he might chop it once more. His cleaver had a blade about two feet long, and he never made but one cut; he made it so neatly, too, that his implement did not smite through and dull itself—there was just enough force for a perfect cut, and no more. So through various yawning holes there slipped to the floor below—to one room hams, to another forequarters, to another sides of pork. One might go down to this floor and see the pickling rooms, where the hams were put into vats, and the great smoke rooms, with their airtight iron doors. In other rooms they prepared salt pork—there were whole cellars full of it, built up in great towers to the ceiling. In yet other rooms they were putting up meat in boxes and barrels, and wrapping hams and bacon in oiled paper, sealing and labeling and sewing them. From the doors of these rooms went men with loaded trucks, to the platform where freight cars were waiting to be filled; and one went out there and realized with a start that he had come at last to the ground floor of this enormous building.

Then the party went across the street to where they did the killing of beef—where every hour they turned four or five hundred cattle into meat. Unlike the place they had left, all this work was done on one floor; and instead of there being one line of carcasses which moved to the workmen, there were fifteen or twenty lines, and the men moved from one to another of these. This made a scene of intense activity, a picture of human power wonderful to watch. It was all in one great room, like a circus amphitheater, with a gallery for visitors running over the center.

The visitors were taken there and shown them, all neatly hung in rows, labeled conspicuously with the tags of the government inspectors—and some, which had been killed by a special process, marked with the sign of the *kosher* rabbi, certifying that it was fit for sale to the orthodox. And then the visitors were taken to the other parts of the building, to see what became of each particle of the waste material that had vanished through the floor; and to the pickling rooms, and the salting rooms, the canning rooms, and the packing rooms, where choice meat was prepared for shipping in refrigerator cars, destined to be eaten in all the four corners of civilization. Afterward they went outside, wandering about among the mazes of buildings in which was done the work auxiliary to this great industry.

There were the men in the pickle rooms, for instance, where old Antanas had gotten his death; scarce a one of these that had not some spot of horror on his person. Let a man so much as scrape his finger pushing a truck in the pickle rooms, and he might have a sore that would put him out of the world; all the joints in his fingers might be eaten by the acid, one by one. Of the butchers and floorsmen, the beef-boners and trimmers, and all those who used knives, you could scarcely find a person who had the use of his thumb; time and time again the base of it had been slashed, till it was a mere lump of flesh against which the man pressed the knife to hold it. The hands of these men would be criss-crossed with cuts, until you could no longer pretend to count them or to trace them. They would have no nails,—they had worn them off pulling hides; their knuckles were swollen so that their fingers spread out like a fan. There were men who worked in the cooking rooms, in the midst of steam and sickening odors, by artificial light; in these rooms the germs of tuberculosis might live for two years, but the supply was renewed every hour. There were the beef-luggers, who carried two-hundred-pound quarters into the refrigerator-cars; a fearful kind of work, that began at four o'clock in the morning, and that wore out the most powerful men in a few years. There were those who worked in the chilling rooms, and whose special disease was rheumatism; the time limit that a man could work in the chilling rooms was said to be five years. There were the wool-pluckers, whose hands went to pieces even sooner than the hands of the pickle men; for the pelts of the sheep had to be painted with acid to loosen the wool, and then the pluckers had to pull out this wool with their bare hands, till the acid had eaten their fingers off. There were those who made the tins for the canned meat; and their hands, too, were a maze of cuts, and each cut represented a chance for blood poisoning. Some worked at the stamping machines, and it was very seldom that one could work long there at the pace that was set, and not give out and forget himself, and have a part of his hand chopped off. There were the "hoisters," as they were called, whose task it was to press the lever which lifted the dead cattle off the floor. They ran along upon a rafter, peering down through the damp and the steam; and as old Durham's architects had not built the killing room for the convenience of the hoisters, at every few feet they would have to stoop under a beam, say about four feet above the one they ran on; which got them into the habit of stooping, so that in a few years they would be walking like chimpanzees. Worst of any, however, were the fertilizer men, and those who served in the cooking rooms. These people could not be shown to the visitor,—for the odor of a fertilizer man would scare any ordinary visitor at a hundred yards, and as for the other men, who worked in tank rooms full of steam, and in some of which there were open vats near the level of the floor, their peculiar trouble was that they fell into the vats; and when they were fished out, there was never enough of them left to be worth exhibiting,—sometimes they would be overlooked for days, till all but the bones of them had gone out to the world as Durham's Pure Leaf Lard!

It was only when the whole ham was spoiled that it came into the department of Elzbieta. Cut up by the two-thousand-revolutions-a-minute flyers, and mixed with half a ton of other meat, no odor that ever was in a ham could make any difference. There was never the least attention paid to what was cut up for sausage; there would come all the way back from Europe old sausage that had been rejected, and that was moldy and white—it would be dosed with borax and glycerine, and dumped into the hoppers, and made over again for home consumption. There would be meat that had tumbled out on the floor, in the dirt and sawdust, where the workers had tramped and spit uncounted billions of consumption germs. There would be meat stored in great piles in rooms; and the water from leaky roofs would drip over it, and thousands of rats would race about on it. It was too dark in these storage places to see well, but a man could run his hand over these piles of meat and sweep off handfuls of the dried dung of rats. These rats were nuisances, and the packers would put poisoned bread out for them; they would die, and then rats, bread, and meat would go into the hoppers together. This is no fairy story and no joke; the meat would be shoveled into carts, and the man who did the shoveling would not trouble to lift out a rat even when he saw one—there were things that went into the sausage in comparison with which a poisoned rat was a tidbit. There was no place for the men to wash their hands before they ate their dinner, and so they made a practice of washing them in the water that was to be ladled into the sausage. There were the butt-ends of smoked meat, and the scraps of corned beef, and all the odds and ends of the waste of the plants, that would be dumped into old barrels in the cellar and left there. Under the system of rigid economy which the packers enforced, there were some jobs that it only paid to do once in a long time, and among these was the cleaning out of the waste barrels. Every spring they did it; and in the barrels would be dirt and rust and old nails and stale water—and cartload after cartload of it would be taken up and dumped into the hoppers with fresh meat, and sent out to the public's breakfast. Some of it they would make into "smoked" sausage—but as the smoking took time and was therefore expensive, they would call upon their chemistry department, and preserve it with borax and color it with gelatine to make it brown. All of their sausage came out of the same bowl, but when they came to wrap it they would stamp some of it "special," and for this they would charge two cents more a pound.

Such were the new surroundings in which Elzbieta was placed, and such was the work she was compelled to do. It was stupefying, brutalizing work; it left her no time to think, no strength for anything. She was part of the machine she tended, and every faculty that was not needed for the machine was doomed to be crushed out of existence. There was only one mercy about the cruel grind—that it gave her the gift of insensibility. Little by little she sank into a torpor—she fell silent. She would meet Jurgis and Ona in the evening, and the three would walk home together, often without saying a word. Ona, too, was falling into a habit of silence—Ona, who had once gone about singing like a bird. She was sick and miserable, and often she would barely have strength enough to drag herself home. And there they would eat what they had to eat, and afterward, because there was only their misery to talk of, they would crawl into bed and fall into a stupor and never stir until it was time to get up again, and dress by candlelight, and go back to the machines. They were so numbed that they did not even suffer much from hunger, now; only the children continued to fret when the food ran short.

Yet the soul of Ona was not dead—the souls of none of them were dead, but only sleeping; and now and then they would waken, and these were cruel times. The gates of memory would roll open—old joys would stretch out their arms to them, old hopes and dreams would call to them, and they would stir beneath the burden that lay upon them, and feel its forever immeasurable weight. They could not even cry out beneath it; but anguish would seize them, more dreadful than the agony of death. It was a thing scarcely to be spoken—a thing never spoken by all the world, that will not know its own defeat.

They were beaten; they had lost the game, they were swept aside. It was not less tragic because it was so sordid, because it had to do with wages and grocery bills and rents. They had dreamed of freedom; of a chance to look about them and learn something; to be decent and clean, to see their child grow up to be strong. And now it was all gone—it would never be! They had played the game and they had lost. Six years more of toil they had to face before they could expect the least respite, the cessation of the payments upon the house; and how cruelly certain it was that they could never stand six years of such a life as they were living! They were lost, they were going down—and there was no deliverance for them, no hope; for all the help it gave them the vast city in which they lived might have been an ocean waste, a wilderness, a desert, a tomb. So often this mood would come to Ona, in the nighttime, when something wakened her; she would lie, afraid of the beating of her own heart, fronting the blood-red eyes of the old primeval terror of life. Once she cried aloud, and woke Jurgis, who was tired and cross. After that she learned to weep silently—their moods so seldom came together now! It was as if their hopes were buried in separate graves.

Jurgis, being a man, had troubles of his own. There was another specter following him. He had never spoken of it, nor would he allow any one else to speak of it—he had never acknowledged its existence to himself. Yet the battle with it took all the manhood that he had—and once or twice, alas, a little more. Jurgis had discovered drink.

He was working in the steaming pit of hell; day after day, week after week—until now there was not an organ of his body that did its work without pain, until the sound of ocean breakers echoed in his head day and night, and the buildings swayed and danced before him as he went down the street. And from all the unending horror of this there was a respite, a deliverance—he could drink! He could forget the pain, he could slip off the burden; he would see clearly again, he would be master of his brain, of his thoughts, of his will. His dead self would stir in him, and he would find himself laughing and cracking jokes with his companions—he would be a man again, and master of his life.

17

Letters from the Great Migration
Emmett J. Scott et al.

These letters to the newspaper The Chicago Defender, *collected by the distinguished African American educator and editor Emmett J. Scott (1873–1957), reflect one of the most important events of American social history, the "great migration" of about half a million African Americans largely from the rural South to Northern cities early in the twentieth century. World War I, both by stimulating business and by cutting off immigration from Europe, created opportunities such as had never before existed for African Americans. The widespread circulation of Chicago newspapers throughout the South, particularly the* Defender, *gave Southern African Americans a picture of the thriving economies and available jobs in Chicago and other Northern cities.*

Reasons for leaving the South were endless: Jim Crow, political disenfranchisement, lynching and other forms of mob violence, and more immediately, injury to the rural economy from floods and boll weevil infestations. The migration northward was a great, leaderless folk movement — the individual decisions of hundreds of thousands to flee the South by whatever means they could find in search of a world offering better schools, greater personal safety and dignity, and the chance for economic improvement.

The migration had enormous long-term effects. In the next half century, six million African Americans left the South, most moving to cities. The migration brought political power and cultural authority to black America and moved many blacks into the American middle class. It also provoked race riots, created vast ghettos, and influenced white movement to segregated suburbs.

BEFORE YOU READ

1. What were the main purposes of the letters to the *Defender?*
2. What were the hopes of these letter writers?
3. To what extent do you think these hopes were realistic?

Sherman, Ga., Nov. 28, 1916

Dear Sir: This letter comes to ask for all infirmations concerning employment in your connection in the warmest climate. Now I am in a family of (11) eleven more or less boys and girls (men and women) mixed sizes who want to go north as soon as arrangements can be made and employment given places for shelter

Emmett J. Scott, "Letters of Negro Migrants of 1916–1918," *Journal of Negro History* (July 1919), pp. 177–80.

and so on (etc) now this are farming people they were raised on the farm and are good farm hands I of course have some experience and qualefication as a coman school teacher and hotel waiter and along few other lines.

I wish you would write me at your first chance and tell me if you can give us employment at what time and about what wages will you pay and what kind of arrangement can be made for our shelter. Tell me when can you best use us now or later.

Will you send us tickets if so on what terms and at what price what is the cost per head and by what route should we come. We are Negroes and try to show ourselves worthy of all we may get from any friendly source we endeavor to be true to all good causes, if you can we thank you to help us to come north as soon as you can.

Anniston, Ala., April 23, 1917

Dear Sir: Please gave me some infamation about coming north i can do any kind of work from a truck gardin[1] to farming i would like to leave here and i cant make no money to leave I ust make enough to live one please let me here from you at once i want to get where i can put my children in schol.

Cedar Grove, La., April 23, 1917

Dear sir: to day I was advise by the defendent offices in your city to communicate with you in regards to the labor for the colored of the south as I was lead to beleave that you was in position of firms of your city & your near by surrounding towns of Chicago. Please state me how is the times in & around Chicago place to locate having a family dependent on me for support. I am informed by the Chicago Defender a very valuable paper which has for its purpose the Uplifting of my race, and of which I am a constant reader and real lover, that you were in position to show some light to one in my condition.

Seeking a Northern Home. If this is true Kindly inform me by next mail the next best thing to do Being a poor man with a family to care for, I am not coming to live on flowry Beds of ease for I am a man who works and wish to make the best I can out of life I do not wish to come there hoodwinked not knowing where to go or what to do so I Solicite your help in this matter and thanking you in advance for what advice you may be pleased to Give I am yours for success.

P. S. I am presently imployed in the Mail Department at Union Station this city.

Brookhaven, Miss., April 24, 1917

Gents: The cane growers of Louisiana have stopped the exodus from New Orleans, claiming shortage of labor which will result in a sugar famine.

Now these laborers thus employed receive only 85 cents a day and the high cost of living makes it a serious question to live.

There is a great many race people around here who desires to come north but have waited rather late to avoid car fare, which they have not got. isnt there

---

1. **truck gardin:** "truck garden," i.e., a garden given over to producing vegetables for the market.

some way to get the concerns who wants labor, to send passes here or elsewhere so they can come even if they have to pay out of the first months wages? Please done publish this letter but do what you can towards helping them to get away. If the R. R. Co. would run a low rate excursion they could leave that way. Please ans.

Savannah, Ga., April 24, 1917

Sir: I saw an advertisement in the Chicago Ledger where you would send tickets to any one desireing to come up there. I am a married man with a wife only, and I am 38 years of age, and both of us have so far splendid health, and would like very much to come out there provided we could get good employment regarding the advertisement.

Sanford, Fla., April 27, 1917

Dear Sir: I have seen through the Chicago Defender that you and the people of Chicago are helping newcomers. I am asking you for some information about conditions in some small town near Chicago.

There are some families here thinking of moving up, and are desirous of knowing what to expect before leaving. Please state about treatment, work, rent and schools. Please answer at some spare time.

Fullerton, La., April 28, 1917

Dear sir: I was reading about you was neading labor ninety miles of Chicago what is the name of the place and what R R extends ther i wants to come north and i wants a stedy employment ther what doe you pay per day i dont no anything about molding works but have been working around machinery for 10 years. Let me no what doe you pay for such work and can you give me a job of that kind or a job at common labor and let me no your prices and how many hours for a day.

De Ridder, La., April 29, 1917

Dear sir: there is lots of us southern mens wants transportation and we want to leave ratway as soon as you let us here from you some of us is married mens who need work we would like to bring our wife with us there is 20 head of good mens want transportation and if you need us let us no by return mail we all are redy only wants here from you there may be more all of our peoples wont to leave here and i want you to send as much as 20 tickets any way I will get you up plenty hands to do most any kind of work all you have to do is to send for them. looking to here from you. This is among us collerd.

Atlanta, Ga., April 30, 1917

Dear Sir: In reading the Chicago Defender I find that there are many jobs open for workmen, I wish that you would or can secure me a position in some of the northern cities; as a workman and not as a loafer. One who is willing to do any kind of hard in side or public work, have had broad experience in machinery and other work of the kind. A some what alround man can also cook, well trained devuloped man; have travel extensively through the western and southern states; A good strong *morial religious* man no habits. I will accept transportation on advance and deducted from my wages later. It does not matter where, that is; as to city, country, town or state since you secure the positions. I am quite sure you will be delighted in securing a position for a man of this description. I'll assure you will not regret of so doing. Hoping to hear from you soon.

Houston, Tx., April 30, 1917

Dear Sir: wanted to leave the South and Go any Place where a man will be any thing Except a Ker I thought would write you for Advise as where would be a Good Place for a Comporedly young man That want to Better his Standing who has a very Promising young Family.

I am 30 years old and have Good Experience in Freight Handler and Can fill Position from Truck to Agt.

would like Chicago or Philadelphia But I dont Care where so long as I Go where a man is a man.

Beaumont, Texas, May 7, 1917

Dear Sir: I see in one of your recent issue of collored men woanted in the North I wish you would help me to get a position in the North I have no trade I have been working for one company eight years and there is no advancement here for me and I would like to come where I can better my condition I woant work and not affraid to work all I wish is a chance to make good. I believe I would like machinist helper or Molder helper. If you can help me in any way it will be highly appreciate hoping to hear from you soon

18

The Trial of Kate Richards O'Hare
Kate Richards O'Hare et al.

In 1917 and 1918, the U.S. Congress passed Woodrow Wilson's Espionage and Sedition Acts, providing up to twenty years in prison to all who would "willfully obstruct the recruiting or enlistment service of the United States" or use seditious language about the form of government. These acts, passed during World War I, were directed primarily at the Socialist Party of America, which in recent years had become a third national party, garnering almost a million votes in the 1912 presidential election. In 1917 its membership voted to oppose the war, declaring it of benefit to capitalists, not workers. This stand, which led to the imprisonment of hundreds of militants and party leaders, stood in contrast to the powerful European labor and socialist parties that had yielded to the pressures of nationalism, proximity to the conflict, and the force of state power by supporting national war efforts.

Kate Richards O'Hare, known as "red Kate," was a fiery leader of the Socialist Party whose evangelical rhetoric had converted poor farmers across the Plains states to socialism. Committed to ending what she believed to be an immoral war, O'Hare had already given dozens of speeches in small towns across America by the time the Espionage Act was passed. Not until July 17, 1917, when she spoke at Bowman, North Dakota, did the law catch up with her. North Dakota was at the time a center of socialism, leftist politics, and prairie populism. In 1915 the Nonpartisan League, a broad farmers' movement that included many socialists, swept into power in the state. Though not explicitly antiwar, the Nonpartisan League had gained popularity partially through its intense criticism of war profiteering. The league's major party enemies, the Democrats, seeking to identify the league with O'Hare's militant and "unpatriotic" opposition to the war, made an issue of her speech, leading to her arrest for obstructing recruitment and enlistments in the armed forces.

At her trial O'Hare faced a judge who had made public statements against both socialism and women who were active in public life. Her jury, selected from a county populated by impoverished farmers committed to the Nonpartisan League, was composed of twelve conservative businessmen, none of whom were members of the league. She was found guilty and the judge, despite his dislike of women in politics, gave her a lighter sentence than many of her fellow Socialist Party members: five years. Her appeal was

The Trial of Kate Richards O'Hare for Disloyalty, Bismarck, North Dakota, 1917, Hon. Martin J. Wade, Judge, reprinted in Robert Marcus and Anthony Marcus, eds., *On Trial: American History through Court Proceedings and Hearings*, Vol. 2 (St. James, NY: Brandywine Press, 1998), pp. 96–98, 100–104.

rejected by a higher court and she served fourteen months in prison before the Department of Justice commuted her sentence in accordance with a nationwide amnesty.

Upon release she helped lead the 1920 presidential campaign of fellow Espionage Act prisoner Eugene V. Debs, who garnered over 900,000 votes from his prison cell. O'Hare's incarceration had made her an ardent advocate of prison reform, a cause she remained active in until her death in 1948. She also founded a school for workers' education and campaigned for her fellow socialist Upton Sinclair in his 1934 race for governor of California.

Before You Read

1. Why did Kate Richards O'Hare oppose America's involvement in World War I?
2. What was O'Hare's defense at her trial?
3. Did O'Hare believe that she was serving her country?
4. Do you think O'Hare received a fair trial?

Mr. Hildreth.[1] Gentlemen of the jury: The Congress of the United States declared war on Germany on the 6th day of April, 1917. The purposes of that war are known to all men. It is to settle the great question as to whether democracy shall rule the world or autocracy. Our soldiers are now crossing the seas. Back of the men who go into the line of entrenchments to do or die must rest the great reserve forces of the Nation.

Our government has called to the colors under the draft act young men between the ages of 21 and 31 years. The man power of the Nation not only is involved, the resources of the Nation are not only involved, but greater than all of these elements of national strength is the spirit of our people. Whatever tends to destroy the spirit of the people, the patriotism of the people, to lessen it here at home while our troops are fighting the battles of the Nation in Europe, lessens our strength as a Nation, minimizes the patriotism of our people, and contributes in no small degree to strengthening the armies of the Central Powers.

One of the methods that have been used in the past in the wars of the Republic to injure the patriotism of the people has been the abuse of free speech. In every war we have been engaged in we have been confronted with the propagandist, the agitator, and the corruptionist. These forces have made it difficult for us to win battles, have prolonged wars, injured the unity of the Nation and been destructive of complete success on the battlefield. It was true of the Revolutionary War, the War of 1812, the Mexican War, and the great Rebellion; and it is true today that in this country, where we have a written Constitution, trial by jury, freedom of the press, and liberty of speech, we are met with a hostility on our own shores far more dangerous than the guns of our European foes.

This great evil was known to all men. Therefore Congress, on the 15th day of June, 1917, passed this Espionage act, and the defendant is charged in this indictment with having violated that act.

---

1. **Mr. Hildreth:** Melvin Hildreth, the prosecuting attorney.

She went to Bowman and before an audience of from 100 to 150 people made a speech which, in some respects, has no parallel in the English language. She said: "Any person who enlists in the army of the United States of America will be used for fertilizer, and that is all that he is good for; and the women of the United States are nothing more or less than brood sows to raise children to get into the army and be made into fertilizer." Search the annals of history and you will find no parallel in any country in the world. It was a direct blow at the spirit of the people, at the patriotism of the people. It was made intentionally and for the purpose charged. It was made to willfully obstruct the enlistment service of the United States, to the injury of the service of the United States, and to obstruct the recruiting service of the United States. . . .

This lecture, this speech, stirred this Commonwealth as no other speech. Why? Because this woman had gone upon the rostrum and, before the people of a great country, had instilled in their hearts and minds that this was [the financier J. P.] Morgan's war and not the war of the United States; that this was a war to protect the investments of financiers and not the democracy of the world; that this was a war that was brought about by moneyed interests; that this was a war not intended to break down the autocracy of Europe, but to build up the moneyed interests of the country; that this war was unjust and was being waged for that purpose and that alone, when she knew that the United States had suffered injury after injury at the hands of the German Government, when she knew that its ships that had a right to sail upon the seas had been sunk and the bodies of thousands of men, women, and children consigned to a watery grave under circumstances of the greatest atrocity and in violation of every principle of the laws of nations and of humanity. And yet she was telling the people that this was a war not in the defense of the American people on the sea and on the land, but that it was a war for the benefit of the moneyed interests of the country. False and pernicious doctrine! A doctrine that, if instilled in the minds of the people of this country, would prevent us from raising armies and navies and would be more potential in behalf of the Central Powers than the soldiers that are across the seas to fight the battles of the Republic. That was her attitude; that was her position; and that is her position here today. She rather justifies her position. She declares that it was a war in behalf of special interests, and not one for the cause of the people of the earth.

Gentlemen of the jury, we are not concerned with the politics of this defendant. We are indifferent as to whether she is a Socialist, a Democrat, or a Republican. But we are not indifferent to her violation of this statute which forbade her efforts upon the rostrum to carry out the evil intentions which this statute was aimed to prevent. . . .

Gentlemen of the jury, this cause is one of the most important that has ever been tried in the United States. The defendant made her speech on the 17th of July, 1917. She has repeated that speech in many places throughout this Commonwealth. Here in this State, where its men and women have been taught to love the land of their adoption, where men and women have been taught that under our system of free schools, universities, and where a million church spires point to heaven, she would instill in the minds of the young, not the patriotism of the fathers of this Republic but the zeal of those who would destroy this Government, destroy its institutions, and drag this flag in the dust of Socialism.

Take the case. Render such a verdict that when the hand that shall write it is traceless in the grave it shall live the embodiment of the hope of a free people and a monument to the stability of our institutions. . . .

THE VERDICT AND SENTENCE

The *Jury* retired, and after a short time, returned to the court room. The foreman handed the following written verdict to the clerk : "We, the jury, find the defendant *guilty* as charged in the indictment.—A. L. Peart, Foreman."

JUDGE WADE. Is there anything to be said now why sentence should not be imposed upon this defendant?

Mrs. O'Hare. Yes, your Honor: I was taught in high school that law was pure logic. Abstract law may be pure logic but the application of the law of testimony in this case seems to have gone far afield from logic. As your Honor knows, I am a professional woman, following the profession of delivering lectures whereby I hope to induce my hearers to study the philosophy of socialism. In the regular course of my profession and work I delivered during this year lectures all over the United States—in North Carolina when the draft riots were at their height; in Arizona two or three days following the deportations from Bisbee, and on the day when the strike vote was taken, when excitement ran high and passions were having their sway; in San Francisco during the Mooney case, and in Portland, Idaho, and the Northwestern lumber regions during the great I. W. W. [Industrial Workers of the World] excitement; and at all of these lectures conditions were as tense as conditions could be. The men who were in the employ of the United States in the Department of Justice were present at my meetings. These men were trained, highly efficient, and highly paid, detectors of crime and criminals. In all these months, when my lecture was under the scrutiny of this kind of men, there was no suggestion at any time that there was anything in it that was objectionable, treasonable or seditious. It was the custom of my meetings to send complimentary tickets to the district attorney and the marshal and deputy marshal of the district in order that they might hear the lecture.

And then in the course of the trip I landed at Bowman—a little, sordid, wind-blown, sun-blistered, frost-scarred town on the plains of Western Dakota. There was nothing unusual in my visit to Bowman, except the fact that it was unusual to make a town of this size. The reason I did was because there was one man whose loyalty and faithfulness and unselfish service to the cause to which I had given my life wanted me to come, and I felt he had a right to demand my services. I delivered my lecture there just as I had delivered it many, many times before. There was nothing in the audience that was unusual except the fact that it was a small audience—a solid, substantial, stolid type of farmer crowd. There was not the great enthusiasm that had prevailed at many of my meetings. There was nothing to stir me or arouse me or cause me to make a more impassioned appeal than usual. There was nothing at all in that little sordid, wind-blown town, that commonplace audience, that should have for a moment overbalanced my reason and judgment and common sense and have caused me to have been suddenly smitten with hydrophobia of sedition. But I found there were peculiar conditions existing at Bowman, and they are common to the whole state of North Dakota. In this State in the last year and a half the greatest and most revolutionary social phenomena that has occurred since the foundation of this Government, has taken place. The story is one that is so well known that I need spend little time on it. Here to these wind-blown, frost-scarred plains came men hard of face and feature and muscle who subdued this desert and made it bloom and produce the bread to feed the world; and these men, toiling in their desperate struggle with adverse conditions and with nature, gradually had it forced on their minds that in some way they were not receiving a just return for the labor expended; that after their wheat was raised and garnered in the processes of marketing, men who toiled not and suffered none of the hardships of production were robbing them of the product of their labor. . . .

And your Honor, it seems to me one of those strange grotesque things that can only be the outgrowth of this hysteria that is sweeping over the world today that a judge on the bench and a jury in the box and a prosecuting attorney should attempt to usurp the prerogatives of God Almighty and look down into the heart of a human being and decide what motives slumber there. There is no charge that if my intent or my motive was criminal that that intent or motive ever was put into action — only the charge that in my heart there was an intent, and on that strange charge of an intent so securely buried in a human heart that no result and no effect came from it, I went to trial. . . .

Your Honor, there are 100,000 people in the United States who know me personally. They have listened to my voice, looked in my face and have worked side by side with me in every great reform movement of the last twenty years. My life has been an open book to them. They know down to this time I have given all that I am, all that I have, from my earliest girlhood, my girlhood, my young womanhood, even my motherhood. And, your Honor, no judge on earth and no ten thousand judges or ten thousand juries can ever convince these hundred thousand people who know me and have worked with me, and these millions who have read my writings, that I am a criminal, or that I have ever given anything to my country except my most unselfish devotion and service. You cannot convince the people who know me that I am dangerous to the United States Government. They are willing to admit I am dangerous to some things in the United States, and I thank God that I am. I am dangerous to the invisible government of the United States; to the special privileges of the United States; to the white-slaver and the saloon-keepers, and I thank God that at this hour I am dangerous to the war profiteers of this country who rob the people on the one hand and rob and debase the Government on the other, and then with their pockets and wallets stuffed with the blood-stained profits of war, wrap the sacred folds of the Stars and Stripes about them and shout their blatant hypocrisy to the world. You can convince the people that I am dangerous to these men; but no jury and no judge can convince them that I am a dangerous woman to the best interests of the United States. . . .

JUDGE WADE. It is never a pleasant duty for me to sentence any one to prison, and it certainly is not a pleasant duty to send a woman to prison; in the course of a trial, in all the years I have been on the bench in the State and Federal courts, I have made it a rule to try to find out who I am sending to prison, because we all make mistakes in this world at times. On the spur of the moment and under excitement, sometimes people are misled and commit offenses, and I have a hard time to reconcile my view of things with heavy sentences in those cases. Therefore, when this case was closed, I made up my mind that I would find out before imposing sentence in this case what were the activities of this defendant.

She testified here to her loyalty, and her support of the President, and I was hoping in my heart that somewhere I would find out that after all, she was such a woman as she has here pictured herself today, and that thus a small penalty for this offense might be adequate, because I realize this is a serious business. The Nation is at war. Every sane man and woman knows that there is only one way that this war can be won, and that is by having men and money and spirit. Those three things are necessary—spirit in the men, in the service, and spirit in the men and women behind the men. And it was because of these absolute essentials that Congress enacted the Espionage law, to reach out and take hold of those who are trying to kill the spirit of the American people, in whole or in part; trying to put in their hearts hate toward this Government and towards the officials of this Government conducting the war. And realizing that this was such a grave matter, I investigated it as far as possible to find out really what character of woman this defendant is, and had been, in her work. I heard the evidence in this case. I had nothing to do with the question of whether she was guilty or innocent. The jury settled that question, and in my judgment, settled it right.

I received information from another town in North Dakota, and this information was given in the presence of counsel for the defendant that at Garrison, in her lecture there, she made the statement that mothers who reared sons to go into the army, were no better than animals on a North Dakota farm; that this war was in behalf of the capitalists, and that if we had loaned our money to Germany instead of to the allies, we would be now fighting with Germany instead of with the allies. That she had boys, but that they are not old enough to go to war, but that if they were, they would not go. That the way to stop the war was to strike, and if the laboring men of this nation would strike, the war would soon be ended. Of course that was an *ex parte* matter. I have heard enough of testimony in my life, and I have seen enough of human nature to know that sometimes these things are stretched because of the feeling on one side or another of the question. So I thought I would go back and see what she had been doing. I wired the Postoffice Department at Washington, and I received a telegram which states:

> Party is on editorial staff of publication, *Social Revolution*, Saint Louis, Missouri, which has been barred from the mails for gross violations of Espionage Act, and is successor to *Ripsaw*. The party appears to be of the extreme type who have attempted to handicap the Government in every way in the conduct of the present war.

That was only a statement of an opinion. I tried to get copies of the *Social Revolution*, and have not succeeded in getting either the number for June or July. At some period during that time the Postmaster General barred this from the mails. I have the April and May numbers. In April they published from Eugene Debs this statement:

> As we have said, the bankers are for bullets—for the fool patriots that enlist at paupers' wages to stop the bullets, while the bankers clip coupons, boost food prices, increase dividends, and pile up millions and billions for themselves. Say, Mr. Workingman, suppose you have sense enough to be as patriotic as the banker, but not a bit more so. When you see the bankers on the firing line with guns in their hands ready to stop bullets as well as start them, then it is time enough for you to be seized with the patriotic itch and have yourself shot into a crazy-quilt for their profit and glory. Don't you take a fit and rush to the front until you see them there. They own the country and if they don't set the example of fighting for it, why should you?'

This was in April, before the war was declared. Up to that time I realize that every person in this country had the right to discuss the war, express their opinions against the war, give any reasons they might have against the war. But you will find here in this statement the note which rings out from the statement of the defendant here in court this afternoon and which forms the foundation of the entire gospel of hate which she and her associates are preaching to the American people: That the Nation is helpless, prostrate, down-trodden by a few capitalists, and that the average man has not a chance on earth; that this war is a war of capitalism; that it was brought about by capital and in the interest of capital; that 100, 200, or 300 millionaires and billionaires if you please, in these United States dominate the souls and consciences of the other 99,000,000 American people. . . .

The Department of Justice furnishes me the following resolutions adopted at a meeting of the extreme wing of the Socialist Party, to which the defendant belongs, at their St. Louis convention after war was declared. The Secret Service, in sending in their report, says in a letter:

> We have been unable to secure anything specific on her that would be a violation of the Federal law in this district, but we have placed her in a class whose hearts and souls we are morally certain are for Germany against our country.

This defendant was chairman of the committee that brought in these resolutions. A newspaper of the city of St. Louis, in describing this convention, states:

> The Socialist Party, in a national convention at the Planters' Hotel last night, adopted resolutions proclaiming its "unalterable opposition to the war just declared by the Government of the United States. The majority report of the committee on war and militarism containing the resolutions received 140 votes. An even more radical report by Louis Boudin, of New York, received 31 votes. The

conservative minority report of John Spargo, of New York, declaring that Socialists should support the war, received only 5 votes. The vote was taken after hours
of speech-making. Thomas William, of California, was hissed when he said he
was an American, charged the delegates with being pro-German, and declared
they did not represent the true sentiment of American Socialists. Mrs. Kate
Richards O'Hare, of St. Louis, defied the Government and civil authorities. She
declared that Socialists would not be molested in St. Louis for what they said because the city was against war, and the authorities were afraid to molest them.

Fine stuff for the boys and girls of the United States to be reading at this hour!

Urban Industrial America

"The photographers of the American city during the nineteenth and early twentieth centuries," writes a historian of the photography of American urbanization, "were explorers in a cultural frontier. . . . They advertised and celebrated change—most fundamentally the transformation of America from a rural and agrarian nation to an urban and industrial one." By the early twentieth century New York City housed over four million people, Chicago over two million, and Philadelphia over one and a half million, making them among the largest cities in the world at that time. Urban life was strange and uncomfortable: vast crowds with foreign languages and unfamiliar manners; furious construction; monumental traffic jams; dense jungles of overhead wires; and the dilemmas of slums, disease, crime, vice, and corruption. At the same time, the city swelled with promise and opportunity: it was a place to escape age-old restrictions; gain new experience; achieve wealth; secure education; discover new entertainments, like amusement parks, dance halls, concerts, and nickelodeons; or simply observe people in venues like the Bowery or Coney Island, where they seemed unusual or glamorous enough to be worth watching.

Photographers helped explore this new territory. Some celebrated the vitality of the urban scene, while others allied with journalists, urban planners, and social workers to bring the problems of the poor and the successes of reform movements to public gaze. Armed with important technological improvements—such as the more convenient dry plate photographic chemistry (which soon gave rise to the popular Kodak camera), crude forms of flash photography, and the halftone process that allowed the direct printing of photographs in books, newspapers, and magazines—these photographers documented their fascination with the changes overtaking the older American scene.

Each spread in this portfolio highlights the work of a different photographer from this classic age of reform and urban photography: Alvin Langdon Coburn, one of the first of his generation to depict the city and industry as subjects worthy of an artist; Jacob A. Riis, who wedded photography to social reform, calculatingly introducing scenes and themes new to the history of American photography; Lewis Wickes Hine, who raised social reform photography to a high art; and Frances Benjamin Johnston, who was a pioneering woman photojournalist.

Plate 1. Alvin Langdon Coburn, "Workers, New York," from Alvin Langdon Coburn, *New York*, 1910

Alvin Langdon Coburn (1882–1936) was a pictorialist photographer, part of a group of early twentieth-century photographers who wished to establish photography as a high art. Working in a style of softened focus that emulated aspects of the Impressionist movement, which was then dominating the other visual arts, Coburn nevertheless turned his camera away from traditional pictorial subjects to the new vistas of the urban landscape. The hard-edged forms of the burgeoning industrial structures helped shape a modernist approach to photography and to art. Coburn sought to capture a sense of the vitality and movement of the new glamorous, urban age. What do you think the smoke in Plates 1, 2, and 3 symbolizes for Coburn? What point is he making in choosing the subjects he does?

Above: Plate 2.
Alvin Langdon
Coburn, "Pillars of
Smoke," Pittsburgh,
1910

Right: Plate 3.
Alvin Langdon
Coburn, "Skyscrap-
ers, Manhattan,"
from Alvin Langdon
Coburn, *New York*,
1910

Left: Plate 4. Jacob A. Riis, "An Ancient Police Station Lodger with the Plank on Which She Slept at the Eldridge Street Station," c. 1898

Below left: Plate 5. Jacob A. Riis, "Shoemaker in Ludlow Street Cellar," c. 1890

Right: Plate 6. Jacob A. Riis, "Baxter Street Court (22 Baxter Street)," c. 1890

Unlike Coburn, who wanted to make art with his camera, journalist Jacob A. Riis (1849–1914) chose to use photography as a tool to provide powerfully convincing visual evidence to document the reality of the statements that he wrote. His images gave an emotional dimension to the statistics and facts that he brought before his audiences in lectures, articles, and books about social problems and the need for reform. Most Americans did not understand the impoverished, overcrowded, disease-ridden world of the slums. Riis's stark, sometimes posed photographs supported his view that these slum dwellers were not, as middle-class people supposed, victims of their own personal shortcomings. Rather, they were engulfed in an environmental disaster that only public action could improve or eliminate. In fact, Riis's campaign led to improvements in sanitation and the demolition of some of the more notorious shanties that he targeted. Study Plates 4, 5, and 6, and try to explain how Riis composed the images to gain viewers' sympathies for his subjects and to persuade them to support housing and sanitary reform.

Above: Plate 7. Lewis Wickes Hine, "Doffer Girl in New England Mill, 1909," from *Lewis W. Hine's Workbooks for the National Child Labor Committee*

Above right: Plate 8. Lewis Wickes Hine, "Young Women in Mill," c. 1910, from *Lewis W. Hine's Workbooks for the National Child Labor Committee*

Below right: Plate 9. Lewis Wickes Hine, "Young Woman outside Mill," c. 1910, from *Lewis W. Hine's Workbooks for the National Child Labor Committee*

Between 1908 and 1917 Lewis Wickes Hine (1874–1940) traveled more than fifty thousand miles as the staff photographer for the National Child Labor Committee to assemble "photographic proof" of the extent of child labor in the United States. All three of these prints are in his *Workbooks for the National Child Labor Committee*, which contain page after page of photographs like these, each with its own negative number so that concerned individuals and groups could purchase copies of the images to use in articles, exhibitions, or posters that argued against the evils of child labor. Yet these photographs are more than propaganda. How does the girl in Plate 7 compare to the figures in Riis's photographs? What details can you find to distinguish the different young mill women in Plate 8? (Hint: Look at their hands.) And how does the young mill woman in Plate 9 relate to her place of employment? How does Hine present these people as individuals maintaining presence and even dignity in difficult circumstances?

Frances Benjamin Johnston (1864–1952), pioneering photojournalist for illustrated magazines, was hired often throughout the 1890s to document the activities of forward-thinking schools and other social agencies that had evolved to cope with the social problems of the day. In 1899 the Hampton Institute, an important agency for educating African Americans and Native Americans, hired her to put together an extensive visual record of their programs and activities. The photos shown in Plates 10, 11, and 12, and others like them, were then used by Hampton in articles, exhibitions, and other fund-raising activities. Her images were designed to express Hampton's highest aspirations. In fact, some critics have complained that Johnston's photos exceed what Hampton actually achieved for its students and graduates. What can you deduce about the programs and aspirations that this school provided for its students? How may Johnston have overstated these scholastic aspirations in her photos?

Above left: Plate 10. Frances Benjamin Johnston, "Carriage Shop, Hampton Institute, Hampton, Va., 1899"

Below left: Plate 11. Frances Benjamin Johnston, "History Classroom, Hampton Institute, Hampton, Va., 1899"

Below: Plate 12. Frances Benjamin Johnston, "Hampton Graduates, Hampton, Va., 1899"

PART FOUR

A New Society

Between the Wars

World War I and its social, political, and technological effects helped to transform the economic organization of America and move it into the "consumer" age. A rapidly expanding advertising industry encouraged Americans to embrace new consumer goods, a trend explored in the visual portfolio "Advertising in the 1920s" (page 197). They responded with alacrity, purchasing cars, radios, and other items for their homes. Many developed doubts about whether the political and cultural values that had worked for a previous generation would work as well for them. These doubts fueled creativity in literature, the arts, and social movements, but also triggered defensive reassertions of nineteenth-century values. These social tensions were displayed in many arenas. The Scopes trial pitted William Jennings Bryan, the hero of rural America, against the renowned defense lawyer Clarence Darrow and other champions of modernism like the critic Joseph Wood Krutch and underscored the chasm in religious and social values held by fundamentalists and modernists. The Harlem Renaissance, which brought Langston Hughes to New York City, revealed new possibilities in race relations exhilarating to some Americans but frightening to many others. And Margaret Sanger's crusade for birth control challenged traditional attitudes in the sensitive areas of family planning and sexuality.

The assumption that modern American life meant unending growth, expansion, and prosperity came into question during the Great Depression of the 1930s. Although citizens everywhere encountered the same overwhelming set of events, the degree to which people were affected by the Depression varied. Some ruminated over fortunes lost on the stock market; others joined radical organizations; still others drifted from place to place. Many wrote plaintive letters to President and Mrs. Franklin D. Roosevelt. And the labor movement evolved a new weapon, the sit-down strike, that created powerful industrywide unions that raised the wages of millions of workers and created a national political base for labor as part of FDR's New Deal.

The Scopes Trial (1925)

19

In Defense of the Bible

William Jennings Bryan
and Clarence Darrow

*In July 1925 John T. Scopes was tried for teaching the theory of evolution in the
Dayton, Tennessee, high school. The first trial in American history to be broadcast
nationally, it was "monkey business" to some and "the trial of the century" to others.
A writer in the* Moody Bible Institute Monthly *considered the case "the mightiest
issue that has ever been joined since the trial of Jesus Christ before Pontius Pilate."*

*The Tennessee legislature in March 1925 had passed the Butler Act making it a
crime to teach in any state-supported school (including universities) "any theory that
denies the story of the Divine Creation of man as taught in the Bible, and to teach instead that man has descended from a lower order of animals." Almost on a whim, a few
Daytonians decided to test the law and persuaded Scopes, a young local high school biol-
ogy teacher, to become the defendant.*

*Larger forces, however, were at work. The Protestant churches were sharply divid-
ing between fundamentalists who believed in the literal truth of the Bible and liberals
who accepted the findings of science. The split corresponded to a division between urban
and rural values, a division that was also sharply reflected in national, and especially
Democratic Party, politics. The South was a stronghold of fundamentalism, and laws
like the Butler Act had much support throughout the region.*

*A famous orator led each legal team. William Jennings Bryan (1860–1925), long
identified with the values of the countryside, had been the Democratic Party candidate
for president in 1896, 1900, and 1908 and had served as Woodrow Wilson's first secretary of state. Clarence Darrow (1857–1938) was nationally famous both as a trial
lawyer and as a lecturer on evolution, the scientific outlook, and various reforms. When
the presiding judge, John T. Raulston, banned the use of expert witnesses on the theory
of evolution, Darrow called Bryan himself to the stand as an authority on the Bible.
Bryan agreed to mount the witness box, and the judge permitted the testimony to pro-
ceed—but without the jury, which the judge had ruled was not to decide matters of the
truth of either evolution or the Bible but only whether Scopes had taught evolution to
his high school class. Yet Darrow made it seem as if Bryan, fundamentalism, and perhaps even the Bible were on trial and revealed Bryan's spotty knowledge of scientific*

Sheldon Norman Grebstein, ed., *Monkey Trial: The State of Tennessee vs. John Thomas Scopes* (Boston:
Houghton Mifflin, 1960).

matters. The following day the judge changed his mind, expunged all of Bryan's testimony, and sent the case to the jury for the inevitable finding of Scopes's admitted guilt.

BEFORE YOU READ

1. Why do you think Bryan agreed to testify?
2. Was Darrow's questioning fair?
3. Could Bryan have made his arguments stronger?
4. What values was Bryan defending?
5. What do you think of Darrow's performance? Was he, as some have said, putting the Bible on trial? Was Darrow's devotion to science in any way deserving of challenge?

The Court: The question is whether or not Mr. Scopes taught man descended from the lower order of animals.

EXAMINATION OF W. J. BRYAN BY CLARENCE DARROW, COUNSEL FOR THE DEFENSE

Q: You have given considerable study to the Bible, haven't you, Mr. Bryan?

A: Yes, sir, I have tried to.

Q: Well, we all know you have; we are not going to dispute that at all. But you have written and published articles almost weekly, and sometimes have made interpretations of various things.

A: I would not say interpretations, Mr. Darrow, but comments on the lesson.

Q: If you comment to any extent, these comments have been interpretations?

A: I presume that any discussion might be to some extent interpretations, but they have not been primarily intended as interpretations.

Q: Then you have made a general study of it?

A: Yes, I have; I have studied the Bible for about fifty years, or some time more than that, but, of course, I have studied it more as I have become older than when I was but a boy.

Q: Do you claim that everything in the Bible should be literally interpreted?

A: I believe everything in the Bible should be accepted as it is given there; some of the Bible is given illustratively. For instance: "Ye are the salt of the earth." I would not insist that man was actually salt, or that he had flesh of salt, but it is used in the sense of salt as saving God's people.

Q: You believe the story of the flood to be a literal interpretation?

A: Yes, sir.

Q: When was that flood?

A: I would not attempt to fix the date. The date is fixed, as suggested this morning.

Q: About 4004 b.c.?

A: That has been the estimate of a man that is accepted today. I would not say it is accurate.

Q: That estimate is printed in the Bible?

A: Everybody knows, at least, I think most of the people know, that was the estimate given.

Q: But what do you think that the Bible, itself, says? Don't you know how it was arrived at?

A: I never made a calculation.

Q: What do you think?

A: I do not think about things I don't think about.

Q: Do you think about things you do think about?

A: Well, sometimes.

The Bailiff: Let us have order.

Mr. Darrow: Mr. Bryan, you have read these dates over and over again?

A: Not very accurately; I turn back sometimes to see what the time was.

Q: You want to say now you have no idea how these dates were computed?

A: No, I don't say, but I have told you what my idea was. I say I don't know how accurate it was.

Q: You say from the generation of man—

Gen. Stewart: I am objecting to his cross-examining his own witness.

Mr. Darrow: He is a hostile witness.

The Court: I am going to let Mr. Bryan control—

The Witness: I want him to have all the latitude he wants, for I am going to have some latitude when he gets through.

Mr. Darrow: You can have latitude and longitude.

The Court: Order.

Gen. Stewart: The witness is entitled to be examined as to the legal evidence of it. We were supposed to go into the argument today, and we have nearly lost the day, your Honor.

Mr. McKenzie: I object to it.

Gen. Stewart: Your Honor, he is perfectly able to take care of this, but we are attaining no evidence. This is not competent evidence.

The Witness: These gentlemen have not had much chance—they did not come here to try this case. They came here to try revealed religion. I am here to defend it, and they can ask me any question they please.

The Court: All right.

Mr. Darrow: Great applause from the bleachers.

The Witness: From those whom you call "yokels."

Mr. Darrow: I have never called them yokels.

The Witness: That is the ignorance of Tennessee, the bigotry.

Mr. Darrow: You mean who are applauding you?

The Witness: Those are the people whom you insult.

Mr. Darrow: You insult every man of science and learning in the world because he does not believe in your fool religion.

The Court: I will not stand for that.

Mr. Darrow: For what he is doing?

The Court: I am talking to both of you.

Gen. Stewart: This has gone beyond the pale of a lawsuit, your Honor. I have a public duty to perform under my oath, and I ask the Court to stop it. Mr. Darrow is making an effort to insult the gentleman on the witness stand and I ask that it be stopped, for it has gone beyond the pale of a lawsuit.

The Court: To stop it now would not be just to Mr. Bryan. He wants to ask the other gentleman questions along the same line.

Gen. Stewart: It will all be incompetent.

The Witness: The jury is not here.

The Court: I do not want to be strictly technical.

Mr. Darrow: Then your Honor rules, and I accept.

Gen. Stewart: The jury is not here.

Mr. Darrow: How long ago was the flood, Mr. Bryan?

A: Let me see Ussher's calculation about it?

Mr. Darrow: Surely.

A: I think this does not give it.

Q: It gives an account of Noah. Where is the one in evidence? I am quite certain it is there.

The Witness: Oh, I would put the estimate where it is, because I have no reason to vary it. But I would have to look at it to give you the exact date.

Q: I would, too. Do you remember what book the account is in?

A: Genesis.

Mr. Hays: Is that the one in evidence?

Mr. Neal: That will have it; that is the King James Version.

Mr. Darrow: The one in evidence has it.

The Witness: It is given here, as 2348 years B.C.

Q: Well, 2348 years B.C. You believe that all the living things that were not contained in the ark were destroyed.

A: I think the fish may have lived.

Q: Outside of the fish?

A: I cannot say.

Q: You cannot say?

A: No, I accept that just as it is; I have no proof to the contrary.

Q: I am asking you whether you believe?

A: I do.

Q: That all living things outside of the fish were destroyed?

A: What I say about the fish is merely a matter of humor.

Q: I understand.

The Witness: Due to the fact a man wrote up here the other day to ask whether all the fish were destroyed, and the gentleman who received the letter told him the fish may have lived.

Q: I am referring to the fish, too.

A: I accept that as the Bible gives it and I have never found any reason for denying, disputing, or rejecting it.

Q: Let us make it definite, 2,348 years?

A: I didn't say that. That is the time given there [*indicating the Bible*] but I don't pretend to say that is exact.

Q: You never figured it out, these generations, yourself?

A: No, sir; not myself.

Q: But the Bible you have offered in evidence says 2,340 something, so that 4,200 years ago there was not a living thing on the earth, excepting the people on the ark and the animals on the ark and the fishes?

A: There have been living things before that.

Q: I mean at that time.

A: After that.

Q: Don't you know there are any number of civilizations that are traced back to more than 5,000 years?

A: I know we have people who trace things back according to the number of ciphers they have. But I am not satisfied they are accurate.

Q: You are not satisfied there is any civilization that can be traced back 5,000 years?

A: I would not want to say there is because I have no evidence of it that is satisfactory.

Q: Would you say there is not?

A: Well, so far as I know, but when the scientists differ from 24,000,000 to 306,000,000 in their opinion as to how long ago life came here, I want them to be nearer, to come nearer together, before they demand of me to give up my belief in the Bible.

Q: Do you say that you do not believe that there were any civilizations on this earth that reach back beyond 5,000 years?

A: I am not satisfied by any evidence that I have seen.

Q: I didn't ask you what you are satisfied with. I asked you if you believe it?

The Witness: Will you let me answer it?

The Court: Go right on.

The Witness: I am satisfied by no evidence that I have found that would justify me in accepting the opinions of these men against what I believe to be the inspired Word of God.

Q: And you believe every nation, every organization of men, every animal, in the world outside of the fishes—

The Witness: The fish, I want you to understand, is merely a matter of humor.

Q: You believe that all the various human races on the earth have come into being in the last 4,000 years or 4,200 years, whatever it is?

A: No, it would be more than that.

[Here Bryan and Darrow engaged in some calculations as to when man was created, according to the chronology Bryan was defending.]

Q: That makes 4,262 years. If it is not correct, we can correct it.

A: According to the Bible there was a civilization before that, destroyed by the flood.

Q: Let me make this definite. You believe that every civilization on the earth and every living thing, except possibly the fishes, that came out of the ark were wiped out by the flood?

A: At that time.

Q: At that time. And then whatever human beings, including all the tribes, that inhabited the world, and have inhabited the world, and who run their pedigree straight back, and all the animals, have come onto the earth since the flood?

A: Yes.

Q: Within 4,200 years. Do you know a scientific man on the face of the earth that believes any such thing?

A: I cannot say, but I know some scientific men who dispute entirely the antiquity of man as testified to by other scientific men.

Q: Oh, that does not answer the question. Do you know of a single scientific man on the face of the earth that believes any such thing as you stated, about the antiquity of man?

A: I don't think I have ever asked one the direct question.

Q: Quite important, isn't it?

A: Well, I don't know as it is.

Q: It might not be?

A: If I had nothing else to do except speculate on what our remote ancestors were and what our remote descendants have been, but I have been more interested in Christians going on right now to make it much more important than speculation on either the past or the future.

Q: You have never had any interest in the age of the various races and people and civilization and animals that exist upon the earth today, is that right?

A: I have never felt a great deal of interest in the effort that has been made to dispute the Bible by the speculations of men, or the investigations of men.

Q: Are you the only human being on earth who knows what the Bible means?

Gen. Stewart: I object.

The Court: Sustained.

Mr. Darrow: You do know that there are thousands of people who profess to be Christians who believe the earth is much more ancient and that the human race is much more ancient?

A: I think there may be.

Q: And you never have investigated to find out how long man has been on the earth?

A: I have never found it necessary—

Q: For any reason, whatever it is?

A: To examine every speculation; but if I had done it I never would have done anything else.

Q: I ask for a direct answer.

A: I do not expect to find out all those things, and I do not expect to find out about races.

Q: I didn't ask you that. Now, I ask you if you know if it was interesting enough or important enough for you to try to find out about how old these ancient civilizations were?

A: No; I have not made a study of it.

Q: Don't you know that the ancient civilizations of China are 6,000 or 7,000 years old, at the very least?

A: No; but they would not run back beyond the creation, according to the Bible, 6,000 years.

Q: You don't know how old they are, is that right?

A: I don't know how old they are, but probably you do. [*Laughter in the courtyard.*] I think you would give preference to anybody who opposed the Bible, and I give the preference to the Bible.

Q: I see. Well, you are welcome to your opinion. Have you any idea how old the Egyptian civilization is?

A: No.

Q: Do you know of any record in the world, outside of the story of the Bible, which conforms to any statement that it is 4,200 years ago or thereabouts that all life was wiped off the face of the earth?

A: I think they have found records.

Q: Do you know of any?

A: Records reciting the flood, but I am not an authority on the subject.

Q: Now, Mr. Bryan, will you say if you know of any record, or have ever heard of any records, that describe that a flood existed 4,200 years ago, or about that time, which wiped all life off the earth?

A: The recollection of what I have read on that subject is not distinct enough to say whether the records attempted to fix a time, but I have seen in the discoveries of archaeologists where they have found records that described the flood.

Q: Mr. Bryan, don't you know that there are many old religions that describe the flood?

A: No, I don't know.

Q: You know there are others besides the Jewish?

A: I don't know whether these are the record of any other religion or refer to this flood.

Q: Don't you ever examine religion so far to know that?

A: Outside of the Bible?

Q: Yes.

A: No; I have not examined to know that, generally.

Q: You have never examined any other religions?

A: Yes, sir.

Q: Have you ever read anything about the origins of religions?

A: Not a great deal.

Q: You have never examined any other religion?

A: Yes, sir.

Q: And you don't know whether any other religion ever gave a similar account of the destruction of the earth by the flood?

A: The Christian religion has satisfied me, and I have never felt it necessary to look up some competing religions.

Q: Do you consider that every religion on earth competes with the Christian religion?

A: I think everybody who does not believe in the Christian religion believes so —

Q: I am asking what you think?

A: I do not regard them as competitive because I do not think they have the same sources as we have.

Q: You are wrong in saying "competitive"?

A: I would not say competitive, but the religious unbelievers.

Q: Unbelievers of what?

A: In the Christian religion.

Q: What about the religion of Buddha?

A: I can tell you something about that, if you want to know.

Q: What about the religion of Confucius or Buddha?

A: Well, I can tell you something about that, if you would like to know.

Q: Did you ever investigate them?

A: Somewhat.

Q: Do you regard them as competitive?

A: No, I think they are very inferior. Would you like for me to tell you what I know about it?

Q: No.

A: Well, I shall insist on giving it to you.

Q: You won't talk about free silver, will you?

A: Not at all. . . .

20

Tennessee's Dilemma

Joseph Wood Krutch

Joseph Wood Krutch (1893–1970), the writer of the following article from The Nation, *was a native of Tennessee who moved to New York after attending the University of Tennessee in the years before World War I. Though he was an iron-willed rationalist committed to the teaching of Darwin's theory of evolution, the series of articles that he published in* The Nation *provide a clarity, generosity, and skepticism that were absent in much of the highly charged and partisan reporting of the Scopes trial. Throughout his coverage of what came to be known as "the trial of the century," Krutch not only criticized the creationists but also chastised his fellow believers in "modern science" for allowing the Butler Act to pass and for failing to take a strong stand in defense of their beliefs due to timidity or political opportunism.*

Krutch, unlike many other commentators, engaged a bigger picture than merely the outcome of the trial. His observations about the problems and challenges of American education, citizenship, and political leadership suggest why many of the issues at stake in the Scopes trial still remain unresolved over seventy-five years later. He went

Joseph Wood Krutch, "Tennessee's Dilemma," *The Nation* 121.3133 (July 22, 1925).

on to become one of America's best-known authors and naturalists, winning the 1955 National Book Award for nonfiction for his book The Measure of Man: On Freedom, Human Values, Survival, and the Modern Temper *(1954).*

BEFORE YOU READ

1. Why does Joseph Wood Krutch believe that "nothing of importance can be decided at Dayton"?

2. Do you believe that the rural-urban divide was as important as Krutch suggests? Is it an important divide now?

3. How serious do you think Krutch was about the danger of fundamentalism?

Those who say that nothing of importance can be decided at Dayton have, at first glance, reason on their side. Even in Rhea County tadpoles will still lose their tails whatever may happen to Mr. Scopes, and, it is to be hoped, the human organism will continue in a similarly unperturbed fashion its evolution toward whatever state Nature has in mind for it. It is now perfectly evident that the question of the constitutionality of the Tennessee law, the only tangible legal issue involved, will not be the chief one discussed, and it might thus appear that the whole discussion threatens to become diffusely inconclusive.

No sooner had Clarence Darrow begun his cross-examination of prospective jurors than it became clear that he proposed to prove that the teaching of the defendant was not irreconcilable with a sufficiently liberal interpretation of the Bible, and hence was not a violation of the law, which specifically forbids only those theories which deny the account in Genesis. The theoretical position of the Bible as final authority upon scientific questions will thus not be questioned, and the right of the State legislature to control the teaching of professors will be left similarly unchallenged.

But the real problem raised is not legal but sociological. No verdict of the jury and no injunction of the Supreme Court can change the fact that the trial is a symptom of the vast gulf which lies between two halves of our population, and that the real question to be settled is the question of how this gulf may be bridged. In the centers of population men have gone on assuming certain bodies of knowledge and certain points of view without realizing that they were living in a different world from that inhabited by a considerable portion of their fellow-citizens, and they have been unconscious of the danger which threatened them at the inevitable moment when the two worlds should come in conflict. In Tennessee the moment has arrived and a single battle will no more settle it than the World War settled the questions from which it arose.

Of the reality of the danger there can be no question. The zeal of the fundamentalists has been enormously quickened by an anticipatory taste of triumph, and they will push any victory they may gain to the fullest possible extent. Already one State legislator has announced his intention of "putting teeth" in the present law by making the penalty for its violation a prison sentence instead of a fine, and various extensions of the principle of State interference with teaching may be confidently predicted. Members of the D.A.R. will, sooner or later, seek to forbid in the schools any historical facts which tend to reflect upon the character or motives of Revolutionary heroes; conservative economists and sociologists will certainly follow their lead; and, unless the movement is definitely checked, the next twenty-five years will see the State schools and universities so shackled with legislation as to make them utterly worthless as institutions for education. The control of learning will pass into the hands of the uneducated, and youth will leave the schools more ignorant than when it entered them.

Doubtless Tennessee is in a condition not much worse than that of the majority of the States in the Union. Her folly consists chiefly in the fact that she has allowed the situation to get out of hand by her cowardly refusal to deal with it as it arose. Neither she nor any other State has been able adequately to educate her citizens—and for that fact she is not to blame, since the task is beyond her financial or other strength. But when people cannot be educated they must be led, and it is in leadership that Tennessee has failed.

Left undisturbed, the rural population would have bothered itself very little over the teachings of the school or the college, since it has that respect for learning natural to all uneducated communities. A few years ago, however, it became evident that it would not be thus undisturbed, for various propagandists of the Bryan school came among it to declaim against what one of the agitators now in Dayton picturesquely calls "Hell in the high schools." Dayton was made aware of a question at issue, it looked for leaders, and it found them on one side alone. Fundamentalists were eager and zealous; educators were at best timid and non-committal, at worst hypocritically evasive. Under the circumstances, Dayton cannot be blamed if she chose to follow those who knew what they stood for.

Even at that very late moment when the anti-evolution bill was introduced into the legislature a little courage might have saved the day. Had the president of the State University gone with his faculty to Nashville, had the editors of the daily papers said what they thought, and had, in general, the enlightened members of the community shown one-half the decision manifest by the other side they might very well have won. Instead they lay low. They declined the challenge; they refused to make any effort to lead; they left their opponents in undisputed possession of the field. Dayton was reasonable to conclude, as undoubtedly it has concluded, that nine-tenths of Tennessee, the only world it knows, is with it and Bryan. It does not even know that the university which it respects is against it, and it is following a sound instinct. It is right to have no great confidence in scientists and educators who ask for nothing except its money. If the time ever comes when they show a disposition to tell what they believe it may possibly listen to them.

In the courtroom at Dayton and in the newspaper reports of the proceedings there Tennessee will be reminded of the situation into which she has drifted, and the ultimate result of the trial will depend upon whether or not she heeds the reminder. Neither John R. Neal, the only native prominently represented upon the defense, nor Messrs. Darrow, Hays, and Malone, his associates, can do much for her if she will do nothing for herself. They may win their case or they may lose it, but an ignorant population, almost wholly without leaders, will remain.

FOR CRITICAL THINKING

1. Bryan, in agreeing to testify at the Scopes trial, had reserved the right similarly to question Darrow. What questions might Bryan have asked? Construct a set of questions and answers between the two men, with Darrow in the witness box and Bryan doing the questioning.

2. Was the Scopes trial really "the trial of the century"? Which issues of the trial are still matters of debate today? In what ways does discussion of these issues today resemble or differ from arguments at the Scopes trial?

3. Imagine yourself a supporter of Bryan and of his rejection of scientific evidence for evolution. Write an editorial objecting to Krutch's characterization of creationists.

21

The Harlem Renaissance

Langston Hughes

"I went up the steps and out into the bright September sunlight," reports the poet Langston Hughes (1902–1967) in his autobiography. "Harlem! I stood there, dropped my bags, took a deep breath, and felt happy again." What was there, in this Upper East Side Manhattan subway stop of 1921, to excite a young black Midwesterner?

By the standards of most white Americans of the time, little enough. While not yet the congested slum it would become during the Great Depression, Harlem was poor. Among the 73,000 Harlemites in 1920 and close to 200,000 a decade later, there was little in the way of a prosperous middle class. In wealth, residences, stability, and order, Harlem fell in some ways behind black sections of several Southern cities. Nor was it the largest concentration of blacks in the North: the greatest migration was to Chicago.

What gave excitement to Harlem was its reputation as a "race capital"—a center of social and cultural independence. For Harlem residents, being a visible part of the great metropolis, tough and streetwise rather than deferential and under the surveillance of suspicious white neighbors and hostile Southern police, was liberating. The main black civil rights organizations and journals were anchored in Harlem. Black American troops had been honored with a parade in New York City for their services during World War I. And the speakeasies and jazz cabarets as well as the rent parties that turned shabby apartments into informal nightclubs blared with the new exciting sound that would soon make both whites and blacks talk about "the Jazz Age."

In 1921, Harlem was in the first stages of an artistic and literary flowering richer than anything African Americans had yet achieved. In the next several years popular musicians like Duke Ellington and Bessie Smith, writers like Langston Hughes (whose memories of this period are excerpted here), artists, and intellectuals would together create a distinctive cultural energy charged with the rhythms and themes of the African American experience.

The Harlem Renaissance and the jazz explosion soon attracted white patronage. Harlem nightclubs and cabarets began to cater to white patrons, and Harlem jazz migrated to Broadway in shows like Shuffle Along. *Irving Berlin's song "Puttin' on the Ritz," later made famous with modified lyrics, was first written in 1929 about going uptown to Harlem:*

> *Have you seen the well-to-do*
> *Up on Lenox Avenue*
> *On that famous thoroughfare*

Langston Hughes, *The Big Sea* (New York: Hill and Wang, 1963), pp. 223–28, 235–40, 243–47.

With their noses in the air
High hats and colored collars
White spats and fifteen dollars
Spending ev'ry dime
For a wonderful time.

If you're blue
and you don't know
Where to go to,
Why don't you go
Where Harlem sits
Puttin' on the Ritz.

Whites provided audiences for black entertainers and patronage for some African American artists and writers. Langston Hughes himself enjoyed the support of a wealthy patroness until his work turned political, and then the relationship ended. The questions raised by these relationships continue to be at issue in American life. How separate from or integrated with white society should black culture be? Is there a separate black aesthetic? Is it appropriate or corrupting to address white audiences and accept white patronage? Does success in the arts and entertainment draw energy from the less glamorous struggle for civil rights, political power, and economic opportunity? Participants in the Harlem Renaissance struggled with all these questions, and the debate continues today.

BEFORE YOU READ

1. What was Langston Hughes's attitude toward the era "when the Negro was in vogue"? What did he like about it, and what did he dislike?

2. What, according to Hughes, was it like to be a writer during the Harlem Renaissance?

3. What was the role of A'Lelia Walker in the Harlem Renaissance? Why does Hughes devote so many paragraphs to her activities? Why does her funeral seem important to him?

EXCERPT FROM
"WHEN THE NEGRO WAS IN VOGUE"

The 1920's were the years of Manhattan's black Renaissance. It began with *Shuffle Along, Running Wild,* and the Charleston. Perhaps some people would say even with *The Emperor Jones,* Charles Gilpin, and the tom-toms at the Provincetown. But certainly it was the musical revue, *Shuffle Along,* that gave a scintillating send-off to that Negro vogue in Manhattan, which reached its peak just before the crash of 1929, the crash that sent Negroes, white folks, and all rolling down the hill toward the Works Progress Administration.

Shuffle Along was a honey of a show. Swift, bright, funny, rollicking, and gay, with a dozen danceable, singable tunes. Besides, look who were in it: The now famous choir director, Hall Johnson, and the composer, William Grant Still, were part of the orchestra. Eubie Blake and Noble Sissle wrote the music and played and acted in the show. Miller and Lyles were the comics. Florence Mills skyrocketed to fame in the second act. Trixie Smith sang "He May Be Your Man But He Comes to See Me Sometimes." And Caterina Jarboro, now a European prima donna, and the internationally celebrated Josephine Baker were merely in the chorus. Everybody was in the audience—including me. People came back to see it innumerable times. It was always packed.

To see *Shuffle Along* was the main reason I wanted to go to Columbia. When I saw it, I was thrilled and delighted. From then on I was in the gallery of the Cort Theatre every time I got a chance. That year, too, I saw Katharine Cornell in *A Bill of Divorcement*, Margaret Wycherly in *The Verge*, Maugham's *The Circle* with Mrs. Leslie Carter, and the Theatre Guild production of Kaiser's *From Morn Till Midnight*. But I remember *Shuffle Along* best of all. It gave just the proper push—a pre-Charleston kick—to that Negro vogue of the 20's, that spread to books, African sculpture, music, and dancing.

Put down the 1920's for the rise of Roland Hayes, who packed Carnegie Hall, the rise of Paul Robeson in New York and London, of Florence Mills over two continents, of Rose McClendon in Broadway parts that never measured up to her, the booming voice of Bessie Smith and the low moan of Clara on thousands of records, and the rise of that grand comedienne of song, Ethel Waters, singing: "Charlie's elected now! He's in right for sure!" Put down the 1920's for Louis Armstrong and Gladys Bentley and Josephine Baker.

White people began to come to Harlem in droves. For several years they packed the expensive Cotton Club on Lenox Avenue. But I was never there, because the Cotton Club was a Jim Crow club for gangsters and monied whites. They were not cordial to Negro patronage, unless you were a celebrity like Bojangles. So Harlem Negroes did not like the Cotton Club and never appreciated its Jim Crow policy in the very heart of their dark community. Nor did ordinary Negroes like the growing influx of whites toward Harlem after sundown, flooding the little cabarets and bars where formerly only colored people laughed and sang, and where now the strangers were given the best ringside tables to sit and stare at the Negro customers—like amusing animals in a zoo.

The Negroes said: "We can't go downtown and sit and stare at you in your clubs. You won't even let us in your clubs." But they didn't say it out loud—for Negroes are practically never rude to white people. So thousands of whites came to Harlem night after night, thinking the Negroes loved to have them there, and firmly believing that all Harlemites left their houses at sundown to sing and dance in cabarets, because most of the whites saw nothing but the cabarets, not the houses.

Some of the owners of Harlem clubs, delighted at the flood of white patronage, made the grievous error of barring their own race, after the manner of the famous Cotton Club. But most of these quickly lost business and folded up, because they failed to realize that a large part of the Harlem attraction for downtown New Yorkers lay in simply watching the colored customers amuse themselves. And the smaller clubs, of course, had no big floor shows or a name band like the Cotton Club, where Duke Ellington usually held forth, so, without black patronage, they were not amusing at all.

Some of the small clubs, however, had people like Gladys Bentley, who was something worth discovering in those days, before she got famous, acquired an accompanist, specially written material, and conscious vulgarity. But for two or three amazing years, Miss Bentley sat, and played a big piano all night long, literally all night, without stopping—singing songs like "The St. James Infirmary," from ten in the evening until dawn, with scarcely a break between the notes, sliding from one song to another, with a powerful and continuous underbeat of jungle rhythm. Miss Bentley was an amazing exhibition of musical energy—a large, dark, masculine lady, whose feet pounded the floor while her fingers pounded the keyboard—a perfect piece of African sculpture, animated by her own rhythm.

But when the place where she played became too well known, she began to sing with an accompanist, became a star, moved to a larger place, then downtown, and is now in Hollywood. The old magic of the woman and the piano and the night and the rhythm being one is gone. But everything goes, one way or another. The '20's are gone and lots of fine things in Harlem night life have disappeared like snow in the sun—since it became utterly commercial, planned for the downtown tourist trade, and therefore dull.

The lindy-hoppers at the Savoy even began to practise acrobatic routines, and to do absurd things for the entertainment of the whites, that probably never would have entered their heads to attempt merely for their own effortless amusement. Some of the lindy-hoppers had cards printed with their names on them and became dance professors teaching the tourists. Then Harlem nights became show nights for the Nordics.

Some critics say that that is what happened to certain Negro writers, too—that they ceased to write to amuse themselves and began to write to amuse and entertain white people, and in so doing distorted and over-colored their material, and left out a great many things they thought would offend their American brothers of a lighter complexion. Maybe—since Negroes have writer-racketeers, as has any other race. But I have known almost all of them, and most of the good ones have tried to be honest, write honestly, and express their world as they saw it.

All of us know that the gay and sparkling life of the so-called Negro Renaissance of the '20's was not so gay and sparkling beneath the surface as it looked. Carl Van Vechten, in the character of Byron in *Nigger Heaven*, captured some of the bitterness and frustration of literary Harlem that Wallace Thurman later so effectively poured into his *Infants of the Spring*—the only novel by a Negro about that fantastic period when Harlem was in vogue.

It was a period when, at almost every Harlem upper-crust dance or party, one would be introduced to various distinguished white celebrities there as guests. It was a period when almost any Harlem Negro of any social importance at all would be likely to say casually: "As I was remarking the other day to Heywood—," meaning Heywood Broun. Or: "As I said to George—," referring to George Gershwin. It was a period when local and visiting royalty were not at all uncommon in Harlem. And when the parties of A'Lelia Walker, the Negro heiress, were filled with guests whose names would turn any Nordic social climber green with envy. It was a period when Harold Jackman, a handsome young Harlem school teacher of modest means, calmly announced one day that he was sailing for the Riviera for a fortnight, to attend Princess Murat's yachting party. It was a period when Charleston preachers opened up shouting churches as sideshows for white tourists. It was a period when at least one charming colored chorus girl, amber enough to pass for a Latin American, was living in a pent house, with all her bills paid by a gentleman whose name was banker's magic on Wall Street. It was a period when every season there was at least one hit play on Broadway acted by a Negro cast. And when books by Negro authors were being published with much greater frequency and much more publicity than ever before or since in history. It was a period when white writers wrote about Negroes more successfully (commercially speaking) than Negroes did about themselves. It was the period (God help us!) when Ethel Barrymore appeared in blackface in *Scarlet Sister Mary!* It was the period when the Negro was in vogue.

I was there. I had a swell time while it lasted. But I thought it wouldn't last long. (I remember the vogue for things Russian, the season the Chauve-Souris first came to town.) For how could a large and enthusiastic number of people be crazy about Negroes forever? But some Harlemites thought the millennium had come. They thought the race problem had at last been solved through Art plus Gladys Bentley. They were sure the New Negro would lead a new life from then on in green pastures of tolerance created by Countee Cullen, Ethel Waters, Claude McKay, Duke Ellington, Bojangles, and Alain Locke.

I don't know what made any Negroes think that—except that they were mostly intellectuals doing the thinking. The ordinary Negroes hadn't heard of the Negro Renaissance. And if they had, it hadn't raised their wages any. As for all those white folks in the speakeasies and night clubs of Harlem—well, maybe a colored man could find *some* place to have a drink that the tourists hadn't yet discovered.

EXCERPT FROM "HARLEM LITERATI"

During the summer of 1926, Wallace Thurman, Zora Neale Hurston, Aaron Douglas, John P. Davis, Bruce Nugent, Gwendolyn Bennett, and I decided to publish "a Negro quarterly of the arts" to be called *Fire*—the idea being that it would burn up a lot of the old, dead conventional Negro-white ideas of the past, *épater le bourgeois*[1] into a realization of the existence of the younger Negro writers and artists, and provide us with an outlet for publication not available in the limited pages of the small Negro magazines then existing, the *Crisis, Opportunity*, and the *Messenger*—the first two being house organs of inter-racial organizations, and the latter being God knows what.

Sweltering summer evenings we met to plan *Fire*. Each of the seven of us agreed to give fifty dollars to finance the first issue. Thurman was to edit it, John P. Davis to handle the business end, and Bruce Nugent to take charge of distribution. The rest of us were to serve as an editorial board to collect mater-

---

1. *épater le bourgeois:* shock the middle class (Fr.).

ial, contribute our own work, and act in any useful way that we could. For artists and writers, we got along fine and there were no quarrels. But October came before we were ready to go to press. I had to return to Lincoln, John Davis to Law School at Harvard, Zora Hurston to her studies at Barnard, from whence she went about Harlem with an anthropologist's ruler, measuring heads for Franz Boas.

Only three of the seven had contributed their fifty dollars, but the others faithfully promised to send theirs out of tuition checks, wages, or begging. Thurman went on with the work of preparing the magazine. He got a printer. He planned the layout. It had to be on good paper, he said, worthy of the drawings of Aaron Douglas. It had to have beautiful type, worthy of the first Negro art quarterly. It had to be what we seven young Negroes dreamed our magazine would be—so in the end it cost almost a thousand dollars, and nobody could pay the bills.

I don't know how Thurman persuaded the printer to let us have all the copies to distribute, but he did. I think Alain Locke, among others, signed notes guaranteeing payments. But since Thurman was the only one of the seven of us with a regular job, for the next three or four years his checks were constantly being attached and his income seized to pay for *Fire*. And whenever I sold a poem, mine went there, too—to *Fire*.

None of the older Negro intellectuals would have anything to do with *Fire*. Dr. Du Bois[2] in the *Crisis* roasted it. The Negro press called it all sorts of bad names, largely because of a green and purple story by Bruce Nugent, in the Oscar Wilde tradition, which we had included. Rean Graves, the critic for the *Baltimore Afro-American*, began his review by saying: "I have just tossed the first issue of *Fire* into the fire." Commenting upon various of our contributors, he said: "Aaron Douglas who, in spite of himself and the meaningless grotesqueness of his creations, has gained a reputation as an artist, is permitted to spoil three perfectly good pages and a cover with his pen and ink hudge pudge. Countee Cullen has written a beautiful poem in his 'From a Dark Tower,' but tries his best to obscure the thought in superfluous sentences. Langston Hughes displays his usual ability to say nothing in many words."

So *Fire* had plenty of cold water thrown on it by the colored critics. The white critics (except for an excellent editorial in the *Bookman* for November, 1926) scarcely noticed it at all. We had no way of getting it distributed to bookstands or news stands. Bruce Nugent took it around New York on foot and some of the Greenwich Village bookshops put it on display, and sold it for us. But then Bruce, who had no job, would collect the money and, on account of salary, eat it up before he got back to Harlem.

Finally, irony of ironies, several hundred copies of *Fire* were stored in the basement of an apartment where an actual fire occurred and the bulk of the whole issue was burned up. Even after that Thurman had to go on paying the printer.

---

2. **Dr. Du Bois:** W. E. B. Du Bois, American educator, sociologist, and a founder of the National Association for the Advancement of Colored People.

Now *Fire* is a collector's item, and very difficult to get, being mostly ashes.

That taught me a lesson about little magazines. But since white folks had them, we Negroes thought we could have one, too. But we didn't have the money.

Wallace Thurman laughed a long bitter laugh. He was a strange kind of fellow, who liked to drink gin, but *didn't* like to drink gin; who liked being a Negro, but felt it a great handicap; who adored bohemianism, but thought it wrong to be a bohemian. He liked to waste a lot of time, but he always felt guilty wasting time. He loathed crowds, yet he hated to be alone. He almost always felt bad, yet he didn't write poetry.

Once I told him if I could feel as bad as he did *all* the time, I would surely produce wonderful books. But he said you had to know how to *write*, as well as how to feel bad. I said I didn't have to know how to feel bad, because, every so often, the blues just naturally overtook me, like a blind beggar with an old guitar:

> You don't know,
> You don't know my mind—
> When you see me laughin',
> I'm laughin' to keep from cryin'.

About the future of Negro literature Thurman was very pessimistic. He thought the Negro vogue had made us all too conscious of ourselves, had flattered and spoiled us, and had provided too many easy opportunities for some of us to drink gin and more gin, on which he thought we would always be drunk. With his bitter sense of humor, he called the Harlem literati, the "niggerati."

Of this "niggerati," Zora Neale Hurston was certainly the most amusing. Only to reach a wider audience, need she ever write books—because she is a perfect book of entertainment in herself. In her youth she was always getting scholarships and things from wealthy white people, some of whom simply paid her just to sit around and represent the Negro race for them, she did it in such a racy fashion. She was full of side-splitting anecdotes, humorous tales, and tragicomic stories, remembered out of her life in the South as a daughter of a travelling minister of God. She could make you laugh one minute and cry the next. To many of her white friends, no doubt, she was a perfect "darkie," in the nice meaning they give the term—that is a naïve, childlike, sweet, humorous, and highly colored Negro.

But Miss Hurston was clever, too—a student who didn't let college give her a broad *a* and who had great scorn for all pretensions, academic or otherwise. That is why she was such a fine folk-lore collector, able to go among the people and never act as if she had been to school at all. Almost nobody else could stop the average Harlemite on Lenox Avenue and measure his head with a strange-looking, anthropological device and not get bawled out for the attempt, except Zora, who used to stop anyone whose head looked interesting, and measure it.

When Miss Hurston graduated from Barnard she took an apartment in West 66th Street near the park, in that row of Negro houses there. She moved in with no furniture at all and no money, but in a few days friends had given her everything, from decorative silver birds, perched atop the linen cabinet, down to a footstool. And on Saturday night, to christen the place, she had a *hand*-chicken dinner, since she had forgotten to say she needed forks.

She seemed to know almost everybody in New York. She had been a secretary to Fannie Hurst, and had met dozens of celebrities whose friendships she retained. Yet she was always having terrific ups-and-downs about money. She tells this story on herself, about needing a nickel to go downtown one day and wondering where on earth she would get it. As she approached the subway, she was stopped by a blind beggar holding out his cup.

"Please help the blind! Help the blind! A nickel for the blind!"

"I need money worse than you today," said Miss Hurston, taking five cents out of his cup. "Lend me this! Next time, I'll give it back." And she went on downtown.

Harlem was like a great magnet for the Negro intellectual, pulling him from everywhere. Or perhaps the magnet was New York—but once in New York, he had to live in Harlem, for rooms were hardly to be found elsewhere unless one could pass for white or Mexican or Eurasian and perhaps live in the Village—which always seemed to me a very arty locale, in spite of the many real artists and writers who lived there. Only a few of the New Negroes lived in the Village, Harlem being their real stamping ground.

EXCERPT FROM "PARTIES"

In those days of the late 1920's, there were a great many parties, in Harlem and out, to which various members of the New Negro group were invited. These parties, when given by important Harlemites (or Carl Van Vechten) were reported in full in the society pages of the Harlem press, but best in the sparkling Harlemese of Geraldyn Dismond who wrote for the *Interstate Tattler*. On one of Taylor Gordon's fiestas she reports as follows:

> What a crowd! All classes and colors met face to face, ultra aristocrats, Bourgeois, Communists, Park Avenuers galore, bookers, publishers, Broadway celebs, and Harlemites giving each other the once over. The social revolution was on. And yes, Lady Nancy Cunard was there all in black (she would) with 12 of her grand bracelets. . . . And was the entertainment on the up and up! Into swell dance music was injected African drums that played havoc with blood pressure. Jimmy Daniels sang his gigolo hits. Gus Simons, the Harlem crooner, made the River Stay Away From His Door and Taylor himself brought out everything from "Hot Dog" to "Bravo" when he made high C.

A'Lelia Walker was the then great Harlem party giver, although Mrs. Bernia Austin fell but little behind. And at the Seventh Avenue apartment of Jessie Fauset, literary soirées with much poetry and but little to drink were the order of the day. The same was true of Lillian Alexander's, where the older intellectuals gathered.

A'Lelia Walker, however, big-hearted, night-dark, hair-straightening heiress, made no pretense at being intellectual or exclusive. At her "at homes"

Negro poets and Negro number bankers mingled with downtown poets and seat-on-the-stock-exchange racketeers. Countee Cullen would be there and Witter Bynner, Muriel Draper and Nora Holt, Andy Razaf and Taylor Gordon. And a good time was had by all.

A'Lelia Walker had an apartment that held perhaps a hundred people. She would usually issue several hundred invitations to each party. Unless you went early there was no possible way of getting in. Her parties were as crowded as the New York subway at the rush hour—entrance, lobby, steps, hallway, and apartment a milling crush of guests, with everybody seeming to enjoy the crowding. Once, some royal personage arrived, a Scandinavian prince, I believe, but his equerry saw no way of getting him through the crowded entrance hall and into the party, so word was sent in to A'Lelia Walker that His Highness, the Prince, was waiting without. A'Lelia sent word back that she saw no way of getting His Highness in, either, nor could she herself get out through the crowd to greet him. But she offered to send refreshments downstairs to the Prince's car.

A'Lelia Walker was a gorgeous dark Amazon, in a silver turban. She had a town house in New York (also an apartment where she preferred to live) and a country mansion at Irvington-on-the-Hudson, with pipe organ programs each morning to awaken her guests gently. Her mother made a great fortune from the Madame Walker Hair Straightening Process, which had worked wonders on unruly Negro hair in the early nineteen hundreds—and which continues to work wonders today. The daughter used much of that money for fun. A'Lelia Walker was the joy-goddess of Harlem's 1920's.

She had been very much in love with her first husband, from whom she was divorced. Once at one of her parties she began to cry about him. She retired to her boudoir and wept. Some of her friends went in to comfort her, and found her clutching a memento of their broken romance.

"The only thing I have left that he gave me," she sobbed, "it's all I have left of him!"

It was a gold shoehorn.

When A'Lelia Walker died in 1931, she had a grand funeral. It was by invitation only. But, just as for her parties, a great many more invitations had been issued than the small but exclusive Seventh Avenue funeral parlor could provide for. Hours before the funeral, the street in front of the undertaker's chapel was crowded. The doors were not opened until the cortège arrived—and the cortège was late. When it came, there were almost enough family mourners, attendants, and honorary pallbearers in the procession to fill the room; as well as the representatives of the various Walker beauty parlors throughout the country. And there were still hundreds of friends outside, waving their white, engraved invitations aloft in the vain hope of entering.

Once the last honorary pallbearers had marched in, there was a great crush at the doors. Muriel Draper, Rita Romilly, Mrs. Roy Sheldon, and I were among the fortunate few who achieved an entrance.

We were startled to find De Lawd standing over A'Lelia's casket. It was a truly amazing illusion. At that time *The Green Pastures* was at the height of its fame, and there stood De Lawd in the person of Rev. E. Clayton Powell, a Harlem minister, who looked exactly like Richard B. Harrison in the famous role in the play. He had the same white hair and kind face, and was later offered the part of De Lawd in the film version of the drama. Now, he stood there motionless in the dim light behind the silver casket of A'Lelia Walker.

Soft music played and it was very solemn. When we were seated and the chapel became dead silent, De Lawd said: "The Four Bon Bons will now sing."

A night club quartette that had often performed at A'Lelia's parties arose and sang for her. They sang Noel Coward's "I'll See You Again," and they swung it slightly, as she might have liked it. It was a grand funeral and very much like a party. Mrs. Mary McCleod Bethune[3] spoke in that great deep voice of hers, as only she can speak. She recalled the poor mother of A'Lelia Walker in old clothes, who had labored to bring the gift of beauty to Negro womanhood, and had taught them the care of their skin and their hair, and had built up a great business and a great fortune to the pride and glory of the Negro race—and then had given it all to her daughter, A'Lelia.

Then a poem of mine was read by Edward Perry, "To A'Lelia." And after that the girls from the various Walker beauty shops throughout America brought their flowers and laid them on the bier.

That was really the end of the gay times of the New Negro era in Harlem, the period that had begun to reach its end when the crash came in 1929 and the white people had much less money to spend on themselves, and practically none to spend on Negroes, for the depression brought everybody down a peg or two. And the Negroes had but few pegs to fall.

---

3. **Mary McCleod Bethune:** African American educator.

22

My Fight for Birth Control
Margaret Sanger

Margaret Sanger (1879–1966) was not the first champion of the right to use contraception, but she was an important organizer of the twentieth-century movement to make "birth control"—an expression she coined in 1914—legal and widely available. Her account of the life and death of Sadie Sacks, presented here as written in her autobiography, she told in countless speeches throughout her career. While the incident did not initiate her concern for birth control access or for the plight of poor women, it did fix her decision to focus her work on this issue, as she did for the rest of her life.

In 1873 Congress had passed the Comstock Act, which imposed fines and imprisonment for providing information to another person "for the prevention of conception or procuring of abortion." The state of New York had a similar statute. So virtually all Sanger's activities to further her cause were against the law. Opening a birth control clinic in 1916 was an act of civil disobedience—much like the acts practiced by the civil rights movement half a century later. Sanger, by violating the law, forced changes in it.

While contraception was to remain illegal in some states into the 1960s, this determined reformer brought about a major change. When she began her crusade, middle-class women had informal access to birth control information and devices, but poor women generally did not. By 1921 when she formed the American Birth Control League—which in 1942 would become Planned Parenthood—courts had already begun to allow doctors to disseminate birth control information and devices to married women, and prosecutions under the Comstock Act virtually ceased.

BEFORE YOU READ

1. Is it, as Margaret Sanger wrote at the beginning of this selection, "futile and useless to relieve . . . misery" if you do not get to its root?

2. When she had her revelation after Mrs. Sacks's death, she wrote, "I could now see clearly the various social strata of our life; all its mass problems seemed to be centered around uncontrolled breeding." Do you agree with this? What are the merits and the dangers of such an argument?

3. What was Sanger's motive for opening the birth control clinic in Brooklyn?

Margaret Sanger, *My Fight for Birth Control* (New York: Farrar-Rinehart, 1931), pp. 46–56, 152–60.

[1912]

Early in the year 1912 I came to a sudden realization that my work as a nurse and my activities in social service were entirely palliative and consequently futile and useless to relieve the misery I saw all about me. . . .

Were it possible for me to depict the revolting conditions existing in the homes of some of the women I attended in that one year, one would find it hard to believe. There was at that time, and doubtless is still today, a substratum of men and women whose lives are absolutely untouched by social agencies.

The way they live is almost beyond belief. They hate and fear any prying into their homes or into their lives. They resent being talked to. The women slink in and out of their homes on their way to market like rats from their holes. The men beat their wives sometimes black and blue, but no one interferes. The children are cuffed, kicked and chased about, but woe to the child who dares to tell tales out of the home! Crime or drink is often the source of this secret aloofness, usually there is something to hide, a skeleton in the closet somewhere. The men are sullen, unskilled workers, picking up odd jobs now and then, unemployed usually, sauntering in and out of the house at all hours of the day and night.

The women keep apart from other women in the neighborhood. Often they are suspected of picking a pocket or "lifting" an article when occasion arises. Pregnancy is an almost chronic condition amongst them. I knew one woman who had given birth to eight children with no professional care whatever. The last one was born in the kitchen, witnessed by a son of ten years who, under his mother's direction, cleaned the bed, wrapped the placenta and soiled articles in paper, and threw them out of the window into the court below. . . .

In this atmosphere abortions and birth become the main theme of conversation. On Saturday nights I have seen groups of fifty to one hundred women going into questionable offices well known in the community for cheap abortions. I asked several women what took place there, and they all gave the same reply: a quick examination, a probe inserted into the uterus and turned a few times to disturb the fertilized ovum, and then the woman was sent home. Usually the flow began the next day and often continued four or five weeks. Sometimes an ambulance carried the victim to the hospital for a curetage, and if she returned home at all she was looked upon as a lucky woman.

This state of things became a nightmare with me. There seemed no sense to it all, no reason for such waste of mother life, no right to exhaust women's vitality and to throw them on the scrap-heap before the age of thirty-five.

Everywhere I looked, misery and fear stalked—men fearful of losing their jobs, women fearful that even worse conditions might come upon them. The menace of another pregnancy hung like a sword over the head of every poor woman I came in contact with that year. The question which met me was always the same: What can I do to keep from it? or, What can I do to get out of this? Sometimes they talked among themselves bitterly.

"It's the rich that know the tricks," they'd say, "while we have all the kids." Then, if the women were Roman Catholics, they talked about "Yankee tricks," and asked me if I knew what the Protestants did to keep their families down.

When I said that I didn't believe that the rich knew much more than they did I was laughed at and suspected of holding back information for money. They would nudge each other and say something about paying me before I left the case if I would reveal the "secret." . . .

Finally the thing began to shape itself, to become accumulative during the three weeks I spent in the home of a desperately sick woman living on Grand Street, a lower section of New York's East Side.

Mrs. Sacks was only twenty-eight years old; her husband, an unskilled worker, thirty-two. Three children, aged five, three and one, were none too strong nor sturdy, and it took all the earnings of the father and the ingenuity of the mother to keep them clean, provide them with air and proper food, and give them a chance to grow into decent manhood and womanhood.

Both parents were devoted to these children and to each other. The woman had become pregnant and had taken various drugs and purgatives, as advised by her neighbors. Then, in desperation, she had used some instrument lent to her by a friend. She was found prostrate on the floor amidst the crying children when her husband returned from work. Neighbors advised against the ambulance, and a friendly doctor was called. The husband would not hear of her going to a hospital, and as a little money had been saved in the bank a nurse was called and the battle for that precious life began.

It was in the middle of July. The three-room apartment was turned into a hospital for the dying patient. Never had I worked so fast, never so concentratedly as I did to keep alive that little mother. Neighbor women came and went during the day doing the odds and ends necessary for our comfort. The children were sent to friends and relatives and the doctor and I settled ourselves to outdo the force and power of an outraged nature.

Never had I known such conditions could exist. July's sultry days and nights were melted into a torpid inferno. Day after day, night after night, I slept only in brief snatches, ever too anxious about the condition of that feeble heart bravely carrying on, to stay long from the bedside of the patient. . . .

At the end of two weeks recovery was in sight, and at the end of three weeks I was preparing to leave the fragile patient to take up the ordinary duties of her life, including those of wifehood and motherhood. Everyone was congratulating her on her recovery. All the kindness of sympathetic and understanding neighbors poured in upon her in the shape of convalescent dishes, soups, custards, and drinks. Still she appeared to be despondent and worried. She seemed to sit apart in her thoughts as if she had no part in these congratulatory messages and endearing welcomes. I thought at first that she still retained some of her unconscious memories and dwelt upon them in her silences.

But as the hour for my departure came nearer, her anxiety increased, and finally with trembling voice she said: "Another baby will finish me, I suppose."

"It's too early to talk about that," I said, and resolved that I would turn the question over to the doctor for his advice. When he came I said: "Mrs. Sacks is worried about having another baby."

"She well might be," replied the doctor, and then he stood before her and said: "Any more such capers, young woman, and there will be no need to call me."

"Yes, yes—I know, Doctor," said the patient with trembling voice, "but," and she hesitated as if it took all of her courage to say it, *"what* can I do to prevent getting that way again?"

"Oh ho!" laughed the doctor good naturedly. "You want your cake while you eat it too, do you? Well, it can't be done." Then, familiarly slapping her on the back and picking up his hat and bag to depart, he said: "I'll tell you the only sure thing to do. Tell Jake to sleep on the roof!"

With those words he closed the door and went down the stairs, leaving us both petrified and stunned.

Tears sprang to my eyes, and a lump came in my throat as I looked at that face before me. It was stamped with sheer horror. I thought for a moment she might have gone insane, but she conquered her feelings, whatever they may have been, and turning to me in desperation said: "He can't understand, can he?—he's a man after all—but you do, don't you? You're a woman and you'll tell me the secret and I'll never tell it to a soul."

She clasped her hands as if in prayer, she leaned over and looked straight into my eyes and beseechingly implored me to tell her something—something *I really did not know.* It was like being on a rack and tortured for a crime one had not committed. To plead guilty would stop the agony; otherwise the rack kept turning.

I had to turn away from that imploring face. I could not answer her then. I quieted her as best I could. She saw that I was moved by the tears in my eyes. I promised that I would come back in a few days and tell her what she wanted to know. The few simple means of limiting the family like *coitus interruptus* or the condom were laughed at by the neighboring women when told these were the means used by men in the well-to-do families. That was not believed, and I knew such an answer would be swept aside as useless were I to tell her this at such a time.

A little later when she slept I left the house, and made up my mind that I'd keep away from those cases in the future. I felt helpless to do anything at all. I seemed chained hand and foot, and longed for an earthquake or a volcano to shake the world out of its lethargy into facing these monstrous atrocities.

The intelligent reasoning of the young mother—how to *prevent* getting that way again—how sensible, how just she had been—yes, I promised myself I'd go back and have a long talk with her and tell her more, and perhaps she would not laugh but would believe that those methods were all that were really known.

But time flew past, and weeks rolled into months. That wistful, appealing face haunted me day and night. I could not banish from my mind memories of that trembling voice begging so humbly for knowledge she had a right to have. I was about to retire one night three months later when the telephone rang and an agitated man's voice begged me to come at once to help his wife who was sick again. It was the husband of Mrs. Sacks, and I intuitively knew before I left the telephone that it was almost useless to go.

I dreaded to face that woman. I was tempted to send someone else in my place. I longed for an accident on the subway, or on the street—anything to prevent my going into that home. But on I went just the same. I arrived a few minutes after the doctor, the same one who had given her such noble advice. The woman was dying. She was unconscious. She died within ten minutes after my arrival. It was the same result, the same story told a thousand times before—death from abortion. She had become pregnant, had used drugs, had then consulted a five-dollar professional abortionist, and death followed.

After I left that desolate house I walked and walked and walked; for hours and hours I kept on, bag in hand, thinking, regretting, dreading to stop; fearful of my conscience, dreading to face my own accusing soul. At three in the morning I arrived home still clutching a heavy load the weight of which I was quite unconscious.

I entered the house quietly, as was my custom, and looked out of the window down upon the dimly lighted, sleeping city. . . .

. . . For hours I stood, motionless and tense, expecting something to happen. I watched the lights go out, I saw the darkness gradually give way to the first shimmer of dawn, and then a colorful sky heralded the rise of the sun. I knew a new day had come for me and a new world as well.

It was like an illumination. I could now see clearly the various social strata of our life; all its mass problems seemed to be centered around uncontrolled breeding. There was only one thing to be done: call out, start the alarm, set the heather on fire! Awaken the womanhood of America to free the motherhood of the world! I released from my almost paralyzed hand the nursing bag which unconsciously I had clutched, threw it across the room, tore the uniform from my body, flung it into a corner, and renounced all palliative work forever.

I would never go back again to nurse women's ailing bodies while their miseries were as vast as the stars. I was now finished with superficial cures, with doctors and nurses and social workers who were brought face to face with this overwhelming truth of women's needs and yet turned to pass on the other side. They must be made to see these facts. I resolved that women should have knowledge of contraception. They have every right to know about their own bodies. I would strike out—I would scream from the housetops. I would tell the world what was going on in the lives of these poor women. I *would* be heard. No matter what it should cost. *I would be heard.*

[1916]

The selection of a place for the first birth control clinic was of the greatest importance. No one could actually tell how it would be received in any neighborhood. I thought of all the possible difficulties: The indifference of women's organizations, the ignorance of the workers themselves, the resentment of social agencies, the opposition of the medical profession. Then there was the law—the law of New York State.

Section 1142 was definite. It stated that *no one* could give information to prevent conception to *anyone* for any reason. There was, however, Section 1145, which distinctly stated that physicians *(only)* could give advice to prevent conception for the cure or prevention of disease. I inquired about the section, and was told by two attorneys and several physicians that this clause was an exception to 1142 referring only to venereal disease. But anyway, as I was not a physician, it could not protect me. Dared I risk it?

I began to think of the doctors I knew. Several who had previously promised now refused. I wrote, telephoned, asked friends to ask other friends to help me find a woman doctor to help me demonstrate the need of a birth control clinic in New York. None could be found. No one wanted to go to jail. No one cared to test out the law. Perhaps it would have to be done without a doctor. But it had to be done; that I knew.

Fania Mindell, an enthusiastic young worker in the cause, had come on from Chicago to help me. Together we tramped the streets on that dreary day in early October, through a driving rainstorm, to find the best location at the cheapest terms possible. . . .

Finally at 46 Amboy Street, in the Brownsville section of Brooklyn, we found a friendly landlord with a good place vacant at fifty dollars a month rental; and Brownsville was settled on. It was one of the most thickly populated sections. It had a large population of working-class Jews, always interested in health measures, always tolerant of new ideas, willing to listen and to accept advice whenever the health of mother or children was involved. I knew that here there would at least be no breaking of windows, no hurling of insults into our teeth; but I was scarcely prepared for the popular support, the sympathy and friendly help given us in that neighborhood from that day to this.

With a small bundle of handbills and a large amount of zeal, we fared forth each morning in a house-to-house canvass of the district in which the clinic was located. Every family in that great district received a "dodger" printed in English, Yiddish and Italian. . . .

It was on October 16, 1916, that the three of us—Fania Mindell, Ethel Byrne and myself—opened the doors of the first birth control clinic in America. I believed then and do today, that the opening of those doors to the mothers of Brownsville was an event of social significance in the lives of American womanhood.

News of our work spread like wildfire. Within a few days there was not a darkened tenement, hovel or flat but was brightened by the knowledge that motherhood could be voluntary; that children need not be born into the world unless they are wanted and have a place provided for them. For the first time, women talked openly of this terror of unwanted pregnancy which had haunted their lives since time immemorial. The newspapers, in glaring headlines, used the words "birth control," and carried the message that somewhere in Brooklyn there was a place where contraceptive information could be obtained by all overburdened mothers who wanted it.

Ethel Byrne, who is my sister and a trained nurse, assisted me in advising, explaining, and demonstrating to the women how to prevent conception. As all of our 488 records were confiscated by the detectives who later arrested us for violation of the New York State law, it is difficult to tell exactly how many more women came in those few days to seek advice; but we estimate that it was far more than five hundred. As in any new enterprise, false reports were maliciously spread about the clinic; weird stories without the slightest foundation of truth. We talked plain talk and gave plain facts to the women who came there. We kept a record of every applicant. All were mothers; most of them had large families.

It was whispered about that the police were to raid the place for abortions. We had no fear of that accusation. We were trying to spare mothers the necessity of that ordeal by giving them proper contraceptive information. It was well that so many of the women in the neighborhood knew the truth of our doings. Hundreds of them who had witnessed the facts came to the courtroom afterward, eager to testify in our behalf.

One day a woman by the name of Margaret Whitehurst came to us. She said that she was the mother of two children and that she had not money to support more. Her story was a pitiful one—all lies, of course, but the government acts that way. She asked for our literature and preventives, and received both. Then she triumphantly went to the District Attorney's office and secured a warrant for the arrest of my sister, Mrs. Ethel Byrne, our interpreter, Miss Fania Mindell, and myself.

I refused to close down the clinic, hoping that a court decision would allow us to continue such necessary work. I was to be disappointed. Pressure was brought upon the landlord, and we were dispossessed by the law as a "public nuisance." In Holland the clinics were called "public utilities."

When the policewoman entered the clinic with her squad of plain clothes men and announced the arrest of Miss Mindell and myself (Mrs. Byrne was not present at the time and her arrest followed later), the room was crowded to suffocation with women waiting in the outer room. The police began bullying these mothers, asking them questions, writing down their names in order to subpoena them to testify against us at the trial. These women, always afraid of trouble which the very presence of a policeman signifies, screamed and cried aloud. The children on their laps screamed, too. It was like a panic for a few minutes until I walked into the room where they were stampeding and begged them to be quiet and not to get excited. I assured them that nothing could happen to them, that I was under arrest but they would be allowed to return home in a few minutes. That quieted them. The men were blocking the door to prevent anyone from leaving, but I finally persuaded them to allow these women to return to their homes, unmolested though terribly frightened by it all.

Crowds began to gather outside. A long line of women with baby carriages and children had been waiting to get into the clinic. Now the streets were filled, and police had to see that traffic was not blocked. The patrol wagon came rattling through the streets to our door, and at length Miss Mindell and I took our seats within and were taken to the police station.

23

Down and Out in the Great Depression
Anonymous

President Franklin D. Roosevelt (1882–1945), in his famous "fireside chats," was the first president effectively to use radio to communicate directly to the nation. And Eleanor Roosevelt (1884–1962) was different from all previous first ladies in her public championing of the underdog. Victims of the Great Depression of the 1930s sometimes wrote to the president, to Mrs. Roosevelt, or to various agencies and administrators responsible for carrying out government-sponsored plans for relief. This was largely a new phenomenon in American life. President Hoover employed one secretary to answer mail from the public; the Roosevelt White House needed fifty.

The archives of the New Deal era contain tens of millions of letters from ordinary people expressing their concerns and frequently asking for help. This trove of information about the forgotten men and women of the 1930s reveals attitudes about government, wealth and poverty, opportunity, and patriotism. Unlike many secondary sources for understanding the ways events affected everyday people, these letters are not articles filtered through the perception of an interviewer or memoirs written long after the events.

Robert S. McElvaine, who edited these letters for publication in Down and Out in the Great Depression *(1983), uses them to understand the real experience of unemployment and destitution in the 1930s.*

BEFORE YOU READ

1. What attitudes toward the government were held by the people writing to the Roosevelts? What attitudes about social class do you find in the letters?

2. Can you identify the prejudices these people had? What groups were they prejudiced against, and for what reasons?

3. What can you infer about the successes and failures of the New Deal?

[Oil City, Penn.
December 15, 1930]

Col Arthur Woods
Director, Presidents Committee
Dear Sir:

. . . I have none of these things [that the rich have], what do they care how much we suffer, how much the health of our children is menaced. Now I

Robert S. McElvaine, *Down and Out in the Great Depression: Letters from the "Forgotten Man"* (Chapel Hill: University of North Carolina Press, 1983).

happen to know there is something can be done about it and Oil City needs to be awakened up to that fact and compelled to act.

Now that our income is but $15.60 a week (their are five of us My husband Three little children and myself). My husband who is a world war Veteran and saw active service in the trenches, became desperate and applied for Compensation or a pension from the Government and was turned down and that started me thinking. . . . [There should be] enough to pay all world war veterans a pension, dysabeled or not dysabeled and there by relieve a lot of suffering, and banish resentment that causes Rebellions and Bolshevism. Oh why is it that it is allways a bunch of overley rich, selfish, dumb, ignorant money hogs that persist in being Senitors, legislatures, representitives? Where would they and their possessions be if it were not for the Common Soldier, the common laborer that is compelled to work for a starvation wage. for I tell you again the hog of a Landlord gets his there is not enough left for the necessaries if a man has three or more children. Not so many years ago in Russia all the sufferings of poverty (and you can never feel them you are on the other side of the fence but try to understand) conceived a child, that child was brought forth in agony, and its name was Bolshevism. I am on the other side of the fence from you, you are not in a position to see, but I, I can see and feel and understand. I have lived and suffered too. I know, and right now our good old U.S.A. is sitting on a Seething Volcano. In the Public Schools our little children stand at salute and recite a "rig ma role" in which is mentioned "Justice to all." What a lie, what a naked lie, when honest, law abiding citizens, decendents of Revilutionary heros, Civil War heros, and World war heros are denied the priviledge of owning their own homes, that foundation of good citizenship, good morals, and the very foundation of good government the world over. Is all that our Soldiers of all wars fought bled and died for to be sacrificed to a God awful hideious Rebellion? in which all our Citizens will be involved, because of the dumb bungling of rich politicians? Oh for a few Statesmen, oh for but one statesman, as fearless as Abraham Lincoln, the amancipator who died for us. and who said, you can fool some of the people some of the time, But you can't fool all of the people all of the time. Heres hoping you have read this to the end and think it over. I wish you a Mery Christmas and a Happy New Year.

Very Truly Yours
Mrs. M. E. B

Phila., Pa.
November 26, 1934

Honorable Franklin D. Roosevelt
Washington, D.C.
Dear Mr. President:

I am forced to write to you because we find ourselves in *a very serious condition.* For the last three or four years we have had depression and *suffered* with my *family* and little children *severely*. Now Since the Home Owners Loan Corporation opened up, I have been going there in order to save my home, because there has been unemployment in my house for more than three years. You can imagine that I and my family have suffered from lack of water supply in my house for more than two years. Last winter I did not have coal and the pipes burst in my house and therefore could not make heat in the house. Now winter is here again and we are suffering of cold, no water in the house, and we are facing to be forced out of the house, because I have no money to move or pay so much money as they want when after making settlement I am mother of little children, am sick and losing my health, and we are eight people in the family, and where can I go when I don't have money because no one is working in my house. The Home Loan Corporation wants $42. a month rent or else we will have to be on the street. I am living in this house for about ten years and when times were good we would put our last cent in the house and now I have *no money, no home* and *no wheres to go.* I beg of you to please help me and my family and little children for the sake of a sick mother and suffering family to give this your immediate attention so we will not be forced to move or put out in the street.

Waiting and Hoping that you will act quickly.
Thanking you very much I remain

Mrs. E. L.

Lincoln Nebraska
May 19/ 34

Mrs Franklin D. Roosevelt
Washington, D.C.
Dear Mrs Roosevelt:

Will you be kind enough to read the following as it deals with a very important subject which you are very much interested in as well as my self.

In the Presidents inaugral adress delivered from the capitol steps the afternoon of his inauguration he made mention of The Forgotten Man, and I with thousands of others am wondering if the folk who was borned here in America some 60 or 70 years a go are this Forgotten Man, the President had in mind, if we are this Forgotten Man then we are still Forgotten.

We who have tried to be diligent in our support of this most wonderful nation of ours boath social and other wise, we in our younger days tried to do our duty without complaining.

We have helped to pay pensions to veterans of some thre wars, we have raised the present young generation and have tried to train them to honor and support this our home country.

And now a great calamity has come upon us and seamingly no cause of our own it has swept away what little savings we had accumulated and we are left in a condition that is imposible for us to correct, for two very prominent reasons if no more.

First we have grown to what is termed Old Age, this befalls every man.

Second as we put fourth every effort in our various business lines trying to rectify and reestablish our selves we are confronted on every hand with the young generation, taking our places, this of corse is what we have looked forward to in training our children. But with the extra ordinary crisese which left us helpless and placed us in the position that our fathers did not have to contend with.

Seamingly every body has been assisted but we the Forgotten Man, and since we for 60 years or more have tried to carry the loan without complaining, we have paid others pensions we have educated and trained the youth, now as we are Old and down and out of no reason of our own, would it be asking to much of our Government and the young generation to do by us as we have tried our best to do by them even without complaint.

We have been honorable citizens all along our journey, calamity and old age has forced its self upon us please donot send us to the Poor Farm but instead allow us the small pension of $40.00 per month and we will do as we have done in the past (not complain).

I personly Know of Widows who are no older than I am who own their own homes and draw $45.00 per month pension, these ladies were born this side of the civil war the same as I, therefore they never experianced war trouble.

Please donot think of us who are asking this assitsnce as Old Broken down dishonorable cotizens, but we are of those borned in this country and have done our bit in making this country, we are folk in all walks of life and businesse.

For example I am an architect and builder I am not and old broken down illiterate dishonorable man although I am 69 years old, but as I put forth every effort to regain my prestage in business I am confronted on every side by the young generation taking my place, yes this is also the case even in the effort of the government with its recovery plan, even though I am qualifyed to suprentend any class of construction but the young man has captured this place also.

What are we to do since the calamity has swept our all away,? We are just asking to be remembered with a small part as we have done to others $40,00 a month is all we are asking.

Mrs. Roosevelt I am asking a personal favor of you as it seems to be the only means through which I may be able to reach the President, some evening very soon, as you and Mr. Roosevelt are having dinner together privately will you ask him to read this. And we American citizens will ever remember your kindness.

Yours very truly.
R. A. [male]

[February, 1936]

Mr. and Mrs. Roosevelt.
Wash. D.C.
Dear Mr. President:

I'm a boy of 12 years. I want to tell you about my family. My father hasn't worked for 5 months. He went plenty times to relief, he filled out application. They won't give us anything. I don't know why. Please you do something. We haven't paid 4 months rent, Everyday the landlord rings the door bell, we don't open the door for him. We are afraid that we will be put out, been put out before, and don't want to happen again. We haven't paid the gas bill, and the electric bill, haven't paid grocery bill for 3 months. My brother goes to Lane Tech. High School. he's eighteen years old, hasn't gone to school for 2 weeks because he got no carfare. I have a sister she's twenty years, she can't find work. My father he staying home. All the time he's crying because he can't find work. I told him why are you crying daddy, and daddy said why shouldn't I cry when there is nothing in the house. I feel sorry for him. That night I couldn't sleep. The next morning I wrote this letter to you. in my room. Were American citizens and were born in Chicago, Ill. and I don't know why they don't help us Please answer right away because we need it. will starve Thank you.

    God bless you.

[Anonymous]
Chicago, Ill.

Dec. 14—1937
Columbus, Ind.

Mrs. F. D. Roosevelt,
Washington, D.C.

Mrs. Roosevelt: I suppose from your point of view the work relief, old age pensions, slum clearance and all the rest seems like a perfect remedy for all the ills of this country, but I would like for you to see the results, as the other half see them.

    We have always had a shiftless, never-do-well class of people whose one and only aim in life is to live without work. I have been rubbing elbows with this class for nearly sixty years and have tried to help some of the most promising and have seen others try to help them, but it can't be done. We cannot help those who will not try to help themselves and if they do try a square deal is all they need, and by the way that is all this country needs or ever has needed: a square deal for all and then, let each one paddle their own canoe, or sink.

    There has never been any necessity for any one who is able to work, being on relief in this locality, but there have been many eating the bread of charity and they have lived better than ever before. I have had taxpayers tell me that their children came from school and asked why they couldn't have nice lunches like the children on relief.

    The women and children around here have had to work at the fields to help save the crops and several women fainted while at work and at the same time we couldn't go up or down the road without stumbling over some of the reliefers, moping around carrying dirt from one side of the road to the other and back again, or else asleep. I live alone on a farm and have not raised any crops for the last two years as there was no help to be had. I am feeding the stock and have been cutting the wood to keep my home fires burning. There are several reliefers around here now who have been kicked off relief, but they refuse to work unless they can get relief hours and wages, but they are so worthless no one can afford to hire them.

As for the clearance of the real slums, it can't be done as long as their inhabitants are allowed to reproduce their kind. I would like for you to see what a family of that class can do to a decent house in a short time. Such a family moved into an almost new, neat, four-room house near here last winter. They even cut down some of the shade trees for fuel, after they had burned everything they could pry loose. There were two big idle boys in the family and they could get all the fuel they wanted, just for the cutting, but the shade trees were closer and it was taking a great amount of fuel, for they had broken out several windows and they had but very little bedding. There were two women there all the time and three part of the time and there was enough good clothing tramped in the mud around the yard to have made all the bedclothes they needed. It was clothing that had been given them and they had worn it until it was too filthy to wear any longer without washing, so they threw it out and begged more. I will not try to describe their filth for you would not believe me. They paid no rent while there and left between two suns owing everyone from whom they could get a nickels worth of anything. They are just a fair sample of the class of people on whom so much of our hard earned tax-money is being squandered and on whom so much sympathy is being wasted.

As for the old people on beggars' allowances: the taxpayers have provided homes for all the old people who never liked to work, where they will be neither cold nor hungry: much better homes than most of them have ever tried to provide for themselves. They have lived many years through the most prosperous times of our country and had an opportunity to prepare for old age, but they spent their lives in idleness or worse and now they expect those who have worked like slaves, to provide a living for them and all their worthless descendants. Some of them are asking for from thirty to sixty dollars a month when I have known them to live on a dollar a week rather than go to work. There is many a little child doing without butter on its bread, so that some old sot can have his booze and tobacco: some old sot who spent his working years loafing around pool rooms and saloons, boasting that the world owed him a living.

Even the child welfare has become a racket. The parents of large families are getting divorces, so that the mothers and children can qualify for aid. The children to join the ranks of the "unemployed" as they grow up, for no child that has been raised on charity in this community has ever amounted to anything.

You people who have plenty of this worlds goods and whose money comes easy, have no idea of the heart-breaking toil and self-denial which is the lot of the working people who are trying to make an honest living, and then to have to shoulder all these unjust burdens seems like the last straw. During the worst of the depression many of the farmers had to deny their families butter, eggs, meat etc. and sell it to pay their taxes and then had to stand by and see the deadbeats carry it home to their families by the arm load, and they knew their tax money was helping pay for it. One woman saw a man carry out eight pounds of butter at one time. The crookedness, selfishness, greed and graft of the crooked politicians is making one gigantic racket out of the new deal and it is making this a nation of dead-beats and beggars and if it continues the people who will work will soon be nothing but slaves for the pampered poverty rats and I am afraid these human parasites are going to become a menace to the country unless they are disfranchised. No one should have the right to vote theirself a living at the expense of the tax payers. They learned their strength at the last election and also learned that they can get just about what they want by "voting right." They have had a taste of their coveted life of idleness, and at the rate they are increasing, they will soon control the country. The twentieth child arrived in the home of one chronic reliefer near here some time ago.

Is it any wonder the taxpayers are discouraged by all this penalizing of thrift and industry to reward shiftlessness, or that the whole country is on the brink of chaos?

M. A. H. [female]
Columbus, Ind.

[no address]
Jan. 18, 1937

[Dear Mrs. Roosevelt:]

I . . . was simply astounded to think that anyone could be nitwit enough to wish to be included in the so called social security act if they could possibly avoid it. Call it by any name you wish it, in my opinion, (and that of many people I know) is nothing but downright stealing. . . .

Personally, I had my savings so invested that I would have had a satisfactory provision for old age. Now thanks to his [F.D.R.'s] desire to "get" the utilities I cannot be sure of anything, being a stockholder, as after business has survived his merciless attacks (*if* it does) insurance will probably be no good either.

[She goes on to complain about the lack of profits.]

Then the president tells them they should hire more men and work shorter hours so that the laborers, who are getting everything now raises etc. can have a "more abundant life." That simply means taking it from the rest of us in the form of taxes or otherwise. . . .

Believe me, the only thing we want from the president, unless or if you except Communists and the newly trained chiselers, is for him to balance the budget and reduce taxes. That, by the way, is a "mandate from the people" that isn't getting much attention.

I am not an "economic royalist," just an ordinary white collar worker at $1600 per. Please show this to the president and ask him to remember the wishes of the forgotten man, that is, the one who dared to vote against him. We expect to be tramped on but we do wish the stepping would be a little less hard.

Security at the price of freedom is never desired by intelligent people.

M. A. [female]

[Mr. Harry Hopkins
Washington, D.C.]
[Dear Mr. Hopkins:]

Will you please investigate the various relief agencies in many cities of the United States. The cities where there are a large foreign and jewish population. No wonder the cities are now on the verge of bankruptcy because we are feeding a lot of ignorant foreigners by giving them relief. And, they are turning against us every day. I would suggest to deport all foreigners and jews who are not citizens over the United States back to any land where they choose to go and who will admit them. As America is now over crowded with too much immigration and it can not feed even its own citizens without feeding the citizens of other foreign nations. I have found out after careful investigation that we are feeding many foreigners who send out their wives to work and who have money in the bank. While the men drink wine and play cards in saloons and cafes. I have spoken to one Italian whom I met. And I ask him what he was doing for a living. He said me drinka da dago red wine and play cards and send the wife out to work. Isn't a very good thing for us to support them. No wonder the taxpayers are grumbling about taxes. Most of them are a race of black hands murders boot leggers bomb throwers. While most of the sheeney jews as they are called are a race of dishonest people who get rich by swindling, faking and cheating the poor people. Besides the jews are responsible by ruining others in business by the great amount of chisling done. And selling even below the cost prices, in order to get all the others business. The foreigners and jews spend as little as they can to help this country. And, they live as cheap as they can. And, work as cheap as they can, and save all the money they can. And when they have enough they go back to their country. Why don't we deport them under the section of the United States Immigration Laws which relates to paupers and those who become a public charge. The Communist Party is composed mostly by foreigners and jews. The jews are the leaders of the movement and urge the downfall of this government. . . .

A Taxpayer

24

The Sit-Down Strikes
Henry Kraus

While the New Deal's reform efforts began to wane after a flurry of legislation in 1935 known as the second hundred days, organized labor's drive in 1936 and 1937 toward national organization levied a powerful tool that both gave the New Deal an institutional base and solidified opposition to it. Labor's new weapon was the sit-down strike.

Early in 1936, the Firestone Rubber Company of Akron, Ohio, fired several unionists for organizing against a proposed wage cut. In defense of their sacked union brothers, workers remained after their work shifts to occupy the factory. Within just two days Firestone gave in. When a similar situation occurred across town at Goodyear, the police deputized 150 strikebreakers to help clear the factory. There they were met by thousands of angry workers from all over Akron. Goodyear, too, surrendered, and the new strategy spread across the nation. Over five hundred sit-downs occurred between 1936 and 1937, achieving more success for unionization in a year than labor had accomplished in decades.

Why did the sit-down strike work? Businessmen were fearful of having equipment dashed along with their hopes of industrial recovery. And the new strategy prevented management from hiring nonunion "scab" workers to replace strikers. Both federal and state governments no longer expected public support for the use of force that had once been their response to labor militancy. So industry after industry yielded to the workers' new aggressiveness. In 1936, before the sit-downs began, scarcely four million workers had belonged to unions. By the end of 1937 the figure was over seven million. The nation entered World War II with over eleven million workers organized.

The most famous sit-down occurred in December 1936 at General Motors' Fisher Body Plant in Flint, Michigan, in response to the firing of two union members. The account of the "Battle of Bull's Run" ("bull" was then current slang for a policeman) excerpted here was written by Henry Kraus, an official of the United Auto Workers who edited the Flint union newspaper and was one of the leaders of the sit-in.

BEFORE YOU READ

1. What was the strategy of the union during the sit-down strike at the Fisher Body Plant? On what support did the workers rely?

2. What was management's strategy for removing strikers from the factory?

3. Why did the sit-down strike succeed?

Henry Kraus, *The Many and the Few: A Chronicle of the Dynamic Auto Workers*, 2nd ed. (Los Angeles: Plantin Press, 1947), pp. 125–42.

BATTLE OF BULL'S RUN

The corporation needed violence. Far more than would have been true in a normal strike it had to produce a situation that would destroy the eminently peaceful and decent impression of the sitdown. . . . An attack on the great Fisher One plant with its hundreds of defenders was out of the question. But in [Flint's] other sitdown plant—Fisher Two—a Pinkerton spy who was among the original strikers had come out to report to the corporation that there were no more than a hundred men in occupation. This plant would be an easy objective.

The Fisher Two factory, located about two miles northwest of Fisher One, was actually a part of the great Chevrolet group. It was by no means a key plant, however—nothing like Fisher One, for example—for there were a dozen others like it assembling Chevrolet bodies in scattered places throughout the country. Hence to recapture this plant would mean little to the corporation in a practical way. But psychologically—it would mean much. And even if the attempt were unsuccessful the resulting violence would lay the basis for the calling of the National Guard. . . .

At noon on January 11th, 200 Flint businessmen met in the Adams Room of the Durant Hotel to talk over the strike crisis. George Boysen, the head of the Flint Alliance, was the feted guest. "Flint is confronted by a movement that is vicious," he warned. "They have taken possession of the plants and the same thing is liable to happen in your business. If they once get Flint, if they succeed in making Flint helpless, then we're all through."

It was a sort of moral preparation for what was to follow later in the day. Immediately after the luncheon, City Manager Barringer and Harry Gault, a General Motors attorney, got together with a few carefully selected men. And simultaneously things began to happen at Fisher Two that led to the strike's most exciting evening.

First the union transporters carrying "dinner" to the Fisher Two men were stopped at the gate by the plant guards. It was the first time anything like this had occurred. . . .

Of course the men had no intention of getting out. The outside pickets got a 24-foot ladder, placed it along the side of the building and the food was run up that way. It was only a momentary victory, however, for . . . soon after, in fact, probably following hurried consultation with the city hall, the plant guards . . . overcame the small picket group defending the ladder and confiscated it.

Then other things began to happen. The plant heat was shut off. And next all traffic approaches to the factory were closed by the police while owners of parked cars within the immediate area were told to remove them. Thoroughly aroused by these moves, the union hastened all available pickets to the plant as well as the sound car which was directed unobserved right through the police cordon over a small unpaved road by a Chevrolet worker.

It was clear that the sitdowners must immediately gain possession of the gate. . . . Twenty Fisher Two men were selected, armed with plant-made billies, to do the job. . . . The rest of the men clustered around the stair-head listening. The exchange of words was brief.

"I want the key to the gate," the squad captain snapped.

"My orders are to give it to nobody," the chief of the company police replied.

"Well, we want that door opened," Manley said. "We've got to get food in here."

The men hesitated a moment. Then they took a firmer grip on their clubs and moved toward the gate.

"Get the hell out of there!" they warned and the guards sided away with alacrity. They disappeared before anyone could notice where they went. Actually they hurried to the ladies' restroom and locked themselves into it while their captain got to a phone and called police headquarters to report—in keeping with the blueprint—that the company guards had been "captured" and were being held prisoner by the strikers.

Meanwhile the sitdowners' special squad approached the locked doors at the gate, put their shoulders to them, and pressed. There was a sound of ripping wood and the doors flew open. The men ran out and a great cheer went up from the pickets. . . .

But while the strikers and their sympathizers were celebrating in this manner things were taking place at police headquarters. As soon as word was received that the Fisher Two men had "acted" in response to the shutting off of the food supply, [Police] Capt. [Edwin H.] Hughes immediately phoned Sheriff Wolcott with the pre-arranged news that the strikers had "kidnapped" the company guards and that there was violence at the plant.

The sheriff hadn't the slightest notion of what was up. . . . On the road he was passed by several speeding police cars and before his own auto had a chance to turn around at the plant and park, he found himself in the midst of a confusion of activity. . . .

And several squad cars, sirens screaming, headed from north and south on Chevrolet Avenue, came to shrieking stops in front of the plant. Instantly a dozen heavily caparisoned men looking like some sort of monstrous prehistoric beetles piled out of the cars and came running toward the main gate, pulling their gas helmets over their faces as they ran. Several gas grenades exploded in the picket line, forcing the picketers to break and dash for safety. At the first alarm, however, the insiders who had been mingling with them had scrambled back to the plant, slammed the doors shut and barred them. The police were there that moment. One of them smashed a pane and inserting his gas gun shot a shell inside.

Meanwhile the sound car had remained temporarily disregarded by the attackers as the riot squad opened the attack. Vic Reuther began shouting over the mike:

"Pickets, back to your posts! Men in the plant, get your fire hose going!"

The wind was from the north, causing the gas that was sent into the picket line to be blown directly back toward the cops—a lucky detail. The pickets themselves had gone but a short distance off, looking about for things to throw. They had been only temporarily discomfited by the gas attack. . . . With whatever they could find these men began to heave, running in closer all the time.

There had been some women and children among the pickets also. The women ran off to deposit their kids in a nearby restaurant and were soon back. Inside, meanwhile, the sitdowners had recovered quickly, unwinding a fire hose and dragging it toward the door. It was a little short but the strikers let fly anyway, blowing the cops back with the force of the stream. The men upstairs had another hose poked through a window and playing on the police outside while two-pound car door hinges began raining down. All this occurred within five minutes or less and now suddenly the officers, several of them drenched through and through, began to retreat unceremoniously toward the Flint River bridge out of range of the water and the hinges.

The sitdowners and pickets yelled in wild triumph. The men on the ground floor hauled out cases of empty [glass] milk and pop bottles for the pickets to use in case of another attack and the boys upstairs dumped quantities of hinges onto the sidewalk for them. Thus the second coming of the police found the plant's defenders completely prepared. The second assault group was several times larger than the first. These men were not masked and besides their clubs were merely armed with gas grenades which they sought to hurl through the upper windows with the object of forcing the sitdowners back from their vantage points. But the men inside would seize these with a gloved hand and quickly douse them in a pail of water which had been brought out for the purpose.

Very few of the police got very close to the building at all this time as they were met by a thick barrage of popular ammunition. . . .

The strikers once more shouted exultantly as the police took to their heels again, this time with the pickets close behind them. Several of the hard-pressed officers drew their pistols as they ran and discharged them indiscriminately into the ranks of their pursuers. The strikers began to fall. Those near them would stop to carry them back but the others kept on, swept forward by the emotion of battle. They came upon the sheriff's car with the sheriff and several deputies still in it. They seized hold of it, rocked it several times and then gave it a big heave and crashed it over on its side. The corpulent old fellow had all he could do to crawl, grunting and whewing, out of the auto but just as he had righted himself on the pavement a hinge came sailing and glanced his temple. . . .

The rout was complete. The police stopped on the bridge about fifty yards south of the plant. Angered by their crushing repulse those in charge began to distribute rifles to the officers. But at this point the sheriff, though incensed at his own reception, interceded.

"There's going to be no shooting here!" he told Chief Wills. "I'm the leading law enforcement officer in the county during any trouble and those are my orders."

The guns were put back.

Nevertheless, soon after one of the men on the low roof suddenly grabbed his side and exclaimed:

"I've been shot."

The boys carried him inside, took his trousers down, and sure enough there was the bullet wound in his hip. Then another chap came in—he'd been hit in the shoulder. And soon the bullets came peppering, splattering against the building and dinging through the windows. Some of this shooting came from the Chevrolet No. 2 side of the street, where police and guards could be seen behind the dark windows. . . .

Vic Reuther, Bill Carney (of the United Rubber Workers) and other organizers had taken turns at the mike [in the sound car] all through the fighting, shouting encouragement and directions to the pickets. Once a woman picket grabbed the mike and hysterically castigated the police: "Cowards! Cowards! Shooting unarmed and defenseless men!" Often the metallic voice coming over the loudspeaker sounded like an unintelligible garble in the noise and commotion but to the fighting men and women its mere presence was an extraordinary support. Though a large group of guards ringed the precious instrument, several times a gas bomb would lodge under the car and the fumes seeping through the floorboard would half-suffocate the inmates. But they never gave up their crucial posts.

Ambulances had meanwhile arrived and the wounded men were carried off. . . . Fourteen of our men had bullet wounds, mostly buckshot, while only one was critically hit. . . . A dozen police and sheriff's deputies were also treated at the hospital for head and other body injuries, the results of well-aimed strikers' brickbats. . . .

Large crowds of onlookers had witnessed the entire battle, standing somewhat beyond the clusters of police on both ends of the street. Despite rumors of a mobilization by the Flint Alliance none of these civilians engaged in the fighting on the side of the attackers. On the contrary, they were clearly sympathetic to the strikers and as those in the sound car directed a steady appeal to them to join the pickets many began coming over.

The police grew fearful of being caught between the several groups of watchers and pickets, particularly as the former began to express more and more openly their sympathy for the strikers. The officers sought to drive them off by shooting gas shells into their midst but the crowds merely jeered, spread out temporarily to allow the gas to thin out and then returned. One heroic policeman sent a shell crashing through the window of the restaurant near the north end of the plant where reporters and spectators had gathered to warm themselves.

At the other end of the factory, as the police slowly retreated up long Chevrolet hill which started at the Flint River bridge, they drove the spectators before them. About half-way up they halted and continued from this point to shoot down into the hollow at the sound car and pickets, now and then turning to explode a shell in the direction of the crowding onlookers. But through it all the voice of the sound car could be heard though several hundred yards away, alternately rising above the turmoil of the exploding guns and sounding like the very soul of courage:

> The corporation has charged the sitdowners with disregard for property. But it is General Motors who tonight through their city police have destroyed property. All during these days the Fisher Body workers have been sitting down peacefully, protecting their jobs; yes, and religiously guarding the machines at which they earn their livelihood. Not a scratch has marred a single object inside the plant until tonight when the police shot their gas and bullets

into it in a cowardly attack upon these unarmed and peaceful men. What could they do but defend themselves as best they could? They must now fight not only for their jobs but for their very lives. Let General Motors be warned, however, the patience of these men is not inexhaustible. If there is further bloodshed here tonight we shall not be responsible for what the workers do in their rage! There are costly machines in that plant. Let the corporation and their thugs remember that!

The brave words coming out of the war-scarred hollow dramatized for the crowds of onlookers the workers' own sense of their struggle, their knowledge of the odds they were fighting against, their dangerous state of siege even in the midst of victory. . . .

As things quieted down everybody got busy making preparations for an all-night vigil. It was considered certain that the police would attack again as soon as they had received a new supply of gas. Reporters told us that the Detroit and Saginaw departments had been contacted for this purpose. (Fortunately for the strikers, there was nothing available from these sources.) We built barricades in the street at both ends of the plant by shoving abandoned cars abreast each other. Meanwhile the cops looked on almost disinterestedly from up the hill. I had taken charge of this work when Gene Richards, another of the Buick boys who had engaged in the night's fighting, protested this use of other people's cars without their permission.

"I don't think that's right," he said. "After all, the owners might object."

"Object!" I shouted melodramatically. "Brother, this is war!"

The street is front of the plant looked like "No Man's Land." It was littered with broken glass, bottles, rocks, hinges. The water blown from the fire hoses had frozen over (the temperature ran around 16 degrees that night), forming a sheet of ice from sidewalk to sidewalk. A heavy aura of gas kept eyes tearing for hours after hostilities had ceased. Inside the plant the ground floor was covered by an inch-deep pool of water. The hose lay uncoiled ready for use. The strikers had taken over the cafeteria and were already setting up their kitchen there despite the heavy tincture of gas prevailing. The room adjoining was appropriated by the strike committee. Upstairs the strikers showed reporters and photographers around, pointing out bullet holes in the windows and walls and posing for pictures. Everyone went about heavily armed and weighted down with throwing material. . . .

The night grew steadily colder and the pickets and strike sympathizers began to fall away rapidly. The crowds in the street had finally dispersed and only a knot of police remained on the hill, stamping in the cold, waiting. A reconnaissance tour of the plant showed an alarmingly small number of men remaining. The upstairs was deserted; downstairs there was only a tiny group in the cafeteria keeping warm. Evidently many of the sitdowners had slipped home for the night, seizing the first opportunity in two weeks to do so. The next day they returned with a multiplied force but this night the plant that had been defended so gallantly was almost abandoned through overconfidence and neglect.

Advertising in the 1920s

Since Volney Palmer opened the first advertising agency in 1841 in Philadelphia, Americans have had a love-hate relationship with advertising. Advertisements are attacked for appealing to our fears and anxieties, imposing arbitrary and impossible-to-attain standards of beauty, fitness, personal hygiene, and affluence, and promoting stereotypical attributes of gender, race, and class. Yet they also help us define our identities by influencing our decisions about the music we listen to, the clothing we buy, the cars we drive, and the places we vacation. There is rarely a day when we do not hear a sales pitch, watch an ad, or read a corporate logo; museums, parks, schools, and many sports and entertainment venues carry the names of corporate sponsors.

Much of the contemporary dominance of advertising originated in the 1920s, when mass production of consumer goods and the growing affluence of the post–World War I era led to national distribution networks and increased competition among rapidly growing corporations like Coca-Cola, Palmolive, and Ford. During this golden age of advertising, companies across the country began to compete for the best artists, writers, and musicians, whom they lured with the promise of regular paychecks and mass recognition for their work. Advertisements in newspapers and magazines, on billboards, and on the radio flooded into every nook and cranny of the built environment. This remarkable rise of advertising as mass communication is reflected in paintings of the period by famous American artists such as Reginald Marsh and Edward Hopper. For these artists, the signs, billboards, and product logos of advertising provided the backdrop and culturescape for visual explorations of the inner worlds of Americans facing the alienation of modernity.

Hated around the world for its sometimes compelling beauty, unapologetic crassness, and power to influence the subconscious, American advertising remains both the best and the worst of U.S. popular culture. The following ads from the 1920s and 1930s are examples of the ways in which advertising has long exploited desires and insecurities.

Right: Plate 1. Listerine advertisement, *Ladies Home Journal,* April 1922

Far right: Plate 2. Palmolive Soap advertisement, *Ladies Home Journal,* January 1922

The advertisements in Plates 1 and 2 use a combination of images and text. In the Listerine ad, a modern young woman approaches her "tragic" thirtieth birthday still single. The problem is "halitosis." Even if the manufacturers of Listerine did not invent this affliction, they certainly popularized it. The ad's presentation has a semi-scientific quality, discussing bad breath as a medical problem that can be treated successfully with Listerine, a "well-known liquid antiseptic." The Palmolive ad in Plate 2 includes images of an attractive young woman looking unhappy and forlorn and an exotic figure bringing beauty secrets from ancient Egypt. The lengthy text teaches readers about skin care. Both advertisements demonstrate how marketing transformed ordinary products into daily necessities; the ads sell by appealing to concerns about attractiveness. How do you account for the poor product placement in the Listerine ad? Is the ad addressed to men or to women? How does each product claim to bring happiness to its consumers? How does each ad shape the public image of the product it is selling?

Often a bridesmaid but never a bride

THE case of Geraldine Proctor was really pathetic. Most of the girls in her set were married, or about to be. Yet not one of them possessed more grace or charm or beauty than she.

And as Miss Proctor's birthdays crept gradually toward that tragic thirty-mark, marriage seemed farther away from her life than ever.

She was often a bridesmaid but never a bride.

* * *

Your mirror can't tell you when your breath is not right. And even your most intimate friends probably won't.

That's the insidious thing about halitosis (the medical term for unpleasant breath). Halitosis creeps upon you unawares. You may even have it for years without knowing so yourself.

That of course is when halitosis is a symptom of some deep-seated organic trouble a doctor must correct. Or maybe a dentist.

But so commonly halitosis is rather a temporary or local condition that will yield to more simple treatment.

Listerine, the well-known liquid antiseptic, possesses wonderful properties as a mouth deodorant. When regularly used, it arrests food fermentation and leaves the breath sweet, fresh and clean.

As such it becomes an indispensable friend to people who wish to enjoy the comfortable assurance that their breath is always beyond reproach.

Listerine will put you on the safe and polite side. Provide yourself with a bottle today and use it regularly as a gargle and mouth wash.

Your druggist has handled Listerine for years, and regards it as a safe, effective antiseptic of great merit.

Start using Listerine today. Don't be in doubt another day about your breath—Lambert Pharmacal Company, Saint Louis, Mo.

For HALITOSIS *use* LISTERINE

This Beauty
Every Girl Can Have

The charm of a fresh, schoolgirl complexion depends more on care than Nature

MANY a girl would be considered pretty if she would only remedy those defects of complexion which so greatly detract from charm. Too often she doesn't realize that a dull, lifeless, sallow skin is fatal to beauty. And that blotches and blackheads affect her popularity and prevent the attention and admiration which every girl craves.

There is no need to have such a complexion—improving it is easy. A little time and care each day will quickly be repaid with becoming freshness, smoothness and fine texture.

What every complexion needs

Thorough cleansing once a day with fine, mild soap on whose soothing properties you can rely. Most women will tell you that this soap is Palmolive.

Massage the profuse, creamy lather well into the pores so that every trace of oil, dirt and perspiration is removed.

Don't be afraid to be thorough—the mild, gentle Palmolive lather soothes while it cleanses. The result is a skin healthfully cleansed from the accumulations which are the original cause of most disfigured skins.

What neglect does

When you fail to cleanse your face thoroughly once a day this is what happens:

The network of pores which compose the surface of the skin becomes clogged with dirt and oil. The pores collect powder and accumulate excess cold cream.

This clogging causes enlargement—your once fine skin becomes coarse. You have blackheads and ugly blotches. Your complexion is dull and sallow.

The day you begin to cleanse with the soothing Palmolive lather you notice decided improvement. Each succeeding day rewards you with a fresher, finer skin.

The safe facial soap

Palmolive is the modern scientific blend of rare oriental oils, famous for 3,000 years as cosmetics. Olive oil contributes softening, relaxing qualities. Richness and body are due to palm oil.

The smooth, creamy Palmolive lather soothes while it cleanses, leaving the skin velvet smooth.

Volume and Efficiency enable us to sell 25c quality for

10c

There is no danger of irritation—the most sensitive skin thrives when cleansed with Palmolive.

Let it do for your body what it does for your face

Because the skin of the face is burned by the sun, roughened and chapped by the wind and made sensitive by temperature changes, the greatest care must be observed in its cleansing. It must be with soap, but such fine, mild soap that the skin is soothed and healed. Such soap is Palmolive, blended from palm and olive oils.

Use Palmolive for bathing, and the dry, rough, itching condition doctors call winter itch will be greatly relieved. It is caused by living in moistureless rooms and bathing with drying soap. The combination exhausts the natural oil supply which lubricates the skin.

Bathe with Palmolive and you remove one cause of discomfort and help the other. The mild lather softens the skin, lessens the dryness and soothes the itching. If you value comfort in cold weather, bathe with Palmolive and let it keep the skin of your body as smooth as your face.

All for 10 cents

If made in small quantity Palmolive would cost at least 25 cents a cake. It is volume that lowers price. Popularity keeps the Palmolive factories working day and night. It compels the importation of the costly oils in vast quantity.

Result, the finest, mildest soap which can be produced at a price which all can afford for every toilet purpose.

THE PALMOLIVE COMPANY
Milwaukee, U. S. A.
THE PALMOLIVE COMPANY OF CANADA, Limited
Toronto, Ont.

Copyright 1921, The Palmolive Company   1418

A Delightful Test

To bring you prettier teeth

This offers you a ten-day test which will be a revelation to you. It will show you the way to whiter, cleaner, safer teeth.

Millions of people of some forty races now employ this method. Leading dentists everywhere advise it. Now you should learn how much it means to you and yours.

Clouded by a film

Your teeth are clouded more or less by film. The fresh film is viscous—you can feel it with your tongue. It clings to teeth, enters crevices and stays. And it forms the basis of dingy coats.

The film absorbs stains, so the teeth look discolored. Film is the basis of tartar. These coats, more or less discolored, spoil the luster of the teeth.

How it ruins teeth

That film holds food substance which ferments and forms acids. It holds the acids in contact with the teeth to cause decay.

Millions of germs breed in it. They are the chief cause of many troubles, local and internal. So most tooth troubles are now traced to that film, and they are almost universal.

Now we combat it

Dental science, after long research, has found two film combatants. Many careful tests have proved their efficiency. Modern authorities endorse them. Leading dentists everywhere urge their daily use.

A new-day tooth paste has been created, called Pepsodent. It complies with modern requirements. And these two great film combatants are embodied in it.

Two other effects

Pepsodent brings two other effects which authority now deems essential. It multiplies the starch digestant in the saliva. That is there to digest starch deposits which may otherwise remain to form acids.

It multiplies the alkalinity of the saliva. That is Nature's neutralizer for acids which cause decay.

An ideal diet, rich in acid-bearing fruit, would bring like effects. But Pepsodent brings them regularly.

Send the coupon for a 10-Day Tube and watch these effects for a while. Note how clean the teeth feel after using. Mark the absence of the viscous film. See how teeth whiten as the film-coats disappear.

Then judge the benefits by what you see and feel. You will be amazed.

Pepsodent
REG. U.S. · PAT. OFF.

The New-Day Dentifrice

Endorsed by modern authorities and now advised by leading dentists nearly all the world over. All druggists supply the large tubes.

10-Day Tube Free 822

THE PEPSODENT COMPANY,
Dept. 724, 1104 S. Wabash Ave., Chicago, Ill.
Mail 10-day tube of Pepsodent to

ONLY ONE TUBE TO A FAMILY

Left: Plate 3. Pepsodent advertisement, *Ladies Home Journal,* April 1922

Right: Plate 4. Colgate's advertisement, *Ladies Home Journal,* April 1934

Plates 3 and 4 show medical science being used again to market a personal hygiene product: toothpaste. In Plate 3 the text emphasizes the advances of dental science, the approval of modern authorities, and the physiological problems that the product addresses. Health problems caused by tooth decay and mouth-related germs can easily be defeated by twice-a-day applications of Pepsodent. Twelve years later Colgate ran the ad in Plate 4, which promises marital bliss and makes scientific claims about its product. The text narrates the story of a husband with roving eyes brought home to his wife when she recaptures her bright, gorgeous smile through the use of Colgate's Ribbon Dental Cream. Colgate's succeeds where other dental creams fail because of its technological innovativeness: it combines polishing action with emulsive action. What are the major differences between these two ads? Which product is based more on scientific research? Explain.

Plates 5 and 6 highlight the public's interest in technology in the 1920s. The name Edison epitomizes early-twentieth-century science, and the ad in Plate 5 boldly displays that name with an image of a frightened child comforted by modern technology. The text provides the setting—"a big strange house full of big strange sounds." The product is "the most perfect which Science has thus developed" and is sold by merchants possessing "accurate standards from which to prescribe *just the right lamp* for every room and every sort of fixture." What quality of life is General Electric selling in this ad? Technology reaches the heart of the family in the Magnavox ad in Plate 6. A fashionable family sits around the Thanksgiving table; a young couple dances in the background. Magnavox is selling not only entertainment and information but also a certain style of living—sophisticated, prosperous, and up-to-date. Is Magnavox selling its radios as "high culture" or "popular culture"? Why does this ad try to link Magnavox with Thanksgiving? What type of programming does Magnavox expect its customers to listen to?

Women sense it immediately ꙮ ꙮ

—that atmosphere of elegance and refinement—those necessary little appointments, noticed but not discussed, which contribute so much to the comfort and well-being of guests and family.

ScotTissue has made a place for itself in well-conducted homes. It is the choice of discriminating women everywhere, because of its hygienic purity and safety.

A highly-absorbent, snow-white, soothing tissue, marvelously soft as fine old linen. Kind to the most sensitive skin. Peculiarly adapted to the needs of women of intuitive daintiness. Ask your doctor.

No conversation. Just say "ScotTissue" to your storekeeper and receive a big, economical, dustproof roll.

Scott Paper Company, Chester, Pa.

Soft as old Linen
ScotTissue
The absorbent soft white Toilet paper
Scott Paper Company
Chester, Pa. U.S.A.

**15 cents
a roll**

Our Offer

If your dealer cannot supply you, send us 5c cents with your dealer's name and we will send you a full size roll of ScotTissue, prepaid.

© S. P. Co.

Another Thirsty Fibre Product
3 rolls 25c

The techniques of advertising can be used to market any product: emphasize class and sophistication and even toilet paper can become a status symbol. The image in Plate 7 presents two refined and fashionable women having tea in a smartly decorated room. The text stresses the elegance and refinement of the setting and touts ScotTissue as the choice of "discriminating women" in "well-conducted homes." The product is described as hygienic, pure, safe, "soft as fine old linen," and "peculiarly adapted to the needs of women of intuitive daintiness." This ad features words and large, detailed illustrations; the product itself is clearly but discretely placed. What is the most distinctive feature of ScotTissue? What image do the two women project, and why would they make you want to buy the product? What is "intuitive daintiness"?

Left: Plate 7. Scot Tissue advertisement, *Saturday Evening Post*, September 11, 1926

Right: Plate 8. Knapp-Felt hat advertisement, *Saturday Evening Post*, September 11, 1926

The advertisement in Plate 8 is selling youth and class through a hat. The image is of a dashing, active young man; the hat's name, the Lord Nelson, sounds British and conveys a sophisticated military air. The text emphasizes youth, grace, fashion, quality, and newness. The focus on youth was novel for the American market at this time, as was the British link through the product name. When you purchase a Lord Nelson hat, what qualities are you buying? What elements of the advertisement give you the impression that the hat has these qualities?

KNAPP-FELT

Here's the Lord Nelson!

THE Knapp-Felt hat for September is the Lord Nelson. It will be shown in the newest colorings for Fall by the principal hatters throughout the United States on

Friday, September tenth

Young men, and those who feel young, will enjoy the smart lines of the crown, the graceful sweep of the brim and the newness of the exclusive trimming.

Seventy-five years of experience in making fine hats in the C & K Shop are in every Knapp-Felt hat. The choice of the finest materials and the expert hand-workmanship of experienced craftsmen guarantee the superb quality.

The Lord Nelson is made in the ten dollar grade only. Other Knapp-Felt styles from $8.00 to $40.00. A catalogue may be had on application.

THE CROFUT & KNAPP COMPANY
JOHN CAVANAGH ~ *President*
620 Fifth Avenue ~ New York City

BOBBED HAIR LOOKS BETTER WHEN TREATED THIS WAY

*B*OBBED HAIR is destined to remain popular. Its convenience, becomingness and gift of youthfulness make it the choice of chic, fashionable women everywhere.

To make bobbed hair look its best, shampoo thoroly and often with MADAM C. J. WALKER'S VEGETABLE SHAMPOO. Rinse in three or four waters, dry with towels and sunlight; apply MADAM C. J. WALKER'S WONDERFUL HAIR GROWER to the scalp to encourage growth or MADAM C. J. WALKER'S TETTER SALVE to combat disease; MADAM C. J. WALKER'S TEMPLE GROWER to grow hair on neck and temples; MADAM C. J. WALKER'S GLOSSINE to add life, lustre and an admirable silky sheen.

Madam C. J. Walker Agents everywhere (there's one near you) and good drug stores will cheerfully supply you with these and other Madam C. J. Walker Preparations. If not, write

THE MADAM C. J. WALKER MFG. CO., INC.
640 N. WEST ST.   INDIANAPOLIS, IND.

The image that Madam C. J. Walker presents in selling hair products in Plate 9 is similar to those used by companies catering to white women. An attractive young African American woman with bobbed (and straightened) hair models the look that Madam Walker promises. The text emphasizes that bobbed hair is popular, convenient, becoming, and youthful and that it is the choice of chic and fashionable women. In contrast to the sophisticated young woman of the Madam Walker ad, the Brer Rabbit Molasses ad in Plate 10 features a smartly dressed young man enjoying his wife's homemade gingerbread. The woman lets the reader know that her husband likes the gingerbread so well because it reminds him of the "plantation molasses he used to have when he was a boy . . . thanks to Brer Rabbit." The ad also features Brer Rabbit dressed up in the clothing worn by servants and seemingly in a hurry to deliver a platter of gingerbread. In what ways do these ads present racist images? Do these ads target blacks or whites, men or women? Note the publication in which each ad appeared. What image is Madam Walker selling? To what sentiment is the Brer Rabbit ad appealing?

Left: Plate 9. Advertisement for Madam C. J. Walker Preparations, *Crisis*, April 1927

Right: Plate 10. Brer Rabbit Molasses advertisement, *Ladies Home Journal*, January 1934

Her Saturday Night *Gingerbread*

brought him back to her

ALICE, after several years of marriage, began to feel that Jack was getting tired of domesticity and just her. In particular, she thought, his eyes wandered all too often in the direction of pink and white Betty Thornton, a recent arrival in town.

Alice, however, had a way with her, too. So she dried her eyes and decided to take steps.

* * *

She found an exotic black satin at Dale's which made her figure look like a movie star's. She bought it.

The next evening, she prepared a dinner of simple, delicious dishes, ending with Jack's favorite dessert—Brer Rabbit Gingerbread, heaped high with whipped cream.

It was while Jack was lifting his third forkful of gingerbread to his mouth that he said what Alice had hoped all evening he would say.

"There's something about this dinner, darling, that makes me feel like a pampered prince! Everything is so perfect—and you look like a princess."

Alice thought, as she smiled across the table into Jack's worshipful eyes, "It's the gingerbread that did the trick . . . he's as crazy about it as a little boy. There's certainly no molasses flavor anywhere like Brer Rabbit."

Soft, delicious gingerbread, made from Brer Rabbit Molasses, is always a great favorite with husbands. They love its pungent flavor, its tang and delicious aroma.

Brer Rabbit Molasses is real New Orleans molasses, made from the finest grade of freshly crushed sugar cane. That's what makes it taste so good. It is a wholesome food, too.

Two kinds: Gold Label—the highest quality light molasses for fancy cookery, fine on pancakes; Green Label—a darker molasses with a stronger flavor.

Try this "Southern Spicy Gingerbread"

You'll see why Jack praised it

2 eggs; ¾ cup brown sugar; ¾ cup Brer Rabbit Molasses; ¾ cup melted shortening; 2½ cups flour; 2 teaspoons soda; 2 teaspoons ginger; 1½ teaspoons cinnamon; ½ teaspoon cloves; ½ teaspoon nutmeg; ½ teaspoon baking powder; 1 cup boiling water.

Add beaten eggs to the sugar, molasses and melted shortening, then add the dry ingredients which have been mixed and sifted, and lastly the hot water. Bake in small individual pans or in a shallow pan in moderate oven (350° F.) 30 to 40 minutes. This recipe makes a light fluffy gingerbread that becomes a party dessert when topped with whipped cream.

BRER RABBIT
REAL PLANTATION *Molasses*

FREE — *Booklet containing more than 90 other Brer Rabbit recipes*

PENICK & FORD, LTD., INC., Dept. LH-13, New Orleans, La. Please send me copy of "Old-fashioned Molasses Goodies."

Name

Address

PART FIVE

"The American Century"

War, Affluence, and Uncertainty

World War II affected virtually every part of American life. Problems of economic depression vanished with the growth of productivity in war industries and—to the surprise of most economists—did not return after peace was declared. The federal government expanded during the war and never returned to its prewar size. Family life changed dramatically: fathers were absent, mothers were working, families moved to crowded centers of war industry, consumer goods were rationed or unavailable, and divorce rates soared. Science was transformed both by its scale of activities and by its subjection to military security regulations. Loyalties and antipathies shifted in extraordinary ways: the communist Soviet Union became one of the United States' most important allies and bore the brunt of the war's casualties, while German and Italian Americans became suspect, and many Japanese Americans were locked in internment camps.

The readings in Part Five sample the drama of World War II. Phyllis Fisher, married to physicist Leon Fisher, recounts the experience of living under the strange new secrecy of science at Los Alamos National Laboratory. J. Robert Oppenheimer, who directed scientific work at Los Alamos, recounts the controversy surrounding the creation of the atomic bomb. Fanny Christina Hill was one of the many women dubbed "Rosie the Riveter" in the newspapers who found new opportunities in the war industries. Ben Yorita and Philip Hayasaka describe the internment camps where they and their families were forced to endure much of the war. Several American soldiers remember how they suffered at the hands of the Japanese during the Bataan death march.

Victory in the war planted seeds of hope and fear. Uncertainties about the future of the United States were accompanied by ideological quarrels with the Soviet Union. The anxious transition to a peacetime economy and then back to the quasi-war footing of the cold war provoked the red scare, the fear of communist espionage that television game show producer Mark Goodson and his conscience struggled with during the 1950s. But as war was replaced not with renewed depression but instead with a prosperity unknown in previous human history, hope was restored for many. For others, however, the 1950s was a period of disappointment and exclusion. Many women and minorities were not as lucky as Fanny Christina Hill in retaining employment and a living wage after the war.

POINTS OF VIEW
Building an Atomic Bomb (1942–1945)

25
Letters from Los Alamos
Phyllis Fisher

"My two great loves," the scientist J. Robert Oppenheimer often told friends, "are physics and New Mexico. It's a pity they can't be combined." Oppenheimer had first visited the Pajarito Plateau in New Mexico in 1922 just before he began college. Two decades later, the nation's need for secrecy and his own longtime affection for the area made it the appropriate site of a great adventure for many physicists and their families.

At Los Alamos, scientists who were accustomed to open communications and sophisticated academic communities lived under the rule of secrecy and military security. They could not tell relatives where they were going or what they were doing; even their spouses might not have known what the laboratory's mission was. Often they did not know what other units in the laboratory were working on, and few knew what the ultimate objective of the project was.

Leon Fisher, a physicist, his wife, Phyllis, and their son, Bobby, came to Los Alamos in October 1944. All mail was censored, so Phyllis Fisher's frequent letters to her parents could not reveal where she was. The first successful explosion of a nuclear device on July 16, 1945, at the "Trinity site" at Alamogordo, New Mexico, had to pass unnoticed in her letters. But after August 6, 1945, when an atomic bomb was dropped on Hiroshima, she could freely write what she thought about the atomic bomb and how scientists at Los Alamos reacted to it.

BEFORE YOU READ

1. What was life like at Los Alamos? What adjustments did people have to make to live there?

2. What was Phyllis Fisher's reaction to the dropping of the atomic bombs in Japan? What were the reactions of scientists and the public, as far as you can tell?

Phyllis Fisher, *The Los Alamos Experience* (Tokyo: Japan Publications, 1985), pp. 24–27, 29–30, 32, 46–50, 115–17, 121–22, 145.

October 4, 1944

We're moving! Believe me, you're not any more surprised than I am! You'd like to know where we're going? So would we! And it isn't that Lee won't tell me. It's hard to believe, but he doesn't know either. The only encouraging thing he could say was that we'll know where we are when we get there. Great!

Lee came home from the university early this afternoon, tossed his briefcase on the couch and said, "Sit down, Phyllis, we've really got to talk." He was so serious that he ignored Bobby, who had toddled across the floor to greet him. He told me of an important phone call that he had made earlier in the afternoon, which . . . will result in our making this sudden move.

Here's what I can tell you. We'll be going "there" next week (less than a day's trip from Albuquerque) to select our living quarters, and we will move "there" sometime between the 26th and 30th of this month. We have been directed to drive to a certain city and report to an inconspicuous address where we will be given further instructions. It's alright with me, so long as we're not met by a bearded mystic, given a piece of thread and instructed to follow it to its end. At this point, nothing would surprise me. . . .

For the time being, let's call the place Shangri-La or Sh-La for short. I'm tired of writing "there" and "the place," and I don't know what to call it. I couldn't tell you its real name if I knew it. Please don't say anything to anyone yet, at least until I tell you what you can or should say. I'll write all I can about Sh-La. Please understand that if I don't answer your questions, there is a reason. I have been told that our mail, both incoming and outgoing, will be censored. If my letters have less coherence than usual, please blame it on the rules and regulations of our future home.

Well, here we go, two so-called adults, one baby and one fox-terrier, heading off to play "hide and seek" for the duration. I'm pretty excited about it, but I'm frightened too. It's very much like stepping off into space and I just hope we land on our feet.

[October, 1944]

Authoritative books on child-rearing warn me that when Bobby is three (or is it four?) he'll ask countless questions, many of them unanswerable. Well, it will take him a full year to ask as many questions as you did in your last letter. The worst of it is, I can't answer anything! I don't know the answers and I couldn't tell you if I did! No, we can never give you the size of the project. They take precautions that this information not be known. For example, we have been told not to transfer what they flatteringly term our "entire bank account" to a bank nearer the project. And, "What kind of work will Leon do?" and "Is it dangerous?" Mom! How can I answer you? Then you ask, "Can you assure us you will stay in New Mexico or, at least in continental U.S.A.?" I can tell you're both worried. I don't know what to say to you.

October 11, 1944

I'm breathless! We've been "there"! Shangri-La is super! We drove up yesterday and stayed just long enough to tour the place, pick out our house and learn some of the rules, regulations and by-laws of this Never-Never-Land. Naturally, the day was not uneventful. In fact, Lee and I are still blushing over our latest butch.[1]

I wrote you that we were given an address in Santa Fe from which we were to receive further instructions. We dutifully followed our little map, found the address alright and stared at it in amazement. The place was a bakery! Once in, we didn't know what to do. A girl behind the counter asked if she could help us and we boobs were tongue-tied. Lee finally stated that we were "told to come here." Silence reigned. More silence. Believe me, I fully expected the girl to break open a loaf of bread, surreptitiously extract from it a message written in code and slyly slip it to us. Instead, a bored voice from the other side of the room said, "You must be looking for the office down the way; people are going in and out of there all the time." We felt like four cents, said our thanks and meekly ambled out. Fine beginning! The office down the way was presided over by Dorothy, a genial, relaxed woman from whom we learned that we were expected and were given our directions to Sh-La. Then we started out on a most spectacularly beautiful drive.

Shangri-La is a streamlined, alpine settlement, size unmentionable, location unmentionable, altitude unmentionable. But it's very complete. We found theater, sports field, playground, and a school. There is even a radio station that picks up programs and adds music. Apparently, we will live in a spot where ordinary radio reception is extremely poor.

Anyway, the inmates assure us that there is plenty here to compensate for the very extreme isolation. We saw notices of picnics, dances, bridge parties, etc. If we get tired of my cooking, and that's entirely possible, we can eat out at the mess hall. We are entitled to use the Army commissary and PX, and they seem quite adequate.

Lee and I were lectured briefly on the importance of developing an antisocial outlook. We're not to be friendly with residents of nearby towns. (I hadn't noticed any nearby towns.) If we go to Santa Fe (which isn't my idea of nearby) we are to keep to ourselves and not talk to outsiders unless it is necessary in the transaction of business, etc. However, we are allowed a half-smile and a slight nod to persons we already know there. "Only this and nothing more." . . .

October 27, 1944

. . . You can tear up the floor plan I sent you. Any resemblance between it and the place we're living in is purely coincidental. Our belongings were unceremoniously dumped in the wrong house, a smaller place (classification: garage style) at about six o'clock this evening. Our chosen home, we were told by a WAC[2] in the housing office, had been assigned by mistake to someone else. Instead, after a great deal of scurrying around, we were deposited here to remain until another batch of houses can be built. The WAC tried to be comforting, assuring

1. **butch:** crewcut.
2. **WAC:** Women's Army Corp member.

us in her most languid southern accent, that it would be but a week or so before these next prefabs would be tossed together, and we could move.

November, 1944

Now, listen to this very carefully and try to understand. I can't. We have a gate here that isn't a gate at all. It consists of a guardhouse and an unfriendly sign-post surrounded by sentries. Regulations governing passage of said "gate" top any screwy regulation of any Army post anywhere. It seems that you can drive past it in an automobile without showing a pass, but you can't walk past it. Pedestrians must show passes. No exceptions.

I drove past the gate (to the vet's) with Fawn and, naturally, wasn't stopped. The veterinary hospital is only about 100 yards beyond and is visible from the gate. After our visit to the vet, I rushed out with my shivering dog, climbed into the car to start back, and—you guessed it—the car wouldn't start. By this time, it was snowing. I began to run as best I could, with Fawn held securely inside my coat. Of course, I was promptly stopped at the gate. I had no pass! In my rush to get Fawn to the vet's and back, I had neglected to take it. I explained to the sentries that my car wouldn't start. I had to get back. My husband had to get to work. My baby would be alone! My dog was dying! None of which made any difference. Only one word seemed to have meaning, the word "regulations." There were, it seemed, no provisions for someone who drove out the gate and had to walk back through it. Too bad. By then the snow was slanting and spinning angrily, and I wasn't getting any warmer. Fawn wasn't getting any lighter. They could see my car standing there, but that didn't make any difference. One MP suggested that I phone someone who could come out and identify me. Fine help! No one I knew had a phone. Lee couldn't be reached by phone until he left Bobby and went to work. And he wouldn't do that (I certainly hope he wouldn't do that) until I was safely home. What to do?

Then through the gloom and the swirling snow, there appeared a jeep, with driver, of course. Through chattering teeth, and right in front of the MPs, I asked the stranger for a lift. He agreed. I climbed into the jeep and in we went with full permission of the guards at the gate!

[November, 1944]

... Our guests were two completely balmy SEDs,[3] Bob and Norman. Bob, an attractive fellow with a nice smile, was in high spirits. He told us that next Wednesday he is going to fall madly in love with a girl named Shirley. A whirlwind romance will follow, culminating in marriage sometime in December. I was most impressed, but a little baffled by it all. But there is an explanation. Military regulations here forbid the wife of an enlisted man to come to live in Sh-La. If Bob goes home to marry his Shirley, he'll have to leave her and return to our little exile alone. However, if Shirley qualifies for a position here, meets Bob here, falls in love here, marries here, why then, she can stay. In fact, she has

---

3. **SEDs:** Special Engineering Detachment members.

to stay! Hence the plotted romance. See? And Shirley has already been hired by the project and will arrive next Wednesday.

[November, 1944]

This evening we were invited to dinner with friends. It was the sort of evening one learns to expect around these parts. Dinner is eaten in a mad rush. The men dash back to work. The wives do the dishes and chat a while. At ten o'clock the men return jabbering a strange language most nearly identified as "scientese." Tonight it was particularly pleasant. We discovered we had many interests in common. In other words, we all are very fond of Mozart and heartily dislike Dewey.[4]

This afternoon a group of Leon's co-workers dropped in. Apparently, they are very charming and comical as well as very bright and interesting. You'll have to take Lee's word for it. You see, they, too, speak little English, but mostly "scientese." The only conversation directed my way was "Hello" and "Goodbye" and oft-repeated moanings about dreading Thanksgiving dinner at the mess hall. Hint, hint.

Monday, August 6, 1945

Please note——LOS ALAMOS, NEW MEXICO

Well, today's news makes everything else seem pretty unimportant! You can't possibly imagine how strange it is to turn on the radio and hear the outside world talking about us today! After all the extreme secrecy, it seems positively unreal to hear stories about the bomb, the site, and everything.

The "gadget" worked better (!) than anyone dare to expect, and Hiroshima, a city we have never heard of, and its population of 350,000 has been wiped out. The radio announcers could hardly control their voices. They told the whole story. How had they gotten the information so quickly? They named names! Who had told them? They described our hill, our hill. They located us on a barren plateau in the mountains north and west of Santa Fe.

They identified us as LOS ALAMOS!

We couldn't believe what we heard! "Over one hundred thousand Japs killed by one bomb," the announcers bragged. They ticked off the figures as though they were reporting scores at a sporting event. But, hey, those are people! A radius of one mile vaporized, they cheered as I shuddered. They are talking about a populated target, a city. And part of me keeps saying, "This can't be real." It's also actually unreal to hear names connected with the project, names like Oppenheimer, Segre, Fermi, Bohr, and others. After months of caution and secrecy, it's too much.

Kaltenborn[5] somehow seemed more detached and more objective than the others. He took time, in spite of the hysteria, to consider the bomb's potential for good or evil. Then he described the first test atomic explosion in the southern "arid part of the state" in New Mexico and named the date, the place, and even the code name, "Trinity."

---

4. **Dewey:** Thomas E. Dewey, Republican presidential candidate.
5. **Kaltenborn:** H. V. Kaltenborn, the conservative radio news commentator.

After "Trinity," days went by while we waited to hear how and when the gadget (maybe I'd better get used to writing the word "bomb") would be used. Which brings us up to today. By comparison the excitement on the hill today has put that of July 16th far down the scale of insane rejoicing. You can't imagine it. I can't describe it. I'm certain that it will take time for the emotional bits in all of us that were triggered by "Trinity" and that blew up with the bomb to settle down into place.

August 10, 1945

Now I am upset! Yesterday's bombing of Nagasaki was shocking! I cannot understand the necessity of a second bomb. The Japanese were known to be suing for peace and trying to negotiate terms that they could accept. Why destroy another city and its inhabitants? Why couldn't both bombs have been dropped over some unimportant unpopulated island as a demonstration of what could happen to Japan?

[August, 1945]

I almost fainted when a traveling salesman knocked at my door. There has never been one here before. He had gotten a temporary pass. Amazing! I was so busy questioning him that he had trouble telling me what he had for sale.

[The following paragraphs describe varying reactions to the success of the project. Some were on the verge of hysteria; others took it more calmly.]

. . . [For] instance, yesterday, Scotty [who works in the tech area and] who lives across the street, called to me at around 9:00 A.M. I went over to his house, found him in bed sobbing convulsively into his pillow. He had turned on his heater, which had exploded and burned about a square inch on his arm and spread soot around the living room. It was just too much and the poor guy was nauseated, dizzy, and completely hysterical. I got him quieted down somewhat, notified his wife, who [also] works in the tech area, and called a doctor.

Lee goes around with a "Cheshire Cat" grin that won't wipe off. He is very tired and has gotten little sleep. He gets up and wanders around at night when he should be sleeping. And I've lost four pounds in all the excitement.

[In October, J. Robert Oppenheimer spoke to the scientists and their families.]

[October, 1945]

. . . And what [Oppenheimer] said was so exactly what I've been feeling but have been unable to express. His talk was short, even faltering. He told us that the whole world must unite or perish. He felt that unless there is a way to prevent wars, the pride we are feeling today will give way to concern and fear for the future. He said that the day may come when "mankind will curse the names of Los Alamos and Hiroshima."

26

To Build a Bomb
J. Robert Oppenheimer

The 1920s were a golden age in theoretical physics. Brilliant and dedicated physicists like J. Robert Oppenheimer (1904–1967) ignored society and politics, living in a separate world of new theories and discoveries in relativity and quantum theory that transformed classic Newtonian physics. Then in the early 1930s, with the rise of dictators such as Hitler, Mussolini, and Stalin, politics began noticeably to intrude even on sciences as remote as theoretical physics. And, far harder to notice, scientific theories and discoveries began ever so slowly to intrude on politics. James Chadwick's discovery of the neutron in 1932 and Albert Einstein's emigration from Germany to the United States in 1933 seemed far less important than the rise of Adolf Hitler or the election of Franklin D. Roosevelt. Yet by 1938, when scientists in Germany at last figured out that neutrons could "split" certain atoms and release great quantities of energy, the fate of people and nations suddenly hung in the balance.

Germany had long been the center of the new physics. Scientists in Great Britain and the United States could only speculate on what progress Hitler's scientists might have been making in harnessing nuclear fission. In June 1942, American and British scientists developed plans for a uranium-based atomic bomb. Full-scale efforts to construct such a bomb, code named the "Manhattan Project," thus began in the shadow of Germany's possible head start. (Only later was Germany's lack of progress discovered.)

The Manhattan Project was actually an activity of the Army Corps of Engineers. Under the direction of General Leslie R. Groves, massive facilities in Los Alamos, New Mexico; Oak Ridge, Tennessee; and Hanford, Washington, were built, involving about 125,000 workers and costing $2 billion. Los Alamos — a site chosen by Oppenheimer — was the scientific capital of the project and was kept relatively independent of the military despite its strict security. Oppenheimer, no longer the detached scholar of the 1920s, recruited scientists worldwide and directed their work in ways they were completely unaccustomed to. Collaborating with larger groups of scientists than had ever gathered before, they worked to the tightest of deadlines: beating the Germans to the bomb. Their success, and the ironies of that success, are the subjects of Oppenheimer's autobiographical sketch and his November 1945 speech.

Jonathan F. Fanton, R. Hae Williams, and Michael B. Stoff, eds., *The Manhattan Project: A Documentary Introduction to the Atomic Age* (New York: McGraw-Hill, 1991), pp. 29–32; Alice Kimball Smith and Charles Weiher, eds., *Robert Oppenheimer: Letters and Recollections* (Cambridge: Harvard University Press, 1980), pp. 315–20, 324–25.

BEFORE YOU READ

1. What changed Oppenheimer from an unworldly scientist to a man who could direct a large and important enterprise?

2. What responsibilities did he see for scientists after the war?

3. After he opposed the development of the hydrogen bomb, Oppenheimer lost his security clearance to engage in or advise government research on nuclear weapons. What foreshadowings of his doubts about nuclear weapons do you see in Oppenheimer's speech?

AUTOBIOGRAPHICAL SKETCH (1954)

I was born in New York in 1904. My father had come to this country at the age of 17 from Germany. He was a successful businessman and quite active in community affairs. My mother was born in Baltimore and before her marriage was an artist and teacher of art. I attended Ethical Culture School and Harvard College, which I entered in 1922. I completed the work for my degree in the spring of 1925. I then left Harvard to study at Cambridge University and in Goettingen, where in the spring of 1927 I took my doctor's degree. The following year I was national research fellow at Harvard and at the California Institute of Technology. In the following year I was fellow of the international education board at the University of Leiden and at the Technical High School in Zurich.

In the spring of 1929, I returned to the United States. I was homesick for this country, and in fact I did not leave it again for 19 years. I had learned a great deal in my student days about the new physics; I wanted to pursue this myself, to explain it and to foster its cultivation. I had had many invitations to university positions, 1 or 2 in Europe, and perhaps 10 in the United States. I accepted concurrent appointments as assistant professor at the California Institute of Technology in Pasadena and at the University of California in Berkeley. For the coming 12 years, I was to devote my time to these 2 faculties.

Starting with a single graduate student in my first year in Berkeley, we gradually began to build up what was to become the largest school in the country of graduate and postdoctoral study in theoretical physics, so that as time went on, we came to have between a dozen and 20 people learning and adding to quantum theory, nuclear physics, relativity and other modern physics.

My friends, both in Pasadena and in Berkeley, were mostly faculty people, scientists, classicists, and artists. I studied and read Sanskrit with Arthur Rider. I read very widely, mostly classics, novels, plays, and poetry; and I read something of other parts of science. I was not interested in and did not read about economics or politics. I was almost wholly divorced from the contemporary scene in this country. I never read a newspaper or a current magazine like *Time* or *Harper's;* I had no radio, no telephone; I learned of the stock-market crash in the fall of 1929 only long after the event; the first time I ever voted was in the presidential election of 1936. To many of my friends, my indifference to contemporary affairs seemed bizarre, and they often chided me with being too much of a highbrow. I was interested in man and his experience; I was deeply interested in my science; but I had no understanding of the relations of man to his society.

Beginning in late 1936, my interests began to change. These changes did not alter my earlier friendships, my relations to my students, or my devotion to physics; but they added something new. I can discern in retrospect more than one reason for these changes. I had had a continuing, smoldering fury about the treatment of Jews in Germany. I had relatives there, and was later to help in extricating them and bringing them to this country. I saw what the depression was doing to my students. Often they could get no jobs, or jobs which were wholly inadequate. And through them, I began to understand how deeply political and economic events could affect men's lives. I began to feel the need to participate more fully in the life of the community. But I had no framework of political conviction or experience to give me perspective in these matters. . . .

Ever since the discovery of nuclear fission, the possibility of powerful explosives based on it had been very much in my mind, as it had in that of many other physicists. We had some understanding of what this might do for us in the war, and how much it might change the course of history. In the autumn of 1941, a special committee was set up by the National Academy of Sciences under the chairmanship of Arthur Compton to review the prospects and feasibility of the different uses of atomic energy for military purposes. I attended a meeting of this committee; this was my first official connection with the atomic-energy program.

After the academy meeting, I spent some time in preliminary calculations about the consumption and performance of atomic bombs, and became increasingly excited at the prospects. At the same time I still had a quite heavy burden of academic work with courses and graduate students. I also began to consult, more or less regularly, with the staff of the Radiation Laboratory in Berkeley on their program for the electromagnetic separation of uranium isotopes. I was never a member or employee of the laboratory; but I attended many of its staff and policy meetings. With the help of two of my graduate students, I developed an invention which was embodied in the production plants at Oak Ridge. I attended the conference in Chicago at which the Metallurgical Laboratory (to produce plutonium) was established and its initial program projected.

In the spring of 1942, Compton called me to Chicago to discuss the state of work on the bomb itself. During this meeting Compton asked me to take the responsibility for this work, which at that time consisted of numerous scattered experimental projects. Although I had no administrative experience and was not an experimental physicist, I felt sufficiently informed and challenged by the problem to be glad to accept. At this time I became an employee of the Metallurgical Laboratory.

After this conference I called together a theoretical study group in Berkeley, in which Hans Bethe, Emil Konopinski, Robert Serber, Edward Teller, John H. Van Vleck, and I participated. We had an adventurous time. We spent much of the summer of 1942 in Berkeley in a joint study that for the first time really came to grips with the physical problems of atomic bombs, atomic explosions, and the possibility of using fission explosions to initiate thermonuclear reactions. I called this possibility to the attention of Dr. Vannevar Bush during the late summer; the technical views on this subject were to develop and change from then until the present day.

After these studies there was little doubt that a potentially world-shattering undertaking lay ahead. We began to see the great explosion at Alamogordo[1] and the greater explosions at Eniwetok[2] with a surer foreknowledge. We also began to see how rough, difficult, challenging, and unpredictable this job might turn out to be. . . .

In later summer, after a review of the experimental work, I became convinced, as did others, that a major change was called for in the work on the bomb itself. We needed a central laboratory devoted wholly to this purpose, where people could talk freely with each other, where theoretical ideas and experimental findings could affect each other, where the waste and frustration and error of the many compartmentalized experimental studies could be eliminated, where we could begin to come to grips with chemical, metallurgical, engineering, and ordnance problems that had so far received no consideration. We therefore sought to establish this laboratory for a direct attack on all the problems inherent in the most rapid possible development and production of atomic bombs.

In the autumn of 1942 General Leslie R. Groves assumed charge of the Manhattan Engineer District. I discussed with him the need for an atomic bomb laboratory. There had been some thought of making this laboratory a part of Oak Ridge. For a time there was support for making it a Military Establishment in which key personnel would be commissioned as officers; and in preparation for this course I once went to the Presidio[3] to take the initial steps toward obtaining a commission. After a good deal of discussion with the personnel who would be needed at Los Alamos and with General Groves and his advisers, it was decided that the laboratory should, at least initially, be a civilian establishment in a military post. While this consideration was going on, I had showed General Groves Los Alamos; and he almost immediately took steps to acquire the site.

In early 1943, I received a letter signed by General Groves and Dr. James B. Conant, appointing me director of the laboratory, and outlining their conception of how it was to be organized and administered. The necessary construction and assembling of the needed facilities were begun. All of us worked in close collaboration with the engineers of the Manhattan District.

The site of Los Alamos was selected in part at least because it enabled those responsible to balance the obvious need for security with the equally important need of free communication among those engaged in the work. Security, it was

---

1. **Alamogordo:** New Mexico site of first detonation of an atomic device.
2. **Eniwetok:** Pacific island used as an atomic test site.
3. **Presidio:** military base in San Francisco.

hoped, would be achieved by removing the laboratory to a remote area, fenced and patrolled, where communication with the outside was extremely limited. Telephone calls were monitored, mail was censored, and personnel who left the area—something permitted only for the clearest of causes—knew that their movements might be under surveillance. On the other hand, for those within the community, fullest exposition and discussion among those competent to use the information was encouraged.

The last months of 1942 and early 1943 had hardly hours enough to get Los Alamos established. The real problem had to do with getting to Los Alamos the men who would make a success of the undertaking. For this we needed to understand as clearly as we then could what our technical program would be, what men we would need, what facilities, what organization, what plan.

The program of recruitment was massive. Even though we then underestimated the ultimate size of the laboratory, which was to have almost 4,000 members by the spring of 1945, and even though we did not at that time see clearly some of the difficulties which were to bedevil and threaten the enterprise, we knew that it was a big, complex and diverse job. Even the initial plan of the laboratory called for a start with more than 100 highly qualified and trained scientists, to say nothing of the technicians, staff, and mechanics who would be required for their support, and of the equipment that we would have to beg and borrow since there would be no time to build it from scratch. We had to recruit at a time when the country was fully engaged in war and almost every competent scientist was already involved in the military effort.

The primary burden of this fell on me. To recruit staff I traveled all over the country talking with people who had been working on one or another aspect of the atomic-energy enterprise, and people in radar work, for example, and underwater sound, telling them about the job, the place that we were going to, and enlisting their enthusiasm.

In order to bring responsible scientists to Los Alamos, I had to rely on their sense of the interest, urgency, and feasibility of the Los Alamos mission. I had to tell them enough of what the job was, and give strong enough assurance that it might be successfully accomplished in time to affect the outcome of the war, to make it clear that they were justified in their leaving other work to come to this job.

The prospect of coming to Los Alamos aroused great misgivings. It was to be a military post; men were asked to sign up more or less for the duration; restrictions on travel and on the freedom of families to move about to be severe; and no one could be sure of the extent to which the necessary technical freedom of action could actually be maintained by the laboratory. The notion of disappearing into the New Mexico desert for an indeterminate period and under quasi-military auspices disturbed a good many scientists, and the families of many more. But there was another side to it. Almost everyone realized that this was a great undertaking. Almost everyone knew that if it were completed successfully and rapidly enough, it might determine the outcome of the war. Almost everyone knew that it was an unparalleled opportunity to bring to bear the

basic knowledge and art of science for the benefit of his country. Almost everyone knew that this job, if it were achieved, would be a part of history. This
sense of excitement, of devotion and of patriotism in the end prevailed. Most of
those with whom I talked came to Los Alamos. Once they came, confidence in
the enterprise grew as men learned more of the technical status of the work;
and though the laboratory was to double and redouble its size many times before the end, once it had started it was on the road to success.

We had information in those days of German activity in the field of nuclear
fission. We were aware of what it might mean if they beat us to the draw in the
development of atomic bombs. The consensus of all our opinions, and every directive that I had, stressed the extreme urgency of our work, as well as the need
for guarding all knowledge of it from our enemies. . . .

The story of Los Alamos is long and complex. Part of it is public history.
For me it was a time so filled with work, with the need for decision and action
and consultation, that there was room for little else. I lived with my family in
the community which was Los Alamos. It was a remarkable community, inspired by a high sense of mission, of duty and of destiny, coherent, dedicated,
and remarkably selfless. There was plenty in the life of Los Alamos to cause irritation; the security restrictions, many of my own devising, the inadequacies
and inevitable fumblings of a military post unlike any that had ever existed before, shortages, inequities and in the laboratory itself the shifting emphasis on
different aspects of the technical work as the program moved forward; but I
have never known a group more understanding and more devoted to a common
purpose, more willing to lay aside personal convenience and prestige, more understanding of the role that they were playing in their country's history. Time
and again we had in the technical work almost paralyzing crises. Time and
again the laboratory drew itself together and faced the new problems and got
on with the work. We worked by night and by day; and in the end the many
jobs were done. . . .

SPEECH TO THE ASSOCIATION
OF LOS ALAMOS SCIENTISTS

Los Alamos, November 2, 1945

I am grateful to the Executive Committee for this chance to talk to you. I should
like to talk tonight—if some of you have long memories perhaps you will regard
it as justified—as a fellow scientist, and at least as a fellow worrier about the fix we
are in. I do not have anything very radical to say, or anything that will strike most
of you with a great flash of enlightenment. I don't have anything to say that will
be of an immense encouragement. In some ways I would have liked to talk to you
at an earlier date—but I couldn't talk to you as a Director. I could not talk, and
will not tonight talk, too much about the practical political problems which are involved. . . . I don't think that's important. I think there are issues which are quite
simple and quite deep, and which involve us as a group of scientists—involve us
more, perhaps than any other group in the world. I think that it can only help to

look a little at what our situation is—at what has happened to us—and that this must give us some honesty, some insight, which will be a source of strength in what may be the not-too-easy days ahead.

The real impact of the creation of the atomic bomb and atomic weapons—to understand that one has to look further back, look, I think, to the times when physical science was growing in the days of the renaissance, and when the threat that science offered was felt so deeply throughout the Christian world. The analogy is, of course, not perfect. You may even wish to think of the days in the last century when the theories of evolution seemed a threat to the values by which men lived. The analogy is not perfect because there is nothing in atomic weapons—there is certainly nothing that we have done here or in the physics or chemistry that immediately preceded our work here—in which any revolutionary ideas were involved. I don't think that the conceptions of nuclear fission have strained any man's attempts to understand them, and I don't feel that any of us have really learned in a deep sense very much from following this up. It is in a quite different way. It is not an idea—it is a development and a reality—but it has in common with the early days of physical science the fact that the very existence of science is threatened, and its value is threatened. This is the point that I would like to speak a little about.

I think that it hardly needs to be said why the impact is so strong. There are three reasons: one is the extraordinary speed with which things which were right on the frontier of science were translated into terms where they affected many living people, and potentially all people. Another is the fact, quite accidental in many ways, and connected with the speed, that scientists themselves played such a large part, not merely in providing the foundation for atomic weapons, but in actually making them. In this we are certainly closer to it than any other group. The third is that the thing we made—partly because of the technical nature of the problem, partly because we worked hard, partly because we had good breaks—really arrived in the world with such a shattering reality and suddenness that there was no opportunity for the edges to be worn off.

But when you come right down to it the reason that we did this job is because it was an organic necessity. If you are a scientist you cannot stop such a thing. If you are a scientist you believe that it is good to find out how the world works; that it is good to find out what the realities are; that it is good to turn over to mankind at large the greatest possible power to control the world and to deal with it according to its rights and its values.

There are many people who try to wiggle out of this. They say the real importance of atomic energy does not lie in the weapons that have been made; the real importance lies in all the great benefits which atomic energy, which the various radiations, will bring to mankind. There may be some truth in this. I am sure that there is truth in it, because there has never in the past been a new field opened up where the real fruits of it have not been invisible at the beginning. I have a very high confidence that the fruits—the so-called peacetime applications—of atomic energy will have in them all that we think, and more. There are others who try to escape the immediacy of this situation by saying that, after all, war has always been very terrible; after all, weapons have always gotten worse and worse; that this is just another weapon and it doesn't create a great change; that they are not so bad; bombings have been bad in this war and this is not a change in that—it just adds a little to the effectiveness of bombing; that some sort of protection will be found. I think that these efforts to diffuse and weaken the nature of the crisis make it only more dangerous. I think it is for us to accept it as a very grave crisis, to realize that these atomic weapons which we have started to make are very terrible, that they involve a change, that they are not just a slight modification: to accept this, and to accept with it the necessity for those transformations in the world which will make it possible to integrate these developments into human life.

. . . It is a new field, in which the position of vested interests in various parts of the world is very much less serious than in others. It is serious in this country, and that is one of our problems. It is a new field, in which the role of science has been so great that it is to my mind hardly thinkable that the international traditions of science, and the fraternity of scientists, should not play a constructive part. It is a new field, in which just the novelty and the special characteristics of the technical operations should enable one to establish a community of interest which might almost be regarded as a pilot plant for a new type of international collaboration. I speak of it as a pilot plant because it is quite clear that the control of atomic weapons cannot be in itself the unique end of such operation. The only unique end can be a world that is united, and a world in which war will not occur. But those things don't happen overnight, and in this field it would seem that one could get started, and get started without meeting those insuperable obstacles which history has so often placed in the way of any effort of cooperation. Now, this is not an easy thing, and the point I want to make, the one point I want to hammer home, is what an enormous change in spirit is involved. There are things which we hold very dear, and I think rightly hold very dear; I would say that the word democracy perhaps stood for some of them as well as any other word. There are many parts of the world in which there is no democracy. There are other things which we hold dear, and which we rightly should. And when I speak of a new spirit in international affairs I mean that even to these deepest of things which we cherish, and for which Americans have been willing to die—and certainly most of us would be willing to die—even in these deepest things, we realize that there is something more profound than that; namely, the common bond with other men everywhere. It is only if you do that that this makes sense; because if you approach the problem and say, "We know what is right and we would like to use the atomic bomb to persuade you to agree with us," then you are in a very weak position and you will not succeed, because under those conditions you will not succeed in delegating responsibility for the survival of men. It is a purely unilateral statement; you will find yourselves attempting by force of arms to prevent a disaster.

I don't have very much more to say. There are a few things which scientists perhaps should remember, that I don't think I need to remind us of; but I will, anyway. One is that they are very often called upon to give technical information in one way or another, and I think one cannot be too careful to be honest. And it is very difficult, not because one tells lies, but because so often questions are put in a form which makes it very hard to give an answer which is not misleading. I think we will be in a very weak position unless we maintain at its highest the scrupulousness which is traditional for us in sticking to the truth, and in distinguishing between what we know to be true from what we hope may be true.

The second thing I think it right to speak of is this: it is everywhere felt that the fraternity between us and scientists in other countries may be one of the most helpful things for the future; yet it is apparent that even in this country not all of us who are scientists are in agreement. There is no harm in that; such disagreement is healthy. But we must not lose the sense of fraternity because of it; we must not lose our fundamental confidence in our fellow scientists.

I think that we have no hope at all if we yield in our belief in the value of science, in the good that it can be to the world to know about reality, about nature, to attain a gradually greater and greater control of nature, to learn, to teach, to understand. I think that if we lose our faith in this we stop being scientists, we sell out our heritage, we lose what we have most of value for this time of crisis.

But there is another thing: we are not only scientists; we are men, too. We cannot forget our dependence on our fellow men. I mean not only our material dependence, without which no science would be possible, and without which we could not work; I mean also our deep moral dependence, in that the value of science must lie in the world of men, that all our roots lie there. These are the strongest bonds in the world, stronger than those even that bind us to one another, these are the deepest bonds—that bind us to our fellow men.

For Critical Thinking

1. Joseph Rothblat, a Polish scientist recruited to work at Los Alamos, insisted on leaving the project at the end of 1944 when it became apparent that there was no danger of any other nation's building a nuclear weapon before the United States. Based on your reading of these two selections, what do you think of his decision? Should other scientists have followed his lead? Why or why not?

2. What are the hazards for scientists and scientific research posed by the sort of secrecy under which work at Los Alamos was done? Did this set a dangerous precedent? According to Oppenheimer, should scientists agree to do work that cannot be freely published? Does this violate a central ethic of science?

3. What role does Oppenheimer think scientists should play in influencing public policies that directly stem from their work, such as the policy regarding the use of nuclear weapons? What similar issues are important today, and what role should scientists play in them?

27

Rosie the Riveter
Fanny Christina Hill

World War II brought with it a massive need for a larger labor force. Millions of men were under arms, and the United States, billing itself the "Arsenal of Democracy" for the Allied forces, strove for giant increases in the production of planes, ships, trucks, tanks, armaments, food, clothing, and all the other supplies that fuel a war. In 1940, 11.5 million women were employed outside the home, principally single women, widows, and wives from poor families. African American women like Fanny Christina Hill expected to work in whatever jobs were available to them — most commonly domestic service.

On Columbus Day 1942, President Franklin D. Roosevelt called for a new attitude in the workplace: "In some communities employers dislike to hire women. In others they are reluctant to hire Negroes. We can no longer afford to indulge such prejudices." Soon women like Hill shifted from "women's jobs" to defense work, prompting others who previously had not worked to adopt these new roles as well.

War production peaked in 1944. By the middle of that year, pressure grew to persuade women to return to their homes even before the war reached its conclusion. Defense plant newspapers replaced features on women production workers with "cheesecake" contests. Tales of neglected children became a theme of popular journalism. Yet seventy-five percent of women surveyed in 1944 and 1945 expressed the desire to continue working after the war. A cultural battle had begun that would outlast wartime.

Before You Read

1. How was Fanny Christina Hill's life affected by her work during the war?
2. Why did she continue working after the war? Was she influenced by the pressure to cease working?
3. What examples of prejudice affecting her life do you find? How did she deal with them?

I went to a little small town—Tyler, Texas. . . . And the only thing I could do there for a living was domestic work and it didn't pay very much. So I definitely didn't like it.

Sherna Berger Gluck, *Rosie the Riveter Revisited* (Boston: Twayne, 1987), pp. 28–33, 35–38, 40–45, 48–49.

But I left Tyler. I was saying, "I don't like it here because you can't make any money." I discovered I didn't have any trade. I had nothing I could do other than just that, and that wasn't what I wanted. So I decided I'd better get out of this town. I didn't like Dallas because that was too rough. Then someone told me, "Well, why don't you try California?" So then I got Los Angeles in my mind. I was twenty and I saved my money till I was twenty-one. In August 1940, I came here.

When I first came, when my aunt met me down at the station, I had less then ten dollars. I went on to her house and stayed. In less than ten days I had found a job living on the place doing domestic work. I stayed there from some time in August until Christmas. I was making thirty-five dollars a month. That was so much better than what I was making at home, which was twelve dollars a month. I saved my money and I bought everybody a Christmas present and sent it. Oh, I was the happiest thing in the world!

I liked to go on outings a lot. So when I first came to California, when I'd have my day off, I'd go to the parks and to the beach and museum. Just go sightseeing; walking and look in the windows. Sometimes my aunt would go along with me or I'd find another girlfriend. But then I had a sister here pretty soon.

Los Angeles was a large city but I adjusted to it real well. It didn't take me long to find a way about it. I knew how to get around, and I knew how to stay out of danger and not take too many chances. I read the *Eagle* and I still get the *Sentinel*[1] once in a while. I have to get it to keep up with what the black people are doing. I used to read those papers when I was a child back home. That's what give me a big idea. I used to read a little paper called the *Kansas City Call*, and they had a *Pittsburgh Courier* that all the Negroes read.

[She returns to Texas to get married.] I stayed there for about nine months until he went into the service. Then I came to Los Angeles. I told my sister, "Well, I better get me a good job around here working in a hotel or motel or something. I want to get me a good job so when the war is over, I'll have it." And she said, "No, you just come on out and go in the war plants and work and maybe you'll make enough money where you won't have to work in the hotels or motels." . . .

I don't remember what day of the week it was, but I guess I must have started out pretty early that morning. When I went there, the man didn't hire me. They had a school down here on Figueroa and he told me to go to the school. I went down and it was almost four o'clock and they told me they'd hire me. You had to fill out a form. They didn't bother too much about your experience because they knew you didn't have any experience in aircraft. Then they give you some kind of little test where you put the pegs in the right hole.

---

1. the *Eagle* and . . . the *Sentinel:* newspapers that covered news events in the African American community.

There were other people in there, kinda mixed. I assume it was more women than men. Most of the men was gone, and they weren't hiring too many men unless they had a good excuse. Most of the women was in my bracket, five or six years younger or older. I was twenty-four. There was a black girl that hired in with me. I went to work the next day, sixty cents an hour.

I think I stayed at the school for about four weeks. They only taught you shooting and bucking rivets and how to drill the holes and to file. You had to use a hammer for certain things. After a couple of whiles, you worked on the real thing. But you were supervised so you didn't make a mess.

When we went into the plant, it wasn't too much different than down at the school. It was the same amount of noise; it was the same routine. One difference was there was just so many more people, and when you went in the door you had a badge to show and they looked at your lunch. I had gotten accustomed to a lot of people and I knew if it was a lot of people, it always meant something was going on. I got carried away: "As long as there's a lot of people here, I'll be making money." That was all I could ever see.

I was a good student, if I do say so myself. But I have found out through life, sometimes even if you're good, you just don't get the breaks if the color's not right. I could see where they made a difference in placing you in certain jobs. They had fifteen or twenty departments, but all the Negroes went to Department 17 because there was nothing but shooting and bucking rivets. You stood on one side of the panel and your partner stood on this side, and he would shoot the rivets with a gun and you'd buck them with the bar. That was about the size of it. I just didn't like it. I didn't think I could stay there with all this shooting and a'bucking and a'jumping and a'bumping. I stayed in it about two or three weeks and then I just decided I did *not* like that. I went and told my foreman and he didn't do anything about it, so I decided I'd leave.

While I was standing out on the railroad track, I ran into somebody else out there fussing also. I went over to the union and they told me what to do. I went back inside and they sent me to another department where you did bench work and I liked that much better. You had a little small jig that you would work on and you just drilled out holes. Sometimes you would rout them or you would scribe them and then you'd cut them with a cutters.

I must have stayed there nearly a year, and then they put me over in another department, "Plastics." It was the tail section of the B-Bomber, the Billy Mitchell Bomber. I put a little part in the gun-sight. You had a little ratchet set and you would screw it in there. Then I cleaned the top of the glass off and put a piece of paper over it to seal it off to go to the next section. I worked over there until the end of the war. Well, not quite the end, because I got pregnant, and while I was off having the baby the war was over.

Some weeks I brought home twenty-six dollars, some weeks sixteen dollars. Then it gradually went up to thirty dollars, then it went up a little bit more and a little bit more. And I learned somewhere along the line that in order to make a good move you gotta make some money. You don't make the same amount everyday. You have some days good, sometimes bad. Whatever you make you're supposed to save some. I was also getting that fifty dollars a month from my husband and that was just saved right away. I was planning on buying a home and a car. And I was going to go back to school. My husband came back, but I never was laid off, so I just never found it necessary to look for another job or to go to school for another job.

I was still living over on Compton Avenue with my sister in this small little back house when my husband got home. Then, when Beverly was born, my sister moved in the front house and we stayed in the back house. When he came back, he looked for a job in the cleaning and pressing place, which was just plentiful. All the people had left these cleaning and pressing jobs and every other job; they was going to the defense plant to work because they was paying good. But in the meantime he was getting the same thing the people out there was getting, $1.25 an hour. That's why he didn't bother to go out to North American [Aircraft Company]. But what we both weren't thinking about was that they did have better benefits because they did have an insurance plan and a union to back you up. Later he did come to work there, in 1951 or 1952.

I worked up until the end of March and then I took off. Beverly was born the twenty-first of June. I'd planned to come back somewhere in the last of August. I went to verify the fact that I did come back, so that did go on my record that I didn't just quit. But they laid off a lot of people, most of them, because the war was over.

It didn't bother me much—not thinking about it jobwise. I was just glad that the war was over. I didn't feel bad because my husband had a job and he also was eligible to go to school with his GI bill. So I really didn't have too many plans—which I wish I had had. I would have tore out page one and fixed it differently; put my version of page one in there.

I went and got me a job doing day work. That means you go to a person's house and clean up for one day out of the week and then you go to the next one and clean up. I did that a couple of times and I discovered I didn't like that so hot. Then I got me a job downtown working in a little factory where you do weaving—burned clothes and stuff like that. I learned to do that real good. It didn't pay too much but it paid enough to get me going, seventy-five cents or about like that.

When North American called me back, was I a happy soul! I dropped that job and went back. That was a dollar an hour. So, from sixty cents an hour, when I first hired in there, up to one dollar. That wasn't traveling fast, but it was better than anything else because you had hours to work by and you had benefits and you come home at night with your family. So it was a good deal.

It made me live better. I really did. We always say that Lincoln took the bale off of the Negroes. I think there is a statue up there in Washington, D.C., where he's lifting something off the Negro. Well, my sister always said—that's why you can't interview her because she's so radical—"Hitler was the one that got us out of the white folks' kitchen."

[She recalls the discrimination faced by black workers at North American Aircraft.] But they had to fight. They fought hand, tooth, and nail to get in there. And the first five or six Negroes who went in there, they were well educated, but they started them off as janitors. After they once got their foot in the door and was there for three months — you work for three months before they say you're hired — then they had to start fighting all over again to get off of that broom and get something decent. And some of them did.

But they'd always give that Negro man the worst part of everything. See, the jobs have already been tested and tried out before they ever get into the department, and they know what's good about them and what's bad about them. They always managed to give the worst one to the Negro. The only reason why the women fared better was they just couldn't quite give the woman as tough a job that they gave the men. But sometimes they did.

There were some departments, they didn't even allow a black person to walk through there let alone work in there. Some of the white people did not want to work with the Negro. They had arguments right there. Sometimes they would get fired and walk on out the door, but it was one more white person gone. I think even to this very day in certain places they still don't want to work with the Negro. I don't know what their story is, but if they would try then they might not knock it.

But they did everything they could to keep you separated. They just did not like for a Negro and a white person to get together and talk. Now I am a person that you can talk to and you will warm up to me much better than you can a lot of people. A white person seems to know that they could talk to me at ease. And when anyone would start — just plain, common talk, everyday talk — they didn't like it.

And they'd keep you from advancing. They always manage to give the Negroes the worst end of the deal. I happened to fall into that when they get ready to transfer you from one department to the next. That was the only thing that I ever ran into that I had to holler to the union about. And once I filed a complaint downtown with the Equal Opportunity.

The way they was doing this particular thing — they always have a lean spot where they're trying to lay off or go through there and see if they can curl out a bunch of people, get rid of the ones with the most seniority, I suppose. They had a good little system going. All the colored girls had more seniority in production than the whites because the average white woman did not come back after the war. They thought like I thought: that I have a husband now and I don't have to work and this was just only for the war and blah, blah, blah. But they didn't realize they was going to need the money. The average Negro was glad to come back because it meant more money than they was making before. So we always had more seniority in production than the white woman.

All the colored women in production, they was just one step behind the other. I had three months more than one, the next one had three months more than me, and that's the way it went. So they had a way of putting us all in [the] Blueprint [department]. We all had twenty years by the time you got in Blueprint and stayed a little while. Here come another one. He'd bump you out and then you went out the door, because they couldn't find nothing else for you to do—so they said. They just kept doing it and I could see myself: "Well, hell, I'm going to be the next one to go out the door!"

So I found some reason to file a grievance.[2] I tried to get several other girls: "Let's get together and go downtown and file a grievance." I only got two girls to go with me. That made three of us. I think we came out on top, because we all kept our jobs and then they stopped sending them to Blueprint, bumping each other like that. So, yeah, we've had to fight to stay there.

When I bought my house in '49 or '48, I went a little further on the other side of Slauson, and I drove up and down the street a couple of times. I saw one colored woman there. I went in and asked her about the neighborhood. She said there was only one there, but there was another one across the street. So I was the third one moved in there. I said, "Well, we's breaking into the neighborhood."

I don't know how long we was there, but one evening, just about dusk, here comes this woman banging on my door. I had never seen her before. She says, "I got a house over here for sale, you can tell your friends that they can buy it if they want to." I thought to myself, "What in the hell is that woman thinking about?" She was mad because she discovered I was there. Further down, oh, about two streets down, somebody burned a cross on a lawn.

Then, one Sunday evening, I don't know what happened, but they saw a snake in the yard next door to us. Some white people were staying there and the yard was so junky, I tell you. Here come the snake. We must have been living there a good little while, because Beverly was old enough to bring the gun. Everybody was looking and they had a stick or something. I don't know how, but that child came strutting out there with the gun to shoot the snake. My husband shot the snake and from that point on, everybody respected us—'cause they knew he had a gun and could use it.

I was talking to a white person about the situation and he said, "Next time you get ready to move in a white neighborhood, I'll tell you what you do. The first thing you do when you pull up there in the truck, you jump out with your guns. You hold them up high in the air." He says, "If you don't have any, borrow some or rent 'em, but be sure that they see you got a gun. Be sure one of them is a shotgun and you go in there with it first. They going to be peeping out the window, don't you worry about it. They going to see you. But if they see those guns going in first, they won't ever bother you."

I did like he said, moved in here with some guns, and nobody come and bothered me. Nobody said one word to me.

Working at North American was good. I did make more money and I did meet quite a few people that I am still friends with. I learned quite a bit. Some of the things, I wouldn't want to go back over. If I had the wisdom to know the difference which one to change and which one not to, I would. I would have fought harder at North American for better things for myself.

---

2. **grievance:** a discrimination complaint filed with the Equal Opportunities Employment Commission.

I don't have too many regrets. But if I had it to do over again, if I had to tamper with page one, I would sure get a better education. I would never have stopped going to school. I took several little classes every so often—cosmetology, photography, herbs. For a little while, I did study nursing. I would have finished some of them. I would have went deeper into it.

We always talking about women's lib and working. Well, we all know that the Negro woman was the first woman that left home to go to work. She's been working ever since because she had to work beside her husband in slavery—against her will. So she has always worked. She knows how to get out there and work. She has really pioneered the field. Then after we've gotten out here and proved that it can be done, then the white woman decided: "Hey, I don't want to stay home and do nothing." She zeroed in on the best jobs. So we're still on the tail-end, but we still back there fighting.

28

Memories of the Internment Camp

Ben Yorita and Philip Hayasaka

During World War II, the United States was more careful about protecting the civil liberties of its citizens than it had been after its entrance into World War I. There was, however, one glaring exception: the internment of 110,000 Japanese Americans in camps euphemistically called "relocation centers." (A similar attempt to relocate Italian and German Americans from areas along the West Coast was quickly recognized as impractical and soon abandoned.) The military director of the internment program declared that the "Japanese race is an enemy race and while many second and third generation Japanese born on United States soil, possessed of United States Citizenship, have become Americanized, the racial strains are undiluted. . . . It, therefore, follows that along the vital Pacific coast over 112,000 potential enemies, of Japanese extraction, are at large today." These people, seventy thousand of them native-born citizens of the United States, were forced to evacuate their homes within forty-eight hours (losing about $500 million in property along with their jobs) and made to live for long periods of time in tar-papered barracks behind barbed wire.

The Supreme Court of the United States, in two major decisions, supported the constitutionality of internment. Justice Robert Jackson warned in a dissenting opinion that the case established a precedent that "lays about like a loaded weapon." In 1988, Congress, in recognition of the wrong that the government inflicted, appropriated compensation for internees.

This reading, from interviews conducted by Archie Satterfield in the 1970s, is about the experiences of two Japanese Americans who suffered through this mockery of American justice.

BEFORE YOU READ

1. What were the main fears aroused among Japanese Americans by the internment?
2. What did Japanese Americans lose by the internment?
3. What were the likely psychological effects on Japanese Americans of the internment?
4. Compare the treatment of Japanese Americans in the United States with that of Jews in Germany. What was similar? What was different?

Archie Satterfield, *The Home Front: An Oral History of the War Years in America, 1941–1945* (New York: Playboy Press, 1981), pp. 330–38.

BEN YORITA

"Students weren't as aware of national politics then as they are now, and Japanese-Americans were actually apolitical then. Our parents couldn't vote, so we simply weren't interested in politics because there was nothing we could do about it if we were.

"There were two reasons we were living in the ghettos: Birds of a feather flock together, and we had all the traditional aspects of Japanese life—Japanese restaurants, baths, and so forth; and discrimination forced us together. The dominant society prevented us from going elsewhere.

"Right after Pearl Harbor we had no idea what was going to happen, but toward the end of December we started hearing rumors and talk of the evacuation started. We could tell from what we read in the newspapers and the propaganda they were printing—guys like Henry McLemore,[1] who said he hated all Japs and that we should be rounded up, gave us the idea of how strong feelings were against us. So we were expecting something and the evacuation was no great surprise.

"I can't really say what my parents thought about everything because we didn't communicate that well. I never asked them what they thought. We communicated on other things, but not political matters.

"Once the evacuation was decided, we were told we had about a month to get rid of our property or do whatever we wanted to with it. That was a rough time for my brother, who was running a printshop my parents owned. We were still in debt on it and we didn't know what to do with all the equipment. The machines were old but still workable, and we had English type and Japanese type. Japanese characters had to be set by hand and were very hard to replace. Finally, the whole works was sold, and since nobody would buy the Japanese type, we had to sell it as junk lead at 50¢ a pound. We sold the equipment through newspaper classified ads: 'Evacuating: Household goods for sale.' Second-hand dealers and everybody else came in and bought our refrigerator, the piano, and I had a whole bunch of books I sold for $5, which was one of my personal losses. We had to sell our car, and the whole thing was very sad. By the way, it was the first time we had ever had a refrigerator and it had to be sold after only a few months.

"We could take only what we could carry, and most of us were carrying two suitcases or duffel bags. The rest of our stuff that we couldn't sell was stored in the Buddhist church my mother belonged to. When we came back, thieves had broken in and stolen almost everything of value from the church.

"I had a savings account that was left intact, but people who had their money in the Japanese bank in Seattle had their assets frozen from Pearl Harbor until the late 1960s, when the funds were finally released. They received no interest.

"They took all of us down to the Puyallup fairgrounds, Camp Harmony,[2] and everything had been thrown together in haste. They had converted some of

---

1. **Henry McLemore:** syndicated columnist for the Hearst newspapers who strongly supported mass evacuation of Japanese Americans from the West Coast to the interior.
2. **Camp Harmony:** temporary assembly center in Puyallup, Washington.

the display and exhibit areas into rooms and had put up some barracks on the parking lot. The walls in the barracks were about eight feet high with open space above and with big knotholes in the boards of the partitions. Our family was large, so we had two rooms.

"They had also built barbed-wire fences around the camp with a tower on each corner with military personnel and machine guns, rifles, and searchlights. It was terrifying because we didn't know what was going to happen to us. We didn't know where we were going and we were just doing what we were told. No questions asked. If you get an order, you go ahead and do it.

"There was no fraternization, no contact with the military or any Caucasian except when we were processed into the camp. But the treatment in Camp Harmony was fairly loose in the sense that we were free to roam around in the camp. But it was like buffalo in cages or behind barbed wire.

"There was no privacy whatsoever in the latrines and showers, and it was humiliating for the women because they were much more modest then than today. It wasn't so bad for the men because they were accustomed to open latrines and showers.

"We had no duties in the sense that we were required to work, but you can't expect a camp to manage itself. They had jobs open in the kitchen and stock room, and eventually they opened a school where I helped teach a little. I wasn't a qualified teacher, and I got about $13 a month. We weren't given an allowance while we were in Camp Harmony waiting for the camp at Minidoka[3] to be finished, so it was pretty tight for some families.

"From Camp Harmony on, the family structure was broken down. Children ran everywhere they wanted to in the camp, and parents lost their authority. We could eat in any mess hall we wanted, and kids began ignoring their parents and wandering wherever they pleased.

"Eventually they boarded us on army trucks and took us to trains to be transported to the camps inland. We had been in Camp Harmony from May until September. There was a shortage of transportation at the time and they brought out these old, rusty cars with gaslight fixtures. As soon as we got aboard we pulled the shades down so people couldn't stare at us. The cars were all coaches and we had to sit all the way to camp, which was difficult for some of the older people and the invalids. We made makeshift beds out of the seats for them, and did the best we could.

"When we got to Twin Falls,[4] we were loaded onto trucks again, and we looked around and all we could see was that vast desert with nothing but sagebrush. When the trucks started rolling, it was dusty, and the camp itself wasn't completed yet. The barracks had been built and the kitchen facilities were there, but the laundry room, showers, and latrines were not finished. They had taken a bulldozer in the good old American style and leveled the terrain and then built the camp. When the wind blew, it was dusty and we had to wear face masks to go to the dining hall. When winter came and it rained, the dust turned into gumbo mud. Until the latrines were finished, we had to use outhouses.

3. **Minidoka:** relocation center in Idaho.
4. **Twin Falls:** transfer city in Idaho.

"The administrators were civilians and they tried to organize us into a chain of command to make the camp function. Each block of barracks was told to appoint a representative, who were called block managers. Of course we called them the Blockheads.

"When winter came, it was very cold and I began withdrawing my savings to buy clothes because we had none that was suitable for that climate. Montgomery Ward and Sears Roebuck[5] did a landslide business from the camps because we ordered our shoes and warm clothing from them. The people who didn't have savings suffered quite a bit until the camp distributed navy pea coats. Then everybody in camp was wearing outsize pea coats because we were such small people. Other than army blankets, I don't remember any other clothing issues.

"The barracks were just single-wall construction and the only insulation was tar paper nailed on the outside, and they never were improved. The larger rooms had potbellied stoves, and we all slept on army cots. Only the people over sixty years old were able to get metal cots, which had a bit more spring to them than the army cots, which were just stationary hammocks.

"These camps were technically relocation centers and there was no effort to hold us in them, but they didn't try actively to relocate us until much later. On my own initiative I tried to get out as soon as I could, and started writing letters to friends around the country. I found a friend in Salt Lake City who agreed to sponsor me for room and board, and he got his boss to agree to hire me. I got out in May 1943, which was earlier than most. In fact, I was one of the first to leave Minidoka.

"Of course I had to get clearance from Washington, D.C., and they investigated my background. I had to pay my own way from Twin Falls to Salt Lake City, but after I left, the government had a program of per diem for people leaving.

"I got on the bus with my suitcase, all by myself, my first time in the outside world, and paid my fare and began looking for a seat, then this old guy said: 'Hey, Tokyo, sit next to me.'

"I thought, Oh, my God, Tokyo! I sat next to him and he was a friendly old guy who meant well."

Yorita's friend worked in a parking garage across the street from the Mormon tabernacle, and the garage owner let them live in the office, where the two young men cooked their own meals. One nearby grocery-store owner wouldn't let them buy from him, and a barber in the neighborhood hated them on sight. Yorita parked a car once that had a rifle and pair of binoculars in the back seat, and he and his friend took the binoculars out and were looking through them when the barber looked out and saw them studying the Mormon tabernacle. He called the FBI, and two agents were soon in the garage talking to the young men.

Yorita wasn't satisfied with his job in Salt Lake City, and soon left for Cincinnati, then Chicago, which he enjoyed because most Chicago people

---

5. **Montgomery Ward and Sears Roebuck:** two mail-order catalog companies.

didn't care what nationality he was. He and a brother were able to find good jobs and a good place to live, and they brought their parents out of the Idaho camp to spend the rest of the war in Chicago.

PHILIP HAYASAKA

Philip Hayasaka was a teen-ager when Pearl Harbor was attacked. Unlike most Japanese-Americans, his parents had been able to find a home in a predominantly Caucasian neighborhood because his father was a wholesale produce dealer and most of his business was conducted with Caucasians. Consequently, when the family was interned, Hayasaka was a stranger to most of the other families.

Still, he and his family understood well the rationale of the Little Tokyos along the West Coast.

"If you could become invisible, you could get along. We were forced into a situation of causing no trouble, of being quiet, not complaining. It was not a matter of our stoic tradition. I've never bought that. We did what we had to do to survive.

"There was a lot of hysteria at the time, a lot of confusion, and the not knowing what was going to happen created such a fear that we became super-cautious. We would hear that the FBI was going into different houses and searching, and we would wonder when they were coming to our house. We just knew that they were going to come and knock on the door and that we wouldn't know what to do when they came.

"A lot of people were burning things that didn't need to be burned, but they were afraid suspicion would be attached to those things. All those wonder-ful old calligraphies were destroyed, priceless things, because they thought someone in authority would believe they represented allegiance to Japan. One time I was with my mother in the house, just the two of us, and there was a knock on the door. My mother had those rosary-type beads that the Buddhists use for prayer, and she put them in my pocket and sent me outside to play and stay out until whoever was at the door left. She was afraid it was the FBI and they would take them away from us. It sounds silly now, but that kind of fear was pervasive then. It was tragic.

"When this happened, my dad's business went to hell. Suddenly all his ac-counts payable were due immediately, but all the accounts receivable weren't. People knew the guy wasn't going to be around much longer, so they didn't pay him. I knew at one time how much he lost that way—we had to turn in a claim after the war—but I've forgotten now. But it was a considerable amount. Those claims, by the way, didn't give justice to the victims; it only legitimized the government. We got about a nickel on the dollar.

"It was kind of interesting how different people reacted when they came to Camp Harmony to see friends, and how we reacted in return. Friends from Seattle would come down to see me, and we had to talk through the barbed-wire fences. [Note: Nobody was permitted to stand closer than three feet to the fence, which meant conversations were held at least six feet from each other, with guards standing and watching.] There was one instance when I saw a close friend from high school just outside the fence, and he had come down to see me. He hadn't seen me inside, so I hid rather than going out to see him. The whole evacuation did funny things to your mind.

"All the leaders of the community were taken away, and my dad was interned before we were and taken to the interrogation camp in Missoula. It was one of the greatest shocks of my life when the FBI came and picked him up. Here was a guy who had followed all the rules, respected authority, and was a leader in the company. And all of the sudden he was behind bars for no reason. He stayed there several months before they let him join us at Minidoka."

When the war ended and the camps were closed, about the only people left in them were young children and the elderly. All who could leave for jobs did so, and the experience had a scattering effect on the Japanese-American communities across the Pacific Coast. Several families settled on the East Coast and in the Midwest, and when those with no other place to go, or who didn't want to migrate away from the Coast, returned to their hometowns, they usually found their former ghettos taken over by other minority groups. Consequently, whether they wanted to or not, they were forced to find housing wherever it was available. It was difficult returning to the cities, however. Everybody dreaded it, and some of the elderly people with no place to go of their own were virtually evacuated from the camps. They had become accustomed to the life there and were afraid to leave.

Some Caucasians, such as Floyd Schmoe and the Reverend Emory Andrews, worked with the returning outcasts to help them resettle as smoothly as possible. A few farms had been saved for the owners, but four years of weeds and brush had accumulated. Schmoe was back teaching at the University of Washington by that time, and he organized groups of his students to go out on weekends and after school to help clear the land for crops again. Some people returning found their former neighbors had turned against them in their absence, and grocery-store owners who had become Jap-haters during the war would not sell them food.

The farmers who did get their crops growing again were often so discriminated against that they could not sell their produce, or get it delivered into the marketplace. Schmoe was able to solve this problem for one farmer by talking a neighbor, a Filipino, into taking the Japanese-American's produce and selling it as his own. Hayasaka's father was able to get back into the wholesale produce business by becoming partners with a young Japanese-American veteran of the famed 442d Regiment, the most highly decorated group in the war. The veteran put up a sign over the office saying the business was operated by a veteran, which made it difficult for buyers to avoid it.

BEN YORITA

"The older people never recovered from the camps. The father was the traditional breadwinner and in total command of the family. But after going into the camps, fathers were no longer the breadwinners; the young sons and daughters were. Most of them couldn't even communicate in English, so all the burdens fell on the second generation. And most of us were just kids, nineteen or twenty. Consequently there was a big turnover of responsibility and authority, and the parents were suddenly totally dependent on their children. When we returned to the cities after the war, it was the second generation again that had to make the decisions and do all the negotiating with landlords, attorneys, and the like."

29

The Bataan Death March
Blair Robinett et al.

In the months immediately after the December 7, 1941, attack on Pearl Harbor — as Japanese Americans were being herded into internment camps — the Axis powers were on the march. Hitler's armies threatened Moscow and the Suez Canal, while his submarine navy was sinking British and American ships far more rapidly than they could be replaced: nearly 750,000 tons a month. In the Pacific, Japan captured the key British naval base of Singapore as well as Burma, most of the East Indies, and the Philippines, where General Douglas MacArthur directed troops in a gallant but futile defense.

When the Philippine stronghold of Bataan fell on April 9, 1942, after a three-month siege, Japanese soldiers forced their prisoners — about seventy thousand Americans and Filipinos — to evacuate quickly and without adequate food or water. Thousands died on this infamous Bataan death march amid tortures and horrors that the following selections only begin to describe.

The death march joined the sneak attack on Pearl Harbor as a focus for many Americans' hatred of all things Japanese. Most Americans believed that the cruelty was deliberate and planned. In reality, as the historian John Toland has written, "There had been no plan at all. About half of the prisoners rode in trucks . . . and suffered little. Some who walked saw almost no brutalities and were fed, if not well, at least occasionally. Yet others a mile behind were starved, beaten and killed by brutal guards." Perhaps seven to ten thousand men died on the march, about 2,330 of them Americans. The Japanese generals, in Toland's view, had seriously underestimated how many soldiers had surrendered as well as how sick and near starvation the prisoners already were. Their responsibility for the general misery as well as the gratuitous violence inflicted on the prisoners stemmed not from some deliberate plan but from indifference to suffering, the habitual brutality of the Japanese army (officers routinely beat enlisted men), and the Japanese officers' lack of control over their own soldiers.

Before You Read

1. What evidence can you find in the readings to corroborate or disprove Toland's view of how the death march occurred?

2. How would you try to explain the way the guards acted?

3. How did the prisoners whose accounts you will read survive the march?

Donald Knox, *Death March: The Survivors of Bataan* (New York: Harcourt Brace Jovanovich, 1981), pp. 122–39.

PFC. BLAIR ROBINETT

Company C, 803d Engineers

My group came up the road from Mariveles another half mile or so when a Jap soldier stepped out, came across, and took my canteen out of its cover. He took a drink, filled his canteen out of mine, poured the rest of my water on the ground, and dropped the canteen at my feet. I thought he was going to walk back to the line of Jap troops standing across the road, so I bent over to pick up my canteen. But he turned around and hit me on the head with his rifle butt. Put a crease in the top of my head that I still have. I fell face down on the cobblestones. I crawled back up to my knees, debating whether to pick up the canteen again. I figured the best course of action was to stand up and leave the canteen alone. Soon as the Jap troops moved off, I squatted down and picked it up. A little later a Jap soldier came over to one of the lieutenants out of our company, and when he found out his canteen was empty he beat the lieutenant to his knees with the canteen. Just kept slapping him back and forth across the face.

We moved down the ridge a ways when we saw this GI. He was sick. I figured he had come out of the hospital that was in tents out under the trees. He was wobbling along, uneasy on his feet. There were Japanese infantry and tanks coming down the road alongside us. One of these Jap soldiers, I don't know whether he was on our side or if he deliberately came across the road, but he grabbed this sick guy by the arm and guided him to the middle of the road. Then he just flipped him out across the road. The guy hit the cobblestone about five feet in front of a tank and the tank pulled on across him. Well, it killed him quick. There must have been ten tanks in that column, and every one of them came up there right across the body. When the last tank left there was no way you could tell there'd ever been a man there. But his uniform was embedded in the cobblestone. The man disappeared, but his uniform had been pressed until it had become part of the ground.

Now we knew, if there had been any doubts before, we were in for a bad time.

CAPT. MARION LAWTON

1st Battalion, 31st Regiment, Philippine Army

When we had marched several kilometers, we came to a large group of prisoners who were all Americans. My little group had increased to about fifty by then. There I found my commanding officer, Colonel Erwin. He was a large fellow, a little over six feet tall and weighed probably 240 pounds. He was the type who believed in having an abundance of everything. I noticed he had a heavy barracks bag with him. I'd thrown away everything except a change of socks, underwear, and toilet articles, because I knew I couldn't carry a lot of stuff. Knowing how heavy Colonel Erwin's bag was, I volunteered to help him, but I warned him that I felt it was a mistake to carry that much. "Oh, no," he said, "I might need this gear." He had extra shoes and uniforms and who knows what else. Hadn't been looted either.

The Japs put us in groups of a hundred, columns of four, and marched us out by groups. I managed to stick with Colonel Erwin. This was April 9, the actual day of surrender. It was as hot as the dickens. The Jap trucks started coming in. And there was just clouds of dust. We started marching. I can't remember hours or specific days, but as we moved on it got hotter and we got more fatigued. After a couple of hours people started faltering. Thirsty, tired, some, like me, already sick. Most everyone was suffering from malaria and diarrhea, all hungry. I'd been pretty well fed, but a lot of these fellows had been on half rations since January and, on top of that, in the confusion of the last few days they had eaten nothing at all. So we were hungry, plus being under pressure of combat. We were emotionally spent, so horribly frightened and depressed and distressed, not knowing what was going to happen to us.

About midday Colonel Erwin, still holding his bag, started slowing down and gradually dropping back. Soon I lost sight of him. I got reports later of what happened. He finally dropped back to the tail of the column and the guards back there started prodding him. He drifted on back further still, until one of the guards stuck him with a bayonet. I guess he was delirious and fevered and exhausted. Finally, a guard pushed him to the side of the road and put his rifle muzzle to his back and pulled the trigger. He was one of the early casualties.

With this exception I didn't see many atrocities, other than people being hit or bayonet prodded. See, I was among the first groups out and all the killings and beatings took place in the later groups, those who were one to three days hungrier and weaker.

CPL. HUBERT GATER

200th Coast Artillery

Suddenly the hill rocked under us. There was a roar to the left, to the right, and then several back to our rear. The Japs had moved their field guns into position around us on Cabcaben Field.

"Why the dirty bastards!" the man next to me said. "They're using us as a shield to fire on Corregidor." It was true. We should have realized then what to expect as their prisoners.

A flight of Jap bombers were flying over Corregidor. Our officers cautioned us not to watch them because if our anti-aircraft fire hit any of them we would cheer in spite of ourself. Our chief worry was, would Corregidor return fire on the guns that surrounded us?

Corregidor didn't, but a gunboat out in the Bay did. I don't know the size of the shells; they were some smaller than our 3-inch. The first shell was to our right. Apparently, a dud. It skidded through the grass and set it on fire. Some of the men flattened out; others stood up ready to run to cover. Our officers motioned us down. There were a lot of Japs around us now.

The second shell burst to the rear and center of us. At the time I thought it had hit some of our men. A Jap soldier got part of his chin tore off. He was a terrible looking sight running around, evidently half out of his mind. From chin to waist he was covered with blood.

A young Jap officer who had been silently watching us motioned with his hand for us to take cover. About 300 of us ran across Cabcaben Field to get behind a hill. The rest ran the other way, up the road.

CPL. HUBERT GATER

200th Coast Artillery

Night came. We had moved across the road into a rice field. Jap soldiers, tanks, big field guns, and horses went by in a steady stream. Occasionally, a Jap would run out and hit one of us with his rifle. No one slept. Most of the night Corregidor was firing their big guns. The only way to describe it—it sounded like freight trains going through the air over our heads. They were firing into the area that the Japanese would use to invade Bataan. During the night a man was sent with some canteens for water. The canteens were taken and he was beat up.

The next morning a steady stream of Filipino civilians began to go by, moving out of Bataan. Old and young, many were evidently sick. I didn't realize so many of them had been trapped on Bataan.

SGT. RALPH LEVENBERG

17th Pursuit Squadron

Eventually they started to systematically put us in groups of about 100 or so and marched us off. There were one, two, sometimes four guards, you never knew.

I was fortunate in two respects. First, I had a new pair of shoes, and second, I had some chlorine pills. The shoes I had kept with me ever since we left the barracks outside Manila, and the chlorine I had just managed to pick up. I don't know why, maybe because of my upbringing, I was taught to be protective of my physical being. I was therefore able from time to time, when we stopped near a creek which had dead bodies and horses floating in it, to get some water and purify it with the chlorine.

One of the tricks the Japs played on us—thought it was funny, too—was when they would be riding on the back of a truck, they would have these long black snake whips, and they'd whip that thing out and get some poor bastard by the neck or torso and drag him behind their truck. 'Course if one of our guys was quick enough he didn't get dragged too far. But, if the Japs got a sick guy. . . .

CAPT. MARK WOHLFELD

27th Bombardment Group

We were all mixed up—privates, officers, Scout officers, 31st Infantry, 192d Tank Battalion, 200th New Mexico Coast Artillery—just a jumbled mass of humanity.

My group stopped at a small bridge up above Cabcaben to let some Jap horse artillery through. They were in a real hurry to get these guns in place and start on Corregidor. Right behind the artillery there arrived a great big 1942 Cadillac equipped with a freshly cut wooden camera platform attached to the roof. As soon as they saw us they stopped and the cameraman jumped out and placed his tripod and camera on the platform. He had his big box camera which he looked down into. A white-shirted Japanese interpreter staged us for the cameraman. He told us to line up and put our hands over our heads. We should look depressed and dejected. That wasn't hard. The cameraman took his pictures and started back down the road in his Cadillac towards Corregidor, while we started marching in the other direction. That picture eventually appeared in *Life* magazine.

An hour or so later we halted and fell out near a ditch where there were about five dead Filipinos lying around. They looked like swollen rag dolls. I used a handkerchief knotted at the four corners to keep the sun from my head. I asked the Japanese guard, part talk, part pantomime, "Can I have a helmet? Dead, Filipino. Sun, hot, hot." He finally gave in, but I wondered whether he'd shoot me when I got as far as the ditch: "Fuck it, I'll try it." There was this dead Filipino lying there, and because his face was so puffed up I could only barely manage to get the chin strap off. He was full of maggots and flies. I finally got the helmet off and wiped out the inside with a part of his uniform that wasn't soiled. Then I hung it from my belt so it would dry. Who cared for germs at a time like that? I came back from the ditch and sat next to Major Small. "Boy," he said, "could I stand a Coca-Cola now." I started thinking about my girlfriend then. She worked in Grand Central Station in a real estate office, and I knew she used to go downstairs on her break and get a nice Coke with lots of ice chips in it. I started to take the helmet off my belt and put it on my head, when I noticed the dead Filipino had scratched the name Mary in his helmet liner. The amazing thing was my girlfriend's name was also Mary!

After a column of trucks carrying landing craft passed us, we resumed our march. We fell in behind another group marching out. We'd gone a little farther when we pulled off to the side of the road again to let some trucks roll by. Some of our young guys started asking the Japs whether they could have a drink of water. I looked to my right and saw a buffalo wallow about fifty yards off the road. It looked like green scum. The guards started to laugh and said. "O.K., O.K." So all these kids, eighteen or nineteen year old enlisted men, run for the water and began drowning each other trying to get a drink. The Japs thought it was hilarious. I noticed at the end of the scum some others drinking through handkerchiefs, thinking that would filter the bacteria out. Finally, a Japanese officer came along and began shouting at the men in the water. There must have been fifty of them, and they scattered and ran back for the road. That wasn't the end of it. This officer found some Jap soldiers who had been watching us and ordered them to pull out of the line any Americans who had water stains on their uniforms. When we marched out, after a short while we heard shooting behind us.

That night when we stopped, most of us had had no water all day. Our tongues were thick with dust. We had come into this abandoned barrio and were now sitting in a field. My small group was made up of some senior officers, even a few full colonels. I noticed one, Col. Edmund Lillie, who had been my reserve unit instructor back in the States ten years before. I went up to him, but of course he didn't remember me. We started to talk and began wondering how we could get some water. There was an artesian well near us that had water dribbling out of it, but we were afraid that we'd be shot if we went to get any. Desperate as we were, Colonel Lillie asked a guard whether we could go and get water. The Jap agreed. Most of these officers did not have canteens, but I spotted an old pail, and since I was only a captain, I went over to get it. Inside the pail, stuck to the bottom, was some dried manure. "Maybe I can rinse it out," I said. Lillie told me, "Don't waste the water rinsing it, just fill it up." When I got to the well, one of the Jap guards kept urging me to hurry up. As soon as I got as much as I could, without running the risk of being bayoneted, I came back to the group. There wasn't much water in the pail, but it was something. Lillie told us we could each have only one full mouthful before we passed the pail to the next man. In those days an officer's word meant something, so that's just what we did. Each of us took one full gulp. That way there was enough for everyone.

CAPT. LOYD MILLS

Company C, 57th Infantry, Philippine Scouts

The nights were the worst times for me. We walked all day, from early morning until dusk. Then we were put into barbed-wire enclosures in which the conditions were nearly indescribable. Filth and defecation all over the place. The smell was terrible. These same enclosures had been used every night, and when my group got to them, they were covered by the filth of five or six nights.

I had dysentery pretty bad, but I didn't worry about it because there wasn't anything you could do about it. You didn't stop on "the March" because you were dead if you did. They didn't mess around with you. You didn't have time to pull out and go over and squat. You would just release wherever you were. Generally right on yourself, or somebody else if they happened to be in your way. There was nothing else to do. Without food it was water more than anything. It just went through me . . . bang.

I was in a daze. One thing I knew was that I had to keep going. I was young, so I had that advantage over some of the older men. I helped along the way. If someone near you started stumbling and looked like he was going to fall, you would try to literally pick him up and keep him going. You always talked to them. Tried to make them understand that if they fell they were gone. 'Course, there was nothing you could do about the people who fell in the back.

STAFF SGT. HAROLD FEINER

17th Ordnance Company, Provisional Tank Group

I don't know if the guards were Korean or Taiwanese. I was so miserable on that Death March that I couldn't tell you what they were. I know one thing about them, though—they were mean, sadistic, brutal. And yet, on "the March" I was befriended.

I had been hit at Cabcaben and had a piece of Corregidor shrapnel in my leg. It was the size of a piece of pencil lead and was laying along my shinbone. I had wrapped an old white towel around it and had managed to walk about fifteen miles, but I was getting weaker and more feverish the further I went. I was in bad shape. Guys had to help me. They would kind of hold onto me. If you fell, you were dead. They bayoneted you right away. No bullshit! If you fell, bingo, you were dead.

We finally stopped for the night near a small stream and I laid down. About an hour later this guy comes crawling along. He looked like an Italian, swarthy, kind of muscular. "Hey, fellows, any of you guys need any help?" he was whispering. "I'm a doctor." Didn't give us his name. When he got to me, he stopped and I told him about my leg. Just then a young guard saw us and came over. The first thing they did was hit you with their rifle butts. He spoke atrocious English and he yelled for us to separate. The doctor kept talking, and asked him would it be all right if he took the shrapnel out of my leg. "Wait, wait, wait," and he ran out into the road to see if anyone was coming. Then he came back and said, "Hurry, hurry." I remember the doctor saying, "Soldier, this is going to hurt. If you can take it, I'll get it out." He never had to worry about me hurting. As soon as he touched it, bam, I passed out. He took it out and wrapped a hand towel around my shin. When he left he said, "Yeah, well, I hope to God you make it. God bless you." He disappeared and I never got to know his name.

The Jap guard came up to me during the night and gave me a cup of sweetened chocolate, tasted like milk. I hadn't had any food and no water for days. I didn't speak one single word of Japanese then, but he could speak a little English, but with a really horrible accent. "Someday me go Hollywood, me going to be movie star." That's the way he talked. He made me laugh. All through the night he gave me something, because he knew I needed strength. In the morning he was gone. His squad had been replaced by another. The orders were given, "Everybody up, up, up." We got in line and I found I couldn't walk. My leg hurt so much. Some guys held me up and I was carried about 100 feet to the road. There we were told to stop and sit down. Then we were told to get up. We waited about a half an hour before we were permitted to sit down again. Then we were turned around and marched back to where we started. Wait . . . rest . . . wait . . . march . . . turn around . . . go back. We did this the whole day. I never had to walk, and by the time we started out the next day I had enough strength to limp along on my own. I'm not a religious man, but God said keep those men there, we want to save that man. I don't know what it was. I know I wouldn't have made it, if I had to march that day.

Maybe a day or so later we came to a river. I was still in fairly bad shape. There were a lot of little rivers, and because it was the dry season, they were shallow. The bridge had been knocked out and the Japanese had reconstructed an engineering bridge. Since their troops were crossing it when we arrived, we were made to march down the bank, cross the river, and march up the other side. Sounds simple. We were told not to touch the water. Some of the guys managed to drag their towels in the water and got some water that way. One man, however, reached over and tried to cup his hands and drink some. He was twelve feet from me. They shot him. Some guards on the bridge just popped him off. Going up the other side was hard for me with my leg. I kept sliding on the slimy clay. Finally some guys helped me up.

When we got to the top of the bank, there was a little bend in the road before it crossed the bridge. At that point some Jap sentries were stationed and they were laughing at our struggles. When I got to the top—mind you, I was still crippled—for some reason, maybe because I needed help, one of the sentries took his rifle by the barrel and swung it at me and broke the ribs on my right side. Then I walked with broken ribs and a wounded leg. But I got to San Fernando. Had lots of help. But, hell, guys got there with less than me.

30

Post–World War II "Red Scare"

Mark Goodson

Following each of the world wars of the twentieth century, American politics shifted from progressive to conservative and went through a "red scare," a heightened fear of communism. While there were real reasons that provoked America's confrontation with the Soviet Union, this eagerness to attribute all evil, perhaps all social change, to a malevolent force emanating from Moscow remains one of the mysteries of American life.

The Truman administration conducted a rigid internal security program to weed out disloyal or potentially subversive federal employees (although it fired many more homosexuals than political activists). And Truman pursued a foreign policy of unparalleled aggressiveness against the Soviet Union. Despite this he was successfully attacked by Republicans as "soft" on communism. Espionage cases from World War II and even earlier stirred fears, but not a single case of a communist committing espionage was ever proved. Teachers and professors were fired for political reasons, but no case of communist indoctrination in the classroom ever emerged in these years. Several state commissions and committees branded the National Association for the Advancement of Colored People an instrument of international communism. And the 1954 landmark decision in Brown v. Board of Education, *which paved the way for the integration of public schools, was regularly cited across the South as evidence of communist infiltration of the U.S. Supreme Court.*

The red scare affected the entertainment industry particularly. Both Hollywood and New York had been centers of political radicalism in the 1930s and during the war. Highly organized citizens' groups pressured the entertainment industry to blacklist writers, directors, and actors, among others. This greatly influenced what Americans did and did not see on television or at the movies and left hundreds of industry workers unemployed. Mark Goodson (1915–1992) was a producer of highly successful game shows such as What's My Line, To Tell the Truth, I've Got a Secret, Password, *and* Family Feud. *His recollections of the era explain how the system of blacklisting worked and illustrate how extensive it was.*

BEFORE YOU READ

1. Ask your parents or grandparents about Goodson's quiz shows. Did they have any political content? What purpose was served by banning certain guests or panelists?

2. Consider the cases of Anna Lee and Abe Burrows. What recourse did they have against the blacklists?

Griffin Fariello, *Red Scare: Memories of the American Inquisition: An Oral History* (New York: Norton, 1995), pp. 320–26.

I'm not sure when it began, but I believe it was early 1950. At that point, I had no connection with the blacklisting that was going on, although I had heard about it in the motion picture business and heard rumors about things that had happened on other shows, like *The Aldrich Family*. My first experience really was when we settled into a fairly regular panel on *What's My Line?* in mid-1950. The panel consisted of the poet Louis Untermeyer, Dorothy Kilgallen,[1] Arlene Francis,[2] and Hal Block, a comedy writer. Our sponsor was Stopette, a deodorant.

A few months into the show, I began getting mail on Louis Untermeyer. He had been listed in *Red Channels.* He was one of those folks who had supported the left-wing forces against Franco in Spain. I know that he also had allowed his name to be affiliated with the Joint Anti-Fascist Refugee Committee and had been a sponsor of the 1948 May Day parade. Back in the early 1920s,[3] he had written articles for *The Masses.* But he was certainly not an active political person, at least as far as I knew.

CBS and Stopette also began receiving letters of protest. First, it was just a few postcards. Then it grew. Members of the Catholic War Veterans put stickers on drugstore windows, red, white, and blue stickers, warning, "Stop Stopette Until Stopette Stops Untermeyer."

We didn't pay too much attention until we got the call from CBS. Untermeyer and I were summoned to Ralph Colin's office, who was the general counsel for CBS at the time. Louis and Colin knew each other. Ralph asked him why he lent his name to the group. "I thought it was a good cause," Untermeyer said. "Louis, you're being very naive. These are very difficult times and you've put us in a bad spot. We're going to have to drop you." Untermeyer was very apologetic, but the decision had been made. He was let go.

I remember leaving that office feeling embarrassed. Untermeyer was in his sixties, a man of considerable dignity. He was a good American poet and I liked him; he was funny and articulate on the show. What's more, I had no political ax to grind.

That was the last of that kind of meeting. Soon afterwards, CBS installed a clearance division. There wasn't any discussion. We would just get the word — "Drop that person" — and that was supposed to be it. Whenever we booked a guest or a panelist on *What's My Line?* or *I've Got a Secret*, one of our assistants would phone up and say, "We're going to use so-and-so." We'd either get the okay, or they'd call back and say, "Not clear," or "Sorry, can't use them." Even advertising agencies — big ones, like Young & Rubicam and BBD&O — had

---

1. **Dorothy Kilgallen:** longtime columnist for the *New York Journal-American.*
2. **Arlene Francis:** singer and radio and television talk-show host.
3. Louis Untermeyer (1885–1977) began publishing his poetry in *The Masses* in 1913. During World War One, the magazine's antiwar position ran afoul of the Postmaster General, who revoked its mailing license under the Espionage Act of 1917. *The Masses'* editors were vindicated in court but lost access to the mails through a legal technicality. The magazine was succeeded by the *Liberator*, which ran until 1924. [Goodson's note.]

their own clearance departments. They would never come out and say it. They would just write off somebody by saying, "He's a bad actor." You were never supposed to tell the person what it was about; you'd just unbook them. They never admitted there was a blacklist. It just wasn't done.

Some fairly substantial names were off-limits—big stars like Leonard Bernstein, Harry Belafonte, Abe Burrows, Gypsy Rose Lee, Judy Holliday, Jack Gilford, Uta Hagen, and Hazel Scott. Everyone, from the stars to the bit-part actors, was checked. We once did a show in California called *The Rebel*, and we used wranglers to take care of the horses—we had to clear all of their names. CBS, in particular, asked for loyalty oaths to be signed by everybody, making sure that you were not un-American. So far as I know, no one ever refused.

In 1952, *I've Got a Secret* got a new sponsor, R. J. Reynolds Tobacco Company, with its advertising agency, William Este. When they came aboard, someone from the agency called me and said, "Please get rid of Henry Morgan," one of the regular panelists on the show. Morgan had been named in *Red Channels*. I had known Henry for a long time; he was one of those young curmudgeons who was acidic at times, but he was by no means a communist. His wife was involved with radical politics, but they were getting a divorce, and to some extent his name was just smeared.

I went to the agency and told them that they were crazy to try and get rid of Henry Morgan. They agreed that the charge in *Red Channels* was absurd, but they said they couldn't take the risk. That was the main thing—mail accusing them of being pro-communist was not going to sell cigarettes. They gave me an ultimatum: dump Morgan or face the show's cancellation.

So I went to Garry Moore, the MC of the show and an established comedian. He was a conservative, a Republican from Maryland. I knew that he liked Morgan. I said that if he'd be willing to back me up, I'd tell the agency I'd do the show without a sponsor. He agreed without hesitation. I phoned up William Este and said, "We're not going to do the show without Henry." The people at the agency were flabbergasted. It was virtually unheard-of to have this kind of confrontation. They told me they'd think about it, and in the end, they actually backed down. The show was not canceled, and some weeks later Morgan's name simply vanished from *Red Channels*.

Morgan never even knew. When I wrote the article about my experience,[4] Henry called me. "I did not know that I was about to be dropped," he said. "I knew I was in *Red Channels* and I was outraged about that, but I didn't know I was about to be dropped." It was a revelation for him.

The Morgan episode was my first act of resistance. It was not something my lawyers ever encouraged. The watchword in the business is "Don't make waves."

The studios and the advertising agencies didn't have to subscribe to *Red Channels*. It was one of about a dozen publications. There were several private lists, and the major agencies and networks exchanged lists, most of which had

4. *New York Times Magazine,* January 13, 1991.

several names each. I'd help you out by giving you my list and you'd help me out by giving me your list. There was a big interchange of listings. A fellow called Danny O'Shea was in charge of the listings at CBS, an ex-FBI man. *Red Channels* would maybe have a couple of hundred names, but there might be on the other list at CBS several hundred more. Anybody could show up on a list, stars, technicians, cowboys.

Faye Emerson was a regular panelist on *I've Got a Secret* around the same time. Faye was a liberal, very attractive actress who was also hostessing a show called *Author Meets the Critics*. It was a show like *Meet the Press*, with a series of critics dealing with a book. On one episode, they discussed a book that advocated the United States' possible recognition of Red China. For the most part, the critics agreed with the author. The show went on the air live. The very next day I got a call from the William Este Agency, the same people who had protested Morgan. They told me to drop Faye Emerson, that, because of what she had said, she was a Red China sympathizer. I said, "It doesn't make any sense. We have no control over what Faye Emerson says on a different show." We stood up and said, "No, we won't drop her." And for some reason, they ended up listening to us. But she could very easily have been cut.

Anna Lee was an English actress on a later show of ours called *It's News to Me*. The sponsor was Sanka Coffee, a product of General Foods. The advertising agency was Young & Rubicam. One day, I received a call telling me we had to drop one of our panelists, Anna Lee, immediately. They said she was a radical, that she wrote a column for the *Daily Worker*. They couldn't allow that kind of stuff on the air. They claimed they were getting all kinds of mail. It seemed incongruous to me that this little English girl, someone who seemed very conservative, would be writing for a communist newspaper. It just didn't sound right.

I took her out to lunch. After a little social conversation, I asked her about her politics. She told me that she wasn't political, except she voted Conservative in England. Her husband was a Republican from Texas.

I went back to the agency and said, "You guys are really off your rocker. Anna Lee is nothing close to a liberal." They told me, "Oh, you're right. We checked on that. It's a different Anna Lee who writes for the *Daily Worker*." I remember being relieved and saying, "Well, that's good. You just made a mistake. Now we can forget this." But that wasn't the case. They told me, "We've still got to get rid of her, because the illusion is just as good as the reality. If our client continues to get the mail, no one is going to believe him when he says there's a second Anna Lee." At that point I lost it. I told them their demand was outrageous. They could cancel the show if they wanted to, but I would not drop somebody whose only crime was sharing a name. When I got back to my office, there was a phone call waiting for me. It was from a friend of mine at the agency. He said, "If I were you, I would not lose my temper like that. If you want to argue, do it quietly. After you left, somebody said, 'Is Goodson a pinko?' You could get yourself a very bad label around town." That would have caused me a lot of trouble. All I had to be was in *Red Channels* myself.

Abe Burrows was a regular panelist on *The Name's the Same,* a show we had on ABC in 1952. The sponsor was the Swanson Foods Company. Burrows was a brilliant comedy writer, a nice round-faced fellow whose big hit was a radio show called *Duffy's Tavern.* During the war years Burrows had apparently taken part in cultural activities sponsored by communists in California. To clear his name, he appeared twice before the House Un-American Activities Committee. They released him from further questioning, apparently cleared. But when he went down to testify, it made headlines, and if you made headlines, you got in *Red Channels.* It wasn't long after we booked him on the show that the protest mail began to roll in.

ABC was a brand-new network at the time and didn't have a clearance department. So I would just take the mail and quietly throw it away. One day I got a call from one of the Swanson brothers. He asked if we were getting mail on Burrows. I said we were. He said they were getting a lot of mail. I said we were getting some. He asked if Burrows was a communist. I said, "I don't think so." "Then why is he in *Red Channels?* Why is he getting this mail?" I said, "I think that a long time ago, during the war, he wrote some stuff that was pro-Russian and once belonged to some very liberal groups." Swanson sounded relieved. "If he's not a communist now, then forget it," he said.

Six months later, he called me back. He said, "Are you familiar with the Johnson Supermarkets up in Syracuse, New York?" I had heard about them. Although Mr. Johnson only owned three markets, he was famous for influencing policy throughout the country in the grocery business.[5] Whenever a "controversial" performer appeared on television, he hung signs over the sponsoring company's goods, warning the public that they employed subversives. Swanson told me that Johnson had put out ballots in the store that said, "Do you want any part of your purchase price of Swanson Foods to be used to hire communist fronters? Vote yes or no." Of course, nobody said yes. They took the ballot and marked no. Then Johnson gathered all these ballots together and sent copies of them to stores all over the country. They began getting rid of all Swanson Foods products.

Swanson said, "Look, we love you, we love Burrows. We would like to be liberal, but we're not going to let our business go down the drain for one man." I said, "I understand." That was the end of Abe Burrows, at least on television. Abe understood completely. Luckily for him, he had a major Broadway hit at

5. By the early 1950s no one worked in radio or television without the consent of Laurence A. Johnson. He and his family monitored all network programming and took down the names of those actors, writers, and directors whose politics were considered offensive. Working in concert with a local American Legion post, Johnson threatened the sponsors of the programs with a consumer boycott of their products unless the artists he named were fired. It was the implied support of the American Legion (and its millions of members) that made him such a powerful figure. Johnson died in 1962 at the age of seventy-three, a few days before the courts awarded radio personality John Henry Faulk $3.5 million in a suit against him and Aware, Inc. [Goodson's note.]

the time called *Guys and Dolls*, so he did not suffer. The people who suffered the most were the ones who had little or no names. Every once in a while, they'd get a part in a theater on Broadway, but basically they just vanished.

It was difficult to get people to stand up against this. The people who did stand up were your conservative friends, like Garry Moore and in the beginning, the Swanson brothers. I can understand that. The more liberal the network, the more frightened they were. CBS, after all, was concerned because in Congress, CBS was being called the Communist Broadcasting System. All three networks were run by Jewish Americans. They were concerned with being thought of as un-American. The first major company to break the blacklist was Ford Motors, with a broadcast of a Leonard Bernstein concert. They were strong enough and conservative enough that nobody could accuse them of anything.

I think it's very important to note that I was not really dealing with communists. I was dealing with people who were being tarred with the brush at a time when it was dangerous to be liberal. That was basically it. Whether I would actually have gone to bat for someone like Paul Robeson, an avowed communist at the time, I don't know.[6]

My life had been apolitical, I had never been involved. I was just operating out of a sense of not wanting to see people pushed around. I did not do it from any ideological point of view, except out of a fairly liberal, centrist position. My lawyers, nice liberal guys, certainly did not advise me to stand up and get involved. Most people looked at the names in *Red Channels* and said, "Somebody says they're left-wing and that's that. We don't want to get into trouble."

You can't know what it was like. Nobody today has any feeling of what the atmosphere was like then, to know that one remark in Jack O'Brien's television column in the *Journal-American* could hurt somebody badly. We were all scared.

6. Robeson, although very close to the Party and to the Soviet Union, denied under oath in 1946 that he was a member. [Goodson's note.]

PART SIX

Contested Boundaries

Moral Dilemmas at Home and Abroad

In the twentieth century an American national culture came to dominate all regions of the country and much of the world. Consumerism ruled national markets, the mass media shaped our most personal aspirations, and active federal and state governments provided services and regulations that were both desired and distrusted. The United States took on the role of global policeman and became an immense military superpower.

In the 1960s African Americans intensified their struggle for equality, unrest among young people led to the rise of a new youth culture, the middle class was greatly enlarged and became more mobile, and vocal political movements reawakened on both the right and the left. Both the idealism and the heartbreak of the decade are reflected in letters sent home by student civil rights workers in Mississippi during the summer of 1964. Betty Friedan's landmark 1963 book, *The Feminine Mystique*, helped ignite an angry and militant women's liberation movement that remained a powerful force in American politics for decades. Throughout the 1970s, a myriad of groups inspired by African Americans, women, and antiwar protesters like the Young Lords, La Raza, and the Gay Liberation Front contested old boundaries and tried to fight their way into the mainstream.

Overshadowing all American lives during this period, however, was the Vietnam War—the nation's longest war. The massacre at My Lai in 1968 became a potent symbol of what the war—and, many feared, the nation—had become. By 1979, when Islamic militants seized the American embassy in Iran and held embassy personnel hostage for over a year, the United States had been defeated on the battlefield by Vietnamese communists, the years of protest were largely over, and a sizable segment of society was calling for the restoration of order and traditional values.

The My Lai Incident
(1968–1970)

31

Disbelief and Corroboration
Ronald L. Ridenhour et al.

Throughout the twentieth century, guerrilla wars have led to atrocities, and Vietnam was no exception. Guerrillas do not obey the international rules of warfare and often control areas through deliberate terror. When the Vietcong (VC, Vietnamese communists) captured the ancient city of Hué during the Tet Offensive of 1968, they murdered hundreds, perhaps thousands, some of whom were buried alive. The attempt to eradicate guerrillas from among a population, any member of whom might be a friend, an enemy, or simply a poor peasant wanting to be left alone, inevitably produces episodes of indiscriminate killing of civilians. One U.S. "pacification" effort in a Mekong Delta province in 1969, for example, produced an official body count of eleven thousand Vietcong killed. That only 748 weapons were captured makes it likely that very many of those dead were noncombatants.

The massacre at My Lai on March 16, 1968, was the most notorious atrocity committed by American soldiers in Vietnam, causing many around the world to forget the discipline and restraint of countless other American troops since the beginning of the intervention. Company C (Charlie) of Task Force Barker, part of the Americal Division, after a particularly forceful briefing in which the men were reminded of previous casualties they had suffered at the hands of the VC, attacked the village of My Lai, known to be a VC stronghold. Finding no enemy forces there, they nevertheless opened fire on the old men, women, and children who remained in the hamlet, killing somewhere between two and four hundred. Rapes preceded several of the killings.

However awful the war in Vietnam and however frequent the atrocities on all sides, the men of Charlie Company and those who heard about My Lai knew that they had done something far out of the ordinary. Neither they nor their superiors wanted to talk about what happened. The standard press release, although written by an eyewitness, made no reference to atrocities. A cover-up had begun that lasted until a year later when Ronald L. Ridenhour (1946–1998), a former infantryman, wrote a letter to Congress, forcing an investigation that made available the documents you will read.

Peers Report, vol. 1, pp. 1–7 to 1–11; *My Lai File*, Army Crimes Records Center, Fort Belvoir, Virginia; *Peers Report*, vol. 4, pp. 299–300; *Peers Report*, vol. 4, exhibit M–21, p. 111.

BEFORE YOU READ

1. Why did Ridenhour write his letter? Does the letter convincingly present the need for an investigation?

2. Are there any indications in the documents that military personnel during the raid objected to what was happening?

3. What did the author of the press release intend to convey? Why do you think he did this?

LETTER TO CONGRESS FROM RON RIDENHOUR

Mr. Ron Ridenhour
1416 East Thomas Road #104
Phoenix, Arizona

March 29, 1969

Gentlemen:

It was late in April, 1968 that I first heard of "Pinkville"[1] and what allegedly happened there. I received that first report with some skepticism, but in the following months I was to hear similar stories from such a wide variety of people that it became impossible for me to disbelieve that something rather dark and bloody did indeed occur sometime in March, 1968 in a village called "Pinkville" in the Republic of Viet Nam.

The circumstances that led to my having access to the reports I'm about to relate need explanation. I was inducted in March, 1967 into the U.S. Army. After receiving various training I was assigned to the 70th Infantry Detachment (LRP), 11th Light Infantry Brigade at Schofield Barracks, Hawaii, in early October, 1967. That unit, the 70th Infantry Detachment (LRP), was disbanded a week before the 11th Brigade shipped out for Viet Nam on the 5th of December, 1967. All of the men from whom I later heard reports of the "Pinkville" incident were reassigned to "C" Company, 1st Battalion, 20th Infantry, 11th Light Infantry Brigade. I was reassigned to the aviation section of Headquarters Company 11th LIB. After we had been in Viet Nam for 3 to 4 months many of the men from the 70th Inf. Det. (LRP) began to transfer into the same unit, "E" Company, 51st Infantry (LRP).

In late April, 1968 I was awaiting orders for a transfer from HHC, 11th Brigade to Company "E," 51st Inf. (LRP), when I happened to run into Pfc "Butch" Gruver, whom I had known in Hawaii. Gruver told me he had been assigned to "C" Company 1st of the 20th until April 1st when he transferred to the unit that I was headed for. During the course of our conversation he told me the first of many reports I was to hear of "Pinkville."

"Charlie" Company 1/20 had been assigned to Task Force Barker in late February, 1968 to help conduct "search and destroy" operations on the Batangan Peninsula, Barker's area of operation. The task force was operating out of

---

1. **"Pinkville":** army slang for the vicinity around My Lai.

L. F. Dottie, located five or six miles north of Quang Nhai city on Viet Namese National Highway 1. Gruver said that Charlie Company had sustained casualties; primarily from mines and booby traps, almost everyday from the first day they arrived on the peninsula. One village area was particularly troublesome and seemed to be infested with booby traps and enemy soldiers. It was located about six miles northeast of Quang Nhai city at approximate coordinates B.S. 728795. It was a notorious area and the men of Task Force Barker had a special name for it: they called it "Pinkville." One morning in the latter part of March, Task Force Barker moved out from its firebase headed for "Pinkville." Its mission: destroy the trouble spot and all of its inhabitants.

When "Butch" told me this I didn't quite believe that what he was telling me was true, but he assured me that it was and went on to describe what had happened. The other two companies that made up the task force cordoned off the village so that "Charlie" Company could move through to destroy the structures and kill the inhabitants. Any villagers who ran from Charlie Company were stopped by the encircling companies. I asked "Butch" several times if all the people were killed. He said that he thought they were, men, women and children. He recalled seeing a small boy, about three or four years old, standing by the trail with a gunshot wound in one arm. The boy was clutching his wounded arm with his other hand, while blood trickled between his fingers. He was staring around himself in shock and disbelief at what he saw. "He just stood there with big eyes staring around like he didn't understand; he didn't believe what was happening. Then the captain's RTO (radio operator) put a burst of 16 (M-16 rifle) fire into him." It was so bad, Gruver said, that one of the men in his squad shot himself in the foot in order to be medivac-ed out of the area so that he would not have to participate in the slaughter. Although he had not seen it, Gruver had been told by people he considered trustworthy that one of the company's officers, 2nd Lieutenant Kally (this spelling may be incorrect) had rounded up several groups of villagers (each group consisting of a minimum of 20 persons of both sexes and all ages). According to the story, Kally then machine-gunned each group. Gruver estimated that the population of the village had been 300 to 400 people and that very few, if any, escaped.

After hearing this account I couldn't quite accept it. Somehow I just couldn't believe that not only had so many young American men participated in such an act of barbarism, but that their officers had ordered it. There were other men in the unit I was soon to be assigned to, "E" Company, 51st Infantry (LRP), who had been in Charlie Company at the time that Gruver alleged the incident at "Pinkville" had occurred. I became determined to ask them about "Pinkville" so that I might compare their accounts with Pfc Gruver's.

When I arrived at "Echo" Company, 51st Infantry (LRP) the first men I looked for were Pfc's Michael Terry, and William Doherty. Both were veterans of "Charlie" Company, 1/20 and "Pinkville." Instead of contradicting "Butch" Gruver's story they corroborated it, adding some tasty tidbits of information of their own. Terry and Doherty had been in the same squad and their platoon was the third platoon of "C" Company to pass through the village. Most of the people they came to were already dead. Those that weren't were sought out and shot. The platoon left nothing alive, neither livestock nor people. Around noon the two soldiers' squad stopped to eat. "Billy and I started to get out our chow," Terry said, "but close to us was a bunch of Vietnamese in a heap, and some of them were moaning. Kally (2nd Lt. Kally) had been through before us and all of them had been shot, but many weren't dead. It was obvious that they weren't going to get any medical attention so Billy and I got up and went over to where they were. I guess we sort of finished them off." Terry went on to say that he and Doherty then returned to where their packs were and ate lunch. He estimated the size of the village to be 200 to 300 people. Doherty thought that the population of "Pinkville" had been 400 people.

If Terry, Doherty and Gruver could be believed, then not only had "Charlie" Company received orders to slaughter all the inhabitants of the village, but those orders had come from the commanding officer of Task Force Barker, or possibly even higher in the chain of command. Pfc Terry stated that when Captain Medina (Charlie Company's commanding officer Captain Ernest Medina) issued the order for the destruction of "Pinkville" he had been hesitant, as if it were something he didn't want to do but had to. Others I spoke to concurred with Terry on this.

It was June before I spoke to anyone who had something of significance to add to what I had already been told of the "Pinkville" incident. It was the end of June, 1968 when I ran into Sargent Larry La Croix at the USO in Chu Lai. La Croix had been in 2nd Lt. Kally's platoon on the day Task Force Barker swept through "Pinkville." What he told me verified the stories of the others, but he also had something new to add. He had been a witness to Kally's gunning down of at least three separate groups of villagers. "It was terrible. They were slaughtering the villagers like so many sheep." Kally's men were dragging people out of bunkers and hootches and putting them together in a group. The people in the group were men, women and children of all ages. As soon as he felt that the group was big enough, Kally ordered an M-60 (machine-gun) set up and the people killed. La Croix said that he bore witness to this procedure at least three times. The three groups were of different sizes, one of about twenty people, one of about thirty people, and one of about forty people. When the first group was put together Kally ordered Pfc Torres to man the machine-gun and open fire on the villagers that had been grouped together. This Torres did, but before everyone in the group was down he ceased fire and refused to fire again. After ordering Torres to recommence firing several times, Lieutenant Kally took over the M-60 and finished shooting the remaining villagers in that first group himself. Sargent La Croix told me that Kally didn't bother to order anyone to take the machine-gun when the other two groups of villagers were formed. He simply manned it himself and shot down all villagers in both groups.

This account of Sargent La Croix's confirmed the rumors that Gruver, Terry and Doherty had previously told me about Lieutenant Kally. It also convinced me that there was a very substantial amount of truth to the stories that all of these men had told. If I needed more convincing, I was to receive it.

It was in the middle of November, 1968 just a few weeks before I was to return to the United States for separation from the army that I talked to Pfc Michael Bernhardt. Bernhardt had served his entire year in Viet Nam in "Charlie" Company 1/20 and he too was about to go home. "Bernie" substantiated the tales told by the other men I had talked to in vivid, bloody detail and added this. "Bernie" had absolutely refused to take part in the massacre of the villagers of "Pinkville" that morning and he thought that it was rather strange that the officers of the company had not made an issue of it. But that evening "Medina (Captain Ernest Medina) came up to me ("Bernie") and told me not to do anything stupid like write my congressman" about what had happened that day. Bernhardt assured Captain Medina that he had no such thing in mind. He had nine months left in Viet Nam and felt that it was dangerous enough just fighting the acknowledged enemy.

Exactly what did, in fact, occur in the village of "Pinkville" in March, 1968 I do not know for *certain*, but I am convinced that it was something very black indeed. I remain irrevocably persuaded that if you and I do truly believe in the principles, of justice and the equality of every man, however humble, before the law, that form the very backbone that this country is founded on, then we must press forward a widespread and public investigation of this matter with all our combined efforts. I think that it was Winston Churchill who once said "A country without a conscience is a country without a soul, and a country without a soul is a country that cannot survive." I feel that I must take some positive action on this matter. I hope that you will launch an investigation immediately and keep me informed of your progress. If you cannot, then I don't know what other course of action to take.

I have considered sending this to newspapers, magazines, and broadcasting companies, but I somehow feel that investigation and action by the Congress of the United States is the appropriate procedure, and as a conscientious citizen I have no desire to further besmirch the image of the American serviceman in the eyes of the world. I feel that this action, while probably it would promote attention, would not bring about the constructive actions that the direct actions of the Congress of the United States would.

Sincerely,

/s/ Ron Ridenhour

TESTIMONY OF ROBERT T'SOUVAS

Q: Have you ever heard of Pinkville?

A: Yes. As far as I remember Pinkville consisted of My Lai (4), My Lai (5), and My Lai (6), and maybe some other Hamlets. The Pinkville area was mostly our area of operation, to my knowledge.

Q: Is there one operation in the Pinkville area that stands out in your mind?

A: Yes. In March 1968 we went on an operation to My Lai (4) which is in the Pinkville area. This area stands out in my mind because there was so many women, children, and men killed.

I do not remember the name of my Platoon Leader or my Platoon Sergeant. After we got out of the helicopters, we organized. As soon as I got out the helicopter threw a smoke bomb and I and my Squad were told to look for the Viet

Cong in the vicinity where the helicopter had dropped the smoke bomb. Names are hard to remember and I do not know at this time who the soldiers were that accompanied me. We searched for the Viet Cong, but we could not find them until the helicopter radioed and hovered at a certain spot right over the Viet Cong. Personnel in our Company went to the busy area and found a weapon. I do not know if they found the Viet Cong. I was there with my machine gun. After this my Platoon moved into the Hamlet and we just had to search and destroy mission. I seen people shot that didn't have weapons. I've seen the hootches burn, animals killed—just like saying going to Seoul and start burning hootches and shooting— a massacre wherein innocent people were being killed, hootches being burned, everything destroyed. They had no weapons and we were told that they were VC sympathizers. To come right to the point, we carried out our orders to the very point—Search and Destroy. In my mind, that covered the whole situation.

Q: How many people do you think was shot by C Company in My Lai (4)?

A: This is hard to say—from my personal observation I would say 80 that I have seen myself.

Q: What did the people that you saw shot consist of?

A: Women, men, children and animals.

Q: Did you at anytime receive hostile fire?

A: I was told that we were fired upon, but I myself did not receive direct fire.

Q: Were there still any people living in the Hamlet when you came through?

A: When we got there there was still people alive in the Hamlet and the Company was shooting them, however, when we left the Hamlet there was still some people alive.

Q: Did you see a trail in the village with a pile of dead women and children?

A: I seen dead women, children and men in groups and scattered on the trails and the rice paddies. I seen people running and just innocently being shot.

Q: Did you shoot 2 wounded children laying on the trail outside of My Lai (4)?

A: I opened up on people that were running. I do not remember that I shot at 2 children that were laying down on the trail. However, I do remember I did shoot a girl that was sitting there amongst 5 or more people, sitting there completely torn apart. She was screaming. I felt just as if it was my mother dying. I shot her to get her out of her misery. She was around 15. This happened inside the hamlet. However, I do not remember about the 2 children laying on the trail. I also shot 5 wounded villagers because they did not give them medical aid. They refused to give them medical aid. . . .

Q: Was the combat assault on My Lai (4) different than any of the others you were on?

A: Yes, I never heard anything so stupid as to search and destroy and to kill all those people.

Q: Is there anything else you would like to say?

A: I wanted to talk about this for a long time—and am glad now that it is off my chest—it is wrong. Even before it was investigated, I wanted to write about it to my Senator, but I didn't know how to go about it. This is all that I know about the incident. It is such a long time ago and it is hard to remember the exact sequence of events and I am not too good a map reader and I will not be able to draw a sketch of the Hamlet and show how we went through the Hamlet.

JOURNAL OF THOMAS R. PARTSCH

Mar. 16 Sat.

Got up at 5:30 left at 7:15 we had 9 choppers. 2 lifts first landed had mortar team with us. We started to move slowly through the village shooting everything in sight children men and women and animals. Some was sickening. There legs were shot off and they were still moving it was just hanging there. I think there bodies were made of rubber. I didn't fire a round yet and didn't kill anybody not even a chicken I couldn't. We are [now] suppose to push through 2 more it is about 10 A.M. and we are taken a rest before going in. We also got 2 weapons M1 and a carbine our final destination is the Pinkville suppose to be cement bunkers we killed about 100 people after a while they said not to kill women and children. Stopped for chow about 1 P.M. we didn't do much after that. . . .

Mar. 17 Sun.

Got up at 6:30 foggy out. We didn't go to Pinkville went to My Lai 2, 3, and 4 no one was there we burned as we pushed. We got 4 VC and a nurse. . . .

Mar. 18 Mon.

We got with company and CA out to Dottie [their base] there is a lot of fuss on what happened at the village a Gen was asking questions. There is going to be an investigation on MEDINA. We are not supposed to say anything. I didn't think it was right but we did it at least I can say I didn't kill anybody. I think I wanted to but in another way I didn't.

CAPTAIN BRIAN LIVINGSTON'S LETTER
TO HIS WIFE

Saturday 16 March 68

Dear Betz,

Well its been a long day, saw some nasty sights. I saw the insertion of infantrymen and were they animals. The[y] preped the area first, then a lot of women and kids left the village. Then a gun team from the shark[s], a notorious killer of civilians, used their minny guns, people falling dead on the road. I've never seen so many people dead in one spot. Ninety-five percent were women and kids. We told the grunts on the ground of some injured kids. They helped them al[l-]right. A captain walked up to this little girl, he turned away took five steps, and fired a volly of shots into her. This Negro sergeant started shooting people in the head. Finally our OH23 saw some wounded kids, so we acted like medivacs [mede-vacs]. Another kid whom the grunts were going to "take care of" was next on our list. The OH23 took him to Quang Nai [Ngai] hospital. We had to do this while *we* held machine guns on our own troops—American troops. I'll tell you something it sure makes one wonder why we are here. I can also see why they hate helicopter pilots. If I ever [hear] a shark open his big mouth I'm going to shove my fist into his mouth.

We're trying to get the captain and sergeant afore mentioned reprimanded. I don't know if we will be successful, but we're trying. Enough for that.

Brian

32

Cover-up and Outcome
General Westmoreland,
President Nixon, et al.

Between March 1968 when the massacre at My Lai occurred and December 1969 when the New York Times *and* Life *magazine broke the story, the Reverend Martin Luther King Jr. and Robert Kennedy were both assassinated; ghettoes across the country erupted in riots; the Democratic National Convention degenerated into violence; Alabama governor George Wallace conducted his divisive presidential campaign; anti-war demonstrations escalated enormously; and despite a strategy of "disengagement" (that was being renamed "Vietnamization") American casualties were greater in 1969 than in any previous year.*

With so much wrong it became difficult to assign responsibility for the massacre. A thorough and careful investigation, directed by the highly respected General William R. Peers, recommended charges against fourteen officers: two generals, two colonels, two lieutenant colonels, four majors, two captains, and two first lieutenants. In the end only Lieutenant William Calley was found guilty of killing. He was convicted of the deaths of "at least" twenty-two people and sentenced to life in prison. Several higher officers suffered administrative penalties: demotions, lost decorations, and letters of censure placed in their files for covering up the incident, although according to military law they could have been held responsible for criminal acts of which they should have been aware. The documents you will read present evidence of the cover-up and some of the reasons that it occurred.

Calley's conviction stirred massive controversy. Some regarded him a scapegoat for higher-ranking officers; others argued that amid the confusion over who was a friend and who was an enemy in Vietnam, his acts could not be considered criminal. Jimmy Carter, then governor of Georgia, thought it unfair to single out Calley for punishment. President Richard Nixon reduced his sentence, and in March 1974 he was paroled. When hearing of Calley's parole, General Peers told reporters: "To think that out of all those men, only one, Lieutenant William Calley, was brought to justice. And

Peers Report, vol. 4, p. 245; *Peers Report*, vol. 4, Exhibit M–22, p. 113; *Peers Report*, vol. 4, pp. 401–05; *Peers Report*, vol. 4, pp. 264–65; *Peers Report*, vol. 3, pp. 261–62; *Peers Report*, vol. 2, bk. 24, pp. 44–50; William C. Westmoreland, *A Soldier Reports* (New York: Doubleday, 1976), pp. 377–78; Richard M. Nixon, *RN: The Memoirs of Richard Nixon* (New York: Grossett, 1978), pp. 449–50.

now, he's practically a hero. It's a tragedy." And in My Lai, Nyugen Bat, a hamlet chief who was not a Vietcong before the massacre, recalled, "After the shooting, all the villagers became Communists."

BEFORE YOU READ

1. Why did the Barker report and the Henderson investigation cover up the events at My Lai? What light does the Vietcong document throw on this question?

2. How does the testimony of Herbert L. Carter help you to understand why participants and observers at My Lai did not reveal what had happened?

3. How does General Westmoreland explain the My Lai incident? How persuasive is his explanation?

4. Why did President Nixon reduce Calley's sentence? Was this the right thing to do?

SERGEANT JAY ROBERTS,
PRESS RELEASE ON MY LAI, 1968

CHU LAI, Vietnam—For the third time in recent weeks, the American Division's 11th Brigade infantrymen from Task Force Barker raided a Viet Cong stronghold known as "Pinkville" six miles northeast of Quang Ngai, killing 128 enemy in a running battle.

The action occurred in the coastal town of My Lai where, three weeks earlier, another company of the brigade's Task Force Barker fought its way out of a VC ambush, leaving 80 enemy dead.

The action began as units of the task force conducted a combat assault into a known Viet Cong stronghold. "Shark" gunships of the 174th Aviation Company escorted the troops into the area and killed four enemy during the assault. Other choppers from the 123d Aviation Battalion killed two enemy.

"The combat assault went like clockwork," commented LTC Frank Barker, New Haven, Conn., the task force commander. "We had two entire companies on the ground in less than an hour."

A company led by CPT Ernest Medina, Schofield Barracks, Hawaii, killed 14 VC minutes after landing. They recovered two M1 rifles, a carbine, a shortwave radio and enemy documents.

CAPTAIN BRIAN LIVINGSTON'S
LETTER TO HIS WIFE

19 March 68

Dear Betz,

. . . You remember I told you about the massacre I witnessed, well I read a follow-up story in the paper. The article said I quote "The American troops were in heavy combat with an unknown number of V. C. Two Americans were killed, seven wounded, and 128 V. C. killed." Thats a bunch of bull. I saw four V. C., that is, those with weapons, and the amazing thing about that, is two of them got away. It made me sick to watch it.

Brian

LIEUTENANT COLONEL FRANK A. BARKER JR., "COMBAT ACTION REPORT" ON MY LAI

28 March 1968

8. *Intelligence:* Enemy forces in the area of operation were estimated to be one local force battalion located in the vicinity of My Lai, BS 728795 as shown in Inclosure 1. This information was based upon previous combat operations in this area, visual reconnaissance, and PW and agent reports. During the operation it was estimated that only two local force companies supported by two to three local guerrilla platoons opposed the friendly forces. The area of operation consisted of six hamlets to varying degree of ruin, each separated by rice paddies which were bounded by a series of hedge rows and tree lines. The area was also honeycombed with tunnels and bunkers. . . .

9. *Mission:* To destroy enemy forces and fortifications in a VC base camp and to capture enemy personnel, weapons and supplies.

10. *Concept of Operation:* Task Force Barker conducts a helicopter assault on 160730 Mar 68 on a VC base camp vicinity BS 728795 with Company C, 1st Battalion, 20th Infantry landing to the west and Company B, 4th Battalion, 3d Infantry landing to the southeast of the VC base camp. Company A, 3d Battalion, 1st Infantry moves by foot to blocking positions north of the base camp prior to the helicopter assault. . . .

11. *Execution:* The order was issued on 14 March 1968. Coordination with supporting arms reconnaissance and positioning of forces was conducted on 15 Mar 68. On 160726 Mar 68 a three minute artillery preparation began on the first landing zone and at 0730 hours the first lift for Co C touched down while helicopter gunships provided suppressive fires. At 0747 hours the last lift of Co C was completed. The initial preparation resulted in 68 VC KIA's in the enemy's combat outpost positions. Co C then immediately attacked to the east receiving enemy small arms fire as they pressed forward. At 0809H a three minute artillery preparation on the second landing zone began and the first lift for Co B touched down at 0815 hours. At 0827 the last lift of Co B was completed and Co B moved to the north and east receiving only light enemy resistance initially. As Co B approached the area of the VC base camp, enemy defensive fires increased. One platoon from Co B flanked the enemy positions and engaged one enemy platoon resulting in 30 enemy KIA. Throughout the day Co B and Co C received sporadic sniper fire and encountered numerous enemy booby traps. . . . At 1715 hours Co C linked-up with Co B and both units went into a perimeter defense for the night in preparation for conducting search and destroy operations the next day. With the establishment of the night defensive position at 161800 March 1968 the operation was terminated.

12. *Results:*

A. Enemy losses:

    (1) Personnel:

        128 KIA
         11 VCS CIA

    (2) Equipment captured:

          1 M-1 rifle
          2 M-1 carbines
        10 Chicom hand grenades
         8 US M-26 hand grenades
     410 rounds small arms ammo
         4 US steel helmets with liners
         5 US canteens with covers
         7 US pistol belts
         9 sets US web equipment
         2 short wave transistor radios
         3 boxes of medical supplies

    (3) Equipment and facilities destroyed:

        16 booby traps
         1 large tunnel complex
        14 small tunnel complexes
         8 bunkers
          numerous sets of web equipment

B. Friendly losses:

         2 US KHA
        11 US WHA

15. *Commander Analysis:* This operation was well planned, well executed and successful. Friendly casualties were light and the enemy suffered heavily. On this operation the civilian population supporting the VC in the area numbered approximately 200. This created a problem in population control and medical care of those civilians caught in fires of the opposing forces. However, the infantry unit on the ground and helicopters were able to assist civilians in leaving the area and in caring for and/or evacuating the wounded.

A VIETCONG LEAFLET ON MY LAI

Since the Americans heavy loss in the spring they have become like wounded animals that are crazy and cruel. They bomb places where many people live, places which are not good choices for bombings, such as the cities within the provinces, especially in Hue, Saigon, and Ben Tre. In Hue the US newspapers reported that 70% of the homes were destroyed and 10,000 people killed or left homeless. The newspapers and radios of Europe also tell of the killing of the South Vietnamese people by the Americans. The English tell of the action where the Americans are bombing the cities of South Vietnam. The Americans will be sentenced first by the Public in Saigon. It is there where the people will lose sentiment for them because they bomb the people and all people will soon be against them. The world public objects to this bombing including the American public and that of its Allies. The American often shuts his eye and closes his ear and continues his crime.

In the operation of 15 March 1968 in Son Tinh District the American enemies went crazy. They used machine guns and every other kind of weapon to kill 500 people who had empty hands, in Tinh Khe (Son My) Village (Son Tinh District, Quang Ngai Province). There were many pregnant women some of which were only a few days from childbirth. The Americans would shoot everybody they say. They killed people and cows, burned homes. There were some families in which all members were killed.

When the red evil Americans remove their prayer shirts they appear as barbaric men.

When the American wolves remove their sheepskin their sharp meat-eating teeth show. They drink our peoples blood with animal sentimentalities.

Our people must choose one way to beat them until they are dead, and stop wriggling.

COLONEL FRANK HENDERSON, REPORT OF INVESTIGATION OF MY LAI INCIDENT

24 April 1968

Commanding General
Americal Division
APO SF 96374

1. (U) An investigation has been conducted of the allegations cited in Inclosure 1. The following are the results of this investigation.

2. (C) On the day in question, 16 March 1968, Co C 1st Bn 20th Inf and Co B 4th Bn 3rd Inf as part of Task Force Barker, 11th Inf Bde, conducted a combat air assault in the vicinity of My Lai Hamlet (Son My Village) in eastern Son Tinh District. This area has long been an enemy strong hold, and Task Force Barker had met heavy enemy opposition in this area on 12 and 23 February 1968. All persons living in this area are considered to be VC or VC sympathizers by the District Chief. Artillery and gunship preparatory fire were placed on the landing zones used by the two companies. Upon landing and during their advance on the enemy positions, the attacking forces were supported by gunships from the 174th Avn Co and Co B, 23rd Avn Bn. By 1500 hours all enemy resistance had ceased and the remaining enemy forces had withdrawn. The results of this operation were 128 VC soldiers KIA. During preparatory fires and the ground action by the attacking companies 20 noncombatants caught in the battle area were killed. US Forces suffered 2 KHA and 10 WHA by booby traps and 1 man slightly wounded in the foot by small arms fire. No

US soldier was killed by sniper fire as was the alleged reson for killing the civilians. Interviews with LTC Frank A. Barker, TF Commander; Maj Charles C. Calhoun, TF S3; CPT Ernest L. Medina, Co Co C, 1–20 and CPT Earl Michles, Co Co B, 4–3 revealed that at no time were any civilians gathered together and killed by US soldiers. The civilian habitants in the area began withdrawing to the southwest as soon as the operation began and within the first hour and a half all visible civilians had cleared the area of operations.

3. (C) The Son Tinh District Chief does not give the allegations any importance and he pointed out that the two hamlets where the incidents is alleged to have happened are in an area controlled by the VC since 1964. CC Toen, Cmdr 2d Arvn Div reported that the making of such allegations against US Forces is a common technique of the VC propaganda machine. Inclosure 2 is a translation of an actual VC propaganda message targeted at the ARVN soldier and urging him to shoot Americans. This message was given to this headquarters by the CO, 2d ARVN Division o/a 17 April 1968 as matter of information. It makes the same allegations as made by the Son My Village Chief in addition to other claims of atrocities by American soldiers.

4. (C) It is concluded that 20 non-combatants were inadvertently killed when caught in the area of preparatory fires and in the cross fires of the US and VC forces on 16 March 1968. It is further concluded that no civilians were gathered together and shot by US soldiers. The allegation that US Forces shot and killed 450–500 civilians is obviously a Viet Cong propaganda move to discredit the United States in the eyes of the Vietnamese people in general and the ARVN soldier in particular.

5. (C) It is recommended that a counter-propaganda campaign be waged against the VC in eastern Son Tinh District.

TESTIMONY OF HERBERT L. CARTER

Q: Did you ever hear anything about an investigation into the My Lai incident?
A: Yes.

Q: What did you hear?
A: I heard that they said if anybody asks around or any questions about what happened at My Lai, to tell them that we were fired upon and say that a sniper round had come in or something.

Q: Whom did you hear this from?
A: I was in the hospital at this time at Qui Nhon, and a couple of guys from the company came over. I'm not bragging, but most of the guys in that company liked me. I didn't bother nobody. I did my job and they did their job. We drank together.

Q: They came to see you in the hospital?
A: Yes. A lot of guys came over. You know, when they came back through, they would come over.

Q: Captain MEDINA told us that soon after this operation he got the company together and told them that there was an investigation and it would be better if nobody talked about it while the investigation was underway. Did your friends say anything about this?

A: No. The way they ran it down to me was like somebody was trying to cover something up or something, which I knew they were. They had to cover up something like that.

Q: I think you know that it took a long time for the story of My Lai to get out. What is your opinion as to why this wasn't reported right at the time? You did mention about some of your friends coming and telling you to keep quiet. Do you know anything else?

A: Like a lot of people wondered how come I didn't say something. Now, who would believe me. I go up to you with a story like that and you would call me a nut. You would tell me I am a nut and that there was nothing like this going on. You would think that nothing like this goes on in the United States. Just like I was in a bar a couple of weeks ago, and there was a drunk in there. He was standing there reading a paper and he was asking me if I believed that things like that actually went on, and I said, "I wouldn't know, pal." It was kind of weird. This happened three different times. One time I was sitting up there with a friend of mine, and my partner told me to be quiet about the whole mess. Some people want to talk that talk all day long, and they just don't know this and that about what they are talking about.

Q: Did you or the other members of the company ever think about these killings as a war crime?

A: Not at that time. No. I didn't want to think about anything at the time.

Q: In your statement to Mr. CASH you spoke of it as murder?

A: Yes.

Q: You looked at it as being murder, but you didn't think about it as being a war crime?

A: That's right. I thought it was just the poor misfortunes of war.

GENERAL WILLIAM C. WESTMORELAND

In the criminal cases, acquittal resulted in all but that of a platoon leader, First Lieutenant William L. Calley Jr. Charged with the murder of more than a hundred civilians, he was convicted on March 29, 1971, of the murder of "at least" twenty-two. He was sentenced to dismissal from the service and confinement at hard labor for life, but the latter was reduced by judicial review to twenty years and further reduced after my retirement by Secretary of the Army Howard Callaway to ten years, an action that President Nixon sustained. The case was subsequently and for a long time under judicial appeal in the federal courts.

Lieutenant Calley was legally judged by a jury whose members all were familiar with the nature of combat in Vietnam and well aware that even the kind of war waged in Vietnam is no license for murder. The vast majority of Americans in Vietnam did their best to protect civilian lives and property, often at their own peril. That some civilians, even many, died by accident or inevitably in the course of essential military operations dictated by the enemy's presence among the people was no justification or rationale for the conscious massacre of defenseless babies, children, mothers, and old men in a kind of diabolical slow-motion nightmare that went on for the better part of a day, with a cold-blooded break for lunch. I said at the time of the revelation: "It could not have happened—but it did."

Although I can in no way condone Lieutenant Calley's acts—or those of any of his colleagues who may have participated but went unpunished—I must have compassion for him. Judging from the events at My Lai, being an officer in the United States Army exceeded Lieutenant Calley's abilities. Had it not been for educational draft deferments, which prevented the Army from drawing upon the intellectual segment of society for its junior officers, Calley probably never would have been an officer. Denied that usual reservoir of talent, the Army had to lower its standards. Although some who became officers under those conditions performed well, others, such as Calley, failed.

An army has a corps of officers to insure leadership: to see that orders are given and carried out and that the men conduct themselves properly. Setting aside the crime involved, Lieutenant Calley's obvious lack of supervision and failure to set a proper example himself were contrary to orders and policy, and the supervision he exercised fell far short.

In reducing standards for officers, both the United States Army and the House Armed Services Committee, which originated the policy of deferments for college students, must bear the blame. It would have been better to have gone short of officers than to have accepted applicants whose credentials left a question as to their potential as leaders.

PRESIDENT RICHARD M. NIXON

On March 29, 1971, just days after the withdrawal of ARVN troops from Laos, First Lieutenant William Calley Jr. was found guilty by an Army court-martial of the premeditated murder of twenty-two South Vietnamese civilians. The public furore over Lam Son had just begun to settle down, and now we were faced with still another Vietnam-related controversy. This one had been simmering since the fall of 1969, when the murders were first revealed.

It was in March 1968, ten months before I became President, that Calley led his platoon into My Lai, a small hamlet about 100 miles northeast of Saigon. The village had been a Vietcong stronghold, and our forces had suffered many casualties trying to clear it out. Calley had his men round up the villagers and then ordered that they be shot; many were left sprawled lifeless in a drainage ditch.

Calley's crime was inexcusable. But I felt that many of the commentators and congressmen who professed outrage about My Lai were not really as interested in the moral questions raised by the Calley case as they were interested in using it to make political attacks against the Vietnam War. For one thing, they had been noticeably uncritical of North Vietnamese atrocities. In fact, the calculated and continual role that terror, murder, and massacre played in the Vietcong strategy was one of the most underreported aspects of the entire Vietnam War. Much to the discredit of the media and the antiwar activists, this side of the story was only rarely included in descriptions of Vietcong policy and practices.

On March 31 the court-martial sentenced Calley to life in prison at hard labor. Public reaction to this announcement was emotional and sharply divided. More than 5,000 telegrams arrived at the White House, running 100 to 1 in favor of clemency.

John Connally and Jerry Ford recommended in strong terms that I use my powers as Commander in Chief to reduce Calley's prison time. Connally said that justice had been served by the sentence, and that now the reality of maintaining public support for the armed services and for the war had to be given primary consideration. I talked to Carl Albert and other congressional leaders. All of them agreed that emotions in Congress were running high in favor of presidential intervention.

I called Admiral Moorer on April 1 and ordered that, pending Calley's appeal, he should be released from the stockade and confined instead to his quarters on the base. When this was announced to the House of Representatives, there was a spontaneous round of applause on the floor. Reaction was particularly strong and positive in the South. George Wallace, after a visit with Calley, said that I had done the right thing. Governor Jimmy Carter of Georgia said that I had made a wise decision. Two days later I had Ehrlichman[1] announce that I would personally review the Calley case before any final sentence was carried out.

By April 1974, Calley's sentence had been reduced to ten years, with eligibility for parole as early as the end of that year. I reviewed the case as I had said I would but decided not to intervene. Three months after I resigned, the Secretary of the Army decided to parole Calley.

I think most Americans understood that the My Lai massacre was not representative of our people, of the war we were fighting, or of our men who were fighting it; but from the time it first became public the whole tragic episode was used by the media and the antiwar forces to chip away at our efforts to build public support for our Vietnam objectives and policies.

For Critical Thinking

1. Why did the My Lai massacre occur? Does the response to it, including both the cover-up and the outcome, suggest why it could occur?

2. What responsibility did higher-ranking officers bear for the massacre? What policies encouraged such an occurrence?

3. Should Calley have been required to serve a larger part of his sentence, or were the actions of President Nixon and other officials the right ones to take?

---

1. **Ehrlichman:** John Ehrlichman, one of President Nixon's closest advisers.

33

Betty Friedan Starts a Revolution

Betty Friedan et al.

By the end of World War II, modernized yet still conservative attitudes were circulating about the role that women should play in American society. Women were told to use newly acquired managerial skills to organize their households, arrange car pools, run the local PTA, and otherwise make a full-time commitment to maintaining their family's mental and physical well-being. The Feminine Mystique, *the title of Betty Friedan's book published in 1963, gave this domestic ideology a name.*

In one vital way, women's behavior was already in sharp conflict with this ideology. The number of female wage earners was higher than before the war, and it continued to rise steadily. But most women worked in what were considered "female" occupations — clerical jobs, domestic service, elementary school teaching — and women were acquiring a smaller proportion of college and professional degrees than they had forty years before. Still, by 1960 the number of women working at other than domestic tasks was almost equal to that of men.

Criticizing the "feminine mystique," Friedan (b. 1921) urged women to find meaningful work or public roles, to return to school, and to develop their own personalities and identities. Her message found many willing listeners. However, as her recollections of that period and the letters to her excerpted here attest, the issue was by no means simple.

BEFORE YOU READ

1. How did Betty Friedan come to write *The Feminine Mystique?*

2. How did the women who wrote to Friedan perceive the past role of women, and how different or similar did they think present roles should be?

3. These letters were written before the new women's movement emerged in the late 1960s. What arguments that defend and attack the goals of that movement do you see foreshadowed in these letters?

ON WRITING THE FEMININE MYSTIQUE

If I hadn't wasted a whole year, 1956–57, doing an alumnae questionnaire of inappropriate and unnecessary depth on the experiences and feelings of my Smith college classmates fifteen years after graduation . . . if their answers had not

Betty Friedan, *It Changed My Life: Writings on the Women's Movement* (New York: Random House, 1976), pp. 17–19; The Friedan Manuscript Collection, Schlesinger Library Manuscript Collections, Radcliffe College, Cambridge, Massachusetts, quoted in Elaine Tyler May, *Homeward Bound: American Families in the Cold War Era* (New York: Basic Books, 1988), pp. 52, 209–17.

raised such strange questions about that role we were all then embracing . . . if the article I finally wrote raising certain of those questions had not been turned down by one woman's magazine (*McCall's*) because its male editor didn't believe it, and rewritten by another (*Ladies' Home Journal*) to deny its evidence so I wouldn't let them print it, and received by a third (*Redbook*), in a shocked rejection note, as something with which "only the most neurotic housewife could possibly identify" . . . I might never have written . . . *The Feminine Mystique.*

During the five years I was writing it, asking other women questions they hadn't asked themselves before, tracing clues from the case histories and puzzled side comments of marriage counselors, psychoanalysts, sociologists and the like, and finally tuning in to the Geiger counter of my own personal truth, I led a double life. I took the bus into the city from Rockland County three days a week, and wrote at my carrel in the Frederick Lewis Allen Room of the New York Public Library, and endured jokes at lunch from the professional writers working in that room because I was writing a book about women, of all things! It was supposed to take one year, and it took five, and neither my husband nor my publisher nor anyone else who knew about it thought I would ever finish it. And when the writing of it took me over completely, I didn't want to waste time taking the bus into the city. I wrote every day, on the dining-room table, while the children were in school, and after they went to bed at night. (It didn't do any good to have a desk of my own; they used it for their homework, anyhow.) The summer I was finishing *The Feminine Mystique*, for some strange reason—maybe a last gasp at denying my seriousness—I dyed my hair blond!

Checking the footnotes in the fall of 1962, I sensed the inescapable implications of the trail of evidence I had followed—that if I was right, the very assumptions on which I and other women were basing our lives and on which the experts were advising us were wrong. I thought, I must be crazy! My then agent refused to handle the book when it was finished, and the publisher only printed several thousand copies. But all along I also felt this calm, strange sureness, as if in tune with something much larger, more important than myself that had to be taken seriously. At first I seemed alone in that awareness.

And then in the spring of 1963, in the weeks and months after the publication of *The Feminine Mystique*, I and other women knew we were not alone. It was a great relief to realize how many others had come up with the same painful questions in trying to live the mystique.

It was a relief, more important to more women than I had even dreamed, to have those questions put into words. The words enabled some women to begin to make changes in their lives almost immediately. And they wrote me personal, impassioned letters, expressing their relief. They also wrote me of the insuperable problems they now had to face trying to move in society not just as "my husband's wife, my children's mother, but as myself."

The emotions that book stirred up in women were not simple. In addition to the dozens, then hundreds, by now thousands of letters of relief, I received many angry letters from women. In fact, I would hear of cocktail parties being broken up by women arguing over my book who hadn't even read it, who in fact seemed afraid to read it. I would hear later that such a woman, attacking me as a destroyerof-the-family, an enemy-of-motherhood, a betrayer-of-femininity, would finally be driven by her own problems that she hadn't dared face before to go back to school, or to look for a job—and she would be passing my book around to her neighbors. I decided that women were sitting on such painful feelings that they didn't dare open the lid unless they knew that they were going to be able to do something about them.

A woman called in to a television program in Detroit where I was publicizing the book. "Tell her to go back and take care of her own children and stop putting ideas into my daughter's head," the woman sputtered angrily. "Being a mother is all women were meant to be; I would never leave any child of mine with a baby-sitter." Thinking to suggest she might feel different a little later, I said, "How old is your youngest child?" "Twenty-three," said the lifelong mother.

Another time, on a program called *Girl Talk*, Virginia Graham,[1] the hostess, turned to the camera and said to the studio audience and the women out there: "Girls, how many of us really need by-lines? What better thing can we do with our lives than to do the dishes for those we love?" Well, I knew that her agent fought for every foot of the size of her by-line on the television screen, and I wondered when the last time was she'd done the dishes for someone she loved. I turned to the camera and said, "Women, don't listen to her. She needs you out there doing the dishes, or she wouldn't have the captive audience for this television program, whose by-line she evidently doesn't want you to compete for." I realized then that this kind of "career woman" didn't really identify with other women at all. For her, there were three kinds of people in the world—men, other women, and herself.

The book was thus strangely threatening to some of those few career women who had defied the feminine mystique in those years to make it, as freaks or exceptions, in man's world. I think they also were sitting on painful feelings—the sacrifices and conflicts and bitter choices some had had to make to get there.

I got very few angry letters from men. From the very beginning, there was much less hostility from men than one might have expected. Many women told me their husbands had bought *The Feminine Mystique* for them to read. It was much more of a threat to women—the challenge, the possibility, the risk and test of moving in society as a person on one's own—than to their husbands. From the beginning, many men seemed to sense that women's liberation would liberate them. It was women who felt the fear—and the relief.

The letters I got came not only from those who had bought the book itself, but also from those who had read excerpts of it printed simultaneously—in unprecedented inexplicable defiance of custom—by the major competing women's magazines whose very feminine mystique I was attacking, the *Ladies' Home Journal* and *McCall's*, and earlier, *Mademoiselle* and *Good Housekeeping*. In this fashion, I suppose the book reached five times the 3,000,000 or so who actually bought it. The unprecedented passion of their response was such that later that year *McCall's* asked me to do an article about the letters.

---

1. **Virginia Graham:** actress and television talk-show host.

LETTERS TO BETTY FRIEDAN

14 May 1963
Brookline, Mass.

My life spans the two eras—the ebb tide of feminism and the rise of the "mystique." My parents were products of the early twentieth century Liberalism and believed firmly that everyone—poor, Negroes, and women too—had a right to have a "rendezvous with Destiny." . . . My feeling of betrayal is not directed against society so much as at the women who beat the drums for the "passionate journey" into darkness. . . . My undiluted wrath is expended on those of us who were educated, and therefore privileged, who put on our black organza nightgowns and went willingly, joyful, without so much as a backward look at the hard-won freedoms handed down to us by the feminists (men and women). The men, in my experience, were interested by-standers, bewildered, amused, and maybe a bit joyful at having two mommies at home—one for the children and one for themselves. . . . My children grew up in the mystique jungle but somehow escaped it.

13 March 1963
Ridgewood, N.J.

. . . [I am] the mother of five and the wife of a successful partner in an investment banking firm. In seeking that something "more" out of life, I have tried large doses of everything from alcohol to religion, from a frenzy of sports activities to PTA . . . to every phase of church work. . . . Each served its purpose at the time, but I suddenly realized that none had any real future. Our children are all in school except for the baby. . . . However, I felt that if I waited until she's in school I'll be too close to forty to learn any new tricks. I've seen too many women say they would "do something" when the last child went to school. The something has usually been bridge, bowling, or drinking.

24 August 1963
Pittsburgh, PA

. . . I entered graduate school at Yale, met a man, left school, and married in 1951. I have since then moved thirteen times, lived in eight states, had four miscarriages, and produced two children. . . . Finally, when I fill out the income tax now, it is occupation: Painter, not housewife. . . . My one advantage over the rest of my generation is, I suppose, the fact that I was raised in a family of feminists. . . . I still tend, belatedly and belligerently, to champion women's rights. The cloying and sentimental public effort of the last decade to raise the prestige of the home and represent it as demanding all that we have to give has more than once precipitated me into incoherent outrage. . . .

21 January 1963
New York City

. . . Since scientific findings reveal the strong effect of the child's environment upon the child, the poor mother has been made to replace God in her omnipotence. It is the terror of this misinterpreted omnipotence that in many cases is keeping women home. I still remember the tear-stained face of a brilliant young woman economist who had earned a Ph.D. in her field when she had to give up a newly discovered exciting job because her pediatrician convinced her that her six- and three-year-old children would become social menaces without her presence 24 hours a day. . . . [*Quoting a school official:*] "Show me a delinquent child and I'll show you a working mother."

Rockaway, New York

. . . What is wrong with the women trapped in the Feminine Mystique is what's wrong with men trapped in the Rat Race. . . . Isn't it true that one of the problems, the biggest really, of our present day society is that there isn't enough meaningful creative work for *anyone* these days? Isn't that one of the reasons fathers are taking their parental role with the seriousness of a career?

23 April 1963
Leicester, Mass.

For the last few years, I have been on the "old housekeeping merry-go-round." . . . I cleaned and I cleaned . . . and then I cleaned some more! All day—every day. My mother had returned to teaching school when I was twelve, and I had resented it, and consequently vowed that when I married and had children I would make it my vocation. I was quite convinced that I was very happy with my role in life as we had our own home and my husband is a good husband and father and a very sufficient provider. However, one night last November, all Hell broke loose in my psyche. I was sitting calmly reading when I became overwhelmed with waves of anxiety. I couldn't imagine what was happening. . . . I visited my family doctor. He put me on tranquilizers and diagnosed it as a mild state of anxiety. However there was no explanation. . . . I see now. . . . I chose security over everything else. . . . I felt I had something more to offer the world and wanted to do something about it. . . . I now have a goal and no longer feel like a vegetable.

23 October 1963
Queens Village, N.Y.

[Written by a woman recalling the realities and perspectives of her emigrant family in the 1930s.]

. . . The emigrant mother often had to work not only in her home, but outside as well, under the most harrowing conditions. . . . For the son, it was important and necessary to obtain an education, so he could escape the sweatshop labor of his father. For the daughter, however, the most precious legacy was an escape from the hard work and drudgery of her mother and the attainment of leisure—the very leisure this emigrant mother never knew herself, and which she so desperately needed. . . . To this emigrant mother, education was only necessary for her son to get a better job, and the daughter, with nothing else besides her femininity, would, with luck, marry well and thereby achieve the leisure her mother never knew.

4 August 1964
Glen Ridge, N.J.

Most of us would be delighted to chuck the wage earning back in our husbands' laps and devote ourselves exclusively to homemaking and community projects. We worry about the children while we're at work. We don't really like to throw the last load of clothes in the washer at 11:30 P.M., and set the alarm for 6:00 so we can iron a blouse for a school age daughter, fix breakfast and school lunches all at the same time, do as much housework as possible before bolting for the office, and face the rest of it, and the grocery shopping and preparing dinner when we get home. This isn't our idea of fulfillment. It doesn't make us more interesting people or more stimulating companions for our husbands. It just makes us very, very tired.

29 May 1964
Folcroft, Pa.

Believe me, a modern woman of today would have to be *four* women to be everything that is expected of her. . . . My husband wants me to work not for the satisfaction I might get out of working, but for the extra money *he* will have for himself. . . . *But*, how about the extra burden it would put on me? I would go out to work if possible, but I cannot do that and come home to a house full of screaming kids, dishes piled in the sink, and mountains of laundry to do. It is no fun to come home and see the sweet, dear, lazy bum asleep on the couch after being on my feet all day. He still likes his home-made pies, cakes, and appetizing meals. . . . I have worked in stores; the post-office; given dinners for a pot and pan outfit; minded children; and sold things door-to-door. At present, I take in sewing and ironing. . . . If I work, then my housework suffers and I get told about that. I would like nothing better than to just do my own work, have some time to myself once in a while so I could just go downtown once in [a] while without having someone else's work staring at me. I get very tired of reading about women working outside the home. . . . I cannot divide myself into more than one person. . . . I have plenty to occupy my time and I happen to enjoy being a house-wife. . . . My husband . . . thinks it's great for women to work, but until men get some of their Victorian ideas out of their heads then I am staying home. Unless he would be willing to help with the housework then I cannot go to work. He thinks he would lose some of his masculinity if anyone saw him hanging out the wash, or washing dishes. And if he had to give up any of his fishing or hunting or running around visiting his buddies to keep an eye on the kids, well, I'm not killing myself for the almighty dollar.

34

Mississippi Freedom Summer

Student Workers

In the summer of 1964, after nearly a decade of civil rights demonstrations, more than a thousand people, most of them white Northern college students, volunteered to travel to Mississippi to help African Americans register to vote and to teach African American children their own history in "freedom schools." The Mississippi Freedom Summer project was a high point and nearly the end of the integrated, nonviolent civil rights movement of the 1950s and 1960s. Although twelve hundred new African American voters registered in the state, it was a hard summer. Consider this macabre score: at least one African American and two white civil rights workers were killed, not including an uncertain number of African American Mississippians who died mysteriously; more than eighty volunteers were wounded and more than a thousand were arrested; thirty-five African American churches were burned; and thirty homes and other buildings were bombed.

But another score can be calculated. Mississippi Freedom Summer contributed to the success of the Voting Rights Act of 1965, which prohibits discrimination in voting practices because of race or color and quickly secured for millions of Southern blacks the right to vote. And the murders of James Chaney, Michael Schwerner, and Andrew Goodman forced federal authorities to infiltrate and destroy the Ku Klux Klan in Mississippi. These letters home from participants in the project (some supplied without attribution) testify to the intensity of the volunteers' experiences that summer.

BEFORE YOU READ

1. Why did these young men and women travel to Mississippi in 1964?
2. What difficulties did they encounter there, and what were their rewards?
3. Had you been a college student in 1964, would you have gone to Mississippi?

Mileston, August 18

Dear folks,

One can't move onto a plantation cold; or canvas a plantation in the same manner as the Negro ghetto in town. It's far too dangerous. Many plantations—homes included—are posted, meaning that no trespassing is permitted, and the owner feels that he has the prerogative to shoot us on sight when we are in the house of one of *his* Negroes.

Elizabeth Sutherland, *Letters from Mississippi* (New York: McGraw-Hill, 1965).

Before we canvas a plantation, our preparation includes finding out whether the houses are posted, driving through or around the plantation without stopping, meanwhile making a detailed map of the plantation.

We're especially concerned with the number of roads in and out of the plantation. For instance, some houses could be too dangerous to canvas because of their location near the boss man's house and on a dead end road.

In addition to mapping, we attempt to talk to some of the tenants when they are off the plantation, and ask them about conditions. The kids often have contacts, and can get on the plantation unnoticed by the boss man, with the pretense of just visiting friends.

Our canvassing includes not only voter registration, but also extensive reports on conditions—wages, treatment by the boss man, condition of the houses, number of acres of cotton, etc. Much more such work needs to be done. The plantation system is crucial in Delta politics and economics, and the plantation system must be brought to an end if democracy is to be brought to the Delta. . . .

Love,
Joel

July 18

. . . Four of us went to distribute flyers announcing the meeting. I talked to a woman who had been down to register a week before. She was afraid. Her husband had lost his job. Even before we got there a couple of her sons had been man-handled by the police. She was now full of wild rumors about shootings and beatings, etc. I checked out two of them later. They were groundless. This sort of rumorspreading is quite prevalent when people get really scared. . . .

At 6 P.M. we returned to Drew for the meeting, to be held in front of a church (they wouldn't let us meet inside, but hadn't told us not to meet outside). A number of kids collected and stood around in a circle with about 15 of us to sing freedom songs. Across the street perhaps 100 adults stood watching. Since this was the first meeting in town, we passed out mimeoed song sheets. Fred Miller, Negro from Mobile, stepped out to the edge of the street to give somebody a sheet. The cops nabbed him. I was about to follow suit so he wouldn't be alone, but Mac's[1] policy was to ignore the arrest. We sang on mightily "Ain't going to let no jailing turn me around." A group of girls was sort of leaning against the cars on the periphery of the meeting. Mac went over to encourage them to join us. I gave a couple of song sheets to the girls. A cop rushed across the street and told me to come along. I guess I was sort of aware that my actions would get me arrested, but felt that we had to show these girls that we were not afraid. I was also concerned with what might happen to Fred if he was the only one.

. . . The cop at the station was quite scrupulous about letting me make a phone call. I was then driven to a little concrete structure which looked like a

---

1. **Mac:** Charles McLaurin, the project director and member of the Student Nonviolent Coordinating Committee, a civil rights group.

power house. I could hear Fred's courageous, off-key rendition of a freedom song from inside and joined him as we approached. He was very happy to see me. Not long thereafter, four more of our group were driven up to make their calls. . . .

Holly Springs

Dear Mom and Dad:

The atmosphere in class is unbelievable. It is what every teacher dreams about—real, honest enthusiasm and desire to learn anything and everything. The girls come to class of their own free will. They respond to everything that is said. They are excited about learning. They drain me of everything that I have to offer so that I go home at night completely exhausted but very happy. . . .

I start out at 10:30 teaching what we call the Core Curriculum, which is Negro History and the History and Philosophy of the Movement, to about fifteen girls ranging from 15 to 25 years of age. I have one girl who is married with four children, another who is 23 and a graduate from a white college in Tennessee, also very poorly educated. The majority go to a Roman Catholic High School in Holly Springs and have therefore received a fairly decent education by Mississippi standards. They can, for the most part, express themselves on paper but their skills in no way compare to juniors and seniors in northern suburban schools.

In one of my first classes, I gave a talk on Haiti and the slave revolt which took place at the end of the eighteenth century. I told them how the French government (during the French Revolution) abolished slavery all over the French Empire. And then I told them that the English decided to invade the island and take it over for a colony of their own. I watched faces fall all around me. They knew that a small island, run by former slaves, could not defeat England. And then I told them that the people of Haiti succeeded in keeping the English out. I watched a smile spread slowly over a girl's face. And I felt the girls sit up and look at me intently. Then I told them that Napoleon came to power, reinstated slavery, and sent an expedition to reconquer Haiti. Their faces began to fall again. They waited for me to tell them that France defeated the former slaves, hoping against hope that I would say that they didn't. But when I told them that the French generals tricked the Haitian leader Toussaint to come aboard their ship, captured him and sent him back to France to die, they knew that there was no hope. They waited for me to spell out the defeat. And when I told them that Haiti did succeed in keeping out the European powers and was recognized finally as an independent republic, they just looked at me and smiled. The room stirred with a gladness and a pride that this could have happened. And I felt so happy and so humble that I could have told them this little story and it could have meant so much.

We have also talked about what it means to be a Southern white who wants to stand up but who is alone, rejected by other whites and not fully accepted by the Negroes. We have talked about their feelings about Southern whites. One day three little white girls came to our school and I asked them to understand how the three girls felt by remembering how it feels when they are around a lot of whites. We agreed that we would not stare at the girls but try to make them feel as normal as possible.

Along with my Core class I teach a religion class at one every afternoon and a class on non-violence at four-fifteen. All my classes are approximately an hour. Both these classes are made up of four to six girls from my morning class and about four boys of the same age group. In religion they are being confronted for the first time with people whom they respect who do not believe in God and with people who believe in God but do not take the Bible literally. It's a challenging class because I have no desire to destroy their belief, whether Roman Catholic or Baptist, but I want them to learn to look at all things critically and to learn to separate fact from interpretation and myth in all areas, not just religion.

Every class is beautiful. The girls respond, respond, respond. And they disagree among themselves. I have no doubt that soon they will be disagreeing with me. At least this is one thing that I am working towards. They are a sharp group. But they are under-educated and starved for knowledge. They know that they have been cheated and they want anything and everything that we can give them.

I have a great deal of faith in these students. They are very mature and very concerned about other people. I really think that they will be able to carry on without us. At least this is my dream. . . .

Love,
Pam

Biloxi, Aug. 16

In the Freedom School one day during poetry writing, a 12-year-old girl handed in this poem to her teacher:

> *What Is Wrong?*
>
> What is wrong with me everywhere I go
>   No one seems to look at me.
> Sometimes I cry.
>
> I walk through woods and sit on a stone.
>   I look at the stars and I sometimes wish.
>
> Probably if my wish ever comes true,
>   Everyone will look at me.

Then she broke down crying in her sister's arms. The Freedom School here had given this girl the opportunity of meeting someone she felt she could express her problems to. . . .

Ruleville

To my brother,

Last night, I was a long time before sleeping, although I was extremely tired. Every shadow, every noise—the bark of a dog, the sound of a car—in my fear and exhaustion was turned into a terrorist's approach. And I believed that I heard the back door open and a Klansman walk in, until he was close by the bed. Almost paralyzed by the fear, silent, I finally shone my flashlight on the spot where I thought he was standing. . . . I tried consciously to overcome this fear. To relax, I began to breathe deep, think the words of a song, pull the sheet up close to my neck . . . still the tension. Then I rethought why I was here, rethought what could be gained in view of what could be lost. All this was in rather personal terms, and then in larger scope of the whole Project. I remembered Bob Moses[2] saying he had felt justified in asking hundreds of students to go to Mississippi because he was not asking anyone to do something that he would not do. . . . I became aware of the uselessness of fear that immobilizes an individual. Then I began to relax.

"We are not afraid. Oh Lord, deep in my heart, I do believe. We Shall Overcome Someday" and then I think I began to truly understand what the words meant. Anyone who comes down here and is not afraid I think must be crazy as well as dangerous to this project where security is quite important. But the type of fear that they mean when they, when we, sing "we are not afraid" is the type that immobilizes. . . . The songs help to dissipate the fear. Some of the words in the songs do not hold real meaning on their own, others become rather monotonous—but when they are sung in unison, or sung silently by oneself, they take on new meaning beyond words or rhythm. . . . There is almost a religious quality about some of these songs, having little to do with the usual concept of a god. It has to do with the miracle that youth has organized to fight hatred and ignorance. It has to do with the holiness of the dignity of man. The god that makes such miracles is the god I do believe in when we sing "God is on our side." I know I am on that god's side. And I do hope he is on ours.

Jon, please be considerate to Mom and Dad. The fear I just expressed, I am sure they feel much more intensely without the relief of being here to know exactly how things are. Please don't go defending me or attacking them if they are critical of the Project. . . .

They said over the phone "Did you know how much it takes to make a child?" and I thought of how much it took to make a Herbert Lee (or many others whose names I do not know). . . . I thought of how much it took to be a Negro in Mississippi twelve months a year for a lifetime. How can such a thing as a life be weighed? . . .

                                                        With constant love,
                                                        Heather

                                                        Tchula, July 16

Yesterday while the Mississippi River was being dragged looking for the three missing civil rights workers, two bodies of Negroes were found——one cut in half and one without a head. Mississippi is the only state where you can drag a river any time and find bodies you were not expecting. Things are really much better for rabbits—there's a closed season on rabbits.

---

2. **Bob Moses:** Robert P. Moses, a young African American high school teacher from New York who organized a team of SNCC workers to join other civil rights workers in Mississippi that summer.

Meridian, August 4

Last night Pete Seeger was giving a concert in Meridian. We sang a lot of freedom songs, and every time a verse like "No more lynchings" was sung, or "before I'd be a slave I'd be buried in my grave," I had the flash of understanding that sometimes comes when you suddenly think about the meaning of a familiar song. . . . I wanted to stand up and shout to them, "Think about what you are singing—people really have died to keep us all from being slaves." Most of the people there still did not know that the bodies had been found. Finally just before the singing of "We Shall Overcome," Pete Seeger made the announcement. "We must sing 'We Shall Overcome' now," said Seeger. "The three boys would not have wanted us to weep now, but to sing and understand this song." That seems to me the best way to explain the greatness of this project—that death can have this meaning. Dying is not an everpresent possibility in Meridian, the way some reports may suggest. Nor do any of us want to die. Yet in a moment like last night, we can feel that anyone who did die for the Project would wish to be remembered not by tributes or grief but by understanding and continuation of what he was doing. . . .

As we left the church, we heard on the radio the end of President Johnson's speech announcing the air attacks on Vietnam. . . . I could only think "This must not be the beginning of a war. There is still a freedom fight, and we are winning. We must have time to live and help Mississippi to be alive." Half an hour before, I had understood death in a new way. Now I realized that Mississippi, in spite of itself, has given real meaning to life. In Mississippi you never ask, "What is the meaning of life?" or "Is there any point to it all?" but only that we may have enough life to do all that there is to be done. . . .

Meridian, August 5

At the Freedom school and at the community center, many of the kids had known Mickey and almost all knew Jimmy Chaney. Today we asked the kids to describe Mickey and Jimmy because we had never known them.

"Mickey was a big guy. He wore blue jeans all the time." . . . I asked the kids, "What did his eyes look like?" and they told me they were "friendly eyes" "nice eyes" ("nice" is a lovely word in a Mississippi accent). "Mickey was a man who was at home everywhere and with anybody," said the 17-year-old girl I stay with. The littlest kids, the 6, 7, 8 years olds, tell about how he played "Frankenstein" with them or took them for drives or talked with them about Freedom. Many of the teen-age boys were delinquents until Mickey went down to the bars and jails and showed them that one person at least would respect them if they began to fight for something important. . . . And the grownups too, trusted him. The lady I stay with tells with pride of how Mickey and Rita came to supper at their house, and police cars circled around the house all during the meal. But Mickey could make them feel glad to take the risk.

People talk less about James Chaney here, but feel more. The kids describe a boy who played with them—whom everyone respected but who never had to join in fights to maintain this respect—a quiet boy but very sharp and very understanding when he did speak. Mostly we know James through his sisters and especially his 12-year-old brother, Ben. Today Ben was in the Freedom School.

At lunchtime the kids have a jazz band (piano, washtub bass, cardboard boxes and bongos as drums) and tiny Ben was there leading all even with his broken arm, with so much energy and rhythm that even Senator Eastland[3] would have had to stop and listen if he'd been walking by. . . .

Meridian, August 11

. . . In the line I was in, there were about 150 people—white and Negro—walking solemnly, quietly, and without incident for about a mile and a half through white and Negro neighborhoods (segregation is like a checkerboard here). The police held up traffic at the stoplights, and of all the white people watching only one girl heckled. I dislike remembering the service—the photographers with their television cameras were omnipresent, it was really bad. And cameras when people are crying . . . and bright lights. Someone said it was on television later. I suppose it was.

Dave Dennis spoke—it was as if he was realizing his anger and feeling only as he spoke. As if the deepest emotion—the bitterness, then hatred—came as he expressed it, and could not have been planned or forethought. . . .

Laurel, August 11

Dear Folks,

. . . The memorial service began around 7:30 with over 120 people filling the small, wooden-pew lined church. David Dennis of CORE,[4] the Assistant Director for the Mississippi Summer Project, spoke for COFO.[5] He talked to the Negro people of Meridian—it was a speech to move people, to end the lethargy, to make people stand up. It went something like this:

"I am not here to memorialize James Chaney, I am not here to pay tribute—I am too sick and tired. Do YOU hear me, I am S-I-C-K and T-I-R-E-D. I have attended too many memorials, too many funerals. This has got to stop. Mack Parker, Medgar Evers, Herbert Lee, Lewis Allen, Emmett Till, four little girls in Birmingham, a 13-year-old boy in Birmingham, and the list goes on and on. I have attended these funerals and memorials and I am SICK and TIRED. But the trouble is that YOU are NOT sick and tired and for that reason YOU, yes YOU, are to blame. Everyone of your damn souls. And if you are going to let this continue now then you are to blame, yes YOU. Just as much as the monsters of hate who pulled the trigger or brought down the club; just as much to blame as the sheriff and the chief of police, as the governor in Jackson who said that he 'did not have time' for Mrs. Schwerner when she went to see him, and just as much to blame as the President and Attorney General in Washington who wouldn't provide protection for Chaney, Goodman and Schwerner when we told them that protection was necessary in Neshoba County. . . . Yes, I am angry, I AM. And it's high time that you got angry too, angry enough to go

3. **Senator Eastland:** James Eastland, a U.S. senator from Mississippi from 1943 to 1978 and an outspoken supporter of segregation.
4. **CORE:** Congress of Racial Equality, a civil rights group.
5. **COFO:** Congress of Federated Organizations, an organization of the civil rights groups operating in Mississippi that summer.

up to the courthouse Monday and register—everyone of you. Angry enough to take five and then other people with you. Then and only then can these brutal killings be stopped. Remember it is your sons and your daughters who have been killed all these years and you have done nothing about it, and if you don't do nothing NOW baby, I say God Damn Your Souls." . . .

Mileston, August 9

Dear Blake,

. . . Dave finally broke down and couldn't finish and the Chaney family was moaning and much of the audience and I were also crying. It's such an impossible thing to describe but suddenly again, as I'd first realized when I heard the three men were missing when we were still training up at Oxford, [Ohio,] I felt the sacrifice the Negroes have been making for so long. How the Negro people are able to accept all the abuses of the whites—all the insults and injustices which make me ashamed to be white—and then turn around and say they want to love us, is beyond me. There are Negroes who want to kill whites and many Negroes have much bitterness but still the majority seem to have the quality of being able to look for a future in which whites will love the Negroes. Our kids talk very critically of all the whites around here and still they have a dream of freedom in which both races understand and accept each other. There is such an overpowering task ahead of these kids that sometimes I can't do anything but cry for them. I hope they are up to the task, I'm not sure I would be if I were a Mississippi Negro. As a white northerner I can get involved whenever I feel like it and run home whenever I get bored or frustrated or scared. I hate the attitude and position of the Northern whites and despise myself when I think that way. Lately I've been feeling homesick and longing for pleasant old Westport and sailing and swimming and my friends. I don't quite know what to do because I can't ignore my desire to go home and yet I feel I am a much weaker person than I like to think I am because I do have these emotions. I've always tried to avoid situations which aren't so nice, like arguments and dirty houses and now maybe Mississippi. I asked my father if I could stay down here for a whole year and I was almost glad when he said "no" that we couldn't afford it because it would mean supporting me this year in addition to three more years of college. I have a desire to go home and to read a lot and go to Quaker meetings and be by myself so I can think about all this rather than being in the middle of it all the time. But I know if my emotions run like they have in the past, that I can only take that pacific sort of life for a little while and then I get the desire to be active again and get involved with knowing other people. I guess this all sounds crazy and I seem to always think out my problems as I write to you. I am angry because I have a choice as to whether or not to work in the Movement and I am playing upon that choice and leaving here. I wish I could talk with you 'cause I'd like to know if you ever felt this way about anything. I mean have you ever despised yourself for your weak conviction or something. And what is making it worse is that all those damn northerners are thinking of me as a brave hero. . . .

Martha

35

The Young Lords
Pablo Guzmán

The Young Lords Party, founded in 1969, was one of the many left-wing urban youth organizations that developed out of the political turmoil of the late 1960s. Modeled after the Black Panther Party, the Young Lords was a loose confederation of Puerto Rican youth groups that skirted the boundary between a civil rights organization, a street gang, and a third world anticolonial liberation army. They brought together a remarkable mix of Puerto Ricans, from upwardly mobile "college kids" to street toughs, prostitutes, and recent immigrants from the island. The Young Lords, along with the Black Panthers, the Brown Berets, and the many Native American youth organizations that sprang up around the same time, articulated the political voice of a generation of nonwhite teenagers that had been shaped by growing up on the excluded margins of the greatest economic boom in world history.

Heavily influenced by the Marxist revolutions in Cuba, Vietnam, and China, the Young Lords attempted to weld traditional ethnic community organizations to their politics of revolution through neighborhood study groups, educational meetings, and the kind of confrontational, direct political action that had made the black power movement so frightening to the authorities. Like the Panthers, they often carried guns and used paramilitary tactics borrowed from third world guerrilla movements to gain attention, patrolling or occupying hospitals, churches, and other public buildings. Their political banditry included commandeering a hospital van to provide free mobile medical services to their communities. They also provided a free breakfast program for school children and produced a weekly radio program, newspapers, and even a coffee-table book.

Their deep ties to neighborhood and community made it very difficult for the police to identify or arrest members. The New York Police Department and the FBI eventually did manage to destabilize the group, but for six years the Young Lords captured the imagination of many in urban America, particularly in New York City with its sizable Puerto Rican community. A large number of the group's leaders went on to become successful journalists, lawyers, television and radio personalities, union organizers, professional political activists, academics, and authors. Pablo Guzmán, the author of this memoir, became a television reporter after his time in the Young Lords.

Pablo Guzmán, "*La Vida Pura*: A Lord of the Barrio," in Andrés Torres and José E. Velázquez, eds., *The Puerto Rican Movement: Voices from the Diaspora* (Philadelphia: Temple University Press, 1998), pp. 155–58, 164–67. Originally appeared in the *Village Voice*, March 21, 1995.

BEFORE YOU READ

1. What were the main objectives of the Young Lords?
2. Why do you think the Young Lords gained support from their community?
3. What does Guzmán reveal about how he now feels about his involvement with the Young Lords?

I had never done anything like this before. Twelve other guys, one woman, myself, and a small handful of people who, until moments before had been spectators, were about to set a barricade of garbage on fire. Garbage in the ghetto sense: rusted refrigerators from empty lots, the untowed carcasses of abandoned vehicles, mattresses, furniture, and appliances off the sidewalk as well as the stuff normally found in what few trash cans the city saw fit to place in *El Barrio*.[1] We were taking on the sanitation department, although it wouldn't be long before firefighters and police became involved—not to mention John Lindsay's[2] city hall.

It was a late Sunday afternoon. Somehow, after gathering the material on the corners of Third Avenue and 110th Street, we had managed to pile it across the wide avenue between green lights, catching the uptown traffic before it moved again. Many drivers cursed, a few were just curious. But though Juan tried explaining through a bullhorn, and though Sonia, Voodoo, David, Mauricio, and a couple of others began waving their purple berets to warn the first drivers to slow down, none of them were prepared when this instant barrier suddenly got torched. I was helping to flip a junked car into the blockade when I saw the gasoline being poured. It was ignited and more gasoline was poured as the flames shot upward. A couple of bystanders I didn't know amazed me with how quickly and professionally they stoked the fire.

When the fire trucks arrived, I should not have been surprised that they were met with bottles and bricks. But it was still unsettling. We had been trying for weeks to rally a crowd and could never draw one, though the week before we had some success on the steps of a church at 111th and Lexington Avenue when David unfurled a Puerto Rican flag. Now, however, this blazing protest had done more than get people's attention. We needed to control what was becoming a mob. Through his bullhorn, Juan González[3] shouted: "The firemen are not our enemy! They're not the problem!" But the firefighters had already gone into reverse.

When the cops arrived minutes later, we had wanted to talk, to explain. That we were making a point, and now we'd clean the mess up. All we had been trying to do after sweeping up the streets on previous Sundays was talk with sanitation about once-a-week pickups and nonexistent trash cans, and about

1. *El Barrio:* Puerto Rican name for "Spanish" or East Harlem.
2. **John Lindsay:** mayor of New York City from 1965 to 1973.
3. **Juan González:** journalist and author.

how to decently treat people asking for help instead of blowing them off with "You spics get the f—— outta here, this space is off-limits. You gotta problem, talk to the mayor." But the cops came out of their cars swinging. We whipped off our berets and tried melting into the crowd. What really saved us, though, was the people on the rooftops, who instantly started hurling missiles from above. As we had prearranged in case of such an emergency, we ran in twos and threes to a spot outside *El Barrio* in Black Harlem. There, we sized up our first battle. I couldn't believe how my chest was pounding from the run. And the rush. About a dozen "civilian" participants had taken off with us, following the purple berets. This took us by surprise. Still, it was an opportunity. So in a playground we explained what we were about and enlisted our first recruits. It was the summer of 1969, and the first stateside organization of radical young Puerto Ricans was announcing itself—we hoped—as a political force.

RAÍCES/ROOTS

We called ourselves the Young Lords Organization. In June 1969, two small groupings from Spanish Harlem and one from the Lower East Side, consisting overwhelmingly of guys between seventeen and twenty-two, decided to merge. I was in the Sociedad de Albizu Campos, named for the leader of the old Nationalist Party of Puerto Rico. Primarily college students, we had begun meeting three months before. I had just returned from a semester of study in Cuernavaca, Mexico, completing the required "in-the-field" half of my freshman year at the State University at the brand-new Old Westbury. I left as Paul Guzman, a nervous only child of a Puerto Rican–Cuban mother and a Puerto Rican father, both of whom were born "here"—stateside. I came back to the states as Pablo Guzmán. The other East Harlem group consisted mostly of high-school dudes who met in an after-school photo workshop run by Hiram Maristany. The Lower East Side group was a mix of college and high-school aged guys who we later found out had already been penetrated by two or three NYPD Red Squad agents.

Immediately after the merger, Mickey, David, and I drove in Mickey's Volkswagen Beetle to Chicago. We didn't know at the time about the Brown Berets or La Raza Unida among the Chicanos and the Mexicans of the West and Southwest. But Mauricio and I had read in that week's *Guardian* about what the Chicago Panthers called a "Rainbow Coalition" they had put together. The Panthers had turned (or were trying to turn) two Chicago gangs, the Young Patriots (poor Whites with Appalachian roots) and the Young Lords (Puerto Ricans and Mexicans), away from 'banging and toward something more constructive. If there was already a Latino group in action, we reasoned, why not throw in together? The Lords' chairman, Cha Cha Jiménez, breezily gave us permission to organize as the New York chapter of the YLO. The affiliation with Chicago was where we got our purple berets—even though they claimed to be moving away from street life, the Lords weren't giving up their colors.

This whole gang thing was fairly jolting. Although to this day people think the New York group was a gang because of that name, we never were, and except for Felipe Luciano (one of the few New Yorkers who had been in a gang himself), we walked lightly around the Chicago boys. Nevertheless, it was a Mexican member of the Chicago Lords, Omar López, who came up with our slogan, *"Tengo Puerto Rico en Mi Corazón"*—"I Have Puerto Rico in My Heart." We loved it, and it soon spread throughout Puerto Rican circles. Only years later did we learn that it contained a slight grammatical error, a testimonial to the bad Spanish most of us "spoke." We were truly examples of Ricans raised in the states.

I wasn't yet nineteen. My folks would have freaked if they'd known what their only child—the altar boy from Our Lady of Pity who was supposed to use his Bronx science diploma and college scholarship to bust out of the ghetto—was really doing on his summer vacation. But it didn't come from nowhere—my parents and my grandparents, after all, had first instilled in me a sense that there was far too long a history of injustice in this society. "Only," as my father would say later at my trial, "your mother and I never thought you would actually try to do something about it. Not on such a scale, anyhow."

By the time of that trial, the Young Lords Party—we split from Chicago in April 1970 because we felt they hadn't overcome being a gang—had been targeted by Hoover's FBI as the Latino version of the Panthers and the Weather Underground. Although we never kept a roster, I tallied our New York membership at the end of 1970, and we had grown to more than a thousand, with storefront offices in *El Barrio*, the Lower East Side, and the South Bronx. We had branches in Newark-Hoboken, Bridgeport, Philadelphia, and Puerto Rico, active supporters in Detroit, Boston, Hawaii, in the military and in the prisons. We published a weekly newspaper, *Pa'lante*. We had organized workers, including medical professionals, in the city's hospitals and had a sizeable following on campuses across the country, where we often spoke. . . .

"WHERE ARE THE DAMN GUNS!"

In early October 1970, two of our members, Bobby Lemus and Julio Roldán, were arrested basically for drinking beer and hanging out with some guys on a stoop one night. This was 1970, remember. The next morning, Julio was found hung in his cell at the "Tombs" (Manhattan House of Detention), the latest in a series of controversial "suicides" in jails and police precincts, often with autopsies returned that did not indicate unassisted death. We had been covering the issue in *Pa'lante*. Julio was a quiet, unassuming little guy of about thirty who joined mainly because he believed in independence. His main contribution was cooking at one of our communal apartments at East Harlem.

Surrounded by five thousand demonstrators, we carried his casket from the González Funeral Home on Madison Avenue and marched to the church on 111th that we had taken over a year before. We took it over again, suddenly, posting armed guards at the entrance and at either side of the casket. The standoff would continue, we said, until conditions in the prisons changed. It was the first time we had ever been connected with weapons. We caught even most of our own organization by surprise. Given the risk involved, and the infiltration we took as a given, we had to. The police, already at war with the "soft" Lindsay administration, were furious, but the mayor did not want a confrontation, and so he negotiated. The cops vented their frustration in other ways.

Very soon after the takeover, the Central Committee received reports from inmates in cells next to Julio indicating that he may have taken his own life. This created a debate that split the leadership. My view was that we should admit to doubts and cut our losses immediately. By this time Felipe was not part of the leadership, and indeed, soon he would be gone altogether. Meanwhile, a hard-liner named Gloria Fontanez, recruited from Gouverneur Hospital in the Lower East Side, had risen rapidly through the ranks. She argued that we should stick with our issue regardless of its actual truth, and the majority went along so as not to undermine the months of work we'd put into the UN march scheduled for October 1970. Because I continued to argue, I was suspended. In five and a half years of hard work, that is the only episode of which I am not proud—that and not doing more to get Gloria tossed out.

The march to the UN came off spectacularly, as it probably would have had we left the church earlier. But when the march was over with, we were still there. Negotiations were ongoing, however, and by God they budged: The Board of Corrections would institute sweeping reforms, and José Torres would get a seat on the board.

So now there was the matter of getting out of the church. Past the ring of cops waiting to bust us for the guns. The deal with the city included an amnesty clause that the city was sure would backfire on us. The cops would be allowed in to make sure there were no guns, and only upon their OK could we walk with no charges against us. Because the police had the place surrounded and had infiltrators inside, they were sure they were going to catch us sneaking guns out. And then, all bets would be off. On the appointed day, the police arrived, and at the front door I had the captain and his escort put up against the wall and frisked. "Sorry, Captain," I said, "but we agreed: no weapons. And that includes you. We don't want to say anybody planted anything, right?" The captain acquiesced, and because this occurred within view of reporters covering the "surrender," the image of the Young Lords telling a police captain to assume the position spread. The PBS (Policemen's Benevolent Association) and indignant editorialists called for his head, on a stake right next to ours.

The cops searched thoroughly and found nothing. To this day, I have had police veterans ask me how we pulled it off. Later that day, I had to break policy and get the story from the Lord in charge, David Pérez. "Never underestimate the power of the people," he said laughing. "The cops stopped everybody they thought looked like a Young Lord a block from the church. 'Where are the damn guns?!' one cop yelled at me. But we've spent the last year and change organizing this whole community, not just a part of it. They've been stopping everyone under thirty-five. We broke the weapons down and hid them under the coats of *las viejitas,* the little old ladies who look like your grandmother. Hey, those little old ladies were down."

GERALDO RIVERA SAVES MY ASS

In April 1970, a seven-month effort by Juan González was to culminate in the takeover of Lincoln Hospital. Juan and his team had organized doctors, nurses, other health-care providers, and patients in Manhattan and the Bronx in revealing exposés of just how poorly the system works for poor folks. From lead poisoning and tuberculosis, we had gone on to report the wave of unnecessary hysterectomies performed on Latin women, organized disgruntled rank-and-file workers within 1199, "liberated" an X-ray truck, promoted preventive medicine, and tried to show the links between the pharmaceutical companies, the AMA establishment, hospitals, and insurance outfits that made up the multibillion-dollar health-care industry. But our immediate plan was to take over Lincoln Hospital in the South Bronx and run it with the help of staff who were fed up with rats in the emergency room, antiquated equipment, meager supplies, and chronic personnel shortages.

Lincoln was a mess. For twenty-five years it awaited demolition, and for twenty-five years the city never funded the construction of its replacement. Getting spics a better hospital was the last thing on their agenda. I was from the South Bronx, and growing up I had heard the stories of a stabbing victim crawling two blocks to the catchment zone where the ambulance would take him to Morrisania (which would eventually be shut down as well). Apocryphal, perhaps, but it reflected Lincoln's street rep.

At dawn, we moved in, sneaking through windows and doors opened by doctors and nurses working with us. From inside, we told the guards they could go on a "lo-o-o-ng" break. A huge Puerto Rican flag was flown from the roof. The city was notified, and acute-care patients were transferred, but all other patients were treated by a reenergized staff. A phalanx of cops in riot gear sealed off the area outside, and the standoff was on. We held a news conference in the hospital auditorium, me in an Afro and white lab coat, and made our case against the city. Deputy Mayor Aurelio sent Sid Davidoff and Barry Gottehrer and their Latino "liaison," Arnie Segarra (who went on to become Dinkins's[4] appointment aide). Negotiations began. By late afternoon, we had won: A new Lincoln would be built. And, of course, the participants would receive amnesty.

The cops were not going for this amnesty bullshit. And they could give a f—— that Lindsay was their boss—he was as hated as Dinkins. So a few blocks from the hospital, I was chased by four detectives in an unmarked car. I thought I had given them the slip, but a dog, a goddamn dog, came nipping after me and slowed me down, and I was collared. Just before they got the cuffs on, I pulled my beret from my back pocket and waved it to the onlookers. "Call the Young Lords!" I vainly cried out. Then my wrists got pinched tight, and my head was slammed on the car roof before I was thrown inside.

They gave me a few more shots, but I knew I was in for a serious beating back at the precinct. As spokesmen, Felipe and I were the biggest targets. On two occasions, cops arrested guys they mistook for me, breaking one's leg and another's

---

4. **Dinkins:** David Dinkins, the first African American mayor of New York City (1989–1993).

arm. In Chicago, I spoke at a rally at the start of the Chicago 7 trial, and as I was finishing, word came that the cops were going to bust me. I managed to escape but learned later that once again the cops grabbed a look-alike and beat the shit out of him. I had been shot at by cops and nearly run over by a squad car in both Chicago and New York. And now my charmed existence had come to an end.

At the 40th Precinct, I was put in a "bing," or holding cell. Louie Perez, who had been assigned as my security when he left Lincoln, was already there. This Negro detective put on a show for his White comrades. They had taken Louie's nunchakus, the "karate sticks" many Lords used. "So, this is what you use against cops, huh?" the lackey said. "Well, let's see how it stands up against this"—and he patted one of the three guns he was visibly packing. His boys laughed, and I knew we were goners. "This is America, c——s——." He was leaning in close through the bars. His hand was at the lock. "And you oughta be taught what happens to punks who want to mess it up for the rest of us." He was going for the key. Louie and I braced ourselves.

Suddenly, there was a commotion. Bustling sounds from below. Shouting, growing louder. Gerry Rivera materialized, with what seemed like half the precinct coming up the stairs behind him, Keystone Kops–style. He dodged a cop, leaped over a railing, dodged another, and got to our cell. "You OK?" he asked. I was ready to kiss his feet. "Yeah, yeah," I panted. "You just made it. Behind you, watch out!" He turned just before the first cop could grab him. "I'malawyerthesearemyclientsyoutouchanyoneofusI'lltakeallyourbadges." Cops froze in mid air.

From an office, a supervisor emerged looking down at some paper. "Jesus! I just got off the phone with headquarters. Do we have some Young Lord here for the hospital thing, they're getting all kinds of calls from the media—" He finally looked up and took the scene in. "What the f—— is all this?" Gerry waded through fifty or so cops and glibly explained. I had to laugh; he was a piece of work.

Gerry burst into our collective lives soon after we had opened the first office, interrupting a meeting with our lawyers to charge that we had no Latino representation, like, for instance, him, even though one of our attorneys was a Puerto Rican he knew personally. Appalled though we were, we admired his chutzpah. But when he tried to join we drew the line. "This is an adventure for you, bro," he was told. "You're not really into the ideology." Still, he had a lot of heat, and he loved the street battles—and the press conferences. Eventually he took advantage of a scholarship to the Columbia School of Journalism that I had turned down because it would have meant leaving the Lords. We wished him well. Once out of Columbia, he got a gig with WABC-TV and hit the ground running. And that's how the Young Lords Party unleashed Geraldo Rivera on an unsuspecting universe. . . .

By our sixth year, it was over. Partly because of destabilization by arrest and government infiltration but mainly because we were young and prone to mistakes—mistakes of leadership, of vulnerability to betrayal, and of the same movement infighting that we had once so despised. But before we dissolved, the Young Lords Party had left its mark:

- A new Lincoln Hospital was built in the South Bronx after we seized a facility that the city had run out of a condemned building for twenty-five years.

- We forced the city to use the lead-poisoning and tuberculosis detection tests gathering dust in some agency's basement after we liberated them and exposed epidemics in both diseases—which are now making comebacks.

- We pushed the Board of Corrections into reforming prison conditions just before the Attica uprising—which our sixteen-year-old chief of staff, Juan "Fi" Ortíz, witnessed as our representative on the negotiation team.

- We encouraged schools to teach Puerto Rican history. Some, at least, now do.

- We created a climate for the start of bilingual education. Never intended as a parallel track, but as a way of mainstreaming Spanish-dominant kids to English proficiency, it has since been sabotaged by educators who were against it from the beginning.

- We produced the first radio show by a New York–born Latino (myself, over WBAI).

- Ask any Latino professional in Nueva York who advanced in government or the corporate world between, say, 1969 and 1984, and you'll be told they owe part of their opportunity to the sea change in perception that the Young Lords inspired.

- We helped raise the understanding, first among Latinos and then the society at large, that Puerto Ricans possessed a culture on a par with anyone's.

An American Hostage in Tehran
Barry Rosen

On November 4, 1979, five hundred Iranian students seized the American embassy in Iran in response to the U.S. government allowing the recently deposed Iranian dictator Shah Reza Pahlevi to enter the United States for medical treatment. It was the beginning of a hostage drama that would last for 444 days, involve fifty-two captive embassy personnel, and bring down a U.S. president, Jimmy Carter. This was not the first time that Americans had been taken hostage for political reasons, but what made the Iran crisis different was that it gave ordinary Americans their first real view of the power and intensity of anti-American sentiment abroad. Though the scars of the Vietnam War were still fresh, Vietnamese Communists had generally avoided anti-American rhetoric, hoping to win support for their cause from drafted soldiers and sympathetic Americans. In Iran it was different. Nightly news coverage showed large angry mobs burning the Stars and Stripes and chanting "death to Carter, death to America" in the streets of Tehran, while Islamic militants paraded members of the U.S. Marine embassy guard, bound and blindfolded, in front of television cameras. For over a year Americans watched in horror as an entire country, led by a revolutionary Islamic government, vented rage against the United States for its support of the shah's brutal and repressive regime.

The Iranian students were not just holding Americans captive, as Islamic militants later did in Lebanon. They were occupying American sovereign territory in flagrant violation of international law and custom. President Carter devoted much of his last year in office to freeing the hostages, trying everything from freezing billions of dollars in Iranian assets and halting oil imports from Iran to undertaking a disastrous military rescue operation, known as "Eagle Claw," which ended before it began with three helicopters crashing in a sandstorm. After the failure of "Eagle Claw," Secretary of State Cyrus Vance resigned, leaving Carter's presidency even more compromised. These failures prepared the way for the victory of the conservative Republican Ronald Reagan in the 1980 election. Carter continued to negotiate with the Iranians until the final minutes of his presidency, bringing a military telephone with him to Reagan's inauguration. The Reagan years began that afternoon with an announcement by the new president that the hostages had been freed.

Barry Rosen, the writer of the following selection, specialized in Persian and Central Asian studies and ran Voice of America's Uzbek service in the 1970s. In November 1978 he became the American embassy press attaché in Tehran and was in the embassy

Barbara and Barry Rosen, with George Feifer, *The Destined Hour: The Hostage Crisis and One Family's Ordeal* (Garden City, NY: Doubleday, 1982), pp. 128–34, 136–38.

when it was taken over. His knowledge of Iranian culture made him a leader among the hostages and he became well known to both Iranians and Americans during his 444 days of captivity.

BEFORE YOU READ

1. Why, according to Barry Rosen, did the Iranian students hate the United States?
2. What did the students hope to accomplish by taking the embassy?
3. What does Rosen reveal about his opinion of the shah in this document?

November 4 dawned a drizzly day that prompted daydreams of Florida with Barbara. It was Sunday, a normal workday in Iran. The embassy staff numbered about eighty now, up from the forty of the early months after the revolution. Many of the additions were on temporary duty; some were assigned to help businessmen who had returned to complete contracts. We did not consider that the beginning of resumption of heavy involvement in the country.

Back in my office from Isfahan, I first checked the press to prepare our report for the morning staff meeting. Most newspapers provided their readers with times and routes of major demonstrations. Apparently nothing anti-American was scheduled for the day. There were just the usual relevant items to summarize for Washington, which on that day were few: no unusually strident charges or complaints against America.

My cable drafted, I took a telephone call from a magazine called *Message of Peace*, based in the holy city of Qom. The journal had a strong anti-Western bias, but the call informed me that I was expected in Qom to discuss the possibility of exchanging Islamic and Christian theological students between Iran and America. Then I pondered how to fulfill a directive from a more exalted ICA [intelligence] officer. He *had* to be exalted—and isolated—in order to have devised this particular project: a blueprint of Iran's current power structure. At my level this seemed like a request to photograph air. Washington naturally wanted outlines and diagrams, but the situation remained so amorphous and fluid that few Iranians themselves had a clear idea of who reported to whom and who was responsible for what. The new order's most characteristic trait still seemed to me that there *was* no power structure. Power was largely up for grabs among the clergy, various revolutionary organs, and street mobs unleashed for specific jobs.

Our ICA offices were now in a small building fifty yards directly inside the Embassy's main gate. Takht-e Jamshid, the street outside the gate, had been renamed Taleghani, in honor of a recently dead progressive ayatollah. At ten o'clock or so, the sidewalks and roadway began to fill up with demonstrators, slowly at first, then with a surge. When their noise grew more clamorous than usual, I got up from my typing and went into my secretary's office for a better view. Several dozen young men and women sporting plastic-covered pictures of the Imam on their chests were visible through the gate. The boys wore old suit jackets over turtleneck sweaters; many of the girls were in black chadors or kerchiefs. Both sexes were in their late teens and early twenties: a collection of types who took their anti-Americanism very seriously.

"God is great!"

"Long live Khomeini!"

Although they seemed no more worked up than earlier protestors, something held me at my secretary's desk, watching the swelling cluster. Suddenly there were not several dozen but several hundred demonstrators. Then twice that or more. No better trained or disciplined than ever, our crew of embassy guards—those we ourselves had hired—were overwhelmed by the new arrivals.

"God is great!"

"Long live Khomeini!"

"Death to America!"

Just as suddenly, a handful of seemingly designated men started climbing over the gates. Their scrambling appeared both preposterous and utterly natural, as if fated. Some had pistols and lead pipes. Another cut the chain with a large bolt cutter. With the gate flung open, a roar of triumph sounded and a rush of demonstrators, more than we'd seen, poured in like a flood of frenzy. The Embassy's defenses had been breached in seconds.

Thick clubs waved in the air, mingling with portraits of Khomeini held high like icons. The rush was now a tidal wave of field jackets, mustaches, sweat, and grimaces of hatred. The roar had become an unholy howl—but for some reason I couldn't yet react seriously. "There goes my great report on the so-called power structure," I smirked to myself. "And there goes Iran. I bet we close the Embassy by tomorrow."

Even though the gate remained wide open, some of the fist-waving men kept demonstrating their valor by climbing over the wall. A hundred bodies were now inside the compound, twitching with menace, lining up in a kind of battle order. A lieutenant of the National Police Force—in whose Academy I had taught—skipped up to embrace the scruffy invaders. The Revolutionary Guards who had taken over as our protectors from Masha'allah had been stationed outside the compound; I could picture them joining the invaders. The game was up. I felt a certain relief at that, mixed with the excitement of observing a historic moment.

When "shock troops" had captured the Embassy nine months before and marched us out of the vault where we had taken refuge, we assumed we were about to be shot in our own blinding tear gas. When they grabbed my beard and ordered me to open safes whose combinations I didn't know, I believed the end was very near. As much as anything else, the invaders' inexperience made me apprehensive. They were so frightened by what they were doing and so amazed by their ease in penetrating the imperialist monsters' outpost that they made themselves doubly dangerous through nervousness. More experienced this time, they also seemed more determined—which, curiously, boded better for our safety than during the previous invasion. I was less worried about getting shot thanks to somebody's jumpiness.

The fifty yards that separated us from the main gate seemed to shrink to ten. We were right on top of the action and totally cut off, since the Chancery was several minutes' run away. The first detachment of boys and girls—I refused to think of them as men and women—rushed directly for our outer door, which I had naturally locked and barred. I instructed my secretary not to open it for anyone, then ran into my own office to search for classified materials that might not have been locked away in the Chancery with the others. The unsettling sounds of my colleagues being routed from nearby offices penetrated the walls while I was searching. Together with their Iranian employees, they were being driven to the Commercial Library in a nearby wing. The "Death to America" chanting was now so violent that its vibrations almost shook my floor.

As I was rushing through the papers in my last desk drawer, the scrape of the bar being removed from my secretary's door stiffened the hairs on my neck. "Mary, what are you doing?" I screamed. "DON'T OPEN THAT DOOR!" But Mary had children. Her husband was unemployed. Most dangerous for her, she was Armenian: a minority who, like the Jews, had been protected under the Shah and now feared for their safety. Good and loyal as she was, it was too much to ask her to jeopardize everything. By the time I had raced back into the outer room, its door was open.

The exultant victors squeezed in too fast to separate them as individuals. My first impression was of unkemptness. I noticed several girls with clubs among the first dozen. They were in chadors or kerchiefs wrapped heavily around their heads.

"GET OUT!" I shouted in Farsi.

"Either you move out of this room or we're going to drag you out," several voices answered simultaneously.

"This is United States property. Get out of this building immediately!"

This was more than bravado. The presence of that mob in my office made me very angry. To sympathize with the revolution's original aim was one thing, but to believe that revolutionaries had a right to violate diplomatic immunity and custom—to commit this barefaced offense against America—was quite another.

But this was probably too abstract and too patriotic to explain my stubbornness. Most of all I was acting on a childish insistence that *I*, which in this case meant my country, be treated with dignity. And although I was quaking, something in me was confident that I wasn't courting death. Perhaps it was naïve, but I reckoned the revolution, despite its anti-foreign passion, had killed very few foreigners.

Half a dozen intruders began ransacking the office, tearing through my press files and news-agency teletape rolls. Mary hunched in a corner, trembling. (She would be released that evening.) But most of the attention was devoted to me. My resistance seemed both to infuriate and, by enhancing their image of themselves as valiant fighters, to please the intruders.

"Leave this room immediately or you will be hurt," barked one of the leaders while his closest assistants waved clubs in the direction of my head. "This is no joke. You are flouting the will of the Iranian people."

"*You* leave immediately. You have no right to set foot in here, any of you. It is totally illegal."

I was also aware of the element of gamesmanship in my defense of principle. Iranians love to bargain and play brinksmanship, pitting one side against the other. Although the outcome was inevitable, I wanted to see how far I could go with *this* game. They respected a show of strength, which I was determined to carry through.

I gave up when the closest clubs swished inches from my nose. A squad led me to join the others in the Commercial Library. If I had dreamed that this was going to be the first of a dozen substitute cells, I would have been appalled and depressed instead of cocky. . . .

"It's going to be a trade: the Shah for you," said one of the group guarding us in the Commercial Library. That was the first hint that we might be in for something longer than the brief encounter of the Embassy's seizure and its personnel's expulsion. Surely Washington wouldn't, and shouldn't, succumb to terrorism by surrendering the Shah. I felt bitter about the staff meeting of October 22, when we were told about the decision to admit him for medical treatment. But once there, he could not be given up on a plate by a humbled American Government. And if he was not, would we in fact be flying home to a nice holiday with our families the next day?

I was in a group of about fifty captives in the Commercial Library. A handful were Americans. Many of our Iranian staff became panicky and pleaded to call home. Something had snapped in Mary's back; she lay on the floor with my jacket to ease the pain. My attempt to soothe and calm lost out to the wailing of our ordinarily cheerful cleaning woman: "You don't know how brutal they can be. I have children; let me out." . . .

. . . Peering out the window, I saw young men and women spray-painting "Nest of Spies" on the chancery walls, while others denounced the Shah through bullhorns. If the Chancery's steel doors held, as I was certain they would, at least some of our staff were calling for help from the government. However, there were no signs of anyone arriving to restore order. After two heavy hours, the Americans in the library were selected to leave, but not to pack our things or for a ride directly to the airport, as I'd half assumed.

As the other Americans were being blindfolded, I kissed Mary good-bye and shook as many Iranian hands as I could. My own blindfold, a piece of khaki that might have been ripped from the uniform of one of our marines, was an outrage—yet I wanted it, in a way. When one guard asked another, "Is he an American too?" I almost shouted, "Yes I am, and take me with the others!" The blindfold was tight, but I could tell I was being led—alone—to the back end of the compound, toward the Ambassador's residence. The guards debated in whispers. I was pulled one way and then another. Apparently only the break-in itself had been organized.

When the blindfold came off, I was in a bedroom of one of the Embassy's Pakistani kitchen staff. From across the hall I heard one of the military attachés answering his captors in single syllables. My own guards, who would answer no question about who they were and whom they represented, took up the argument about the United States handing over the Shah.

"Whatever *you* say, your government will give in. You're more important to them than the Shah, that blood-sucking dictator, that animal!"

"I might agree with some things you say about the Shah, but our policy is not to surrender to terrorism—which is what you're engaged in."

"Do any of you Americans, even now, have any idea of what the Shah committed?"

"I can't answer for his mistakes or supposed mistakes. Have *you* made any? Are you going to answer for the one you're committing today?"

After our little debate, my guards posted themselves outside the door, and I strained to hear a radio playing in a nearby room. A local news broadcast announced with near glee that our captors called themselves Students Following the Line of the Imam and that support for their brave and righteous action was pouring in from all over the country. The implication that the seizure might be more, or become more, than an impulse of a band of irate zealots was a glum new hint that our confinement might not end in time for dinner. . . .

They were still unsure about who was who among embassy personnel, and still totally disorganized as to which brother or sister was responsible for which duties with respect to us. But they settled on a simple answer to their chaos. After breakfast I was moved again, this time to the large reception room of the Ambassador's residence, which was on the same floor. Blindfolded again, I could not count the Americans there, but coughing, shuffling, and occasional words suggested we numbered fifteen to twenty. I wondered whether the ghosts and goblins from last week's Halloween party were enriching the Iranians' imagination about our sinister activities. That day and the next, we were tied to chairs, our blindfolds remaining on. I got a masterpiece of modern design with a strip of leather for the seat and another supposedly to support the back. It was fairly torturous after the first few hours, but less than my thoughts of what this frenzied treatment might lead to.

A prohibition against talk accompanied the physical bondage. With shouts and threats we were ordered to say nothing except in answer to guards' questions. During the day I was fed a handful of dates while my blindfold remained on. Totally powerless, with ropes cutting into my hands and feet, I did not seriously consider disobeying. Still, it was demoralizing and shaming that we did obey. The only sentence in English I heard throughout the day was, "I'd like to go to the bathroom." I ate supper with the blindfold off in the already filthy kitchen. Contempt for myself was growing together with growing hatred for *them.*

They examined our watches for two-way radios. They checked our heels for hidden . . . what? Their nervousness was not totally misplaced: From their tone and from everything I knew about them, they were, despite their triumphant bluster, amazed by their success and frightened that American retribution for it was already on the way. But from what I knew about them too, they were operating on a knowledge of America that came chiefly from fantasies stimulated by spy thrillers. . . .

Returning from the bathroom on the third day, I asked a young escort if I might see something from the press. Apparently he hadn't heard or understood the leaders' directive against this, for he gave me a copy of *Kayhan*, which bulged with copy about the seizure. The burning of the American flag and the "liberation" of our Iranian secretaries and drivers were featured among the saga of the Iranian people's glorious victory. Most depressing was the total absence of mention—and apparently of perception—that the take-over was a stunning violation of diplomatic immunity. As with the students themselves, the editorialists I read might never have heard of international law. It meant nothing whatever to them. It was a Western, not an Iranian concept, a concept invented to aid the rape of Third World countries. And Iranians were *finished* with everything Western; the seizure itself was proof of that.

What the newspaper did declare, and what the average Iranians surely felt, was that America had for too long used its laws—and not only laws—to oppress Iran. When I understood that the Embassy's seizure was regarded as no wrong, certainly not a crime, I felt a sharp stab of longing to leave the country forever.

PART SEVEN

New World Order?

Angry Realignments after the Cold War

When the Berlin Wall came down in 1989, most historians agreed that it was the end of one period and the beginning of another. Some commentators called it globalization, others postmodernity, and the U.S. president George H. W. Bush described it as a "new world order." The American political scientist Francis Fukuyama attempted a more precise definition in his 1989 article "The End of History?" where he argued that mankind's evolution through monarchy, fascism, communism, and other political ideologies was finally over and that Western liberal democracy would be "the final form of human government." He went on to argue that "economic calculation, the endless solving of technical problems, environmental concerns, and the satisfaction of sophisticated consumer demands" would replace the conflicts over ideologies of the past.

For a time it seemed that Fukuyama was right. The Soviet Union peacefully dissolved, Palestinians and Israeli Jews signed a peace accord, Irish Catholics and Protestants agreed to settle their differences, and South Africa achieved black majority rule. There was still, as Fukuyama had predicted, ethnic conflict, civil war, and a few isolated dictatorships but none of the ideological battles that had characterized the cold war. Though violent, these conflicts seemed like Fukuyama's "technical problems to be solved." In 1991, an international coalition of more than twenty countries, many of which had been enemies only a few years earlier, joined forces to liberate Kuwait from Iraqi occupation, as multinational peacekeeping forces fanned out across the globe.

At home Americans began to reap the benefits of a peace dividend. Though the Los Angeles riots of May 1992 that followed the Rodney King verdict were some of the worst in American history, they passed quickly as the nation elected its first baby-boomer president, the young and charismatic Bill Clinton, who promised inclusion, consensus, and prosperity. Americans still fought over social issues like abortion, religion in the schools, and the death penalty. Bias attacks like the one that killed gay college student Matthew Shepard also continued, but the widespread support for his family, as well as the president's public appearance with Shepard's mother to announce new hate-crime laws, suggested a growing consensus around tolerance, liberalism, and civil rights.

The "economic calculation" described by Fukuyama set the tone for Clinton's post–cold war America. Economists sharing Fukuyama's triumphalism claimed that cyclical economic downturns were a thing of the past. The economy boomed as trillions of dollars flowed into the stock market from around the world. The information superhighway created a "new economy," producing "dot-com" millionaires, software billionaires, and millions of CEOs, MBAs, and workplace "daytraders." This was also the period of "emerging markets," when free-trade policies ended protectionist tariffs and forced the sale of state-sector industries, drawing new capital to modernize aging, inefficient production facilities and forcing the layoff of redundant workers. As new wealth was created, skyscrapers and modern metropolises grew in distant places like Kuala Lumpur and Jakarta, while many American inner cities "gentrified." But most of the world's population missed the boom, experiencing instead displacement, poverty, and blocked ambition. Many took the traditional path out of misery, leaving home and family to migrate to a wealthier region. Mexico lost millions of people as the 1994 devaluation of the peso greatly increased the migration stream described in "Crossing the Rio Grande," bringing landless peasants, laid-off workers, and suddenly impoverished professionals to the United States.

As the decades-long battle between communism and capitalism receded, people across the globe increasingly looked to the past. For some, like Bulgarians, who elected their British-born former king as prime minister in 2001, neomonarchism promised a return to the traditions of a nationalistic past. Others, like antiglobalization protesters at the 1999 "Battle of Seattle," wanted to return to a time when products were made in local communities. Finally, many yearned for a world ordered by ancient religious principles. On the morning of September 11, 2001, a series of coordinated suicide attacks by nineteen fundamentalist Muslims in hijacked jetliners killed almost three thousand people and destroyed one of the great symbols of modernity, the twin towers of the World Trade Center in New York City. The visual portfolio "9/11" (page 335) documents the reactions of public figures and private citizens to the attacks. As the American public and the media attempt to understand the events of September 11, old concerns like the debate over racial profiling, discussed in the following documents, and the anti-Americanism of the previous generation's Tehran hostage crisis have even greater significance in a frightening new era.

37

Driving While Black

James Campbell

African Americans have, for many years, used the acronym DWB ("driving while black") to describe racially biased traffic stops. However, it was not until New Jersey State Police opened fire on a van carrying four nonwhite teenagers to a North Carolina basketball tryout in the summer of 1998 that racial profiling hit the national headlines. Two troopers stopped the van to search for illegal drugs, and as they approached, it rolled backwards. The policemen responded by firing twelve bullets into the van, badly wounding all four teenagers and putting an end to their hopes of basketball careers. The young men filed a lawsuit, leading to a federal investigation that revealed systematic racial profiling and deep cleavages between white and black police officers. The four victims received a $12.95 million settlement, and there were subsequent legal actions by African American motorists throughout the United States.

The two policemen involved each received a $250 fine and were banned for life from police work. Civil rights activists were enraged by the light penalties, while many police and law enforcement advocates complained that an unfair example was being made in banning the two officers. They defended the practice of pulling over young African American and Hispanic men, arguing that the war on drugs that had started in the 1980s could not be won if police could not stop and search the most likely participants in narcotics trafficking. Across the United States there was shock and dismay at the revelations of racial profiling and attempts were made to revamp and improve policing practices. Even the advice column "Dear Abby" took a stand against racial profiling.

James Campbell, the writer of this column, is an African American journalist from Houston who received national attention in 1991 when he became involved in a First Amendment dispute involving the right of reporters to protect their news sources. The following editorial was published in the Houston Chronicle *in September 1998 as part of the national debate that emerged after the New Jersey Turnpike incident.*

James Campbell, "'Driving while black' still gets you stopped," *Houston Chronicle*, September 14, 1998, <http://webadv.chron.com/ads/ads_i/insidestory/editorial/driving.html>.

1. Do you believe James Campbell gives a fair account of the risks of "driving while black"?

2. Do you think there are other groups that are profiled by police?

3. Do you believe that hiring more African American police officers would help solve the problem outlined by Campbell?

There's nothing like a firsthand experience, especially when an old-school uncle is attempting to make a point to his hip-hop nephew.

The subject was "driving while black" —a rite of passage conversation that many black men eventually have with their sons or nephews.

It was February. My nephew was three months from high school graduation and six months from entering college. It was time. My father gave his spiel on the subject when I was 16, fresh out of a driver's education class and ready to take ownership of an environmentally incorrect 1961 Ford Falcon.

It was the early '70s. The distrust of police in Houston's black community was high and well founded. In those days, being stopped by police could prove unhealthy. If you said the wrong thing or showed the faintest degree of attitude, your head was a candidate for the nightstick rumba or worse . . .

My father wanted to make damn sure I understood that. Don't ride around with more than one friend because a carload of black teenage boys invited stops by police, he told me. Of course, it hardly mattered how many were in the car, being stopped by police was an inevitability, particularly if you were black.

The best policy, my father would say, is to ride only with your girlfriend. Wrong. At the time, I dated a fair-skinned black girl with blond hair. That was trouble. White cops going in the opposite direction would U-turn to stop us just to see if she was OK. It was comical.

When I worked as sports editor for a weekly newspaper in the Humble-Kingwood area, police would routinely stop me for no good reason. Never ticketed; just questioned and let go. That was a relief.

Over the years, I've forgotten how many times I've been stopped by police but never the experiences or the feelings of anger, frustration, and despair. It really is a "black thang," and I can't imagine that any white person could relate.

I understood that my father's advice was meant more as a system of survival for "driving while black" than as proper driving etiquette. And so the conversation about the subject with my 18-year-old nephew.

We were en route to New Orleans for Mardi Gras and stopped at a nondescript eatery outside of Lafayette, Louisiana, for breakfast. We talked about life and aspirations. He wants to be an engineer. At a point that I don't recall, the conservation segued to "driving while black."

Mario, whose father is deceased, is a good suburban kid, well mannered and with good grades, a good citizen. All that doesn't matter, I told him, when you're "driving while black." All that matters is that you survive it. I related my experiences and gave him almost the same speech my father had given me. I think he got it, but I wasn't sure.

Not long after getting back on the interstate, we were pulled over by a Louisiana state trooper. I wasn't speeding and hadn't changed lanes recklessly. Only moments earlier, a pleasant-looking white couple sped past us in obvious view of the trooper.

I waited motionless as the trooper approached, knowing that a slight movement might give him the impression that something was amiss. He ordered me out of the car and asked to see my driver's license and proof of insurance. I respectfully complied as Mario sat quietly in the car.

I protested—gently—that I wasn't speeding and asked what I had done. He said I changed lanes without using my turn signal. I wanted to laugh out loud, but my good sense prevailed. He then asked where I was going, how long I planned to stay, and who my passenger was. I answered, respectfully.

He then asked to look inside the car. No problem, I said. He ordered Mario out of the car and asked to see his driver's license. No problem. We both just wanted this to be over. Finally, he let us go—no ticket, no nothing.

I wanted to be angry, but I couldn't. I was relieved. I figured from Mario's silence that he now understood what his old-school uncle had tried to put into words only minutes earlier.

This wasn't an anecdote. This was real. And so are the many stops of black and Hispanic men by police all over this country. The evidence is overwhelming.

Consider a 1992 American Civil Liberties Union study of a 48-mile portion of Interstate 95 from just north of Baltimore to Delaware's border. That study showed blacks made up 14 percent of traffic but 72 percent of those stopped by police.

In 1995, a *Chronicle* analysis of millions of tickets reported to the Texas Department of Public Safety between September 1, 1991, and August 31, 1994, showed that traffic citations issued statewide closely paralleled the ethnic proportions in the state's population.

However, the *Chronicle's* analysis also found that in many cases, minorities were ticketed only for driver's license offenses or for no insurance, raising questions about what initiated the stop. And blacks were more than three times as likely as whites to be ticketed in Harris County's small municipalities.

A move is afoot in Congress to prove unequivocally what I've known for years: that minorities are unfairly targeted for traffic stops. A so-called "driving while black" bill has cleared the U.S. House and is pending in the Senate. It would require the Justice Department to collect data on traffic stops and searches.

Predictably, police oppose the bill, arguing that it would create an undue onus on law enforcement officers and wouldn't necessarily prove anything. Perhaps, perhaps not.

From this point of view, I'm for anything that will keep my nephew from having a "driving while black" conversation with his son.

38

Let Them Profile Me

Fedwa Malti-Douglas

Like much in American political life, the issue of racial profiling came to be framed in a very different way after the terror attacks of September 11, 2001. Though many Americans have long harbored deep personal concerns about the relationship between race and crime, prior to September 11 few felt comfortable openly defending a practice that so clearly singled out individuals for their skin color or region of ancestry. All that has changed.

The attack by nineteen Middle Eastern Muslims punished thousands of people for merely living and working in the United States. The arbitrary nature of the attack combined with the apparent sympathy for the attackers in parts of the Islamic world suggested to many Americans that their ideals of openness and fairness might be naïve and dangerous in a complicated world. Racial profiling suddenly seemed necessary and justifiable to many who had previously viewed it as unacceptable and "un-American."

After September 11, some men of Middle Eastern appearance were attacked by angry mobs, and the FBI detained over one thousand people, sometimes for reasons as flimsy as having the same last name as one of the hijackers. Arab American families, some of whom had lived in the United States for generations, suddenly found their loyalty to their country being questioned. In Florida, a twenty-mile stretch of highway was closed and three Middle Eastern men detained after a tip from a waitress who claimed she heard them joking about the attack. Soon after September 11, the FBI asked police departments across the country to question thousands of Middle Eastern men. A few police chiefs such as African American Andrew Kirkland of Portland, Oregon, refused, claiming that this violated laws against racial profiling, but most complied.

Arab American organizations along with civil liberties activists fought the new racial profiling, arguing that such breaches of human rights were not even effective. In the post–September 11 world, however, even many African Americans were wary of raising their voices against the practice. The following piece, written by Fedwa Malti-Douglas, a professor of law and humanities at Indiana University, is typical in the arguments it advances in favor of racial profiling but unusual in its source: an Arab American scholar with strong ties to the Middle East.

BEFORE YOU READ

1. Do you think that Fedwa Malti-Douglas's views are representative of people of Middle Eastern origin in the United States? What factors might make her views different?

Fedwa Malti-Douglas, "Let Them Profile Me," *New York Times*, February 6, 2002, Op. Ed. article, p. 21.

2. Do you think security is reduced by the fear of accusations of bias?
3. Why do you think the author decided to write this piece?

I have probably been through more ethnic profiling at airports than anyone who has protested the practice on television. My American passport says I was born in Lebanon. I have an unusual name and a classic Mediterranean appearance. And for my research in Middle Eastern studies, I have hopped between Iraq and Tunis; Syria and the United Arab Emirates; Kuwait, Egypt and Morocco. Trips like these leave telltale marks on your passport, and even my fair-haired, blue-eyed husband, traveling with me, has been subject to lengthy interrogations.

In my experience, every country profiles. In Paris I made the mistake of speaking with a security official in French. Finding my fluency suspect, he called over an American who questioned me in English and declared me a fellow citizen when he saw that I was using frequent flier miles.

In Zurich, transferring on the way home from Egypt, I was pulled out of line and taken to a large, bare hangar where my luggage was taken apart. I eventually found out that I had been taken to the isolated building in case a bomb was in my luggage. Was I surprised and upset? Who would not be? But I wanted to get home safely, too.

Once while flying on El Al from Cairo to Tel Aviv, my husband and I were seated in the front and the crew watched our every move. And at Heathrow, I was interviewed at great length about what I would be doing in London. I was staying with a friend.

My most harrowing experience was in Cairo. After a flight from Tunis, my husband was passed through while I was held back and my passport confiscated, perhaps because I had made the mistake of speaking Arabic. After an hour of my beseeching, a kindly older man finally located my passport and gave it back to me.

Despite the inconvenience to me, I believe this scrutiny is a defensible tactic for picking out potential problem passengers. Although I am not a terrorist, others do not necessarily know it. The airline security procedures I ran into also protect me from terrorism. In the last few years, I saw less profiling by American carriers, perhaps because concerns had been raised about discrimination. That laxity continued until September 11.

Security officials need to keep an open mind about national origins. There will be more Richard Reids and John Walker Lindhs, who will not be found through profiling. Yet it is a fact that the particular terrorist group sworn to our destruction, Al Qaeda, is made up largely of Middle Easterners. It is not unreasonable to direct increased attention to passengers with some connection to the Middle East.

Arab Americans like me want to be safe when we fly. Cooperating with security procedures, even when we suspect that we are getting more attention than our fellow citizens, makes sense. Does anyone really want a security official to hesitate before stopping a suspicious passenger out of fear of an accusation of bias?

FOR CRITICAL THINKING

1. Is it possible to oppose the type of racial profiling Campbell describes while condoning the measures described by Malti-Douglas?

2. Do you think African Americans, Latinos, and whites would differ in their support of racial profiling in the "war against terrorism"?

3. Does racial profiling work?

39

Crossing the Rio Grande
Al Santoli

Throughout American history waves of immigration have shaped the nation's life. Only in the period from 1924 to 1965, when federal racial and ethnic quotas were severely enforced, did migration become somewhat less influential. Since the mid-1960s the historic American pattern has reasserted itself, with immigrants—particularly from Asia, the Caribbean, and Latin America—again shaping American social, economic, and cultural life.

The new Americans are at least as varied as the old: Mexicans, Central Americans, Filipinos, Koreans, Indians, Iranians, Jamaicans, Taiwanese, Vietnamese, and others fill the stream of legal immigrants. In addition, large numbers of illegal aliens from Mexico and elsewhere in Latin America have swelled the populations of Florida, Texas, Arizona, New Mexico, and southern California. All have different stories, motives, and prospects. Some have been viewed as essential labor, others as potential welfare cases, and still others as entrepreneurs who will fuel a rebirth of economic growth. The U.S. government has recognized the value of this new immigration by granting citizenship to those who have resided in this country for a number of years—the "amnesty" José Luis mentions in his interview. The interviews collected in Al Santoli's New Americans: An Oral History, *published in 1988, suggest that we are still a nation of immigrants.*

BEFORE YOU READ

1. What goals do Rosa and José pursue? How do these goals compare with those of people born in the United States?

2. What kind of work do Rosa and José do? Are they competing for jobs with U.S. citizens?

3. What is the role of the *migra?*

4. What arguments can you think of for and against allowing Rosa and José to become citizens of the United States?

Rosa María Urbina, age thirty-five, crossed the muddy Rio Grande in 1984 with the hope that she could earn enough money as a housecleaner in El Paso to take her three children out of an orphanage. A widow, she had to place her children in an institution because the $14 a week she earned on a factory assembly line in Juárez was not enough to feed them.

Al Santoli, *New Americans: An Oral History* (New York: Viking, 1988), pp. 266–74.

Each morning she joined hundreds of other young to middle-aged women from the hillside *colonias*,[1] who walked down to the concrete riverbank and paid men called *burros* to ferry them across the river on their shoulders—and back to the squalor of Juárez in the evening. On one of these excursions, she met a handsome farm worker, José Luis, age twenty-six, with dark mestizo[2] features. It was fate, they believe. Within months, Rosa's children joined them in a two-room apartment on the American side of the river.

I was introduced to José and Rosa during a tour of overcrowded tenement buildings in South El Paso that house many of the city's fifty thousand illegal residents. In Mexican slang, they are called *mojados*, or "wets," the river people.

My guide, Julie Padilla, a public-health nurse from the Centro de Salud Familiar La Fe clinic, visits the Urbinas to give their two-month-old baby, José Luis Jr., a postnatal checkup. We walked up a dark stairwell to a dimly lit landing decorated with a colorful gold-framed mural of Our Lady of Guadalupe, the religious patron of all Mexican Catholics. There are sixteen apartments with ripped screen doors along a narrow graffiti-covered corridor. On the back fire escape is a closet-sized communal toilet. Julie said, "There used to be one bathtub that every family on the corridor shared. But in the past year, that's been taken out. I don't know where they bathe now."

Rosa María, José, and the children have the luxury apartment. Half of the 12-foot-square room is taken up by a bed covered by a magenta Woolworth blanket. On the wall, above a calendar of the Good Shepherd, is a portrait of Pope John Paul II. A Winnie the Pooh blanket serves as a makeshift closet door. On a miniature two-tiered nightstand, alongside baby bottles and a green plant, are metal-framed elementary-school photos of the children. Their seven-year-old daughter's Honor Roll certificate is proudly displayed on a mirror above an all-purpose foldout table.

During winter months, José Luis is out of farm work. The baby is Rosa's full-time chore. They survive on $58 a month in food stamps earmarked for the baby, who is an American citizen by virtue of his birth in El Paso. And WICC, the Women, Infant and Children Care program, provides a bag of groceries each week. Although the children attend public school, José and Rosa seldom leave the apartment. They fear that border patrolmen will send them back across the river to the squalor of Juárez.

José: The majority of the people in our apartment building have the same problem as my family. All of us are in El Paso without legal papers. I have been living here since 1981.

Rosa: I came in 1984, to find work. After José and I were married and we found a place to live, I brought my children from a previous marriage. We lived across the river, in Juárez. But I was born further south, in Zacatecas.

José: My hometown is Juárez. Since I was nine years old, I've been coming to El Paso to work. At first I did gardening in people's yards, but I have stayed in El Paso constantly since 1981, going out to the fields to do farm work. I used

---

1. *colonias:* ramshackle housing projects.
2. **mestizo:** a person of mixed European and native ancestry.

to go to Juárez to visit my relatives at least one day each month. But in the last year, I haven't gone, because of the immigration law. To visit Juárez I have to swim across the river. I can't cross the bridge or the *"migra"*[3] can catch me right there.

During the past few months, the river has been very high and fast. That's one reason why not so many people have been crossing lately. I am not working now, because it isn't the growing or harvesting season on the big farms. On February 15, we usually begin to plant onions. That is when the main agricultural season begins. But during a three-month period between planting and harvesting, there is no work.

We haven't paid our rent since December. If we're lucky, I can find some part-time work to pay for food. Our baby, José Luis, is two months old. Because he was born in El Paso, he is an American citizen. We can only get food assistance for him. Once in a while, I find a job as a construction laborer, house painter, whatever is available. We use the money to buy food for the baby and the other three children first.

Rosa: I haven't been able to work lately, because the baby is so small. My other children are all in school. Lorenzo is twelve years old, José Rubén is ten, and Miriam is seven. From the time I came to El Paso, I have worked as a housekeeper and minding homes for people. I am not used to staying in the apartment every day, but I have no other choice, because of my small baby.

I have known many changes in my life. I moved to Juárez from a farm in Zacatecas when I was seven years old. My mother and father were split up. After mother remarried, my stepfather took us to Juárez. We lived in an adobe house in the *colonias* up in the hills.

When I was a teenager, I worked as a hairdresser in a beauty salon, cutting hair. My first husband was a mechanic, fixing cars. We made a good living. But my husband spent the money he made drinking in the *cantinas*. And after a while, he wouldn't let me work, because I had young children to take care of. When he died in 1984, he left me nothing at all. He drank too much and died from cirrhosis of his liver. I had no money . . . nothing. My children were nine, seven, and three years old. I had to find a way to pay rent and feed them.

At that time, the economy in Mexico had become horrible. Inflation was going crazy. The peso jumped to 500 per dollar. Today it is still climbing at 1,000 per dollar. I found a job working on an assembly line at a factory. We produced rubber gloves for hospitals and medical supplies like little caps for syringes. I would go into work at 4:30 in the afternoon and stay until 2:00 A.M. I was paid only 7,000 pesos [$14] each week. That was not enough to feed my kids. And I didn't have any relatives or friends to watch the kids while I worked. So I had no other choice but to put them in a special institution, like an orphanage, for children without parents. This upset me very much. But with my husband dead, and no other form of support, there was nothing I could do.

My only hope was to cross the river to the United States. If I could find a job that paid enough money, my children could join me. I wanted them to have an education and a proper life . . . to be someone.

3. *migra:* U.S. Border Patrol officers.

After I made up my mind to cross the river, I met José Luis. It was like fate—we just found each other. You could say it was love at first sight. [*Laughs.*] I had two young boys who needed a good man to learn from. When he asked me to live with him, I said yes.

José: Before I met Rosa, I lived with my grandmother in Juárez. I would go back and forth across the river to work in El Paso or the farms in New Mexico. After Rosa and I fell in love, we decided to rent this apartment in El Paso and live together.

Rosa: Before I met José, I crossed back and forth across the river five days each week to my housekeeping jobs in El Paso. On weekends, I took my children out of the orphanage. Then I had to reluctantly return them to the orphanage on Sunday evenings and prepare to go back across the river.

For a while, I traveled alone, which can be dangerous. But after I met José Luis, we crossed together. There are men who carry people across the river on their shoulders. The water is kind of rough, but that's what these men do to make a living. They charge passengers 1,500 to 2,000 pesos [$1.50 to $2.50]. The water is up to their chests, but they manage to hold us up on their shoulders so we can get to work dry.

José: Crossing the river can be very dangerous, especially if you cross alone. There are fast water currents, and sometimes the water is quite high. If you don't know how to swim, the undercurrents can pull you right down. And in places the bottom of the river is like quicksand that can trap you. The water turns into kind of a funnel that can drag you down. Some friends of mine have died.

Rosa: I don't know how to swim. I relied on José Luis, who is a good swimmer. We were both very lucky. I can clearly remember an incident where we almost drowned. It began on a Sunday evening, which is a customary time for crossing. At the time, a man was running loose who was raping and killing women who crossed alone. So there were a lot of American border patrolmen and Mexican police along both banks.

After the sun went down and it became quite dark, José and I waited for a while near the riverbank, but it seemed hopeless to try to cross the river undetected. We waited until the next morning to try again.

When the sun came up, we saw that the men who carried people across on their shoulders weren't working, because of all the police. When we noticed that the border patrolmen had left the area, we decided to try to cross by ourselves. That was a big mistake. The current was very fast that day. In the middle of the river, we lost our balance and began to be dragged downstream. I felt helpless and began to panic. Fortunately, another man who was a strong swimmer came to our rescue. He pulled us to the shore.

After José and I began living together in El Paso, I decided to bring my children across the river. The water was too high and swift to risk men carrying them on their shoulders. So I had the children taxied across on a rubber raft.

José: Another danger for people who cross the river is crime. Packs of men hang around the riverbank like wolves. They try to steal people's knapsacks or purses. Sometimes they demand that you give your wallet or wristwatch. If you don't obey them, they will knife you.

Were we ever caught by the *migra* when we crossed the river together? Oh, yes. [*Laughs.*] Lots of times. But the patrolmen are really okay people. They arrest you, ask the usual questions. If you get rough, they will get rough, too. Otherwise they are fine. It all depends on the person who arrests you. If he has a mean personality, he will treat you rudely, whether you are impolite or not. But most of the time, it is a routine procedure.

When the *migra* catch us, they just put us in their truck and take us to their station. They ask our name, address, where we were born. They keep us in a cell maybe three or four hours. Then they put us in a bus and drive us back to Juárez. They drop the women off very near the main bridge. The men are taken a little further away from town.

Our favorite place to cross the river is close to the Black Bridge, which is not far from downtown El Paso. Many of us would stand on the Juárez riverbank and wait for the change of Border Patrol shifts. Each morning, the shift changes between seven-thirty and eight-thirty, sometimes nine-thirty. We learn by observing over long periods of time. And all of our friends have been held in the immigration station. We observed certain patrolmen coming in to work and others checking out after their shifts.

Experienced river crossers pass this information to new people who are just learning the daily routines. Over a period of time, we learn the shift changes by recognizing different officers' faces. Some Mexican people even know the *migra* by name.

Rosa: Suppose I am caught by the patrolmen at seven-thirty in the morning. They will take me to the station and hold me for a few hours, then bus me back to Juárez. I would walk back to a crossing point and try once again. It is like a game. I think the most times I was ever caught by the *migra* was six times in one day. No matter how many times they catch me, I keep coming back.

The majority of the people in the *colonia* where I lived in Juárez worked in El Paso, mostly as housekeepers, construction workers, or helpers in the fields. In the United States there is a lot of work, but in Mexico we have nothing.

José: The men, like myself, who work in the fields come across the river at around 2:30 A.M. to meet the buses that take us to the fields from El Paso. The transportation is owned by the *padrone* of the farms, or by the labor-crew chiefs who hire and pay the workers. In the evenings, we ride the buses back to the river. Sometimes I work twelve hours in a day and earn $20. I've learned to check around to see which farms pay the best. Some pay up to $35 a day.

Farm-labor jobs are not very steady. We just grab whatever is open at the moment. I accept anything, any time, as long as it is work. But suppose I take a job that only pays me $12 a day. It would only be enough to cover my transportation and meals in the field. I must find jobs that pay enough to feed my family.

In order to make $25, I must pick seventy-two buckets of chili peppers. That could take me four or five hours; it depends on how fast my hands are. The total amount of buckets we pick depends upon the amount contracted by the big companies in California. For a big contract, we work as long as necessary to complete the order. But the most I can earn in a day is $35.

During the summer, it gets very hot in the fields, up to 110 degrees. We work for eight hours with a half-hour break for lunch. To save money, I bring my lunch from home. The companies usually provide us with a thermos bottle of cold water. The farthest we travel from El Paso is to Lordsburg, New Mexico. That is around three and a half hours by bus. We leave El Paso at 3:00 A.M. For Las Cruces we leave at 5:00 or 5:30 A.M.

Rosa: To my housekeeping jobs I can take a regular El Paso city bus at 7:00 or 8:00 A.M. I usually come home around 3:30 or 4:00 P.M. each day. For a long while, I worked at one house—a Mexican American family. They started me at $20 a day. Eventually they increased my wages to $25. They live near a large shopping center in the eastern part of town. The job was a little bit easier than working in the factory in Juárez, and paid much better.

In the factory, a whistle blows to let us know when to start, when to stop, when to eat dinner, and when to resume work. Doing housecleaning, I can rest a little when I need to take a short break.

To compare our apartment in El Paso with where I lived in Juárez, I prefer it a little better over there, because in the *colonia* I had a place to hang my clothes after I washed them. The bathroom was outside of the house. But we don't have a bathroom in our apartment here, either. All of the apartments in this part of the building share a toilet on the back stairwell. But in this apartment we have electric appliances, which makes life better than my previous home.

José: The landlord who owns this building is very generous. He lets us owe him rent for the months that I am not working. He understands how tough our life is. We pay whatever we can, even if it's only $50. And he knows that, if the day comes where we are raided by immigration officers, we will run.

The rent for this apartment is $125 a month plus electricity. We all live and sleep in this one room. The two boys sleep on the couch. Our daughter, Miriam, sleeps with us on the bed. And the baby sleeps in a crib next to our bed. Fortunately, we have a kitchen, and a closet in this room. Living conditions in Juárez were better, but there was no work at all.

If it is possible, Rosa and I would like to become American citizens. I would have my documents, and the government wouldn't be after us. All we want is to be able to work in peace.

Our dream is to be able to give our children the best of everything. We know that, for them to have a better future and purpose in life, they need a good education. Of the three children in school now, Miriam is the fastest learner. She received an award for being an honor student, the best in her classroom.

We hope the children can finish high school and have the career of their choice. We are going to sacrifice for them, so that they can have the profession that they desire.

I was only allowed to finish grammar school. I am the oldest in my family, of five sisters and two boys. I had to stop going to school when I was twelve, to work with my father to support the family. I would have liked to finish school, but my parents needed me to work. They chose my sisters to study. So I gave up my studies to support my sisters.

At first, I liked working better than going to school. But after a while, I wanted to attend junior high school. But my mother told me that the family couldn't afford for me to go, and she said my sisters seemed to like the books better than I did. So I continued working. My father had a fruit-and-vegetable business. We sold from a pushcart in downtown Juárez, and I came across the river to do some gardening.

Even though I've come to work in Texas and New Mexico for many years, I've never learned to speak much English. I would like to learn, but I've never had the chance to study. I have a lot of responsibility now to provide for the children. It is more important that they have school, so I must work.

The dreams that Rosa María and I had of living in the U.S. and reality are not the same. We hoped to find a job and live comfortably. Now that we are here, our main purpose is to survive.

I worry about our status under the new immigration law. In the previous place where I lived, I paid the rent all the time, but the landlord threw away all of the receipts. So we have no proof that we have been living here enough years to qualify for amnesty.

On the farms where I worked, my employers or crew bosses didn't keep pay records, because I only worked temporarily at each place. And, besides, I was illegal. So what was the use? If the police showed up, we would be in trouble whether or not the employer had a record. And the employers wanted to protect themselves. They didn't pay us with checks; it was always cash.

Fortunately, the last farmer I worked for took taxes and Social Security out of our wages. He is sending me a W-2 form as proof. I am waiting for it now. But things are getting worse, because the immigration police are putting pressure on people who hire undocumented workers. If the police catch illegals on a job site, the boss can be arrested under the new law. So most places have stopped hiring illegals. For example, my last job in El Paso, I was fired because the *migra* would raid the construction site every day. We would have to stop working and run.

When the planting season begins on the farms, I hope the immigration police don't show up. They raid a farm with a truck and four or five police cars. They position themselves outside the entrance to the farm and wait for us to walk by. They ask us for identification. If we cannot show proof that we are legal, we've had it. They'll take us away.

On the farms where I work, some people are legal and others aren't. If you drive your own car, the police usually won't question you. But if you come to work in the employer's bus, they'll take you away.

Rosa: In town, we don't feel comfortable walking on the street. If the immigration officers see us, they will grab us. We are not afraid for ourselves, because we are accustomed to it. But I worry about the children. They have just begun studying in school here in El Paso. They like it very much. My sons are in the sixth and fifth grades, and Miriam is in second grade. They are learning English very quickly. My oldest boy, Lorenzo, likes social studies and mathematics; he would like to be a doctor. My other son likes the army a lot. He could probably be a good soldier.

José: If we become citizens and the United States government asks them to spend time in the army, we would be honored if they are chosen to serve. We would be very proud of our children for doing their duty for their country.

Rosa: My daughter, Miriam, received a certificate from her teacher. You can ask her what she would like to do when she finishes school.

Miriam: [*Big grin.*] I like to study English and mathematics. Some day I would like to be a teacher.

Rosa: In the buildings on this block, the majority of the people are families. In each apartment there are three or four children. This is the only area we found where the landlords don't mind renting to families with kids. The kids play outside, in the alley behind our building. Not many cars pass on this street at night, so it is pretty quiet. But other neighborhoods are more active and there is more crime on the streets.

We would like to have an ordinary life, but our problems with the *migra* are nothing new. If they catch me again and send me back to Juárez, I will just come back across the river.

40

Rodney King and the Los Angeles Riots
Stan Chambers

Shortly after midnight on March 3, 1991, the noise of a helicopter and police sirens outside his Los Angeles condominium awakened George Holliday, the manager of a plumbing company. On the street below, he saw a large group of police watching four officers beating and kicking an African American man who was writhing on the ground. He grabbed the video camera he had just purchased, fumbled with the switches and wires, and got it running in time to tape a minute and a half of footage that would be watched over and over again on television throughout the world.

Despite what looked like an open-and-shut case of police brutality to most people who had seen the tape, fourteen months later the four white police officers who had administered the beating to Rodney King were acquitted, touching off the worst domestic disturbances since the 1960s. In three days of rioting, fifty-five people were killed, nearly twenty-five hundred injured, and fifteen thousand arrested, with property damage estimated at nearly $1 billion. Federal troops and the California National Guard occupied South Central Los Angeles, and rioting spread to cities across the country. Twelve years of conservatism under Presidents Reagan and Bush would unravel in those few days in May. The nation watched a passive and paralyzed president unable to gain control of the ghettoes of Los Angeles, while Bill Clinton, a charismatic young presidential candidate, waded into crowds amid the still smoldering ruins, confidently assuring all that this would never happen again if he were elected.

Many people argued about what had gone wrong. Some, like Clinton, blamed the Reagan revolution's cuts to social programs, which particularly affected African Americans and Latinos. They argued that Bush's use of the case of a recidivist African American rapist and murderer, Willie Horton, as an appeal to conservatism during his 1988 electoral campaign had ensured four years of racial strife. On the other side, Republicans insisted that the rioting was the product of Democratic Party social support programs of the 1960s, which had encouraged lack of self-discipline, weak family values, and single parenting. In an unusual campaign speech shortly after the riots, Vice President Dan Quayle implied that some of the blame lay with the popular television show Murphy Brown, *whose title character, played by Candice Bergen, chose to have a baby out of marriage.*

Regardless of which side was correct, the King incident had been badly mismanaged at every step. The morning after the beating, Holliday's wife had been rudely dismissed

Stan Chambers, *News at Ten: Fifty Years with Stan Chambers* (Santa Barbara: Capra Press, 1994), pp. 11–16.

by police when she inquired about the incident, leading her to send the tape to the news media. When charges were brought against the four policemen for assault and use of excessive force on King, who sustained eleven skull fractures along with permanent brain and kidney damage, the trial venue was moved from Los Angeles, where the incident occurred, to Simi Valley, a largely white suburb that was home to many LAPD officers. Finally, more than a week passed following the verdict before the president came to Los Angeles to inspect the riot damage and reassure the shaken population.

More than a year later, a federal trial would send two of the four officers involved to prison for thirty months on the charge of violating Rodney King's civil rights. In this selection, Stan Chambers, a longtime KTLA television reporter who covered the Watts riots of 1965, recounts the initial reactions to the videotape of the beating of Rodney King and his view of the riots from a helicopter a year later.

BEFORE YOU READ

1. Do you think the officers who beat Rodney King would have been brought to trial if the beating had not been caught on videotape?

2. What else besides the Rodney King verdict do you think caused the riots?

3. What does Chambers's piece reveal about how journalists affect the events they report?

4. Do you think Chambers regrets the decision to air the video on television?

RODNEY KING VIDEO — MARCH 4, 1991[1]

My three-to-eleven o'clock shift is always full of surprises. Most of the scheduled stories have already been covered, so we turn our attention to what has just happened. I never know what my assignments are going to be when I drive to work listening to the news radio stations. . . .

Our assignment editor, Rosalva Skidmore, looked up from her phone call, smiled and waved a greeting. I scanned the newswire copy on her desk while she finished the call. . . .

"Stan, when you get a chance, will you take a look at this freelance video that we got today and see what you think we can do with it. It's an amateur home video, but it is really quite powerful. Take a look at it."

It was an unusual request so I put it in a play-back video unit right away. I looked at the pictures and felt a flow of adrenaline surge through my body. I had never viewed anything like this before. Although shot the night before in the San Fernando Valley Foothill Police Division, it looked like something that might have happened in Tiananmen Square in Beijing or in a poor black township in South Africa but not in Los Angeles.

The first part of the video was blurred and it was difficult to tell what was happening, but when the photographer found his focus, I saw an incredible

1. Order of narration changed from the original for chronological clarity.

scene of police officers hitting a man with batons, over and over again. The beating didn't stop. It continued at a frenzy. The man was on the ground reeling around. He seemed submissive, but the blows continued. I put the VCR in reverse and watched the blows bounce away from the victim. Then I put it on "play" and looked in disbelief as they pounded him again and again.

"How did we get this?" I asked.

"Some guy with a new home video camera shot this from his patio and he wants to sell it to us as a freelance news story," Rosalva answered.

I kept running the tape back and forth. More than a dozen officers had surrounded the person and three of them were hitting him with batons or kicking him. The others just seemed to stand around.

"Are we the only ones to have it? What's the background?" I asked.

"There was a pursuit on the Foothill Freeway. The guy tried to get away. When he finally stopped, he got out of the car and tried to take on the whole force," she answered.

Several others in the newsroom came over, clustered around the monitor and watched the videotape playback over and over again. Everyone had a pained expression.

"Better show this to the police first. We've got to get their reaction," I said to Rosalva.

The tape had been left off at the main gate by a viewer named George Holliday. He had taken the video when he heard shouting and yelling on the street in front of his apartment. He began videotaping the action and the violent beating sequence unfolded in front of him. Our news director, Warren Cereghino, had watched it many times before I saw it. He agreed that we had to show it to the police department brass before we put it on the air.

I called Lieutenant Fred Nixon in the press relations department and told him what we had.

"Bring it down, Stan. I'll have some of the staff take a look at it with me." . . .

The officers were waiting for me when I arrived with a copy of the tape at their sixth floor office of Parker Center about six o'clock that evening. They watched silently as the tape was played and replayed. It seemed to me they could not believe what they were seeing, but their official reaction was calm and noncommittal.

Lieutenant Nixon did an on-camera interview with me and said that they would have to investigate the circumstances and try to determine what had happened. He said there was no way he could comment on the tape until he knew more about the circumstances. It wasn't much of a reaction from the police department, but we could use it on the air when we ran the tape that night. Several other high-ranking officers saw the tape before I left that evening. These screenings gave the department a chance to get ready for the storm that was about to engulf them. I left a copy of the tape and was assured that the investigation would start immediately.

I had no idea about the impact of the beating tape, but I knew it would be bad. . . .

THE LOS ANGELES RIOTS — APRIL 29, 1992

Our helicopter whirled in a tight circle over Florence and Normandie in South Central Los Angeles. Pilot Mike Tamburro kept the ship at a constant bank. I was in the left seat next to the pilot and had a clear view of the rampaging clutter on the street below. Cameraman Martin Clancey, strapped in a shoulder harness, was hanging out of the helicopter. He had opened the left side door, placed his mini-cam on his shoulder and was recording the helter-skelter action. This was the early evening of April 29, 1992. The Los Angeles riots were erupting below us.

We began to get more reports of scattered violence shortly after we had watched on television the barbaric videotape of motorists being ripped out of their cars, hammered, pounded and chased by rock-throwing men on the ground. The image of a man, later identified as Reginald Denny, being pulled from his truck by thugs, still burned in my mind. My memory was seared by the vivid imprint of the motionless, beaten man, lying on the ground, being kicked and brutalized. I was still filled with rage at the sight of one of the assailants picking up a large piece of cinder-block and throwing it at Denny's apparently lifeless body, smashing him in the head. After the savage beating, the attacker appeared to do a dance, raise his hands towards the helicopter overhead and flashed a gang sign. Then, to my utter disbelief, another person on the street reached into the pocket of the fallen driver and stole his wallet.

This was my television memory; now I was seeing first hand what was really happening.

I peered through my side-window as the copter continued to circle in a steep bank. I could see that traffic was moving through the intersection below us. I watched as various cars whipped in a U-turn to avoid the chaos ahead. There were clusters of people milling around. They were throwing rocks and bottles at the passing cars. There were no police around, just an unruly mob venting hate on innocent motorists who happened to find themselves in the wrong place at the wrong time.

Other figures on the street were darting in and out of a liquor store at the corner, taking what they wanted. The looting, the beating and the hysteria was going on right below me.

My mind went back 27 years to when I covered the Watts riots in 1965. I tried to draw similarities that might help my reports on what was going on below. I remember telling myself that the big difference was that in Watts, they had fires.

Soon after, I noticed white smoke beginning to build in the street at the corner. A single overturned car had just been torched and was beginning to smoke and burn. Within moments, I could see more smoke pouring out of the front windows of the liquor store where looters were still running wild. It was a light smoke, wispy and barely visible from 700 feet above.

As we circled, Martin, peering into the viewfinder of his Sony camera, shouted over the radio communications system, "I think that liquor store is on fire."

Our pilot nodded and refocused the flight circle to the smoking corner building below. Things began to develop in a chaotic and rapid manner. An appliance store just east of Normandie, a short distance from the liquor store, showed the tell-tale light white smoke.

It wasn't long before large flames were shooting out the doors and windows of the first liquor store. The overturned car continued to burn. The appliance store seethed with heavy white smoke that slowly turned to rolling black clouds fed by billowing flames eating their way through the collapsing roof.

My thoughts again flashed back to 1965. I remember being in the newsroom watching pilot-reporter Larry Scheer in the KTLA Telecopter broadcasting the first fire pictures from Watts. My reaction tonight was the same as it had been a quarter of a century ago: I can't believe this is happening, but I am afraid it's only going to get worse. The light of dusk was now completely gone, the sky was black and the lights of South Central Los Angeles sparkled below.

By this time, the station had pre-empted all programs and was in full riot coverage. Hal Fishman, Larry McCormick and Jann Carl were at the anchor desks, Ron Olson was in the middle of the rioting crowd outside police headquarters at Parker Center, Steve Lentz and Marta Waller were covering other parts of the city as the riots seemed to spread.

Fires were breaking out over a widespread area below our helicopter. Dark plumes of smoke were ominously spreading to different spots of the city. New fires exploded on Manchester, Vermont, Figueroa, Martin Luther King Jr., Crenshaw, Jefferson, Rodeo and Century Boulevards. Our pilot broke off from our tight flying circle as we spotted flare-ups. He pulled the stick in one direction and cut a diagonal path across the sky to the next erupting blaze. Each one was a startling surprise. The numbers of separate fires grew from five or six to a dozen, to two dozen. They were now breaking out over a wide part of the city. This was not Watts of 1965 where the fires erupted in a relatively small area. These conflagrations were not limited to Watts and South Central Los Angeles. Roaring, rolling, intense flames were burning in all directions. The targets were varied, but very much the same. Supermarkets, Thrifty Drug Stores, Chief Auto Parts, liquor stores, swap meets, Korean businesses, restaurants and mini-malls miles apart ignited under the arsonist's torch.

Often, our copter would arrive when a fire was just starting. We watched countless buildings where the light wisps of smoke smoldered, then grew heavy, then went gray, then black, then erupted into consuming flames of intense orange. It didn't take long. Flames would roll through the roof of one building, then the fire would spread to a structure next door. Many mini-malls were completely wiped out when fire exploded in one of the stores, then raced through the attic which adjacent businesses shared.

Firemen could not respond to many of these early fires because snipers were shooting at them. Later, police escorts went in with them. KTLA remained on the air for hours. Countless times during the night, I kept repeating to myself: I can't believe this is happening.

I have lived all my life in Los Angeles and know it well. So many places I grew up with were burning. It was heart-rending to be over my city as these structures melted down into ash heaps. . . .

41

Homophobia in the Heartland
Dennis W. Shepard

On October 12, 1998, Matthew Shepard, a twenty-one-year-old University of Wyoming student majoring in political science and foreign relations, died from head trauma and internal injuries suffered five days earlier in a gay-bashing incident. Lured into a truck by two men he had met at the campus bar, Shepard believed he was going with them to discuss gay-liberation politics. Once inside the truck, the men told the 5'2", 102-pound Shepard that they were not gay. They robbed, beat, and tied him to a split-rail fence, where he was found eighteen hours later, barely breathing, with a crushed skull and blood covering his face except for where his tears had washed it away. The image of the gentle and delicate Shepard tied to a fence post and left for dead became a national symbol in the fight against intolerance.

The outrage at the attack and the outpouring of sympathy for Shepard's parents suggested how far most of the country had come in its tolerance of sexual minorities. The trial prosecutor sought the death penalty for Shepard's murderers, despite its unpopularity in Wyoming and the pressure exerted on him by the Roman Catholic Church. Across the nation and around the world, people organized tributes and memorial services for Matthew Shepard. President Clinton held a press conference at the White House where he and Judy Shepard, Matthew's mother, spoke out in support of a federal Hate Crimes Prevention Act. Many states have since passed their own hate crimes laws.

There were, however, many reminders that homosexuality still remains controversial and far from universally accepted. At Matthew Shepard's funeral, parishioners of a Kansas City Baptist congregation disrupted the occasion with signs that read "God hates fags" and "No fags in heaven." Though the trial judge disallowed a "gay panic" defense—that one of the killers had been humiliated as a child by homosexual experiences, which compelled him to commit the crime—the compromise defense, that Shepard's sexual advances had triggered a murderous rage, struck a chord with many Americans who believed homosexuality to be immoral and wrong. Additionally, many people objected to the new hate crimes laws, arguing that they create a two-tiered justice system and punish ideas as well as actions.

The following selection comes from a statement by Dennis Shepard, Matthew's father, that he read to the court after the second of his son's killers, Aaron McKinney, received two life sentences without parole.

Dennis W. Shepard, victim impact statement, November 4, 1999, <http://www.gaylawnews.com/shepardfatherstmt.html> (28 November 2002).

BEFORE YOU READ

1. Why did this case become so important to so many people?
2. Why do you think Dennis Shepard gave this speech?
3. Do you think hate crimes laws might have prevented the death of Matthew Shepard?

Your Honor, Members of the Jury, Mr. Rerucha,
I would like to begin my statement by addressing the jury. Ladies and gentlemen, a terrible crime was committed in Laramie thirteen months ago. Because of that crime, the reputation of the city of Laramie, the University of Wyoming, and the state of Wyoming became synonymous with gay bashing, hate crimes, and brutality. While some of this reputation may be deserved, it was blown out of proportion by our friends in the media. Yesterday, you, the jury, showed the world that Wyoming and the city of Laramie will not tolerate hate crimes. Yes, this was a hate crime, pure and simple, with the added ingredient of robbery. My son Matthew paid a terrible price to open the eyes of all of us who live in Wyoming, the United States, and the world to the unjust and unnecessary fears, discrimination, and intolerance that members of the gay community face every day. Yesterday's decision by you showed true courage and made a statement. That statement is that Wyoming is the Equality State, that Wyoming will not tolerate discrimination based on sexual orientation, that violence is not the solution. Ladies and gentlemen, you have the respect and admiration of Matthew's family and friends and of countless strangers around the world. Be proud of what you have accomplished. You may have prevented another family from losing a son or daughter.

Your Honor, I would also like to thank you for the dignity and grace with which this trial was conducted. Repeated attempts to distract the court from the true purpose of this trial failed because of your attentiveness, knowledge, and willingness to take a stand and make new law in the area of sexual orientation and the "gay panic" defense. By doing so, you have emphasized that Matthew was a human being with all the rights and responsibilities and protections of any citizen of Wyoming.

Mr. Rerucha took the oath of office as prosecuting attorney to protect the rights of the citizens of Albany County as mandated by the laws of the state of Wyoming, regardless of his personal feelings and beliefs. At no time did Mr. Rerucha make any decision on the outcome of this case without the permission of Judy and me. It was our decision to take this case to trial just as it was our decision to accept the plea bargain today and the earlier plea bargain of Mr. Henderson. A trial was necessary to show that this was a hate crime and not just a robbery gone bad. If we had sought a plea bargain earlier, the facts of this case would not have been known and the question would always be present that we had something to hide. In addition, this trial was necessary to help provide some closure to the citizens of Laramie, Albany County, and the state. . . .

My son Matthew did not look like a winner. After all, he was small for his age—weighing at the most 110 pounds and standing only 5'2" tall. He was rather uncoordinated and wore braces from the age of thirteen until the day he died. However, in his all too brief life, he proved that he was a winner. My son, a gentle, caring soul, proved that he was as tough as, if not tougher than, anyone I have ever heard of or known. On October 6, 1998, my son tried to show the world that he could win again. On October 12, 1998, my first-born son, and my hero, lost. On October 12, 1998, my first-born son, and my hero, died. On October 12, 1998, part of my life, part of my hopes, and part of my dreams died, fifty days before his twenty-second birthday. He died quietly, surrounded by family and friends, with his mother and brother holding his hand. All that I have left now are the memories and the mementos of his existence. I would like to briefly talk about Matt and the impact of his death.

It's hard to put into words how much Matt meant to family and friends and how much they meant to him. Everyone wanted him to succeed because he tried so hard. The spark that he provided to people had to be experienced. He simply made everyone feel better about themselves. Family and friends were his focus. He knew that he always had their support for anything that he wanted to try.

Matt's gift was people. He loved being with people, helping people, and making others feel good. The hope of a better world, free of harassment and discrimination because a person was different, kept him motivated. All his life he felt the stabs of discrimination. Because of that, he was sensitive to other people's feelings. He was naïve to the extent that, regardless of the wrongs people did to him, he still had faith that they would change and become "nice." Matt trusted people, perhaps too much. Violence was not a part of his life until his senior year in high school. He would walk into a fight and try to break it up. He was the perfect negotiator. He could get two people talking to each other again as no one else could.

Matt loved people and he trusted them. He could never understand how one person could hurt another, physically or verbally. They would hurt him and he would give them another chance. This quality of seeing only good gave him friends around the world. He didn't see size, race, intelligence, sex, religion, or the hundred other things that people use to make choices about people. All he saw was the person. All he wanted was to make another person his friend. All he wanted was to make another person feel good. All he wanted was to be accepted as an equal.

What did Matt's friends think of him? Fifteen of his friends from high school in Switzerland, as well as his high school advisor, joined hundreds of others at his memorial services. They left college, fought a blizzard, and came together one more time to say goodbye to Matt. Men and women coming from different countries, cultures, and religions thought enough of my son to drop everything and come to Wyoming—most of them for the first time. That's why this Wyoming country boy wanted to major in foreign relations and languages. He wanted to continue making friends and, at the same time, help others. He wanted to make a difference. Did he? You tell me.

I loved my son and, as can be seen throughout this statement, was proud of him. He was not my gay son. He was my son who happened to be gay. He was a good-looking, intelligent, caring person. There were the usual arguments and, at times, he was a real pain in the butt. I felt the regrets of a father when he realizes that his son is not a star athlete. But it was replaced with a greater pride when I saw him on the stage. The hours that he spent learning his parts, working behind the scenes, and helping others made me realize he was actually an excellent athlete, in a more dynamic way, because of the different types of physical and mental conditioning required by actors. To this day, I have never figured out how he was able to spend all those hours at the theater, during the school year, and still have good grades.

Because my job involved lots of travel, I never had the same give-and-take with Matt that Judy had. Our relationship, at times, was strained. But, whenever he had problems, we talked. For example, he was unsure about revealing to me that he was gay. He was afraid that I would reject him immediately so it took him a while to tell me. By that time, his mother and brother had already been told. One day, he said that he had something to say. I could see that he was nervous so I asked him if everything was all right. Matt took a deep breath and told me that he was gay. Then he waited for my reaction. I still remember his surprise when I said, "Yeah? Okay, but what's the point of this conversation?" Then everything was okay. We went back to being a father and son who loved each other and respected the beliefs of the other. We were father and son, but we were also friends.

How do I talk about the loss that I feel every time I think about Matt? How can I describe the empty pit in my heart and mind when I think about all the problems that were put in Matt's way that he overcame? No one can understand the sense of pride and accomplishment that I felt every time he reached the mountaintop of another obstacle. No one, including myself, will ever know the frustration and agony that others put him through, because he was different. How many people could be given the problems that Matt was presented with and still succeed, as he did? How many people would continue to smile, at least on the outside while crying on the inside, to keep other people from feeling bad?

I now feel very fortunate that I was able to spend some private time with Matt last summer during my vacation from Saudi Arabia. We sat and talked. I told Matt that he was my hero and that he was the toughest man that I had ever known. When I said that I bowed down to him out of respect for his ability to continue to smile and keep a positive attitude during all the trials and tribulations that he had gone through, he just laughed. I also told him how proud I was because of what he had accomplished and what he was trying to accomplish. The last thing I said to Matt was that I loved him and he said he loved me. That was the last private conversation that I ever had with him.

Impact on my life? My life will never be the same. I miss Matt terribly. I think about him all the time—at odd moments when some little thing reminds me of him; when I walk by the refrigerator and see the pictures of him and his brother that we've always kept on the door; at special times of the year like the first day of classes at UW or opening day of sage-chicken hunting. I keep wondering almost the same thing I did when I first saw him in the hospital. What would he have become? How would he have changed his piece of the world to make it better?

Impact on my life? I feel a tremendous sense of guilt. Why wasn't I there when he needed me most? Why didn't I spend more time with him? Why didn't I try to find another type of profession so that I could have been available to spend more time with him as he grew up? What could I have done to be a better father and friend? How do I get an answer to those questions now? The only one who can answer them is Matt. These questions will be with me for the rest of my life. What makes it worse for me is knowing that his mother and brother will have similar unanswered questions. . . .

Matt officially died at 12:53 A.M. on Monday, October 12, 1998, in a hospital in Fort Collins, Colorado. He actually died on the outskirts of Laramie, tied to a fence that Wednesday before when you beat him. You, Mr. McKinney, with your friend Mr. Henderson, killed my son.

By the end of the beating, his body was just trying to survive. You left him out there by himself but he wasn't alone. There were his lifelong friends with him—friends that he had grown up with. You're probably wondering who these friends were. First, he had the beautiful night sky with the same stars and moon that we used to look at through a telescope. Then he had the daylight and the sun to shine on him one more time—one more cool, wonderful autumn day in Wyoming. His last day alive in Wyoming. His last day alive in the state that he always proudly called home. And through it all, he was breathing in, for the last time, the smell of Wyoming sagebrush and the scent of pine trees from the Snowy Range. He heard the wind—the ever-present Wyoming wind—for the last time. He had one more friend with him. One he grew to know through his time in Sunday school and as an acolyte at St. Mark's in Casper as well as through his visits to St. Matthew's in Laramie. He had God. I feel better, knowing that he wasn't alone.

Matt became a symbol—some say a martyr—putting a boy-next-door face on hate crimes. That's fine with me. Matt would be thrilled if his death would help others. On the other hand, your agreement to life without parole has taken yourself out of the spotlight and out of the public eye. It means no drawn-out appeals process, [no] chance of walking away free due to a technicality, and no chance of a lighter sentence due to a "merciful" jury. Best of all, you won't be a symbol. No years of publicity, no chance of a commutation, no nothing—just a miserable future and a more miserable end. It works for me. . . .

Matt's beating, hospitalization, and funeral focused worldwide attention on hate. Good is coming out of evil. People have said, "Enough is enough." You screwed up, Mr. McKinney. You made the world realize that a person's lifestyle is not a reason for discrimination, intolerance, persecution, and violence. This is not the 1920s, '30s, and '40s of Nazi Germany. My son died because of your ignorance and intolerance. I can't bring him back. But I can do my best to see that this never, ever happens to another person or another family again. As I mentioned earlier, my son has become a symbol—a symbol against hate and people like you; a symbol for encouraging respect for individuality, for appreciating that someone is different, for tolerance. I miss my son but I'm proud to be able to say that he is my son. . . .

. . . Every time you celebrate Christmas, a birthday, or the Fourth of July, remember that Matt isn't. Every time that you wake up in that prison cell, remember that you had the opportunity and the ability to stop your actions that night. Every time that you see your cell mate, remember that you had a choice, and now you are living that choice. You robbed me of something very precious, and I will never forgive you for that. Mr. McKinney, I give you life in the memory of one who no longer lives. May you have a long life, and may you thank Matthew every day for it.

Your Honor, Members of the Jury, Mr. Rerucha,

Thank you.

September 11 and the Aftermath

Kimberly Morales, Daniel Harris, Diana Hoffman, Amber Amundson

On the morning of September 11, 2001, three hijacked airplanes filled with people and jet fuel were intentionally piloted into the 110-story twin towers of the World Trade Center and a section of the Pentagon. A fourth hijacked plane, headed for Washington, D.C., was brought down in a field in Pennsylvania during a struggle between the hijackers and passengers. Almost three thousand people were killed on this bright and sunny fall morning that altered the course of American history.

Around the world people reacted with shock, mourning the staggering death toll and marveling at the sight of a New York City skyline suddenly bereft of its signature twin towers. Nearly everybody who lived through what came to be called "9/11" knew it was a major historic event with profound implications for world politics and American social and cultural life. Like the 1941 bombing of Pearl Harbor and the 1963 assassination of John F. Kennedy, most people of a certain age are likely to remember forever what they were doing when they first heard of the tragedy.

Beyond the shared moment when people across the world sat together in front of television sets watching the same shocking video footage over and over again, there has been little agreement on what the attacks mean, what has changed and what remains the same, and how history should remember September 11. This is one challenge of history: an event may be significant, but it takes many years to figure out how it fits into the story of a nation.

Long before the dust settled at "ground zero," as the site of the World Trade Center came to be called, nearly everybody with any access to media or public opinion attempted to make some sense of what had happened. President Bush, who gave two brief statements during the day from undisclosed safe locations in the Midwest, returned to Washington in the evening to express the shock and anger that many felt. He declared a "war on terrorism," and two days later, the Congress passed a resolution encouraging

Kimberly Morales, "A College Student's Unplanned Lesson in Suicide," in Dean E. Murphy, ed., *September 11: An Oral History* (New York: Random House, 2002), pp. 125–28; Daniel Harris, "The Kitschification of September 11," in the editors of Salon.com and David Talbot, comps., *Afterwords: Stories and Reports from 9/11 and Beyond*, (New York: Simon and Schuster/Washington Square Press, 2002), pp. 203, 205–8; Diana Hoffman, "The Power of Freedom," <http://911neverforget .tripod.com/neverforgotten/id3.html> (5 December 2002); Amber Amundson, "Our Grief Is Not a Cry for War," letter read at "After September 11: Paths to Peace, Justice and Security," conference organized by the American Friends Service Committee and Tufts University's Peace and Justice Studies Program and Peace Coalition, Medford, Mass., December 7 and 8, 2001, <http://www.afsc .org/nero/pesp/amundson.htm> (5 December 2002).

every U.S. citizen to display the flag. Religious leader Jerry Falwell claimed that America had brought the attacks on itself through its godlessness, and Islamic fundamentalist Osama Bin Laden, believed to have planned the attacks, appeared on television to warn Americans that they would know no peace.

As the nation tried to reclaim daily life, artists, writers, academics, politicians, media personalities, and ordinary Americans attempted to remember and analyze what had happened. They grappled with the difficult questions of how to return to normalcy, what normalcy is, and what should come next for America. The following documents represent some of these struggles to define the meaning of September 11. The first is the recollection of a student who watched the destruction of the World Trade Center, the second is one person's reflections on the public's reactions to the attacks, and the last two represent some of the political divisions over the government's response.

BEFORE YOU READ

1. How different was the experience of firsthand witnesses, like Kimberly Morales, from that of the millions who watched the events unfold on television?

2. Why do you think Morales blames politicians at the end of her account?

3. Do you think that Daniel Harris is being fair in his criticism of the responses to the World Trade Center attack?

4. Many family members of victims of the September 11 attacks have made statements that have gained much publicity. Do you think their views should be given more weight than those of other members of the public?

5. What do you think the writers of the last two pieces want to see the government do in response to September 11? Do you agree with either of them?

6. Do you think the United States changed after September 11? If so, how?

7. What relation does the recent war in Iraq have to the events of September 11?

KIMBERLY MORALES

A College Student's Unplanned Lesson in Suicide

The lady in the floral dress was poking her head out the window. She was one hundred stories up in the sky. There was smoke and fire all around her. She disappeared for a few seconds. Then she was there again, sticking her head out even further. She was far away, but I could tell she was taking big breaths of air. I watched, helpless to do anything but that. I could have closed my eyes, but I didn't. It was like she needed to be seen. Maybe it would help keep her alive. She was gone again. Then back. This time almost her whole body was hanging out. Oh no. I could see what she was thinking. Or maybe I just knew it. The smoke was rushing around her. The flames were at her back. She looked into the building and then looked out again. Then she did it. Down, down, down she went, her pretty floral dress clinging to her body: 90. 80. 70. 60. 50. My eyes followed her until she was gone. I barely had time to consider what she had just done, when it started all over again. More people in the windows. More smoke. More jumping.

I watched those people killing themselves on my way to school. I was supposed to be at work in the counseling department on the third floor at nine A.M. My first class wasn't until 12:15. But I never made it into the building. I stood there at the main entrance on Chambers Street with a crowd of professors, administrators, students and security staff, watching in horror and disbelief as the North Tower burned uncontrollably and desperate people chose to jump rather than burn with it. Behind that tower, but mostly blocked from our view, was the South Tower. It had just been hit too. That crash I saw myself. A few minutes earlier, I was riding the 2 train from my home in the Bronx, unaware of any of this. I had my headset on, listening to some rhythm and blues, when we pulled into Chambers Street. I always turn down the volume when I get to the station, and this time I could hear the conductor making an announcement. "Due to an emergency at the World Trade Center, this will be the last stop." I was getting out there anyway, like I always do, so I didn't pay too much attention to what he had said and I headed up the stairs.

When I got to the sidewalk at Broadway and Chambers, I was still listening to my CD. I don't think I even noticed the great rumble of the low-flying jet above me, but I certainly saw the jet itself. It was banking and it was flying far too low. I could see a little bit of space between its nose and the South Tower. And then they came together in a big explosion and a huge ball of fire. It was instant. Glass was breaking everywhere and papers came spitting out from the windows. I felt my whole body freeze. I couldn't move. Or maybe I didn't want to move. I was terrified. I stood there on the sidewalk for about two minutes. Everything around me was going crazy. People were running everywhere and screaming about two planes. So that was why the North Tower was burning too. The traffic on the street stopped. I watched a man in a jogging suit rush out of his red Toyota and leave his car running.

Your instincts say this shouldn't be happening, a plane crashing into a skyscraper, and then a second one, so you immediately start thinking about what might happen next. I finally broke from my trance and decided the safest place to go was my school. The subway was right behind me, but I figured that would be a dangerous place at a time like this. I didn't want to find myself in a tunnel somewhere when things went bad again. I wanted to be on the ground, able to see around me and know exactly what was going on. I ran to BMCC [Borough of Manhattan Community College] as fast as I could. My friend, Angela, was standing outside. She was crying and was so upset that she could barely even speak. I had to drag the words out of her. She had been there for both planes. She saw it all. She was shaken up beyond belief. Later I saw one of my professors from my early childhood education class. She was frantic. She was trying to go down Broadway toward the World Trade Center. She had a student doing an internship in one of the day-care centers there. But the authorities wouldn't let her get past. It was far too dangerous. We did lose some students, but that one got away safely.

I stayed outside the school, which was being taken over by the police and firefighters as a triage and command center. Rescue workers would rest there. It would be more than three weeks before we would be able to get back inside for classes. I think I watched six people jump to their deaths. I kept thinking, What was going on in their minds? Would I be doing the same thing? I thought of the smoke, and how much they must have been coughing. I thought about the flames getting bigger and how hot they were. Then I thought about their families. These weren't just unknown people caught in the most horrible situation I've ever seen. They were mothers and fathers and grandmothers and grandfathers. They were brothers and sisters and sons and daughters. I thought about how their days had started, probably just like mine, how they woke up not knowing any of this would happen, how they said goodbye thinking they would be back home that night. And I thought about how I was watching them die. It was all really hard to swallow.

Some security guards at the college realized that things were getting threatening, that the towers could fall or pieces of debris could come our way. So they told us to leave and start walking north away from the World Trade Center. "Just keep walking and don't look back," one of them said. I teamed up with six of my girlfriends and got as far as 14th Street when the first building collapsed. We kept going, eventually getting as far as 34th Street. I had heels on my shoes and one of my girlfriends was seven months pregnant, so we weren't moving that fast. Suddenly we heard airplanes again. We had stayed away from the Empire State Building and had no intention of going near Times Square for fear of another attack. We looked up. "They're F16s," one of my friends said. "They're friendly." I knew F16s were our planes, but any plane in the sky made me nervous. We had to sit down, so we went into a Wendy's. I am not sure why I even ordered any food because my nerves were all over the place and I couldn't eat. After about a half hour, they told us to leave. They were closing the restaurant. We continued on to 38th Street, where I got a bus that eventually got me home to the Bronx. My girlfriends all left for Brooklyn.

It was an emotional trip home. I thought a lot about politics. I was really mad and didn't know where to direct my anger. Where were the people in our government whose jobs were to prevent things like this? Were they off in their million-dollar yachts and their fancy vacations while we were suffering through this? When I got home and got into bed, it was hard to fall asleep. I closed my eyes. But I kept seeing the lady with the floral dress.

DANIEL HARRIS

The Kitschification of September 11

Within minutes after the collapse of the World Trade Center, inspirational songs, propagandistic images designed to feed the fires of patriotic fury, and poetry commemorating the victims began to proliferate on radio, television, and the Internet. The Dixie Chicks performed an a cappella rendition of "The Star Spangled Banner"; car-window decals appeared featuring a lugubrious poodle with a glistening tear as large as a gum drop rolling mournfully down its cheek; refrigerator magnets of Old Glory flooded the market ("buy two and get a third one FREE!"); and the unofficial laureates of the World Wide Web brought the

Internet to a crawl by posting thousands of elegies with such lyrics as "May America's flag forever fly unfurled, / May Heaven be our perished souls' 'Windows on the World'!" Gigabytes of odes to the lost firemen and celebrations of American resolve turned the information superhighway into a parking lot:

> *My Daddy's Flag*
>
> Arriving home from work and a trip to the store,
> My 5 year old daughter greeted me at the door.
> "Hi daddy!" she smiled, "what's in the bag?"
> "Well, daddy has brought home the American flag."
>
> With a puzzled look she asked "What does it do?"
> I answered, "it's our country's colors, red, white and blue.
> This flag on our house will protect you my dear,
> It has magical powers to keep away fear."

Does an event as catastrophic as this one require the rhetoric of kitsch[1] to make it less horrendous? Do we need the overkill of ribbons and commemorative quilts, haloed seraphim perched on top of the burning towers and teddy bears in firefighter helmets waving flags, in order to forget the final minutes of bond traders, restaurant workers, and secretaries screaming in elevators filling with smoke, standing in the frames of broken windows on the ninetieth floor waiting for help, and staggering down the stairwells covered in third-degree burns? Perhaps saccharine images of sobbing Statues of Liberty and posters that announce "We will never forget when the Eagle cried" make the incident more palatable, more "aesthetic" in a sense, decorated with the mortician's reassuringly familiar stock in trade. Through kitsch, we avert our eyes from tragedy, transforming the unspeakable ugliness of diseases, accidents, and wars into something poetic and noble, into pat stories whose happy endings offer enduring lessons in courage and resilience.

And yet while kitsch may serve to anesthetize us to the macabre spectacle of perfectly manicured severed hands embedded in the mud and charred bodies dropping out of windows, it may conceal another agenda. The strident sentimentality of kitsch makes the unsaid impermissible and silences dissenting opinions, which cannot withstand the emotional vehemence of its rhetoric. It not only beautifies ghoulish images, it whitewashes the political context of the attack which, when portrayed as a pure instance of gratuitous sadism, of inexplicable wickedness, appears to have had no cause, no ultimate goal. Four months into Bush's "crusade," despite clear successes, we remain far from certain about what, in the long run, we hope to achieve.

Ignoring geopolitics, we sealed the incident off in an ideologically sterile vacuum, the perfect incubator for kitsch, which thrives on irrational simplifications of moral complexities. Rather than making sincere efforts to understand the historical origins of the event in a protracted international conflict, we erect

---

1. **kitsch:** artistic or literary material held to be of low taste and marked especially by empty sentimentality.

a schematic narrative that pitted absolute evil against absolute good, our own unwavering rationality against the delirium of crazed fanatics. On the electronic bulletin boards on the Internet, the terrorists became cartoon villains whose "insane and beastly acts" were both unmotivated and unaccountable, the result of nothing more explicable than "malevolence," of the "dastardly cowardice" of "an inhuman . . . group that has no place in the universe." These "depraved minions of a hate-filled maniac" who subscribed to "the toxic theology [of] suicidal barbarism," "watched from a distance / And laughed in a hauty [sic] tone" at this "ungodly intrusional [sic] violation of human life," this "psychotic" prank ostensibly staged out of sheer spite.

If the perpetrators are monsters, the victims are not just innocent but angelic, diaphanous seraphs with harps who, after being crushed in the collapse, "rose again, / Through the smoke, and dust and pain. / To fly. To play above again / In the blue American sky. / The perfect, blue American sky." R&B vocalist Kristy Jackson has hit the charts with a commemorative single entitled "Little Did She Know" about a woman who, on the morning of September 11, sent her fireman husband off to work with a peck on his cheek, heedless of the fact that he would never return:

> Little did she know she'd kissed a hero
> Though he'd always been one in her eyes
> But when faced with certain death
> He'd said a prayer and took a breath
> And led an army of true angels in the sky.
>
> Little did she know she'd kissed a hero
> Though he'd always been an angel in her eyes
> Putting others first, it's true
> That's what heroes always do
> Now he doesn't need a pair of wings to fly. . . .

Instead of conducting open and uninhibited discussions, we state our opinions through symbols, through saber-rattling images of American eagles sitting on stools sharpening their claws; screen savers of rippling flags captioned "these colors don't run"; computer-manipulated photographs of the tear-streaked face of the Man of Sorrows superimposed on the Statue of Liberty; and votive candles that morph into the burning buildings themselves. It is appropriate that President Bush, a man known for the endlessly inventive infelicities of his speech, should communicate to the American public largely by means of symbols, by displaying the badges of dead policemen and staging photo-ops in which, bull horn in hand, he hugs firemen on piles of rubble and leads squirming first-graders in the Pledge of Allegiance after admiring a bulletin board of their drawings titled "The Day We Were Very Sad."

Symbols are the language spoken by those who are uncomfortable with words. Our leaders use them when they seek to stimulate, not thought, but adrenaline. They are the weapons of emotional obscurantism, paralyzing dialogue before we are plunged into war where doubts and hesitations have potentially disastrous consequences and where our actions must be swift, decisive, and unthinking. So much of the "discussion" of the World Trade Center is based on button-pushing, on a barrage of symbols designed to trigger reflexive, Pavlovian reactions, bringing us to our feet against our wills to salute the flag and burst as one into song, our intellectual independence shot down by salvos of patriotic kitsch. . . .

DIANA HOFFMAN

The Power of Freedom

I know you're celebrating
what your evil deeds have wrought
But with the devastation
something else you've also brought

For nothing is more powerful
than Americans who unite
Who put aside their differences
and for freedom fight

Each defenseless victim whose
untimely death you caused
And every fallen hero
whose brave life was lost

Has only served to strengthen
our national resolve
Each freedom-loving citizen
will surely get involved

You've galvanized our nation
into a force so strong
We'll end your reign of terror
although the fight is long

For every heart that's broken
ten million will stand tall
and every tear that's falling
is the mortar for it all

And when this war is over
one thing I know is sure
Our country will be greater
and our freedom will endure

AMBER AMUNDSON

A Widow's Letter to President Bush

On November 26, I stood before the White House and read this letter:

Dear President Bush, my name is Amber Amundson. I'm a twenty-eight-year-old single mother of two small children. The reason I am a single mother is because my husband was murdered on September 11, while working under your direction. My husband, Craig Scott Amundson, was an active duty, multimedia illustrator for your deputy chief of staff of personnel command, who was also killed.

I am not doing well. I am hurt that the United States is moving forward in such a violent manner. I do not hold you responsible for my husband's death, but I do believe you have a responsibility to listen to me and please hear my pain. I do not like unnecessary death. I do not want anyone to use my husband's death to perpetuate violence.

So, Mr. President, when you say that vengeance is needed so that the victims of 9/11 do not die in vain, could you please exclude Craig Scott Amundson from your list of victims used to justify further attacks. I do not want my children to grow up thinking the reason so many people died following the September 11 attack was because of their father's death. I want to show them a world where we love and not hate, where we forgive and do not seek vengeance.

Please Mr. Bush, help me honor my husband. He drove to the Pentagon with a "Visualize World Peace" bumper sticker on his car every morning. He raised our children to understand humanity and not to fight to get what you want. When we buried my husband, an American flag was laid over his casket. My children believe the American flag represents their dad. Please let that representation be one of love, peace, and forgiveness. I'm begging you for the sake of humanity and my children to stop killing. Please find a nonviolent way to bring justice to the world.

Sincerely,
Amber Amundson

VISUAL PORTFOLIO

9/11

In the first hours after the September 11 attack on the World Trade Center and the Pentagon, the video footage of the twin towers collapsing was broadcast over and over again on television around the planet. People stood in front of television sets in their houses and workplaces looking, in disbelief, at something they had seen many times before in disaster movies: the New York skyline crumbling after an attack from the sky. Yet this time it was real. The footage showed people covered from head to toe in white dust trying to leave the smoky pea-soup haze of the canyons of lower Manhattan's financial district. Some were running with purpose, and others seemed to be drifting in a daze, looking for lost workmates and loved ones or just too stunned to know where to go. Around the world, everyday life came to a halt as offices closed, public spaces and tall buildings were evacuated, and people stayed close to home, joining friends, family, and neighbors to share in what everybody immediately knew was a historical moment.

In New York City people turned to television for information and comfort but found confusing and contradictory reports from newscasters who were struggling to get information and put together a story. There were rumors of more hijacked planes, additional targets, and U.S. Air Force fighter planes intercepting commandeered passenger jets throughout the country. One television reporter nearly created a panic by telling people to evacuate New York City and head for the mainland. Everybody speculated about who was to blame for the attack. One report wrongly blamed Palestinians, another report suggested the Iranian-led Hezbollah, and throughout the Middle East rumors surfaced that Israel's intelligence agency, the Mossad, had staged the whole thing to discredit Arabs.

With President Bush safely hidden in an undisclosed location in the middle of the country and the Secret Service and the army working to ensure the security of the White House, America looked to New York City mayor Rudolph Guiliani to make sense out of the chaos. From his hourly press conferences inside the disaster zone to shaky footage of him sprinting down a street ahead of a cloud of dust and debris coming from the first collapsing tower, Guiliani provided the city and the nation with leadership and a sense that somebody was in charge. He instructed people where to go and what to do and counseled New Yorkers to be calm and tolerant and not to look for someone to blame.

Plate 1. New York *Daily News*, front page, September 12, 2001, Special Edition

The next morning, newspapers across the world struggled to put a few words to the pictures of the burning towers that were on their covers. Many followed the lead of the president in his evening press conference, their headlines proclaiming "WAR" in giant bold letters, while others focused instead on the horror of the attack or the number of people believed to be dead. The front page of the New York *Daily News*, shown in Plate 1, was emblematic of front covers around the world on the morning after the attack, showing the remarkable photograph of a second plane flying into the already burning World Trade Center.

The Awful Toll

Thousands
Still Buried
In the Rubble
Of the World
Trade Center

Monica Iken awaits word on her husband, Michael Iken, a broker in WTC's Tower Two.

Bush Calls the Attacks on Nation 'Acts of War'

FBI Identifies Most of the Airline Hijackers

68 Pages of Coverage

Plate 2. New York *Newsday*, front page, September 13, 2001

On September 13, *Newsday*, a Long Island newspaper, published the image depicted in Plate 2, addressing the emotional devastation wrought by the attack. What editorial choices do you think go into deciding on the makeup of the front page of a newspaper? Why do you think some newspapers included the word *war* in their headlines while others focused on the human toll? What is the relationship between newspaper covers, the way people came to view September 11, and the government's response?

Plate 3. President George W. Bush and Secretary of Defense Donald Rumsfeld at the Pentagon, September 12, 2001

In the days that followed, the visual imagery shifted from pictures of the burning buildings to portraits of people. The president and his secretary of defense Donald Rumsfeld, pictured in Plate 3 in front of the damaged Pentagon, came to be the ones that Americans looked to on the nightly news for information and a sense of where the nation was headed. President Bush became a symbol to many Americans that the government was working to restore order and right a situation that had gone terribly wrong. Do you think that politicians consider visual imagery in their decisions about what places they visit and where they give press conferences?

In that same first week, intelligence sources concluded that the attacks had been the work of Muslim fundamentalists connected to an organization named Al Qaeda, headquartered in Afghanistan. A new menace entered America's orbit—Osama Bin Laden, Al Qaeda's leader. A Saudi Arabian of Yemeni descent, Bin Laden was a Western-educated engineer, with advanced technical knowledge, who had been implicated in previous bombings of U.S. embassies in East Africa. He was a veteran of the war against the Soviet Union in Afghanistan, but after the cold war he turned his wrath on his former allies, declaring a holy war against America. In the weeks after the attacks, handmade posters carrying his photo and the legend "Wanted Dead or Alive" appeared in public places throughout the United States. Plate 4 depicts the original FBI

FBI TEN MOST WANTED FUGITIVE

MURDER OF U.S. NATIONALS OUTSIDE THE UNITED STATES;
CONSPIRACY TO MURDER U.S. NATIONALS OUTSIDE THE UNITED STATES;
ATTACK ON A FEDERAL FACILITY RESULTING IN DEATH

USAMA BIN LADEN

Date of Photograph Unknown

Aliases: Usama Bin Muhammad Bin Ladin, Shaykh Usama Bin Ladin, the Prince, the Emir, Abu Abdallah, Mujahid Shaykh, Hajj, the Director

DESCRIPTION

Date of Birth:	1957	**Hair:**	Brown
Place of Birth:	Saudi Arabia	**Eyes:**	Brown
Height:	6' 4" to 6' 6"	**Complexion:**	Olive
Weight:	Approximately 160 pounds	**Sex:**	Male
Build:	Thin	**Nationality:**	Saudi Arabian
Occupation:	Unknown		
Remarks:	Bin Laden is the leader of a terrorist organization known as Al-Qaeda, "The Base." He is left-handed and walks with a cane.		

CAUTION

USAMA BIN LADEN IS WANTED IN CONNECTION WITH THE AUGUST 7, 1998, BOMBINGS OF THE UNITED STATES EMBASSIES IN DAR ES SALAAM, TANZANIA, AND NAIROBI, KENYA. THESE ATTACKS KILLED OVER 200 PEOPLE. IN ADDITION, BIN LADEN IS A SUSPECT IN OTHER TERRORIST ATTACKS THROUGHOUT THE WORLD.

CONSIDERED ARMED AND EXTREMELY DANGEROUS

IF YOU HAVE ANY INFORMATION CONCERNING THIS PERSON, PLEASE CONTACT YOUR
LOCAL FBI OFFICE OR THE NEAREST U.S. EMBASSY OR CONSULATE.

REWARD

The Rewards For Justice Program, United States Department of State, is offering a reward of up to $25 million for information leading directly to the apprehension or conviction of Usama Bin Laden. An additional $2 million is being offered through a program developed and funded by the Airline Pilots Association and the Air Transport Association.

www.fbi.gov

June 1999
Poster Revised November 2001

Plate 4. "FBI Ten Most Wanted Fugitive" poster of Osama Bin Laden, 2001

poster that was issued long before September 11. Why do you think that so many people made their own wanted posters of Bin Laden?

Above: Plate 5. Rescue workers at Ground Zero, September 13, 2001

Left: Plate 6. A priest blesses a cross of steel beams found in the rubble of the World Trade Center as rescue and construction workers look on, October 4, 2001

Right: Plate 7. A woman places a candle in the center courtyard of the World Trade Center in Long Beach, California, September 14, 2001

As the weeks passed, the political images that emerged from September 11 were dwarfed by human images that seemed to provide more comfort. To most Americans, pictures from the war in Afghanistan that started on October 7, 2001, were of less interest than ones of the home front. The

nation took particular pride in photos of firemen, police officers, and other rescue workers who projected a sense of strength, courage, and determination. The photo in Plate 5, taken two days after the attack, is one of many to capture rescue workers' round-the-clock efforts to find survivors amid the rubble at Ground Zero. The American flag and religious symbols provided comfort for many Americans. Photos such as the one pictured in Plate 6 were reproduced across the country on posters and calendars and in books. Why do you think that the kind of images pictured in Plates 5 and 6 were important to so many Americans after September 11? How do you think these images fit into Daniel Harris's discussion of the kitschification of September 11 (Selection 42)?

Finally, people across the country seemed to need to come together publicly and share feelings, impressions, and sorrows. Memorial services and gatherings like the one pictured in Plate 7 were held throughout the United States, as people attempted to repair the wounded psyche of their country.

Acknowledgments (continued from p. iv)

[17] "Letters from the Great Migration" from Emmett J. Scott, "Letters of Negro Migrants of 1916–1918" from *Journal of Negro History:* 177–80. Copyright © by the Association for the Study of Afro-American Life and History. Reprinted with the permission of the publishers.

[18] "The Trial of Kate Richards O'Hare" from Robert Marcus and Anthony Marcus, eds., *On Trial: American History through Court Proceedings and Hearings*, Vol. 2. Copyright © 1998. By permission of Brandywine Press.

[19] "In Defense of the Bible" from Sheldon Norman Grebstein, ed., *Monkey Trial: The State of Tennessee vs. John Thomas Scopes.* Copyright © 1960 by Sheldon Norman Grebstein. Reprinted by permission.

[20] "Tennessee's Dilemma" by Joseph Wood Klutch, Reprinted with permission from *The Nation* 121.3133, July 22, 1925.

[21] Lyric excerpt of "Puttin' on the Ritz" by Irving Berlin. Copyright © 1928, 1929 by Irving Berlin. Copyright © renewed. International copyright secured. All rights reserved. Reprinted by permission. "The Harlem Renaissance" from Langston Hughes, *The Big Sea: An Autobiography.* Copyright © 1940 by Langston Hughes. Renewed © 1969 by Arna Bontemps and George Houston Bass. Reprinted with the permission of Hill & Wang, a division of Farrar, Straus and Giroux, LLC.

[22] "My Fight for Birth Control" from Margaret Sanger, *My Fight for Birth Control.* Copyright © 1931 by Margaret Sanger. Reprinted with permission of Sanger Resources and Management, Inc.

[23] "Down and Out in the Great Depression" from Robert S. McElvaine, *Down and Out in the Great Depression: Letters from the "Forgotten Men."* Copyright © 1983 by the University of North Carolina Press. Used by permission of the publisher.

[24] "The Sit-Down Strikes" from Henry Kraus, *The Many and the Few: A Chronicle of the Dynamic Auto Workers*, 2nd ed. Copyright © 1947 by Henry Kraus. Used with the permission of the University of Illinois Press.

[25] "Letters from Los Alamos" from Phyllis Fisher, *The Los Alamos Experience.* Copyright © 1985 by Phyllis Fisher. Reprinted with permission of the author.

[27] "Rosie the Riveter" from Sherna Berger Gluck, *Rosie the Riveter Revisited.* Copyright © 1987 Sherna Berger Gluck. Reprinted by permission of The Gale Group.

[28] "Memories of the Internment Camp" from Archie Satterfield, *The Home Front: An Oral History of the War Years in America, 1941–1945.* Copyright © 1981 by Archie Satterfield. Used by permission of Playboy Press.

[29] "The Bataan Death March" from Donald Knox, *Death March: The Survivors of Bataan.* Copyright © 1981 by Donald Knox. Reprinted by permission of Harcourt, Inc.

[30] "Post–World War II 'Red Scare'" from Griffin Fariello, *Red Scare: Memories of the American Inquisition: An Oral History.* Copyright © 1995 by Griffin Fariello. Reprinted by permission of W. W. Norton & Company, Inc.

[32] "Cover-up and Outcome": Westmoreland excerpt from William C. Westmoreland, *A Soldier Reports*, copyright © 1976 by William C. Westmoreland, reprinted with the permission of the author. Nixon excerpt from *RN: The Memoirs of Richard M. Nixon*, copyright © 1978 by Richard Nixon, reprinted by permission of Warner Books, Inc., New York, USA.

[33] "Betty Friedan Starts a Revolution" first published in Betty Friedan, *It Changed My Life: Writings on the Women's Movement.* Copyright © 1963, 1964, 1968, 1970, 1971, 1972, 1973, 1974, 1975, 1978, 1985, 1991, 1998 by Betty Friedan. Originally published by Random House, Inc. Reprinted by permission of Curtis Brown, Ltd.

[34] "Mississippi Freedom Summer" from Elizabeth Sutherland, *Letters from Mississippi.* Copyright © 1965 by McGraw-Hill Companies. Reprinted with the permission of the publishers.

[35] "The Young Lords" from Pablo Guzmán, "La Vida Pura: Lord of the Barrio," as it appears in Andrés Torres and José E. Velázquez, eds., *The Puerto Rican Movement: Voices from the Diaspora.* Copyright © 1998 by Temple University (except Chapter 1, copyright 1998 by Andrés Torres, Chapters 3 and 5, copyright 1998 by José E. Velázquez, and Chapter 12, copyright by Iris Morales). Reprinted by permission of Temple University Press. All rights reserved.

[36] "An American Hostage in Tehran" from Barbara and Barry Rosen, with George Feifer, *The Destined Hour: The Hostage Crisis and One Family's Ordeal.* Copyright © 1982 by Barbara and Barry Rosen. Reprinted by permission of Doubleday, a division of Random House, Inc.

[37] "Driving While Black" from James Campbell, "Driving while black still gets you stopped," *Houston Chronicle*, September 14, 1998. © 1998 Houston Chronicle Publishing Company. Reprinted with permission. All rights reserved.

[38] "Let Them Profile Me" from Fedwa Malti-Douglas, *New York Times*, February 6, 2002, Op. Ed. article, p. 21. Copyright © 2002 by The New York Times Company. Reprinted by permission.

[39] "Crossing the Rio Grande" from Al Santoli, *New Americans: An Oral History.* Copyright © 1988 by Al Santoli. Used by permission of Viking Penguin, a division of Penguin Putnam, and the author, c/o Janklow & Nesbit Associates.

[40] "Rodney King and the Los Angeles Riots" from Stan Chambers, *News at Ten: Fifty Years with Stan Chambers.* Copyright © 1994 by Stan Chambers. Reprinted by permission of Capra Press, Santa Barbara.

[41] "Homophobia in the Heartlands" from November 4, 1999, victim impact statement read by Dennis W. Shepard at the sentencing of Aaron J. McKinney, *Gay Law News*, <http://www.gaylawnews.com/shepardfatherstmt.html> (28 November 2002).

[42] "September 11 and the Aftermath": "Kimberly Morales: A College Student's Unplanned Lesson in Suicide" from Dean J. Murphy, ed., *September 11: An Oral History.* Copyright © 2002 by Dean J. Murphy. Reprinted by permission of Random House, Inc. "The Kitschification of September 11" by Daniel Harris from *Afterwords: Stories and Reports from 9/11 and Beyond*, compiled by the editors of *Salon.com* and David Talbot. Copyright © 2002 by Daniel Harris. Reprinted by permission of Simon & Schuster/Washington Square Press. "The Power of Freedom" by Diana Hoffman, *Never Forgotten*, <http://911neverforget .tripod.com/neverforgotten/id3.html> (5 December 2002). "A Widow's Letter to President Bush" from Amber Amundson, "Our Grief Is Not a Cry for War," a letter read at "After September 11: Paths to Peace, Justice and Security" conference on December 7 and 8, 2001, Medford, Massachusetts, conference organized by the American Friends Service Committee & Tufts University's Peace and Justice Studies Program and Peace Coalition.

Visual Portfolios

The Western Landscape

[Plate 3] Caravan of Emigrants to California Crossing the Great American Desert in Nebraska, from Henry Howe, *Historical Collections of the Great West: Containing Narratives of the Most Important and Interesting Events in Western History*, 1857. Courtesy of Visual Studies Workshop.

[Plate 9] Hydraulic Mines, Gold Run, Colorado Territory, c. 1870s. Courtesy of Visual Studies Workshop.

[Plate 10] No. 65. North from Barthold Pass, *U.S. Geological Survey of the Territories. Department of the Interior, Professor F. V. Hayden in Charge*, 1874. Courtesy of George Eastman House.

[Plate 11] Beautiful View, c. 1885. Erdlen's Photographic Gallery, Salida, Colorado. Courtesy of Visual Studies Workshop.

Urban Industrial America

[Plate 2] Pillars of Smoke, Pittsburgh, 1910. Courtesy of George Eastman House.

[Plate 4] An Ancient Police Station Lodger with the Plank on Which She Slept at the Eldridge Street Station, c. 1898. Museum of the City of New York, The Jacob A. Riis Collection.

[Plate 5] Shoemaker in Ludlow Street Cellar, c. 1890. Museum of the City of New York, The Jacob A. Riis Collection.

[Plate 6] Baxter Street Court (22 Baxter Street), c. 1890. Museum of the City of New York, The Jacob A. Riis Collection.

[Plate 7] Doffer Girl in New England Mill, 1909, from *Lewis W. Hine's Workbooks for the National Child Labor Committee*. Library of Congress.

[Plate 8] Young Women in Mill, c. 1910, from *Lewis W. Hine's Workbooks for the National Child Labor Committee*. Library of Congress.

[Plate 9] Young Woman outside Mill, c. 1910, from *Lewis W. Hine's Workbooks for the National Child Labor Committee*. Library of Congress.

[Plate 10] Carriage Shop, Hampton Institute, Hampton, Va., 1899. Hampton University Archives.

[Plate 11] History Classroom, Hampton Institute, Hampton, Va., 1899. Hampton University Archives.

[Plate 12] Hampton Graduates, Hampton, Va., 1899. Hampton University Archives.

Advertising in the 1920s

[Plate 1] Listerine advertisement. Reprinted with permission of Pfizer.

[Plate 2] Palmolive Soap advertisement. Reprinted with permission of Colgate Palmolive.

[Plate 4] Colgate's advertisement. Reprinted with permission of Colgate Palmolive.

[Plate 5] Edison Mazda Lamps advertisement. Reprinted with permission of General Electric.

[Plate 6] Magnavox Radio advertisement. Reproduced with permission of Koninklijke Philips Electronics N.V. All rights reserved.

[Plate 7] ScotTissue advertisement. Reprinted with permission of Kimberly-Clark.

[Plate 10] Brer Rabbit Molasses advertisement. Reprinted with permission of B&G Foods.

9/11

[Plate 1] New York *Daily News*, front page, September 12, 2001, Special Edition. Copyright 2002 Daily News L.P. AP/Wide World Photos.

[Plate 2] New York *Newsday*, front page, September 13, 2001. © 2001 Newsday, Inc. Reprinted with permission.

[Plate 3] President George W. Bush and Secretary of Defense Donald Rumsfeld at the Pentagon, September 12, 2001. AP/Wide World Photos.

[Plate 4] "FBI Ten Most Wanted Fugitive" poster of Osama Bin Laden, 2001. Courtesy of the FBI.

[Plate 5] Rescue workers at Ground Zero, September 13, 2001. © Fred George (Contact Press Images).

[Plate 6] A priest blesses a cross of steel beams found in the rubble of the World Trade Center as rescue and construction workers look on, October 4, 2001. AP/Wide World Photos.

[Plate 7] A woman places a candle in the center courtyard of the World Trade Center in Long Beach, California, September 14, 2001. AP/Wide World Photos.